New Woman strategies

Sarah Grand
Olive Schreiner
Mona Caird

Published in our
centenary year
≈ **2004** ≈
MANCHESTER
UNIVERSITY
PRESS

To Mark Llewellyn and Heidi Heilmann

New Woman strategies

Sarah Grand
Olive Schreiner
Mona Caird

ANN HEILMANN

Manchester University Press

Manchester and New York

distributed exclusively in the USA by Palgrave

Copyright © Ann Heilmann 2004

The right of Ann Heilmann to be identified as the author of this work has been asserted
by her in accordance with the Copyright, Designs and Patents Act 1988

Published by Manchester University Press
Oxford Road, Manchester M13 9NR, UK
and Room 400, 175 Fifth Avenue, New York, NY 10010, USA
www.manchesteruniversitypress.co.uk

Distributed exclusively in the USA by
Palgrave, 175 Fifth Avenue, New York, NY 10010, USA

Distributed exclusively in Canada by
UBC Press, University of British Columbia, 2029 West Mall,
Vancouver, BC, Canada V6T 1Z2

British Library Cataloguing-in-Publication Data
A catalogue record for this book is available from the British Library

Library of Congress Cataloging-in-Publication Data applied for

ISBN 0 7190 5758 2 *hardback*
ISBN 0 7190 5759 0 *paperback*

First published 2004

13 12 11 10 09 08 07 06 05 04   10 9 8 7 6 5 4 3 2 1

Typeset in Minion
by Koinonia, Manchester
Printed in Great Britain
by Biddles Ltd, King's Lynn

Contents

List of illustrations

Acknowledgements

This book has had a long gestation, and I am grateful to friends, family, colleagues and academic institutions for their sustained support. In particular, I wish to thank the University of Wales Swansea and the Arts and Humanities Research Board for their research leave awards in the academic session 2001–2, and the University of Tübingen, Germany for funding the original research from which this project developed. Thanks are also due to the good humour and keen interest of my students, on whom I tried out many of my ideas; to Gillian Kersley and Huguette Henryson-Caird for their sharing of ideas and photographs; to Sally Ledger for her helpful comments; to Alison Kelly for her careful copy-editing, and to Matthew Frost and the staff of Manchester University Press. My most heartfelt thanks go to Mark Llewellyn for his unstinting enthusiasm, constructive criticism, encouragement, assistance with indexing, and always ready support.

Some of the thoughts developed in this study were first outlined in the following essays: '"Over that Bridge Built with our Bodies the Entire Human Race Will Pass": A Rereading of Olive Schreiner's *From Man to Man* (1926)', *European Journal of Women's Studies*, 2 (1995) 33–50; 'Mona Caird (1854–1932): Wild Woman, New Woman, and Early Radical Feminist Critic of Marriage and Motherhood', *Women's History Review*, 5:1 (1996) 67–95; 'Dreams in Black and White: Women, Race and Self-Sacrifice in Olive Schreiner's Allegorical Writings', in Heloise Brown, Madi Gilkes and Ann Kaloski (eds), *White? Women: Critical Perspectives on Gender and Race* (Raw Nerve Books, 1999), pp. 181–99; 'Narrating the Hysteric: *Fin-de-siècle* Medical Discourse and Sarah Grand's *The Heavenly Twins* (1893)', in Angelique Richardson and Chris Willis (eds), *The New Woman in Fiction and in Fact: Fin-de-siècle Feminisms* (Palgrave, 2001), pp. 123–35. I am indebted to Sage Publications, Triangle Journals, Raw Nerve Books and Palgrave for granting me permission to draw on this material.

List of abbreviations

In all bibliographical references the place of publication is London unless otherwise stated.

'AD'   Vernon Lee, 'Amour Dure: Passages from the Diary of Spiridion Trepka', *Hauntings* (1890), repr. in Vernon Lee, *Supernatural Tales: Excursions into Fantasy* (Arena, 1988), pp. 86–126.

AF   Olive Schreiner, *The Story of an African Farm* (1883; Virago, 1989).

AML   George Moore, *A Modern Lover* (Scott, 1883).

AO   Sarah Grand, *Adnam's Orchard* (Heinemann, 1912).

B   Sarah Grand, *Babs the Impossible* (Hutchinson, 1900).

BB   Sarah Grand, *The Beth Book* (1897; Bristol: Thoemmes, 1994).

BCL   Christine de Pizan, *The Book of the City of Ladies*, trans. Rosalind Brown-Grant (French original 1405; Penguin, 1999).

D   Olive Schreiner, *Dreams* (1890; Fisher Unwin, 1895).

DD   Mona Caird, *The Daughters of Danaus* (1894; New York: Feminist Press, 1989).

DE   Sarah Grand, *A Domestic Experiment* (Blackwoods, 1891).

'DL+RL'   Olive Schreiner, 'Dream Life and Real Life; A Little African Story', *Dream Life and Real Life* (Fisher Unwin, 1893), pp.11-38.

DR   Bram Stoker, *Dracula* (1897; Oxford: Oxford University Press, 1983).

EM   Sarah Grand, *Emotional Moments* (Hurst and Blackett, 1908).

FMTM   Olive Schreiner, *From Man to Man* (1926; Virago, 1982).

GW   Mona Caird, *The Great Wave* (Wishart, 1931).

HT   Sarah Grand, *The Heavenly Twins* (1893; Heinemann, 1908).

ID   Sarah Grand, *Ideala: A Study from Life* (1888; Richard Bentley, 1889).

LOS   S. C. Cronwright-Schreiner (ed.), *The Letters of Olive Schreiner 1876-1920* (Fisher Unwin, 1924).

LVMQ   Ann Heilmann (ed.), *The Late-Victorian Marriage Question: A Collection of Key New Woman Texts*, 5 vols (Routledge Thoemmes, 1998). [Number of volume indicated by Roman numerals].

'M'   Amy Levy, 'Medea (A Fragment in Drama Form, After Euripides)',
         Cameo Series (T. Fisher Unwin, 1891), accessed via the Victorian
         Women Writers Project, *http://www.letrs.indiana.edu/cgi-bin/*
         vwwp-query.pl?type=HTML&rgn=DIV1&idno=InU-AHG2203&byte
         =22389125&q1=Medea

MD   Virginia Woolf, *Mrs Dalloway* (Hogarth Press, 1929).

'MML'   Sarah Grand, 'Mamma's Music Lessons', *Aunt Judy's Magazine for*
         Young People (June to July 1878) 489–95, 527–36, repr. in *SSPSG*,
         III, pp. 57–75. [Page numbers refer to the original publication and,
         in the second instance, the reprinted edition.]

MOM   Mona Caird, *The Morality of Marriage* (George Redway, 1987), repr.
         in *LVMQ*, I.

MS   Christa Wolf, *Medea. Stimmen* (Munich: Luchterhand, 2001).

NGS   George Gissing, *New Grub Street* (Eveleigh Nash & Grayson, 1891).

OMN   Sarah Grand, *Our Manifold Nature* (Heinemann, 1894).

OSL   Richard Rive (ed.), *Olive Schreiner Letters, vol. 1: 1871–1899*
         (Oxford: Oxford University Press, 1988).

OTW   [Mona Caird], *One That Wins: The Story of A Holiday in Italy*, 2
         vols (Fisher Unwin, 1887). [Number of volume indicated by
         Roman numerals.]

POG   Mona Caird, *The Pathway of the Gods* (Skeffington, 1898).

PSJ   Alice Walker, *Possessing the Secret of Joy* (Cape, 1992).

ROM   Mona Caird, *A Romance of the Moors* (Bristol: J. W. Arrowsmith,
         n.d. [1891]).

SD   Sarah Grand, *Singularly Deluded* (Edinburgh: Blackwood's, 1893).

SMW   Ella Hepworth Dixon, *The Story of a Modern Woman* (Heinemann,
         1894).

SOS   Mona Caird, *The Stones of Sacrifice* (Marshall, Simpkin, 1915).

'SR'   Sarah Grand, 'School Revisited', *Aunt Judy's Magazine for Young*
         People (June 1880) 473–81, 537–46, repr. in *SSPSG*, III, pp. 77–98.
         [Page numbers refer to the original publication and, in the second
         instance, the reprinted edition.]

SSPSG   Ann Heilmann and Stephanie Forward (eds), *Sex, Social Purity and*
         Sarah Grand, 4 vols (Routledge, 2000). [Number of volume
         indicated by Roman numerals].

'TD'   Olive Schreiner, 'Three Dreams in a Desert', *Dreams* (1890; Fisher
         Unwin, 1895), pp. 65–85.

TDLF   Frances E. McFall [Sarah Grand], *Two Dear Little Feet* (Jarrold and
         Sons, 1873).

THQ   Sarah Grand, *The Human Quest: Being some thoughts in*
         contribution to the subject of the art of happiness (Heinemann,
         1900), repr. in *SSPSG*, I, pp. 155–79.

TPH   Olive Schreiner, *Trooper Peter Halket of Mashonaland* (Fisher
          Unwin, 1897).
U   Olive Schreiner, *Undine*, with an introduction by S. C. Cronwright-
          Schreiner (Ernest Benn, 1929).
V   Sarah Grand, *Variety* (Heinemann, 1922).
VID   Jean Rhys, *Voyage in the Dark* (1934; Penguin, 1967).
W&L   Olive Schreiner, *Woman and Labour* (1911; Virago, 1987).
WNL   G. Noel Hatton [Mona Caird], *Whom Nature Leadeth*, 3 vols
          (Longmans, Green, 1883).
WOA   Mona Caird, *The Wing of Azrael*, 3 vols (Trübner, 1889). [Number
          of volume indicated by Roman numerals.]
WV   Sarah Grand, *The Winged Victory* (Heinemann, 1916).
'YDR'   Mona Caird, 'The Yellow Drawing-Room' (1891), in Angelique
          Richardson (ed.), *Women Who Did: Stories by Men and Women,
          1890-1914* (Penguin, 2002), pp.21-30.
'YW'   Charlotte Perkins Gilman, *The Yellow Wallpaper* (1892; Virago,
          1993).

Introduction:
the m/others of (feminist) art

[O]ne of the most important, most indispensable services to Social Reform [will] have to be undertaken by the Writers.

The magnificent platform work being done from various centres must be supplemented and farther spread about the world through the medium of the written word. I don't mean merely by frankly propagandist writing (though I am the last to deny the importance of that), but even more valuable is, I think, the spirit of fairness and of nobler thinking about women ...

It is the business (the business as well as the high privilege) of men and women writers to correct the false ideas about women that many writers of the past have fostered. (Elizabeth Robins, 'To the Women Writers' Suffrage League', 4 May 1909)[1]

[N]ineteenth-century women writers frequently both use and misuse (or subvert) a common male tradition or genre ... a 'complex vibration' occurs between stylised generic gestures and unexpected deviations from such obvious gestures, a vibration that undercuts and ridicules the genre being employed. Some of the best-known recent poetry by women openly uses such parody in the cause of feminism: traditional figures of patriarchal mythology like Circe, Leda, Cassandra, Medusa, Helen, and Persephone have all lately been reinvented in the images of their female creators, and each poem devoted to one of these figures is a reading that reinvents her original story. But though nineteenth-century women did not employ this kind of parody so openly and angrily, they too deployed it to give contextual force to their revisionary attempts at self-definition. (Sandra M. Gilbert and Susan Gubar, *The Madwoman in the Attic*, 1979)[2]

The close alliance between literature and social reform that Elizabeth Robins, herself a major player in the Edwardian women's movement, identified as the linchpin of first-wave feminism was of central importance to the New Woman writers of the *fin de siècle*. '[T]hanks to our efforts', Sarah Grand wrote in 1896, 'the "novel with a purpose" and the "sex novel" are more powerful at the present time, especially for good, than any other social influence'.[3] One of the defining characteristics of New Woman fiction was its challenge to and subversion of the conventional dichotomies between literature and political writing, art and popular culture.[4] At the intersection of cultural politics and political activism, New Woman fiction opened up a largely gynocentric space for the discussion and dissemination of feminist thought. The 1880s and 1890s saw the rise of the feminist protest novel, a genre intimately linked, for the first time in British history, to an organised women's movement. Born from this movement and reflecting its concern with inequality in marriage and professional life, with the moral double standard and sexual violence, and with women's political disenfranchisement, but also adapting and transforming these issues to deal with the specifically cultural and aesthetic scripts with which women writers and artists had to contend and giving voice to a new spirituality that subverted dominant Western theological frameworks, New Woman fiction established a tradition of feminist political literature written for and consumed by a female mass market. The social function of popular literature, to 'both stimulate and allay social anxieties',[5] was thus inverted by writers who directed women readers' desires and fantasies not towards domestic or sentimental closure, but towards feminism.

Although New Woman fiction as a genre experienced various trans-mutations after the turn of the century and disappeared with the demise of first-wave feminism in the late 1930s, it laid the foundation for the resurgence of popular feminist fiction in the 1960s and 1970s, when once again feminist literary production and consumption were connected with and informed by political activism and spawned a 'spiritual revolution'.[6] While no direct link can be established between the New Woman writing of the 1890s and the feminist literature – critical-theoretical or narrative – of the twentieth-century women's liberation movement, there are conspicuous affinities in their conceptual frameworks[7] and discursive strategies. One of these is the political imperative of literary revisionism, what Adrienne Rich calls the 'act of looking back, of seeing with fresh eyes, of entering an old text from a new critical direction',[8] foreshadowed in Robins' speech to the Women Writers' Suffrage League as the need to 'correct the false ideas about women that many writers of the past have fostered'.

As Sandra Gilbert and Susan Gubar point out, the feminist revisionist project which in contemporary women's writing frequently assumes the form of parodic reinscriptions of patriarchal mythology found a more subtle expression in Victorian women writers' subversion of 'male' genres or tradi-tions. In this book I offer close readings of the work of three central agents of first-wave literary feminism in order to argue that New Woman fiction navigates the 'complex vibrations' between mimicry and mockery, the invoca-tion and implosion of hegemonic structures in culture and literature and, in Bakhtinian terms, the collision of 'authoritative' and 'internally persuasive' discourses[9] in rather more direct, carefully controlled and even flamboyant ways than might be assumed. Certainly what I aim to achieve is to reclaim New Woman fiction from the Woolfian category of moralistic, stuffy, sensually repressive and intellectually regressive Victorianism which continues to haunt modern criticism, a spectre resurfacing in Elaine Showalter's recent verdict that it is '[i]mpossible' to conceive of 'humorless' first-generation New Women like Olive Schreiner 'writing about women and play, or imagining pleasures, let alone joys, outside of the twin spheres of principle and duty'.[10] What is remarkable is not so much the fact that a writer like Grand, for example, deployed the by the end of the century well-tested feminist strategy of invoking women's higher morality as evidence of their rightful claim to social and political authority, but that she combined social purity discourses with an at times spectacular exploration of female libidinal desire, creating pointedly ambiguous and contradictory femininities in the process. Assumptions about the monolithic or one-dimensional, static nature of New Woman fiction, rooted as they are in the misrecognition of the complex discursive and performative manoeuvres that first-wave literary feminism executed in its de/reconstruction of models of femininity, only serve to reaffirm the binary oppositions ('art' versus 'politics', 'literature' versus 'social reform', 'purpose' versus 'pleasure') that New Woman writers were for the most part engaged in exploding.

Since its rediscovery during the heyday of the second women's movement in the 1970s,[11] the fiction of the New Woman has received increasing scholarly attention. Feminist literary critics like Ann Ardis, Rita Kranidis, Sally Ledger, Jane Eldridge Miller, Patricia Murphy, Lyn Pykett and others have drawn attention to the cultural and sexual politics,[12] feminist-decadent taxonomies[13] and proto-modernist experimentation[14] of New Woman fiction, and recent work by Angelique Richardson scrutinises the New Woman's investment in – or more rarely, opposition to – the eugenics movement.[15] The critical focus on the generic parameters of New Woman fiction – formal hybridity, textual instability, gendered multivocality – has been complemented by Gerd Bjørhovde's comparative and Carolyn Burdett's and Teresa Mangum's single-author studies, which place major New Woman writers within the wider socio-cultural, literary and political contexts of the turn of the century.[16]

New Woman strategies also approaches the genre through a close study of three of its key exponents, but brings a distinctly new conceptual methodology to the subject by privileging *textuality* over cultural-historical investigation. My central emphasis in this book is on the discursive strategies of the writers in order to tease out the productive instabilities that shaped the genre's fluid politics and revisionist poetics. The main critical lens through which I read New Woman fiction is French feminist theory, whose engagement with mimicry, femininity, self-reflexivity, subversion, libidinality and performativity is particularly apt in throwing into relief the writerly acts of New Woman authors. The performative strategies which configured and framed New Woman fiction have tended to be neglected in critical studies, and yet it is this very performativity which points to the writers' self-conscious negotiation of their position within the literary marketplace and the adroitness with which they addressed diverse readerships, from the popular and conservative to the 'high brow' and advanced.

My choice of writers was determined by the incisiveness of their impact on the shaping of the genre. The Anglo-Irish Sarah Grand,[17] the South-African born English Olive Schreiner[18] and the Anglo-Scottish Mona Caird[19] can jointly be credited with implanting the New Woman on the *fin-de-siècle* cultural landscape. If Schreiner wrote the first New Woman novel (*The Story of an African Farm*, 1883), Grand's heated exchange with Ouida in the *North American Review* in 1894[20] established the terms of the debate in the periodical press, where in 1888 Mona Caird's article on 'Marriage' launched the emerging theory discourse of the New Woman movement in the shape of an erudite, historically grounded and fiercely radical analysis of the patriarchal system. The 'bomb of dynamite' that W. T. Stead ascribed to Grand's *The Heavenly Twins* in 1893[21] had its equivalent in the 'flaming bomb' Caird's essay constituted in Annie S. Swan's estimation.[22] Among the flood of reader responses prompted by the article were enthusiastic endorsements of the author:

> every woman … should bless her and call her friend. She is not afraid to expose the wretched marriage tie in all its mockery, but does her best to give happiness and fair-play to her sex. She speaks the truth in every line, and there is not a woman in England or Ireland who will not secretly own to that fact … Women are afraid to speak for themselves and their rights. Mrs Caird has made a beginning.[23]

Like Caird, Grand and Schreiner had an extraordinarily profound and far-reaching impact on a remarkably wide spectrum of contemporary readers. Schreiner received 'almost hundreds of letters about [*African Farm*] from all classes of people, from an Earl's son to a dressmaker in Bond Street, and from a coalheaver to a poet';[24] one of her readers, a Lancashire working woman, declared that 'there is hundreds of women what feels like that but can't speak it, but *she* could speak what we feel'.[25] Similarly, Grand recorded that she was 'often told, especially by women, that [she had] exactly expressed what they [had] always thought but could not express, and that that [was] why they like[d her] books'.[26]

Principal spokeswomen in the New Woman debates, Grand, Schreiner and Caird also gained considerable prominence as first-wave activists. They were charter members of the Women Writers' Suffrage League from its inception in 1908.[27] Committed to the cause of constitutional suffragism, Grand founded the Tunbridge Wells branch of the Women's Citizens' Association and in 1898 became, as her biographer Gillian Kersley records, 'Vice-President of the Women's Suffrage Society, President of the local branch of the National Council of Women, and President and Chairman … of the Tunbridge Wells branch of the NUWSS' (Millicent Garrett Fawcett's National Union of Women's Suffrage Societies).[28] Caird paid subscriptions to the central committee of the National Society for Women's Suffrage in 1878 and to the Pankhursts' Women's Social and Political Union in 1907, after joining the council of the Women's Emancipation Union in 1891; in 1909 she became a member of the London Society for Women's Suffrage.[29] A founding member and then vice president of the South African Women's Enfranchisement League established in 1907, Schreiner resigned from the organisation when black women were excluded from its terms.[30]

Their thorough immersion in suffrage circles, the feminist club movement (such as the Sesame and especially the Pioneer Club),[31] and other progressive causes like anti-vivisection, personal rights and pacifism meant a degree of association, though there does not appear to have been much of a friendship between Grand and Caird, who unequivocally disapproved of *Ideala*.[32] Nor would Grand have thought much of Caird's and especially Schreiner's actual (as opposed to her own subliminal and exclusively textual) sexual liberalism; women who entered 'free' unions, she declared, were 'acting against [their] own interests, and doing a great wrong to [their] possible children'.[33] Caird and Schreiner would have been more congenial company; they corresponded on the topics discussed in Karl Pearson's Men and Women's Club, of which Schreiner was a member.[34]

Central to the work of all three writers was the subjection of women in marriage and the family; where they differed was in the emphasis they placed on specific aspects of Victorian patriarchy: the sexual double standard and male degeneration (Grand), the reproduction of the dominant gender/power relations through the institutionalisation of motherhood (Caird), and the analogies between sexual and racial hegemonies (Schreiner). While Caird linked the potential for constructive mother–child relationships to women's life outside the home, Schreiner extolled the spirit of motherhood as an inherently female principle even as she dramatised the collapse of mothering in her fiction, and Grand attached great importance to women's domestic and maternal responsibilities, yet relieved her successful heroines of cumbersome offspring. Caird and Schreiner enjoined women to demand 'both sides of the apple of life',[35] calling for female economic independence and shared childcare arrangements;[36] Grand, who in her journalistic work tended to reaffirm the concept of separate spheres, created female characters with an irrepressible urge for blurring and exploding the boundaries between public and private, masculine and feminine, sex and gender. These differences and contradictions, between the three writers and within the work of each, were to a crucial extent shaped by the multiplicity of femininities they explored in their endeavour to find narrative solutions to the problems the New Woman had to tackle, especially when she was an artist.

Lyn Pykett notes that the woman artist, in female New Woman fiction, functioned as a figure of authorial 'self-reflexivity': an intruder into the masculine sphere of art, she was the cultural equivalent of the feminist, and also served as a vehicle for 'figuring a conflicted feminine interiority, ... for exploring some of the contradictions involved in dominant definitions of (middle-class) femininity' and for 'celebrating female desire'.[37] In her 'multiple significations'[38] the female artist thus came to embody the New Woman and her multifaceted challenge to the dominant ideology. However, at a time when cultural traditions sustained by degeneration discourses defined misrecognised genius and a neurotic personality as the hallmark of the 'true' artist, New Woman writers were often placed in a precarious double bind. By constructing the artist as a woman of genius, they could lay claim to women's 'intellectual and creative equality with men and to the highest aesthetic achievements', but as Penny Boumelha points out, this could only be achieved 'at the cost of dedicating the heroine to failure if she [was] convincingly to represent authentic cultural values'.[39] This dilemma is couched by Grand, Schreiner and Caird in diverse symbolic figurations. As I discuss in Chapter 3, Grand modelled her creative woman on the conventional concept of the artist possessed of innate genius, only to fracture the patriarchal archetype in three essential ways: in associating creative with spiritual energy, she reconceived art as the province of the feminine, aligning it with artisanship and feminist activism, hence collapsing the traditional dichotomy between aesthetics and ethics. Schreiner, too, feminised the artist-as-genius paradigm and, as Chapter 4 explores, enacted a slippage between women's creative and procreative faculties, but like Caird she dramatised the failure of the artist. Caird concentrated on the artist as a misunderstood genius tragically thwarted by patriarchal society, its institutions and ancient, myth-laden traditions (Chapter 6). All three writers countermanded patriarchal taxonomies in art and culture with the feminist aesth/ethic of purpose.

My specific aim in this book is therefore to conduct an in-depth comparative analysis of Grand, Schreiner and Caird in order to investigate their discursive configurations of 'femininity' and 'feminism' in relation to their conceptualisations of this female and feminist aesthetic. The emphasis on the writers' discursive strategies facilitates closer attention being paid to the gaps, shifts, inconsistencies and performative acts which marked the ideological and textual self-positionings of each writer, highlighting the fluidity of the politics adopted and adapted, both across time and in relation to differing modes of publication addressed to differing target markets. My central focus lies on each writer's representation of the woman artist. In their endeavour to explore a new feminine-cum-feminist poetics, Grand, Schreiner and Caird defined political activism as an expression of female creativity, and distanced themselves to varying degrees from existing movements in art aligned with 'high-cultural' aestheticism and catering for a predominantly male-dominated market (*fin-de-siècle* decadence). As I argue, the emphasis on spirituality, and especially

spiritualism and theosophy, offered alternative discourses which accommo-
dated the needs of a female counter-culture and whose neo-religious language
and rhetorical appeal lent itself to feminist encodings of the socially committed female artist. Seeking to revise and revolutionise, for a feminist framework,
authoritative cultural and aesthetic discourses, each writer drew on, mimicked,
feminised and ultimately transformed traditional literary and cultural tropes
and paradigms: femininity (Grand), allegory (Schreiner), mythology (Caird).

I begin by examining the ideological instabilities so pointedly manifest in
the work of Sarah Grand. In Part I ('Femininities') I use French feminist
theory to examine Grand's mimicry of femininity, a political and aesthetic
strategy that served substantially different objectives in journalistic and early
narrative writings targeted at the mainstream ('outsider') public, from work
addressed to a feminist ('insider') readership. The textual dialectics between
'insider' and 'outsider' perspectives are reflected in the use of colliding points
of view, figured as the clash between 'male' and 'female', authorial and
narratorial/'editorial' perspectives. Although this is an important feature of
the work of all three writers, Grand provides the most complex example of
textual instability and for this reason has been allocated the largest space in my
book. Chapter 1 surveys her journalism and early fiction, drawing on Bakhtin's
concept of heteroglossia and dialogic discourse to interrogate Grand's expert
performances as a New Woman with traditional values, a feminist iconoclast
and an experimental writer who, in her portraits of the teenager (*Babs the
Impossible*) and the young wife (*Singularly Deluded*) probed into the hidden
springs of female desire. Chapters 2 and 3 are concerned with Grand's feminist
trilogy. To what extent is it possible to read *Ideala*, a novel which frames a
separatist feminist message with a male narrator's perspective, as a meta-
fictional vignette of the New Woman writer's project of self-affirmation
within male-dominated literary frameworks? The ideological incoherences of
this text are, I suggest, exploded in *The Heavenly Twins*, whose eponymous
characters stage the rejection of conservatism. Here, Grand introduces a male
first-person narrator only to call his account into question. In what sense,
then, can the plural perspectives of *The Heavenly Twins* be seen as a calculated
exploration of the clash between female interiority and male authority,
internally persuasive and authoritative discourses? As I argue in Chapter 3, *The
Beth Book* constitutes the final stage in Grand's narrative journey of artistic
and ideological self-invention through the representation of multiple
femininities. In her portrait of the artist as feminist creatrice, Ideala's male
super-ego is converted into a celebration of the protagonist's female 'super
ego', the superior being sprung from the union of theosophist high priestess
and woman of genius.

The genius of woman is a central metaphor invoked in Olive Schreiner's
allegorical approach to the New Woman. Part II ('Allegories') engages with

what I call the 'transitional' aspects of Schreiner's work, both in relation to her neo-biblical construction of the feminist struggle for selfhood as one that culminates, paradoxically, in self-sacrifice, and in terms of the middle ground Schreiner inhabited between Grand's and Caird's feminist politics and poetics. Much more progressive than Grand in her synthesising of the woman, labour and race questions, Schreiner did not share the most radical aspects of Caird's sexual politics. My main concern in this part of the book is to tease out the complex parameters of Schreiner's negotiation of theological and aesthetic frameworks in order to investigate the nature of her ideological self-division. If, as Deborah Madsen affirms, for a woman to 'appropriate for feminine use dominant genres would be to alter fundamentally those genres by disrupting the hidden masculinist agenda that shapes the literary categories that are discussed as gender-neutral and purely aesthetic',[40] what textual and conceptual transformations are engendered by Schreiner's use of biblical allegory? Chapter 4 examines two of her 'dreams' ('Three Dreams in a Desert' and 'Dream Life and Real Life') in order to scrutinise Schreiner's secularised metaphysical quest, so evocative of Hélène Cixous's sanctification of creative work as dream work, with reference to the *raced* female body, before moving on to an analysis of the transfiguration of the *gendered* body in *The Story of an African Farm* and the *maternal* body in *From Man to Man*. In what sense can femininity offer the potential for male self-reconstruction and spiritual transfiguration if it remains premised on the idea of sacrifice, and how does this overriding principle of Schreiner's work affect her allegorical novel of the mother as the paradigmatic female artist?

Closely aligned with Schreiner in her emphasis on human rights, Caird substantially differed from her in her determined rejection of self-sacrifice – a concept validated by Grand, too, if only for political purposes – and developed an aesthetic premised upon establishing a balance between women's rights and responsibilities. Part III ('Mythologies') examines Caird's radical sexual and textual politics, which set her apart from the other two writers in the specific conclusions she drew from her exploration of spiritualist-aesthetic discourses. This is exemplified in *The Pathway of the Gods* and *The Stones of Sacrifice*, texts which reveal the all-too-close alliance between alternative theologies, corresponding aesthetic paradigms, the (re)subjection of women, and political dictatorship. Chapter 5 applies Adrienne Rich's concept of re-vision and Carol Gilligan's notion of the 'different voice' of femininity to Caird's historical and narrative work on marriage, while Chapter 6 interrogates the theme of female 're-membrance' (the recollection/rememorisation of the maternal roots which permits the re-membering of the dissevered body of mother and daughter) in her two artist-novels. *One That Wins* stages the self-assertion of the woman artist through the symbolic reconciliation between artist-'mother' and artist-'daughter'. In *The Daughters of Danaus* the complex negotiation of both ancient and contemporary myth enables Caird to reconstruct and decriminalise one of the most monstrified figures in Classical mythology, Medea, and to reclaim her as the paradigmatically wronged woman of genius.

In 1883, a few years before Caird's *One That Wins* and Grand's *Ideala* and contemporaneous with the publication of Schreiner's *African Farm*, George Moore charged contemporary women writers with their failure to develop a distinctive voice of their own. 'If they have created anything new', his male artist demands,

> how is it that their art is exactly like our own? I defy anyone to say that George Eliot's novels are a woman's writing ... I defy you to show me a trace of feminality in anything they ever did, that is the point I raise. I say that women as yet have not been able to transfuse into art a trace of their sex; in other words, unable to assume a point of view of their own they have adopted ours. ... They arrange, explain, but they do not create; they do not even develop a formula ... No, not only are they not fathers, but in art are not even mothers. (*AML*, 39–40)

As the resplendent outlook of Caird's 'Yellow Drawing-Room' indicates, the New Woman artist was able to transfuse into art more than just a trace of her sex. In their subversions and feminist reconstructions of patriarchal foundation myths, Grand, Schreiner and Caird created a new generation of New Women who imploded the cultural and aesthetic frameworks of the fathers in order to construct female creativity as the mother principle of artistic genius.

Part I

Femininities:
Sarah Grand

(1854–1943)

1

Playing with voices/speaking in tongues: journalism and early novels

Personally, I have no doubt as to what is the ideal life for the average married woman. She can have nothing better than a good husband and ample leisure for her household duties. When she is so happy as to have children, they must be her primary consideration. ... There are unfortunately some abnormal women who have ... no aptitude for motherhood, and the best thing that can happen to their children is to be brought up by better hearts; but such women are the exception. They are people who have been perverted themselves for the most part by uncongenial homes. Among them are many who recognise the defect of their nature, and do their best to remedy it by securing women more generously endowed to bring up their children: in this way they do their duty to the best of their ability, and ... feel themselves at liberty to follow special pursuits. As wives and mothers I should count these women failures, and should say that they are quite entitled to try something else. Let them take up law, literature, medicine, or art, if they like, and distinguish themselves if they can. Any honourable profession should be open to them. But if they are affluent and no necessity constrains them to make money, any attempt to do so should be discountenanced for the sake of those who must work to live. (Sarah Grand, 'Should Married Women Follow Professions?', 1899)[1]

A virtuoso in the art of harmonising conflicting ideological positions, Sarah Grand (Figure 1) gained enormous prominence on the *fin-de-siècle* literary and periodical marketplace not least because of her consummate skill in mediating between disparate audiences. Always in the centre of the New Woman debates even when marginalising the radical ideas she had helped put in currency, and engaged in alternately, at times simultaneously, electrifying, horrifying or mollifying her readership, Grand presents a hybrid between a feminist Mrs Grundy and a feminine trickster. Her response to the *Young Woman*'s investigation into the compatibility of marriage and professional life, an extract from which heads this chapter, may serve as a case in point, illustrating as it does the multiple shifts and instabilities in Grand's project of marshalling traditionalist values for feminist agendas. Starting with a discussion of her article, this chapter aims to interrogate Grand's positioning within current criticism through the close reading of selected periodical writings and two early fictions.

1 Sarah Grand in her late thirties.

A social purist who promoted eugenic solutions to societal problems,[2] Grand was without doubt a conservative thinker; her feminist vision embraced social renovation, not wholesale political transformation. Recent research has nevertheless drawn attention to the 'middlebrow militancy' evidenced in her effort to mobilise a conventional-minded middle-class readership for New Woman thought.[3] But Grand was more than a middlebrow feminist. Just as she sought to enhance the status of women's political writing by establishing the concept of a feminine aesthetics premised on the dynamic fusion of art and politics,[4] feminism and spiritualism, so she cut across seemingly anti-pathetic ideological frameworks in combining her virulent critique of contemporary (male) sexual morality with a startlingly modern, sensual exploration of female desire. Baffling as it was for contemporary readers, 'The Strange Case of Sarah Grand'[5] should alert us to the dangers of applying monolithic interpretative paradigms to the sexual politics of New Woman writing. There is some indication that Grand self-consciously experimented with her shifting subject positions: 'Which one of me?' she quipped when told that her acolyte Gladys-Singers Bigger kept a diary about her, and in a humorous autobiographical piece written in 1909 she vouched that in her 'last' interview she would 'remov[e] the various disguises' she had assumed or been assigned by her critics.[6] Her writings, and in particular her periodical press articles, are showpieces of ideological shape-shifting; 'Should Married Women Follow Professions' offers a good example of what I call Grand's 'playing with voices'.

The article is representative of much of what Grand wrote for journals of the 'general illustrated' type (such as *Young Woman* and especially *Woman at Home*) targeted at a broadly middle-class, predominantly domestic female audience.[7] It begins with Grand's assertion of her authority as an 'expert' which is accompanied by an immediate disclaimer: 'In dealing conscientiously with social subjects one finds that it is unsatisfactory to generalise, and difficult to discriminate.'[8] Claim and counter-claim conjointly orchestrate the 'both and neither' tenor of the piece. Grand suggests that, however 'conscientiously' a 'careful expert' deals with the question, 'dogmatism' is counterproductive to any endeavour of arriving at 'the truth' which, in any case, 'all depends' and is subject to personal prerogatives and cultural change: 'What is good to-day may be bad for to-morrow ... It is essentially a matter of circumstances altering cases.'[9] The destabilisation of truth claims and collective imperatives in favour of individualist solutions is followed by the reaffirmation of normative codes, domesticity and motherhood being pronounced the 'ideal' for the 'average married' woman. Yet Grand's emphasis on her 'personal' standpoint effectively undermines her categorical statement, for even those readers who remained unaware of the author's separation from her husband and (by then adult) son in 1890 could not have ignored the persistent message of her novels that marriage and motherhood did nothing to benefit a woman's life: at best subjected to infantilism at the hands of a paternalist husband, the 'average married' woman of her fiction is forever in danger of being assailed by madness or syphilitic infection.

Essentialising women's domestic and child-rearing functions, Grand castigated all those deficient in these qualities as freaks of nature, only to undercut her biologically determinist argument with a battery of qualifiers: as these individuals were the exception rather than the rule, there was no cause for concern, especially if the upbringing of their children was entrusted to more suitable, professionally trained carers (a proposition consistently promoted by the much more radical Mona Caird). Once they had performed their civic duty to the best of their ability, women biologically or psychologically unequipped for motherhood had every right to follow their individual bent, and should be encouraged to make their contribution to society through professional rather than domestic channels. Castigating these women as 'failures' on the personal front enabled Grand to soften the feminist demand for full access to the professions (a point made far more forcefully elsewhere, as when she offered a modern feminist analysis of gender segregation through the imposition of 'masculine' and 'feminine' spheres: 'the division was … arbitrary … anything that paid was "masculine"').[10] By reproving wealthy, upper-class women for crowding the labour market, she implicitly drew attention to the necessity for many women of the middle classes to seek gainful employment for existential reasons. Grand thus addressed a middle-class audience composed of family-centred as well as career-oriented, comfortably placed as well as materially constrained women, suggesting that they were all right in their respective life choices and all acting in a socially responsible manner.

Did Grand want to be all things to all women (readers)? Was she, as Angelique Richardson suggests, essentially a conservative angered by the sexual double standard and the lack of civic virtue in men which endangered women and children, but otherwise largely complicit with the language and thought of the fathers?[11] Or did she see herself as a firmly 'middlebrow' writer primarily engaged on an 'educational project', aiming to introduce moderately feminist ideas to married, non-militant, middle-class women?[12] A generation later, in the 1920s, Vera Brittain used similar discursive strategies on discovering that 'direct propaganda, however accomplished, [was] ineffective': 'subversive doctrines', she concluded, were best transmitted 'through the medium of light dissertations upon innocent-looking domestic topics', and the titles of the articles with which she plied her mainstream audience (such as 'The Age of Marriage') are strongly reminiscent of Grand ('At What Age Should Girls Marry?').[13] Grand's and Brittain's strategic focus on a middle-class readership found a recent echo in Elaine Showalter's remark that if she were to start all over again, 'I would write more for the general public rather than an academic audience. … [A]cademic feminism much too quickly cut off from the mainstream.'[14]

Was it all a clever Irigarayan-style masquerade, then, a deliberately preposterous flaunting of the 'feminine role' with the objective of converting 'a form of subordination into an affirmation, and thus to begin to thwart it', by making '"visible", by an effect of playful repetition, what was supposed to remain invisible: the cover-up of a possible operation of the feminine in language'?[15] The 'worst kind of the New Woman', an Old Woman remarks in Grand's *Babs the Impossible*, was 'the kind that lure men by – er – by the – er – misuse of – er – feminine charm' (*B*, 145). Of the three writers examined in this book, Grand was without doubt the one most consistently concerned with celebrating, mimicking, staging, de/reconstructing and subverting the multiple feminine faces of the New Woman. The ideological inconsistencies that arose from this preoccupation often make her appear the feminist counterpart of 'antis' like Eliza Lynn Linton, Mary Ward and Arabella Kenealy, women who devoted themselves to prominent public careers while at the same time lending their voice and authority to the backlash by maintaining that a woman's place was in the home. In Grand, too, a regressive vision warred with the powerful assertion of her own personality; unlike these other writers, however, she was patently aware of the self-serving hypocrisy underpinning female anti-feminism: '[H]as it ever struck you', she asked an interviewer in 1897, 'how many of the worst enemies to the theory of the making of a career by women are women who have made such a career themselves, and who would be unable to stab their fellow-women in the back if they had not the standing and the authority of that career to give them the weapon which they so treacherously use?'[16] Of equal importance was her recognition of the wider political dimension of her individual need for self-determination, which led her to draw analogies between her personal situation and the general condition of women, coupled with her growing conviction that society could only be transformed by collective political action.

To some extent, the ideological instability of Grand's articles is due to the specific print medium which she favoured: the femalestream, not the more explicitly feminist, periodical press. As Margaret Beetham has argued, the New Woman and the 'new', female-oriented press of the *fin de siècle* interacted in significant ways in redefining fashionable femininity.[17] The commodification of the female reader as a participant of mass consumerism went hand in hand with the commodification of the periodical by a mass community of middle-class women keen to participate in contemporary culture while making a living out of writing. Quick to perceive the propagandist value of a medium which foregrounded female experience and appealed to women's feelings, feminists like Grand strove to transform the individualised wish to embellish private bodies and domestic environments into the political impulse to improve the body politic and domestic power structures of the state. Invoking the values of a traditional readership in order to radicalise it, Grand was able to mobilise the cult of femininity fostered by these periodicals for her feminist purposes, but ultimately she remained constrained by the ideological frameworks she sought to subvert.

Womanliness as a masquerade

In harnessing domestic values to the dictates of civic duty and the New Woman's desire for self-improvement, Grand reconfigured the patriarchal concept of femininity by both politicising and glamorising its 'New Aspect'[18] under modern womanhood. As a responsible citizen, dedicated to 'the sanctity of marriage and the perfecting of the home',[19] the New Woman was justified in claiming full citizenship rights for her sex, for these rights devolved from her maternalistic role as the moral guardian of the nation. In her endeavour to naturalise women's socio-political mandate, Grand utilised a standard feminist device of the time, drawing on domestic housekeeping as a metaphor for women's public mission: 'It is for us to set the human household in order.'[20] The New Woman project of moral and social regeneration was of central importance at a time when 'the man of the moment'[21] remained arrested in an earlier developmental stage or worse, was moving in a retrograde direction: it had always been 'the woman's place and pride and pleasure to teach the child', and this principle naturally extended to the relationship between the sexes, for 'man morally is in his infancy'.[22] The female bid for political power was thus portrayed as a quasi-biological imperative, the natural outcome of women's nurturing and home-making instincts. The endeavour to 'raise the man' reflected a woman's authentically 'womanly' qualities.[23] Like other social purists such as Charlotte Perkins Gilman and many of the later suffragettes, Grand invoked traditional arguments of sexual difference, incorporating them into the new taxonomies of masculinist science in order to invert the dominant gender hegemonies. Paradoxically, her feminist attack on modern masculinity was thus conducted through the patriarchal rhetoric of imperialist eugenics, an ideology which defined women as vessels for the reproduction of male power: with New Women 'for the mothers of men', Grand wrote, 'the English-speaking races could rule the world'.[24]

Much of the appeal of what Bakhtin calls 'authoritative discourse' – discourse 'connected with a past that is felt to be hierarchically higher' – resides in the status it confers on the speaker: consequently, by engaging with 'the word of the fathers',[25] Grand was able to invest her arguments with scientific authority. However, as more radical feminists like Mona Caird were quick to point out, male-centred ideological constructs, even when purloined for feminist purposes, were bound to bolster patriarchal paradigms in the family, marriage and motherhood from which feminists aimed to liberate women. Nonetheless, Grand went to great lengths to turn the woman-as-homemaker concept into an 'internally persuasive', glamorous discourse,[26] exalting the femininity of both its traditional incarnation (the wife and mother) and its public-political equivalent (the feminist, the nation's housekeeper), and arguing that her high moral seriousness was a quality which did not diminish but heightened the New Woman's personal magnetism. Using her own persona as a showcase, Grand impressed on her readers that, however daring her views might be, the New Woman was in tune with the latest fashion and was in fact the arbiter of elegance. Interviewers were urged to emphasise Grand's 'truly feminine love of dress' and to assure readers that, as 'one of the most tastefully dressed members' of the Pioneer Club, she could be consulted 'on questions of the toilet with as much confidence' as on literary and social matters.[27]

Grand's strategic deployment of femininity is most clearly and explicitly outlined in 'The Morals of Manner and Appearance' (1893), which exhorted feminists to be mindful of their 'duty to be prepossessing' and rebuked the older generation of women's rights activists for alienating the public with their careless appearance and brusque manners. Since it was 'not by arguments but by feelings that the world [was] swayed', the best policy of overcoming conservative preconceptions about the unsexing effects of political agitation on women was by 'rous[ing]' senses before addressing intellectual sensibilities: 'To succeed all round, you must invite the eye, you must charm the ear, you must excite an appetite for the pleasure of knowing you and hearing you by acquiring … the reputation of being a pleasing person.' Once captured by the spell of the feminine mystique, even the most resistant of opponents were likely to lend an ear to feminist arguments. If cultivated, this strategy constituted a powerful means of 'kicking against the pricks'.[28] With a keen eye to her audience's subliminal fantasies, Grand thus turned the New Woman into an object of desire, implying at the same time that there was only a thin dividing line between the ideal and real-life contingencies by casting the role model as the reader's mirror image, a traditional homemaker.[29] If Joan Riviere was to argue in 1929 that the performance of femininity enabled many professional women who faced male disapprobation 'both to hide the possession of masculinity and to avert the reprisals expected if … found to possess it',[30] Grand suggested that it could also serve as a cover to introduce traditional-minded women to feminist thought.

Promoting the New Woman as a feminine superstar, while advising aspiring feminists to refine their seduction skills, Grand constructed femininity at one and the same time as an innate quality *and* a performative act, as both an essential feature of evolution's showpiece, modern womanhood, and as 'a part of art'[31] which, like the paraphernalia of the actress, feminists did well in perfecting: a costume a woman could 'put on … with her gloves' ('Vanity and Vexation', *V*, 67). Her articles thus served a doubly didactive purpose, in that they were aimed at seducing female middle-class readers to feminist ideas (however diluted), while offering an object lesson to feminists on how best to market the cause. In her journalistic work (in which I include interviews, which always bear her strategic imprimatur) the glossy image of the New Woman was the product of complex textual masquerades sustained by sophisticated pictorial *mises-en-scène* of her multiple personae. As a reviewer in the *Woman's Signal* was astute enough to grasp, 'She [was] her own most striking creation.'[32] Grand's stagings of the self are particularly pointed in Jane Stoddart's 'Illustrated Interview' of 1895. In this article she comes down on the side of 'noble purity' – both *vis-à-vis* the literary currents of the time (Realism/

2 'Madame Sarah Grand', from photograph by H. S. Mendelssohn, Notting Hill, in Jane T. Stoddart, 'Illustrated Interview: Sarah Grand', *Woman at Home*, 3 (1895) 247.

Naturalism), and in relation to some factions within the women's movement (free love and divorce advocates) – only to alert readers to the futility of seeking consistency in a writer's discursive explorations of different subject positions:

> So many people suppose … that when an author develops a character with great care and fullness, his own views may be safely identified with those expressed by that character. … The views of Evadne or Angelica, for example, are not neces-sarily to be accepted as my views, in fact cannot be, for they are even opposed to each other, yet people frequently write, wondering how I can possibly defend such opinions.[33]

The 'real' Sarah Grand did not exist, a point already advertised by her pseudonym, which framed the 'individual' woman, 'Sarah' – an adopted name – within abstract and impersonal markers of authority, 'Madame' and 'Grand'.

3 'The Drawing-Room', in Jane T. Stoddart, 'Illustrated Interview: Sarah Grand',
Woman at Home, 3 (1895) 248.

In stressing that she was not to be subsumed into her protagonists' voices,
Grand also destabilised the authenticity of her journalistic pronouncements,
implying that these were just as much to be regarded as impersonations and
variations of her authorial persona as her fictional characters; this is substantiated by a closer look at the illustrations accompanying Stoddart's interview.
Whereas some of Grand's early work, especially when it appeared in malestream publications,[34] reflects the ideological clash between illustration and
copy which Graham Law considers a central feature of the representation of
the New Woman in late-Victorian periodical literature,[35] she later used her
standing to influence the selection of pictorial material. Each of the six pages
in Stoddart's 'Illustrated Interview' carries a photograph, alternately of
'Madame Sarah Grand' (Figures 2, 4 and 6) and her Kensington flat (Figures 3,
5 and 7), the site of her subject-constitution as an independent woman, prominent feminist figure and notable writer. Grand had moved to Kensington in
1891 after leaving her husband the previous year;[36] by 1895, four novels and
one collection of short stories had established her as a major figure on the
cultural and socio-political landscape of the *fin de siècle*. Casting herself in
three separate poses located in three highly semiotic settings – a feature replicated in other interviews[37] – Grand subtly signposted the fluidity and versatility

4 'Madame Sarah Grand', in Jane T. Stoddart, 'Illustrated Interview:
Sarah Grand', *Woman at Home*, 3 (1895) 249.

of New Woman femininities. The article is headed by a 'profile' of the author as
an aesthetically dressed, introspective young woman, whose sensual and yet
carefully contained hairstyle (the loose and decorative curls on her forehead
being juxtaposed to the full hair tied back at the neck) mimics and mocks Pre-
Raphaelite iconography, all pointing to a dreamy nature sensitive to art and
beauty, yet governed by a strong purpose, signified by the pointed concen-
tration of mind with which she is studying the book (or journal?) in her hand
(Figure 2). This representation of Grand as a feminine intellectual is reinforced
by the second illustration, which shows a comfortably furnished drawing
room (Figure 3), a place of artistic recreation (adorned by pictures and equipped with a piano) as well as a workspace, the books in the foreground hinting
at the writing process going on in the background (implied by the sheets of
paper covering the bureau and by discarded manuscript pages on the floor).

5 'The Entrance Hall', in Jane T. Stoddart, 'Illustrated Interview:
Sarah Grand', *Woman at Home*, 3 (1895) 250.

The portrait of the artist as a young woman (Figure 2) is followed by a full-face
and torso photograph of a stylised Victorian lady in elegant attire (Figure 4)
who, with a demure and oddly under-confident expression, clutches a banister
and touches the leaves of a plant (possibly an ironic reference to Grand's 1894
story 'The Yellow Leaf', which chronicles the demise of a decadent society
hostess). Was this meant to signify the New Woman in the making, an emblem
of the fashionable reader and erstwhile Old Woman contemplating the journey
into self-discovery, albeit with some apprehension? This idea may also be
encoded by the next illustration, the entrance hall (Figure 5), which pointedly
leads from darkness into light. The final set of photographs feature a poised,
well-groomed lady with an imposing hat (Figure 6), a woman whose serene
gaze indicates strength of mind and self-assurance in the knowledge of her
public success; an impression substantiated by her sitting room (Figure 7), its
near-austere refinement counter-balanced by the presence of the writer's tools
barely visible on a desk placed in the background.

6 'Madame Sarah Grand', in Jane T. Stoddart, 'Illustrated Interview:
Sarah Grand', *Woman at Home*, 3 (1895) 251.

By interpolating feminine with feminist positions, behavioural codes and
linguistic (ideological) consciousnesses, Grand could be said to have been
engaged in constructing a Bakhtinian dialogic premised on 'hybridization': the
'mixture of two social languages within the limits of a single utterance, an
encounter, within the arena of an utterance, between two different linguistic
consciousnesses'.[38] A Bakhtinian reading helps to explain the clash between
Grand's conservative rhetoric in pieces written for the domestic market (which
resemble the problem-and-advice pages of the less glamorous of today's
women's magazines) and the politically explosive tone of her novels and those
of her articles addressed to an advanced readership interested in intellectual
debate (published in the *Fortnightly Review*, the *Humanitarian*, the *North
American Review*). If her journalistic *oeuvre* is treated, in Bakhtinian terms, as
a 'single utterance', Grand's 'two social languages' become immediately apparent

7 'The Sitting-Room', in Jane T. Stoddart, 'Illustrated Interview:
Sarah Grand', *Woman at Home*, 3 (1895) 252.

in two diametrically opposed articles both entitled 'The Modern Girl'.[39] The
North American Review version of 1894 calls for university training and sex
education for girls, condones female sexual desire as a 'healthy'[40] instinct, and
challenges the idea that all women are born mothers; its 1898 counter-piece in
the *Temple Magazine* rebukes readers for neglecting their responsibilities as
'mother[s] of men who will keep us in our proud place as the dominant race'
and attacks the selfish, aggressively self-assertive, pleasure-loving 'girl of the
period' in the polemic style cultivated three decades earlier by Eliza Lynn
Linton.[41] Another instance of hybridisation can be found in Grand's use of the
first-person pronoun, which shifted significantly in semiotic import between
the *Young Woman*'s statement that '*Personally, I* have no doubt as to what is the
ideal life for the average married woman' and the *North American Review*'s
counter-affirmation that '*many amongst us* are not suited for the sacred office'.[42]
Grand's journalism also reflects the other two determinants of the Bakhtinian
dialogic, stylisation and dialogue. Her authorial masquerades correlate with
Bakhtin's two 'individualized linguistic consciousnesses' – 'one that *represents*
(that is, the linguistic consciousness of the styliser) and the one that is *represented*, which is stylised'.[43] However much Grand repudiated '"style" and "art"'
in its decadent configuration – *l'art pour l'art* was but 'the mere mechanics of

literature', she declared in *The Beth Book* (*BB*, 374, 461) – she was an accomplished stylist when it came to staging New Womanhood. By entangling her
readers within the web of her 'internally persuasive' discourse of femininity,
she brought about the process which Bakthin describes as 'coming to know
one's own language as it is perceived in someone else's language, coming to
know one's own belief system in someone else's system'.[44] Judging by contemporary accounts, Grand's strategy of marketing feminism through spec(tac)ular-
ising its feminine glamour held lasting appeal, for even at the time of her death
she was remembered as much for her exquisite womanliness as for her daring
views: as Rebecca West's sister Letitia Fairfield recalled in 1943, she was
'pleasant to look at, charmingly dressed, gentle in voice and manner. She had
an unforgettable air of dignity and inward strength which made one little girl
her lifelong admirer'.[45] Having 'thought of her as something militant', Katherine
Tynan was surprised to find her 'soft-voiced, gentle, delicately feminine, and
most lovable'.[46] If her writing was still associated with all that was 'revolutionary
feminism in the [Victorian] novel', obituarists also stressed that in her 'private
life there was nothing aggressive about Sarah Grand … a charming, well-dressed,
and rather beautiful woman'.[47] That at the height of her career, in 1897, even
confirmed anti-feminists like the critic Hugh Stutfield – otherwise known for
his scathing remarks about the New Woman's 'Tommyrotics'[48] – felt inclined
to applaud the 'Sarah Grandian school' for its 'modern incarnation of the
feminine spirit'[49] testifies to the allure of Grand's feminine mystique. Within
the space of three years her representational strategies had advanced her from
the status of literary terrorist – an 'aboriginal', 'shrieking', 'anarchist woman'[50] –
to that of an authority known for her high moral tone and 'feminine' ethics,
which could be held up as a standard to which other women writers ought to
aspire. The policy of embracing aspects of traditional gender discourse to
prepare the Victorian public for the reception of more explosive sexual politics
was not without its drawbacks, however. Thus the 'Grandian school' served as
a boundary marker between respectability and impropriety, mapping the
discursive space within which the New Woman could be contained (Stutfield
drew on Grand only in order to attack women writers bent on exploring the
'sexual emotions of young ladies').[51] Moreover, Grand remained caught within
the wider ideological framework of the authoritative discourses she aimed to
dismantle, for even if in the course of her writing career she learnt to challenge
the language of the medical fathers, she never fully disengaged herself from the
discursive paradigms of their eugenic sons. Her last two novels, *Adnam's
Orchard* (1912) and *The Winged Victory* (1916), revisit the eugenic concerns of
her *fin-de-siècle* career with a vengeance: ultimately the ideological maze of her
contradictory visions became so confounding even to her own mind that she
was unable to complete her eugenic trilogy.[52] Her early work, by contrast,
offers more subversive revisions of authoritative discourses.

The ventriloquist's tale: from patrocentric voiceover
to matrocentric 'Voix du Ciel'

At the outset of her writing career in the 1870s, Grand was strongly influenced by dominant (male-centred) discourses, particularly medical taxonomies. This was perhaps inevitable, given her marriage, at barely 16, to an army surgeon more than twenty years her senior. The greatest attraction of the match, she later acknowledged, was the prospect of unlimited access to books and the scope for serious and concentrated study.[53] After a mere two years of formal schooling and on the rebound from the 'mental misery'[54] of one institution and the superficiality of the other, with only an uncongenial home to return to, Grand threw herself into this opportunity for self-improvement and exotic adventure (the first five years of her marriage were spent in South East Asia). As a result of her husband's profession and her own growing interest in the 'philosophy of medicine',[55] she was to become the most well-informed and deeply read of all the British New Woman writers on medical matters. Keenly imbibing all available factual knowledge (which she transcribed with enthusiastic detail into her first book, *Two Dear Little Feet*), she also took on board the scientific bias against women:

> At that time I was but a mere girl, and took without question the reiterated prophecy ... that if a woman became a doctor or did anything of an intellectual and capable kind, or made a career for herself, she must become hideously ugly, and hard, and utterly horrid, and like a man ... And I didn't want to be just like a man, and all the other dreadful things they prophesied ... and I believed all I read in print ...[56]

She thus found herself in the paradoxical position of a woman liberated by her private studies in an academic discipline which indoctrinated her with the belief that studying was harmful to women. Under the impact of her own experience, this contradiction could only have sensitised her to the clash of interests between medical men and (married) women, eventually turning her into the fiercest literary opponent of the turn-of-the-century medical establishment on this side of the Atlantic. The conflict between medical and feminist values is personified in her fiction – and that of other New Woman writers like Ella Hepworth Dixon (*The Story of a Modern Woman*, 1894) and Charlotte Perkins Gilman ('The Yellow Wallpaper', 1892) – by the recurring figure of the male doctor and his female subject in her dual role as patient and object of desire. The gradual transformation of the physician from authority figure (*Two Dear Little Feet*, 1873) to villain (*The Beth Book*, 1897) is indicative of Grand's mental journey into ideological independence, reflecting as it does her recognition of the institutionalisation of male power through marriage and medicine.

In *Two Dear Little Feet* the plot – the decline of a vain girl who ruins her health and good looks by wearing incapacitating boots – serves as the narrative background for factual passages which offer medical information on the human body and explicitly link Chinese footbinding and Western fashion.[57] Although the text foreshadows important aspects of her later work – dress reform, the correlation between women's physical and mental health, the pleasures of 'authentic' as opposed to the pains of 'artificial' femininity – the medical profession and its representative, the male doctor, are still cast as credible authority figures. In her recognition of the mother's function as patriarchal gatekeeper, Grand laid the blame on the older woman who, instead of providing a positive role model, leaves her daughter to the designs of a silly maid, who encourages her folly for self-mutilation. Prefiguring Grand's later representation of gender as performance, the book throws into relief the culturally constructed nature of beauty codes, while equating the fashion for feminine frailty with disability and racial inferiority. To interfere with the natural shape of European feet, Grand suggested, was to slide back down the evolutionary scale: 'African negroes, Bushmen of Australia, and, indeed, all low savage races, have broad, flat feet, thick ankles near the ground, low heels, and badly formed calves to their legs; while in the higher races the feet and legs are well-formed' (*TDLF*, 29). The textual hybridity of this early work – a medical primer crossed with the conduct literature of earlier times (warning little girls of the dire consequences of behaving badly: Laura ends by having some of her toes amputated) – is indicative of Grand's divided loyalties. The analogies between women's cramped bodies and atrophied minds signal her developing feminist (and firmly Eurocentric) vision, yet the voice of reason and narrative approbation is that of the elderly male physician, whose wish to see 'a clean bill of health' (*TDLF*, 114) being made a precondition for marriage is levelled at women, not, as would be the case in Grand's subsequent work, at men. The doctor's contempt for 'foolish mothers' and the 'butterfly beauties' they produce (*TDLF*, 59, 51) is reminiscent of Wollstonecraft's *Vindication of the Rights of Woman*, as is the narrator's call for a 'revolution in female manners'[58] through rational, purposeful education: 'if only she had bestowed half as much courage and determination on the pursuit of knowledge' as on the crushing of her feet, Laura, we are informed, might have achieved something in her life (*TDLF*, 53–4). The unmistakable element of *Schadenfreude* in the omniscient narrator's account of Laura's demise, however, cancels out the feminist overtones of the little girl's refusal to 'sit still' and healthy habit of throwing 'her little body about in all directions … in order to grow strong' (*TDLF*, 17). Ultimately, the narrator's anger at 'what treatment of the innocent I have witnessed, and what unnecessary suffering I have seen inflicted' (*TDLF*, 12) is directed at women, not the patriarchal system, whose spokesmen (the doctor and, to a lesser extent, the father) are in effect presented as well-meaning, albeit powerless guardians wishing to protect women and girls from their self-destructive impulses.

If the protagonist of her first novel wrecks herself as a result of ignoring medical advice, in Grand's later work it is their reliance on and fatal attraction to their physicians which proves injurious to women: in *Ideala* the heroine is almost seduced into an adulterous relationship with her physician, in *The Heavenly Twins* Evadne's nervous prostration deepens after she marries her doctor, and in *The Beth Book* the physician-husband is exposed as an adulterer, lock hospital keeper and vivisectionist. By the 1890s, Grand attributed healing qualities no longer to the medical profession but instead to the political potential of women's solidarity. Thus Janey, the title heroine of an 1891 story reprinted in *Our Manifold Nature* (1894),[59] recovers from her 'hysterical paralysis' (a condition severely aggravated by medical neglect and mismanagement) with the help of a female friend who conjures up a feminist vision, a procession of women who (in anticipation of the suffragettes and Ethel Smyth's battle hymn) march to the song 'To us! to us it is given to do great deeds!' (*OMN*, 230, 240–1).

Although Grand's disenchantment with the medical establishment did not find expression in print until the publication of *Ideala* in 1888, the late 1870s saw her experiment with alternative scripts from which male authoritative (medical) discourses were patently absent. This is particularly interesting in light of her contemporaneous work on *Ideala* (written in 1879, revised and completed in 1881),[60] a novel which highlights the difficulties even a strong-minded woman is apt to face when struggling free from male plots and paradigms. In stark contrast, 'Mamma's Music Lessons' (1878) and 'School Revisited' (1880) invest authority in wise and progressive female mentors. Written for the adolescent female market (*Aunt Judy's Magazine*), they thematise the positive repercussions on female character development of a constructive, intellectually stimulating and pleasurable learning experience shaped by a supportive older woman. These stories can be read as a critique of traditional models of girls' education whose emphasis on mechanical drill and rote-learning discouraged methodological study and analytical thinking. They also represent Grand's personal response to her own uncongenial experience.[61] A product of her traditional upbringing, her mother, Margaret Bellenden Clarke, strongly disapproved of her daughter's unconventional impulses, reproving the 11-year-old for sending some songs she had composed to a publisher by impressing on her that 'ladies only work for charity', and otherwise taking little interest in her three daughters while expending her energies, affection and material possessions on her two sons and their expensive private education.[62] In *The Beth Book* (1897) – a text which, she noted, contained a portrait of her mother[63] – Grand exorcised her memories of a difficult relationship by spotlighting the dysfunctional mothering to which her heroine is exposed. Beth suffers emotional as well as bodily neglect (her bedstead – a cot so small that she cannot stretch her legs – yet another instance of the close

connection between the physical and mental confinement of girls): 'her mother
… checked her mental growth again and again instead of helping her to
develop it' (*BB*, 27). With Dickensian detail Grand records the physical violence
to which Beth is subjected when she attempts to take her learning in hand:

> Beth was a piteous little figure, crouched on the piano-stool, her back bent
> beneath her mother's blows, and every fibre of her sensitive frame shrinking
> from her violence; but she made no resistance, and Mrs. Caldwell carried out her
> threat. When she could beat Beth no longer, she told her to sit there until she
> knew that [musical] sign, and then she left her. (*BB*, 159–60)

Beth, who has attempted to play a musical composition her mother considers
too advanced for her level, is beaten for her ignorance in attempting to execute
signs whose meaning she has never been taught. Metaphorically speaking, she
is punished for her desire to make sense of and derive personal pleasure from a
linguistic (artistic) formation into whose structure she is denied insight on the
grounds of occupying an inferior (feminine) subject position. Like one of
Tennyson's six hundred, one in the army of girls trained to become obedient
wives, hers is not to make reply nor to reason why, hers is but 'to do and die', to
internalise her mother's lesson that she is not good enough to proceed on her
own and to 'die' into subservience.

In tracing the damaging impact of feminine socialisation in her tomboy
protagonists, Grand drew attention to the silencing of girls in puberty and the
repercussions of sex-role conditioning on female psychological development.
A century later her insights were substantiated by sociological studies like Lyn
Mikel Brown and Carol Gilligan's *Meeting at the Crossroads* (1992), which
attributes the disempowerment of women to their loss of confidence in early
adolescence. Around the age of puberty the vast majority of the schoolgirls
sampled by Brown and Gilligan suffered a process of inner dissociation that
left them intensely frightened by the disruptive consequences of confronta-
tional situations and therefore willing to sacrifice their own needs for the sake
of an illusionary harmony. While at age 10 or younger, girls felt able to express
negative emotions and were apt to display considerable energy and imagination in making themselves and their feelings heard,[64] the same girls experienced enormous difficulties with voicing dissent and anger with the onset of
adolescence. Faced with feminine role expectations, they learned to abandon
their childhood resistance as tomboyish, unfeminine, inappropriate behaviour.
Adult women – female teachers and mothers – were central to this process of
discouragement. In *The Beth Book* and elsewhere, Grand thematised girls' loss
of voice as a result of their mothers' complicity with patriarchal structures.

Some girls in Brown and Gilligan's study proved resistant to such gender
conditioning. Frequently these were girls whose ethnicity and class origins set
them apart from the rest and who had therefore had to acquire survival skills

early on in life; even more significantly, many of them had strong and supportive mothers who approved of their daughters' spirited self-assertiveness. If *The Beth Book* provides chilling insights into the psychological and even physical abuse that girls were likely to suffer at the hands of male-identified, patriarchal mothers, 'Mamma's Music Lessons' constitutes a guide to the opposite model: female-centred mothering which aims at confidence-building through self-directed learning. It is no coincidence that both texts rely on the same plot device as a conduit for conveying a didactic message to readers, the 'music lesson' encoding conventional feminine training in the decorative arts as well as artistic subject-formation. In sharp contradistinction to Mrs Caldwell, the mother in this story encourages her daughter to shape her own learning experience through experimentation and, importantly, sensual exploration: 'I want to open a new road to pleasure for you' ('MML', 492/62). For this purpose she calls a halt to her daughter's regular exercises, raising her self-esteem by offering her the use of her own grand piano, and breaking the monotony of conventional piano practice by allowing her space to improvise, awakening her curiosity through skilfully prompting her to think about a musical piece whose apparent simplicity reveals great force and complexity of feeling. The mother's passionate execution and stimulating conversations about composers and their creative processes succeeds in ensuring the daughter's lasting enthusiasm: 'She never told me to practise, never asked me to play; but her teaching had inspired me with such a love for music that I needed no urging to study' ('MML', 535/74). The daughter's realisation that 'music is a language' ('MML', 532/71) generates a desire for self-expression, which in turn leads to the constitution of an authentic self. Asked to perform to an audience, she becomes carried away 'playing an accompaniment … to my own thoughts alone' ('MML', 536/75). The 'moral' of 'Mamma's Music Lessons', then, is twofold: music (art) acts as a catalyst for female self-realisation; with the guidance of a congenial female mentor, education effects the writing into being of the female and feminine self.

This self-exploratory, sensually receptive educational process can be decoded as an expression of *écriture féminine*, replacing Bakhtin's authoritative (male-identified, male-dominated) discourse of domestication and repression with the internally persuasive discourse of the feminine 'Voix du Ciel' (the title of the musical composition initiating the daughter into self-discovery):

> The Voice is soft, but clear and penetrating … Again the Voice speaks. Again it pauses. … [W]hen the Voice has finally ceased to speak there is another murmur. Then the crowd separates. It breaks up into groups, and the many voices are heard, speaking very softly at first, but growing gradually louder and louder, until they seem to shout! ('MML', 530/69)

The 'voyage in' which releases the voice of the individual feminine self also has a liberating effect on the collectivity, hence the chorus of voices; a point later echoed in the Prologue to *The Heavenly Twins* (*HT*, xi).

Sensual self-exploration is ultimately ineffective, however, unless it is allied to a strong sense of an object. This is the message conveyed by Grand's second story, 'School Revisited'. Here, the acquisition of merely decorative knowledge and superficial 'accomplishments' is contrasted with the notion of learning as intellectual and moral self-improvement. Schools fail girls if they do not instil in them an interest in knowledge for its own sake and a sense of a purpose, and the best student is not the one most compliant with the system but the most challenging individual. Of the five friends who visit their former teacher three years after leaving school, the only one to have done something with her life is the one who was the most flippant and mischievous-minded pupil: an obvious representation of Grand herself, she has become a didactic feminist writer. Significantly, the central argument of Evelyn's latest book – 'that the life of a high-spirited, energetic girl, will be a burden to herself, and that she will be a nuisance to her friends, until she feels she lives for a purpose – until she has an object in life, and a good motive to urge her on till she attains it' ('SR', 544/95) – is associated with a body radiant with health and energy, suggesting that, whatever doctors might proclaim to the contrary, women flourished under the impact of intellectual stimulation. Evelyn's hedonistic gestures – she 'gathered a whole handful of rose-leaves that had dropped on her lap from a flower she had in her waist-belt, and threw them across the room to Mrs Morley; but they scattered in the air as they flew' ('SR', 475–6/81–2) – invalidate the notion that deep thinking and a purposeful life have a dampening effect on women's good looks, sense of humour and sensuality. Fulfilled in body and mind, and replenishing herself through her rhythmic, cyclical motion – 'tatting and swinging leisurely backwards and forwards in the little rocking-chair' ('SR', 540/91) – the woman with a purpose is able to savour, and pass on to others, the *jouissance* of her writing the feminine self, the inscription of herself into the textual body.

These early stories suggest that, in coming into her own as a feminist writer who called into question the authority of male regulatory practices and discourses, Grand invoked and experimented with a counter-language which, by coupling the seemingly incongruous – pleasure and purpose, sense and sensibility, femininity and feminism – subverted the binary structures of patriarchal logic. This counter-language is central to *Babs the Impossible* and *Singularly Deluded*.

Consuming appetites: *Babs the Impossible* (1900)

Conceived as an entertaining romp, *Babs* articulates many of the concerns of the New Woman – girls' education, the close correlation between healthy bodies and minds, the injurious effects of dysfunctional mothering, the dangers of sexual ignorance, the hypocrisy of the moral double standard, the need for a purposeful occupation besides and beyond marriage, anti-vivisection, the ethics of social responsibility – through what Heather Evans has called the 'gastronomical semiotics'[65] of a plot revolving around characters' picaresque pursuit of pleasure. The anarchic spirit of the heroine and the comical escapades of a middle-aged ex-barman cultivating the role of rural Romeo serve to spice up the feminist message: an early instance of the 'allopathic pill' meant to be 'mistaken for a bonbon and swallowed without a suspicion of its medicinal properties', the strategy Grand devised for the *Heavenly Twins*.[66] Indeed, one reviewer writing for the arch-conservative *Athenaeum*, relieved at the low-key approach to feminist didacticism, even considered *Babs* Grand's 'best book';[67] it was the only one of her novels to be produced on the stage.[68]

Published in 1900, *Babs* was written, Grand recalled in 1931, 'as a serial very quickly, before *Ideala*'.[69] The erotic subtext of this second (possibly third) novel[70] may suggest that its composition falls in the first years of her marriage, the early to mid-1870s, a time when she still felt attracted to David Chambers McFall and was enjoying their physical relationship. Exuberant, rumbustious and transgressive, Babs has much in common with Grand's later protagonists Angelica and Beth, and indeed the history of the novel frames Grand's most productive writing phase culminating in the 1890s with the publication of the second and third parts of her feminist trilogy (*The Heavenly Twins* and *The Beth Book*). In contradistinction to Angelica and Beth, however, Babs's story concentrates on one developmental stage only, puberty, ending at the juncture at which her entry into the adult world positions her at the crossroads between marriage and New Womanhood (thus taking her to the point where Ideala's story begins). While there is no closure, with Babs's ultimate direction being left to the reader's imagination, the text implies that a congenial husband is a panacea for women's problems: Babs's aunt, Lorraine Kingconstance, is cured from her boredom-induced hysteria as soon as an attractive neighbour becomes eligible. The narrative counterpart to many of Grand's articles, this 'pot-boiler'[71] was targeted at a conventional readership, whose expectation of romance and love entanglements was met, only to be undercut by a series of events which problematised the marriage plot. The empty life and famished body of the 'superfluous' spinster Miss Spice, who subsists on a starvation diet of sentimental day-dreams and not much else besides, pinpoints the dangers of romanticising marriage as the end-all and be-all of a woman's existence, and so does the self-satisfied, gluttonous narcissism of widows like Babs's mother, Mrs Kingconstance, who despite over-abundant supplies 'tasted every morsel of her food too scrupulously when it was specially to her liking – which it generally was' (*B*, 12).

Intriguingly, the text draws on a sophisticated range of culinary images to expose the emotional and mental damage inflicted on women by a life wasted for the lack of a purpose and mental food. Heather Evans has drawn attention to the fact that, in this novel at least, the woman question is not so much the marriage question, as Grand asserted in 'The New Aspect of the Woman Question' (1894),[72] as more essentially a question of food provision and deprivation: material, mental and moral.[73] In 1852 Florence Nightingale had drawn analogies between the literal and symbolical under-nourishment of women when she wrote in 'Cassandra' that 'To have no food for our heads, no food for our hearts, no food for our activity [amounts to] ... DEATH FROM STARVATION!'[74] Grand, too, associates the general condition of Danehurst's female population with the long-term effects of malnutrition:

> The men had the best education, the best chance for cultivating their minds by travel and experience, and the most amusement; the women were pretty generally *skimped* in everything that did not tend to increase the pleasure or vouch for the importance of their lords. As the young girls grew up, *a sort of blight* seemed to settle upon them; their *beauty faded*, their possibilities *shrank to nothing*, and they became for the most part *subdued and joyless*. (*B*, 43; emphases added)

Though most pronounced in this novel, the food metaphor is a recurrent motif in Grand's fiction and journalism; thus in *The Beth Book*, the young Beth boosts her own and her sisters' meagre diet by hunting rabbits while Mrs Caldwell spends their food allowance on supporting her sons' expensive cravings for tobacco and alcohol. At a time when, as Evans points out, the periodical press reacted to the socio-political challenge of the New Woman by denouncing her rapacious and unsexing appetites,[75] Grand stressed that the New Woman's impulse was not for self-indulgence – this was the monopoly of the Old Man and Woman – but rather for self-development and wider social regeneration: her project constituted a quasi-evolutionary 'effort of nature to raise the race a step higher in the scale of being'.[76] Like 'healthy, hungry children', women had become aware of the inequities of their position and were demanding their full share in the world's affairs; yet this did not mean that they hungered for modern man's insalubrious tastes:[77] 'The New Woman despises any intemperance; besides, she has no time to do more than sip a wholesome draught'.[78] To help herself to the more uplifting ingredients of the male diet, however, was vital for female emancipation, as even George Sand 'did not succeed till she gave herself a man's opportunities' – and, one might add, his plentiful food – 'to develop her powers'.[79]

While underplaying the New Woman's sensual desire, Grand nonetheless advised fellow writers not to lose sight of the fact that 'we are complex beings, with several senses to be satisfied by our food, whether it be the physical food of the body or that other spiritual food which is to stimulate the intellect ... and strengthen the heart'.[80] Just as she subverted the conservative caricature of

the virago by turning feminine chic into a trademark of the New Woman, so –
within the limits demarcated by the concept of 'wholesomeness' – she
reclaimed the pleasures of the body for feminist purposes: 'We require pleasure
as much for our mental health and strength as we require salt with our food'
(*THQ*, 26). 'We are Epicurean, we women', she declared when upholding
women's right to interfere with men's reprehensible body economies for the
'happiness ... of mankind'.[81] Urging feminists to cultivate a 'delicate aroma' in
order to whet the public's appetite for women's rights – for what 'should we
think of a cook who sent up a side dish perfectly cooked but ungarnished?'[82] –
she candidly admitted to adulterating her own writing with plenty of 'sugar ...
to sweeten the pill of evils exposed'.[83]

One of these sugar bonbons is undoubtedly Jellybond Tinney's comic
seduction of Mrs Kingconstance by means of elaborate gourmet dishes and
mouth-watering cocktails. If his sybaritic temperament has the immediate
effect of producing a 'well-fed, vitalising atmosphere, charged with energy and
suggestive of temporal pleasures', leading to 'a sudden increase of appetite in
others' (*B*, 41), his impact on women is of a more specifically eroticising
nature. 'Mr Jellybond loved to be *sauce piquante* to a lady's life – to any number
of them' (*B*, 67). While spicing up provincial life by turning the head of each
and every one of Danehurst's love-starved ladies, his attention soon centres on
wealthy Mrs Kingconstance, whose ample proportions bespeak her not so
dainty palate. Their affair progresses speedily from the invocation of delicious
hors-d'oeuvres of the Parisian *haute cuisine* to exquisite dishes served in the
exotic ambience of a clairvoyant's cottage, finally to culminate in an orgiastic
banquet *à deux* which peaks on a cordial with orgasmic propensities:

> She held her own being in suspense so as to lose no movement of the liquid
> delight as it spread insidiously, taking gradual possession of every nerve in her
> body, and suffusing her at the same time with a strange, warm glow, which was
> succeeded by a sensation of bliss, a dreamy state, a kind of stupor, although full
> consciousness was never suspended. ... It played *crescendo* upon the emotions and
> then evaporated, leaving only a certain languor which yielded to ... such a recol-
> lection of its effect as should make it to be greatly desired for evermore. (*B*, 113)

In her sensual abandon, Mrs Kingconstance unfortunately resembles nothing so much as a 'comfortable ... cow' (*B*, 45), the very emblem of the Old
Woman castigated in Grand's 'New Aspect of the Woman Question'.[84] Struck
by the spectacle of feminine excess and its dehumanising effect (reluctant to
disrupt her idyll, Mrs Kingconstance disregards the news of her son's serious
illness), even the hedonistic Jellybond feels discomposed: 'the idea of
proposing that night melted from his mind' (*B*, 114). Grand thus explores the
potential of sexual pleasure in women only to bracket it together with an
appropriately developed sense of moral responsibility and the capacity for
upholding a healthy balance between the two.[85] Mrs Kingconstance is as

imbalanced sensually as her niece Lorraine is mentally; both are the product of a gender training which atrophies faculties essential to individual human growth. As dynamic as her mother is indolent, and endowed with a strong sense of social responsibility entirely absent in her self-absorbed female relatives, Babs is in no danger of responding with Mrs Kingconstance's bovine indifference to the well-being of others, nor is she at risk of hysterical inertia like Lorraine Kingconstance or humble self-effacement like Miss Spice; she does, however, have to find a happy medium between indulging her 'beautiful appetite' (*B*, 33) and 'living for her senses alone' (*B*, 159). In the course of her moral education through sensual misadventure Babs learns that her love of pleasure needs to be tempered by 'moderation', 'intelligence' and 'principle' (*B*, 70, 151) if she is to evolve into the mature, self-reliant, passionate yet proudly disciplined New Woman represented by Barbara Land, Babs's enlightened teacher.

The need for a healthy equilibrium between physical and spiritual needs also and especially applies to Babs's burgeoning eroticism. Against the background of her hearty appetite ('Glory! What a delight it is to eat good things!', *B*, 33) and resistance to feminine enculturation ('I don't feel any pride in an attenuated body. Nor shall I shirk my food ... nor squeeze my foot ... I'm here to have my own idea of a good time', *B*, 156), Babs discovers how much she enjoys other sensual pleasures like kissing, and sets about tasting 'the endless variety of earthly joys ... I want to try them all' (*B*, 31). While Grand's later heroines learn to control their erotic desire, moving from sensuality to sensibility, Babs's senses overrule her sense: 'I don't want to think – I want to feel' (*B*, 36). Like Angelica, she has no qualms about propositioning the men she fancies – 'I like to look at you ... You *are* nice to look at!' (*B*, 33, emphasis in original) – but more bodily aware than Angelica, Babs cannot see any reason why she should not be on kissing terms with two men at the same time, or marry them for that matter: 'I want you both. I should like to have Cadenhouse for my Sunday lover and you for my everyday one' (*B*, 153). If Babs's love of petting is a reflection of her sexual desire, Grand was presenting a remarkably libertarian vision with almost a hint of approval towards premarital experimentation; for, as her heroine declares, 'how can one choose a husband until one knows which man one likes to kiss best?' (*B*, 134).

Not only did the Grandian New Girl thus claim the right to attend fully to her bodily needs, in her desire to stimulate a politically effective reading experience, Grand also implicitly offered her heroine up for sexual consumption – a fact that did not escape contemporary critics, who condemned Babs as 'a refined reproduction of the Yahoo maiden'.[86] With her 'abominable ideas about the freedom of her sex' as 'revolting' as her all-too-frank account of the 'physical dissatisfaction' (meaning sexual frustration) of Danehurst's women, Grand represented 'a kind of literary Babs herself' in the eyes of one reviewer, who concluded that the author clearly did 'not really care for social purity'.[87]

8 'Sarah Grand and "Mere Man"', *Harper's Weekly*, 2 November 1901, 1104.

What proved so unnerving to male readers in particular was that Grand's social purist message was embedded in an exceptionally candid exploration of female sensual awakening. Both *Babs the Impossible* and *The Beth Book* constitute an early feminine writing of the body, and critics were only too aware of the 'wicked, cruel charm' of the 'extraordinarly clear and shameless way in which the reader is compelled to see the growth of a girl's soul'.[88] There was more than 'an element of vivisection' in all of this, W. T. Stead observed, adding a note of cannibalism to Grand's use of the food metaphor by implying that the reader's visual feasting on the heroine was brought about by an authorial *mise-en-scène* of her body which was tantamount to anatomical dissection; thus Beth was 'scampering up and down with nothing on, the naked-souled child, until the spectator himself cries out against such frank revealings. It is as Eve before the Fall, without even the fig-leaf.'[89] Orchestrated and controlled as it was by Grand the writer, this dynamic of sensual interchange between spectator and heroine had the effect of placing the reader in the position of a voyeur unnerved by the sudden realisation that in his scrutiny of the 'naked-souled child' he himself became the object of the feminist writer's stripping, probing, penetrating gaze (as caricatured in a cartoon of 1901, see Figure 8). Such a quasi-feminine exposure of the 'naked' masculine self proved disconcerting even to the author of the 'Maiden Tribute' articles.[90] Indeed, while Stead's discomposure may have originated in his recollection of his more than equivocal role in investigating and simultaneously participating in the sexual trafficking of girls, some male readers may have traced an uncomfortable likeness in the figure of the sexually experienced Jeffrey Wylde who, 'judging Babs by conventional standards, ... was taking advantage of her in the conventional way' (*B*, 180) and then condemned her for his own preconceptions and desires; a projection of licentious impulses of the self onto the Other which may have shaped the *Independent* critic's response to Grand's novel.

Within the first decade of her writing career Grand had thus moved from patriarchal mimicry to feminist mockery of authoritative discourses. Just as she reclaimed femininity for feminism, so she valorised women's desire for bodily pleasure as a healthy and, if free from corrupting male influences, 'innocent' instinct, while at the same time attacking the sexual objectification of women through her choice of male characters and marriage plots. In her spiritual journey to New Womanhood her heroine must not only steer clear of a plethora of negative female role models, she must also resist the temptation to imitate patriarchal libidinal and appropriatory practices. Babs's slaughter of her fowls to alleviate the poverty of a disgraced female servant is condemned by the narrative voice, who draws attention to the false logic underlying altruistic impulses carried into action by violent means: 'had she transferred a scrap of the pity for suffering humanity to her poor old hens – she could not have done it' (*B*, 78). Babs's post-lapsarian horror – she 'seized the hatchet, raised it, and brought it down with all her might. The instant it fell, however, she let it go, and rushed from the place' (*B*, 78) – signals her realisation that women's empowerment cannot be brought about through patriarchal abuse of power; in Lordean terms, 'the master's tools will never dismantle the master's house'.[91] At the same time, however, by flinging the beheaded fowls in Jellybond's face and thus in Kristevan terms forcing a figure representing masculinity literally to 'face' the abjected (female) body,[92] Babs symbolically confounds and destabilises patriarchal conceptualisations of femininity. In 'Castration or Decapitation?' Hélène Cixous cites a Chinese story in which women's resistance to masculine law and order is punished by decapitation, in order to argue that, if 'man operates under the threat of castration, if masculinity is culturally ordered by the castration complex, it might be said that the backlash, the return, on women of this castration anxiety is its displacement as decapitation, execution, of woman, as loss of her head'.[93] Babs's decapitation and disposal (abjection) of the fowls ('foul', male-defined femininity) consolidates a process which leads from 'feminine disorder'[94] to the 'inward vision' of the emerging subjectivity of the New Woman: 'that voice that speaks to me ... here, in myself, directing me ... I want to know about this pleasure, and this power – this something in me' (*B*, 51).

This inner power is put to the test in Grand's next novel. If *Babs* is about the need for women to find the right medium between pleasure and purpose, *Singularly Deluded* explores what happens when a wife's desire becomes so overwhelming for the husband that he seeks refuge in the feminine subject position of the hysteric.

Tarantellas of desire: *Singularly Deluded* (1892)

While on holiday, Gertrude Somers (whose initials are an inversion of Grand's[95]), is, presumably 'in jest', tied to a telegraph post next to a railway line by her husband Leslie, a barrister suffering from work-related stress, who then mysteriously disappears, leaving their son, a toddler, playing on the tracks. The son remains miraculously unharmed by two approaching trains, and mother and child are shortly after rescued by a passer-by, the physician Jeffrey Mansell, who introduces Gertrude to the wealthy Lord Wartlebury. Assisted by the two men, she starts an intensive search for her husband which soon turns into a frantic hunt across the Channel and through half of France in pursuit of a shady character who eventually turns out to be her husband's dissipated *Doppelgänger*. Back in Britain, the couple are reunited, and the mystery is resolved in truly sensational style when Leslie explains that he dislocated his ankle as a result of falling into a hole in the ground, after which he was held captive by an over-protective, deaf-mute shepherd.

As Teresa Mangum points out, the novel reflects Grand's developing resistance to the marriage plot by means of a narrative exploration of role reversal and revenge fantasies.[96] Parodying the male adventure novel from within the 'female' genre of sensation fiction, Grand casts the wife as the intrepid hero, braving fire, shipwreck and wrongful imprisonment without so much as battering an eyelid, while the husband is assigned a passive role: susceptible to depression and nervous prostration, the paradigmatic 'female malady' of the nineteenth century,[97] he is prescribed a rest cure (hence their holiday), rebels against his feminine disempowerment by immobilising his wife, only to be punished with confinement to the home of another man. The shepherd's possessive care of and watchful guard over his reluctant charge mimic the power structures inherent in patriarchal marriage, presenting the reader, Mangum notes, with 'discomfiting insights into a wife's view of a paternalistic husband'.[98] As in Charlotte Perkins Gilman's story 'The Yellow Wallpaper' (1892), relief from marital oppression can be achieved only through a metaphorical regression into infancy, with both Leslie and Gilman's released wallpaper woman forced to crawl into freedom (*SD*, 265–6; 'YW', 31).

In conjunction with the husband's disturbing behaviour towards his wife and his desertion of his family at the beginning, the images of captivity and escape which frame and structure the novel, though typical plot components of adventure and sensation fiction, assume meaning beyond the formal attributes of these genres, possibly reflecting the author's own sense of entrapment in a marriage that had begun to jar in the late 1870s, when she was first working on this book. With its Jekyll-and-Hyde theme, the text would certainly have enabled Grand to express her concern about a husband whose marital conduct had become unaccountable and distressing. Thus at one point Gertrude tracks down her fugitive spouse, only to be horrified by his transformation into

> an uncultured man of low tastes, with a good brain much weakened by dissipation and drink ... He confessed gross sins and ignorances without shame or reserve, but seemed to know the possibility and recognise the advantages of leading a better life ... He was weak, however, and sensual, caring for nothing really but constant excitement, and only remorseful when this was not to be obtained and he became subject to the depression consequent upon its absence. (*SD*, 238)

If Gertrude's relief at finding that 'That man ... is not – my husband!' (*SD*, 250) is emblematic of Grand's own hope of being proved wrong in her assessment of McFall, the happy ending with its reunion of the couple embraces a distinctly cautionary message, hinting at the possibility of men behaving badly only to find the tables turned on them in future. Thus the husband's return to the marital home is contrasted with his wife's notable absence from it, throwing him into the very state of 'speechless' bewilderment (*SD*, 269) and suspended animation which he had inflicted on her at the outset of the story: 'There was ... nothing for Leslie to do but lie there day after day, a prey to the most anxious suspense, and wait' (*SD*, 271). With *Singularly Deluded* Grand had embarked on her feminist deconstruction of marriage.

It is indicative of Grand's emerging voice of feminine alterity that this deconstructive message is allied to a subtle exploration of female desire couched in elaborate nature imagery. Thus the couple's seaside holiday is orchestrated by the sensual delights of a 'delicious' second honeymoon: 'And then there were the nights! ... the moon would rise triumphant ... till the air seemed faint with ... pleasure' (*SD*, 5). That this orgasmic experience has a particularly rousing effect on the wife is signalled by the explicitly female libidinal economy of the countryside, whose 'seemingly dry barren' soil is 'nothing ... but a rugged surface', hinting at the hidden springs in the female body which, like the heath with its 'heights and hollows', proves to be

> full of life and cheery voices, the babble of numberless streams, the merry chirp and twitter of restless birds, the hum of busy bees, and the voice of myriads of insects – the dominant chord, made of numberless notes, of the whole melody – *sinking* as they settled in showers upon the leaves, *swelling* as they rose again to pursue their gambols in the air, and *sinking* once more as they again subsided, fatigued by their aerial dances, for another moment's rest ... everything was

throbbing to the heat of the summer sun, *glowing response to his ardent kiss; the whole broad bosom* of the heath outspread, ... *a thymy couch for him to rest upon,* warmed into life and *rapture* by his rays, and *uttering, in the joy of his caress, a low, varied, blissful, inarticulate sob of deep ecstatic pleasure.* (*SD*, 11-12, emphases added)

First enchanted, then unnerved by this 'strange new land' (so reminiscent of Donne's new-found-land, the emblem of the female body as seen through the male gaze),[99] the husband places his son on his shoulders, as if, by towering above the voluptuous landscape, he seeks to reaffirm his masculine authority over the bodyscape that threatens to engulf him – for as Mangum notes, the enclosure into which he will shortly after disappear bears an uncanny resemblance to a vulva (*SD*, 12).[100] Unperturbed by his impulse towards separation and domination (the rope which he swings in one hand will later serve to immobilise her), his wife continues 'singing softly to herself', 'laughingly' feeding strawberries to the child, an act which metaphorically feminises the male body by turning it into a 'crimson orifice ... every now and then presented to her for fresh supplies' (*SD*, 13). The phallic empowerment of the wife is further implied in the husband's discovery of a 'double line of rails', so evocative of the penetrative force of trains and thus indicative of her virile (clitoral) sexuality. Located in the very heart of an abundantly female landscape, the track is 'quite invisible till you were close ... you would scarcely have expected to find [it] there ... hiding itself ... beneath the luxuriant herbage that fringed it thickly on either hand, as if it knew it had no business there' (*SD*, 13–14).

Faced with the fearful synchronicity of feminine and masculine libidinal economies in the now unhallowed maternal body of Nature and Woman, both father and son respond with a disciplining impulse. While the son begins to 'deal death and destruction to every winged creature within his reach' (*SD*, 14), scourging the anarchic female body of its dangerous potential (the flights of ecstasy signified by the insects in the passage cited above), the husband returns insurgent (virile) femininity to the narrow confines of the Law of the Father: 'Presently her husband came up behind her with that piece of rope, and ... wound it round and round her and the telegraph-post, till she stood pinioned like a victim tied to a stake' (*SD*, 14).

Trapped in the stranglehold of phallic signifiers, the wife for the first time becomes aware of her subject position: 'all at once she felt a shiver ... of loneliness and helplessness' (*SD*, 15). With her subsequent release at the hands of Doctor Mansell initiating her journey into 'masculine' agency, she never loses the insight gained during her captivity that she cannot do without the support of kindly men: the noble aristocrat who places his money and yacht at her disposal; the heroic sailor and intrepid coach-driver who, on two separate occasions, save her from drowning; the officer and gentleman who effects her discharge from prison. Ultimately, Gertrude learns that there is no getting away from patriarchy. Her frantic activity is as much a means of blocking out the memory of her subjection as it is a screen concealing the proto-feminist's – the hysteric's – rage.

In *The Newly Born Woman* Catherine Clément describes the specifically ritualistic form such an 'abreaction' of painful reminiscences can take. In southern Italy the Tarantella dance serves to provide cathartic relief from the psychological wounds inflicted by patriarchy as symbolised in the tarantula spider's bite. By 'transforming the tarantula-body of the one bitten into an instrument body and then into a rhythmic and melodic body', the hysteric-as-dancer is able to turn her suffering into '[s]pectacle, music, acrobatics, abreaction' and thus to overcome it, if only temporarily.[101] In Grand's *Singularly Deluded*, the various stages of Gertrude's journeyings from an unspecified seaside resort to London, London to Southampton, Southampton to St Malo, Mont St Michel, back to Southampton, and from there to the Bay of Biscay and the Mediterranean, are accompanied by rhythmic convulsions that invoke both Gertrude's earlier *jouissance* on the heath and the Sicilian tarantella dance.[102] Whether in tune with the reeling motion of the train – 'on, and on, and on, rattle, and clatter, and rumble, shriek of whistle and rush of steam, the mighty crank and the quivering wheel' (*SD*, 57) – or the lapping of the waves, her body is alternately galvanised and soothed by a rhythm which acts as a 'substitute for orgasm, mimed in all the forms of displacement':[103] 'Rock, rock, rock, rock – from side to side, slowly and with every now and then just a perceptive pause … the rocking never ceased – rock, rock, rock, rock, with a sort of running accompaniment and gurgle and splash of water in response to the swaying, and the sound of voices … muffled' (*SD*, 144). Just as after the tarantella the dancer rests 'immobile on the bed',[104] so at the end of her Odyssey Gertrude takes to her berth below deck. This metaphorical return to the womb completes the spider dance's cycle of inversion enacted by the triad of 'madwoman, wildwoman, childwoman'. In contradistinction to the patriarchal trinity of 'madman, wildman, and child' (represented by Leslie Somers, Lawrence Soames and the deaf-mute shepherd, and the toddler) – figures who, because they 'always simultaneously signify origin, exclusion, and the future norm',[105] are all disempowered in Grand's novel (in that they face lameness, suffer from speech impediments and are subjected to near-fatal accidents) – the heroine recovers her energy and appetite for life in the course of performing her spectacular tarantella: 'She ordered a small bottle of champagne, and drank more than half a tumbler of it right off … [Then] she became so hungry, that the leg of a gigantic fowl, with tepid ham and cold potatoes, not only satisfied but pleased her' (*SD*, 113). If the tarantella's mimicry of a 'feast, binge, drunkenness, dissolute ingestion of food, and regurgitation' signals that 'it is not simply a matter of getting unusual pleasures but of pushing them to their very limit',[106] this liminality is explored in both its personal (sensual) and public (occupational) dimensions in Grand's novel: 'Gertrude's anxiety had given way now to a state of excitement that was almost pleasurable ... if she ever had to work for herself, she would be a detective' (*SD*, 86).

The transgressive delights that speak from this text's exploration of female self-pleasuring feed into *A Domestic Experiment* (begun in 1885, published in 1891),[107] a novel which, as Mangum points out, tentatively probes the potential of lesbian desire.[108] As this chapter has suggested, the notion which so often dogs current scholarship that New Woman writers were 'victims of a feminism that was ... confining, Victorian, and self-punishing'[109] in its denial of women's impulse for pleasure and erotic fulfilment is not borne out by closer attention to Grand's early narrative work. This is all the more intriguing in light of her simultaneous engagement with the more conservative aspects of social purity feminism. The Bakhtinian concept of hybridisation and French feminist theories of *écriture féminine* help to elucidate the sophisticated discursive strategies of seduction and the performance of selves which underpinned Grand's conflicting ideological positions, enabling her to move seamlessly from male ventriloquism through feminine subversion to feminist populism. Her journalistic stagings of multiple and contradictory New Woman identities, her experimentation with a plurality of female, feminine and feminist voices, and her early revisionary reworkings of the conventional paradigms of sensation fiction, the domestic novel and medical pamphlet literature point the way forward to her mature work, her trilogy combining the three genres to create an explosive cocktail which lent mass market appeal to her maturing feminist vision.

2

Narrative cross-dressing: *Ideala* (1888) and *The Heavenly Twins* (1893)

Women do things more easily than men, but they do not penetrate below the surface, and if they attempt to do so the attempt is but a clumsy masquerade in unbecoming costume. In their own costume they have succeeded as queens, courtesans, and actresses, but in the higher arts, in painting, in music, and literature, their achievements are slight indeed – best when confined to the arrangements of themes invented by men – amiable transpositions suitable to boudoirs and fans. (George Moore, *Modern Painting*, 1897)[1]

I told you nothing that was not absolutely true ... from Diavolo's point of view. I assumed his manner and habits when I put these things on, imitated him in everything, tried to think his thoughts and looked at myself from his point of view; in fact my difficulty was to remember that I was not him. I used to forget sometimes and think I was. ... [It was] not a bit more marvellous in real life than it would have been upon the stage – a mere exercise of the actor's faculty under the most favourable circumstances; and not a bit more marvellous than to create a character as an author does in a book; the process is analogous. (Sarah Grand, *The Heavenly Twins*, 1893)[2]

Nothing allows us to rule out the possibility of radical transformation of behaviours, mentalities, roles, political economy ... Let us simultaneously imagine a general change in all the structures of training, education, supervision – hence in the structures of reproduction of ideological results. And let us imagine a real liberation of sexuality, ... a transformation of each one's relationship to his or her body (and to the other body), an approximation to the vast, material, organic, sensuous universe that we are. This cannot be accomplished, of course, without political transformations that are equally radical. ... Then 'femininity' and 'masculinity' would inscribe quite differently their effects of difference, their economy, their relationship to expenditure, to lack, to the gift. (Hélène Cixous, 'Sorties', 1975)[3]

As the last chapter has argued, Sarah Grand's success with a broad readership was largely due to the skill with which she experimented with producing what George Moore calls 'amiable transpositions suitable to boudoirs and fans' in order to muster popular support for contemporary feminist sexual politics.

Anything but a 'clumsy masquerade in unbecoming costume', her playful mimicry of authoritative discourses was instrumental to her subversion of patriarchal definitions of femininity by writing into being a new female libidinal economy which destabilised the dominant gender taxonomies. In *The Heavenly Twins* Grand posits gender as an essentially fluid category, a performative act which, with its imaginative interplay of impersonation and identification processes, resembles the work of the actor and writer. By associating the art of the performer with the creativity of the artist, Grand also implies that New Woman conceptualisations of art and the artist differ significantly from those embraced by male writers who, like Moore, draw a sharp distinction between the production (creation) and reproduction (imitation) of identities. Grand's endeavour to map a New Woman poetics whose voice of feminine-feminist alterity would pose a challenge to male-stream art criticism is central to her artist-novel *The Beth Book* and will be the subject of my next chapter. This chapter examines Grand's performance of shifting gender/actor/narrator positions, exploring, in Hélène Cixous's terms, the liberatory potential of radical transformation through gender-transgressive behaviour in relation to the first two parts of Grand's feminist artist/activist trilogy, *Ideala* and *The Heavenly Twins*.

One of the most striking aspects of *Ideala* and *The Heavenly Twins* is the friction between female and male voices as orchestrated by the narrative structure. Both texts present their (predominantly female) readership with a hall of mirrors in which New Woman protagonists are reflected through the prism of male eyes by narrators whose reliability readers are implicitly called upon to question, given the considerable emotional investment they have in the heroine and her story: thus Ideala's spiritual journey from discontented wife to allegorical 'mother ... of the race' (*ID*, 300) resonates with her mentor's fantasies of the 'ideal' woman, the object of his not-so-veiled desire, while Evadne's 'case' of hysteria is framed by the medical-cum-personal notes of her physician-husband. Like her early fiction, Grand's mature work ventriloquises authoritative voices with the aim of undercutting the patriarchal claim to objectivity with the feminist concept of relativity, arguing the centrality of gender in determining point of view and shaping truth perceptions. Each novel contains a meta-fictional subplot subjecting the personal agenda and sexual politics of the male narrator to close scrutiny. The cover plot, which Sandra Gilbert and Susan Gubar identify as a central strategy of earlier nineteenth-century women writers endeavouring to placate patriarchal hostility while shattering the literary looking-glass of male-engendered plots and femininities,[4] here becomes the subject of careful narrative attention. As Teresa Mangum notes,[5] Grand went to considerable lengths to problematise reading processes in her novels, and it is this meta-fictional concern with what Judith Fetterley has called the 'resisting reader'[6] in conjunction with her gender-bending subplots that invested her fiction with much of its politically subversive potential. As an act of resistance, the practice of reading (and writing) against the grain is, in Grand's texts, thematically and conceptually linked with the performance of deviant gender identities, a connection also underscored by Cixous in her remark that 'Femininity and bisexuality go together ... Writing is the passageway, the entrance, the exit, the dwelling place of the other in me – the other that I am and am not, that I don't know how to be, but that I feel passing, that makes me live.'[7] To Grand as to Cixous, the crossing of gender boundaries was instrumental to political transformation; the struggle for political change and the destabilisation of gender were closely aligned.

What distinguishes *Ideala* and *The Heavenly Twins* from Grand's earlier writings is this call for full-scale socio-political transformation underpinned by a sense of women's collective purpose; previous texts, by contrast, offered all but individual solutions to general problems. With her feminist trilogy Grand addressed the New Woman question from four different personal-and-political angles, exploring a spectrum of responses to private and public patriarchy: dis-eased rebellion (Evadne's hysteria), masquerade (Angelica's cross-dressing), social purity separatism (Ideala's sexual withdrawal and move into feminist social reformism), and cultural protest as political protest (Beth's fusion of feminist art and activism). By granting these strategies varying degrees of success or failure, Grand indicated her own priorities, in particular her strong belief in the imperative of direct public action. Those of her heroines who opt for private solutions only are unable to break free from male control: Edith is fatally infected with syphilis contracted from her husband, and Evadne's retreat into nervous illness amounts to self-erasure. Like her playful subversion of gender, Angelica's political speeches are attached to marital strings. Only Ideala and Beth, their development shaped by their recognition of the close relationship between personal and political female emancipation, are rewarded with a measure of success. *Ideala* and *The Beth Book*, the first and last parts of Grand's trilogy, can thus be considered feminist blueprints, framing a warning, embedded in *The Heavenly Twins*, about the futility of feminist resistance which remains detached from the wider political framework. Subversive gestures may afford temporary gratification to the individual concerned but are always ultimately ineffective as a means of women's self-liberation.

It is an apt reflection of Grand's interest in the construction of antithetical discourses that her radical message about women's need to extricate themselves from patriarchal superstructures is undermined by her choice of male narrators. Of the three novels, only *The Beth Book* articulates an unmediated female point of view: a perspective born out of the exorcism of authoritative discourses in the preceding texts. *Ideala* in particular thematises the struggle for a woman to come into her own while being constrained by the straitjacket of male narrative paradigms.

Breaking the bounds of the master discourse: from 'ideal' woman to 'femme divine'

Ideala maps the eponymous heroine's transition from traditionalism to feminism, focusing on one of the central themes of Grand's trilogy: women's enforced choice between sexual and social roles, personal fulfilment and political activism, home-bound femininity and public feminism. Most intriguingly, the novel represents the narrative oxymoron of a feminist separatist message transmitted by a patriarchal voice.

In structure and in content *Ideala* is largely shaped by patriarchal parameters. The protagonist may end a rebel, but she certainly begins her narrative existence by positioning herself in opposition to the women's movement, expressing misogynist views on the unsexing effect on women of the political struggle for equality and the folly of trying to defy the constraints of the female body and mind. Thus in the second chapter, Ideala defines 'three classes' of modern women, two of whom she sharply attacks (the woman's righter and the decadent writer), aligning herself with the third group, women disenchanted with men and the old world order but indecisive about any action that could or should be taken:

> There are, first of all, the women who in their struggles for political power have done so much to unsex us. They have tried to force themselves into unnatural positions, and the consequence has been about as pleasing and edifying as an attempt to make a goose sing. They clamour for change, mistaking change for progress ... The people I speak of are not those who have so nobly devoted themselves to the removal of the wrongs of women, though they work together. But the object of all this class is good. They wish to raise us, and what they want ... is a little more common sense – as is shown in their system of education, for instance, which cultivates the intellectual at the expense of the physical powers, girls being crammed as boys ... just when nature wants all their strength to assist their growth; the result of which becomes periodically apparent when a number of amiable young ladies are let loose on society without hair or teeth. But the thing they clamour for most is equality. There is a great deal to be said in favour of placing the sexes on an equal footing, and if social conventions are stronger and more admirable than natural instincts ... the thing should be done; but the innate perversity of women will make it difficult – for ... whatever the position of a true woman, and however much she may clamour for equality with men in general, the man she herself loves in particular will always be her master ...
>
> Their ideas, shorn of all good intention, have resulted in the production of a new creature; and have made it possible for women who have the faults of both sexes and the virtues of neither to mix in society ... These are the women ... who

spend their time and talents on the production of cleverly-written books of the most corrupt tendency …

Besides these two classes there is the third, which is more difficult to define. It is the one on which our hope rests. The women who belong to it are dissatisfied like the others, but they are less decided, and therefore their dissatisfaction takes no positive shape … They do good and evil indiscriminately, and for the same motive: they find distraction in doing something – anything. But the desire to do good is latent in all of them; show them the way, and it will make itself apparent. (*ID*, 18–20)

Like other New Woman writers and journalists, Grand was keen to distance the feminist project of social regeneration from the stereotype of the 'shrieking sisterhood' in order to enlist reader sympathies for the 'right' kind of rights-with-duties discourse; the critic Elizabeth Rachel Chapman also framed her support for the women's movement with a repudiation of 'the exaggerations and aberrations of a small minority of impatient and ill-balanced minds', which she contrasted with the 'reasonable claims and aspirations' of the 'Best Woman'.[8] That Grand was in tune with the broad spectrum of contemporary female thought – Ideala's tripartite system of women bears analogies with anti-vivisectionist feminist Frances Power Cobbe's categories of the feminist, decadent and old-style woman in *Duties of Women* (1881),[9] and her equation of women's higher education with physical degeneration correlates with similar statements made in May Sinclair's Edwardian suffrage tract *Feminism* (1912)[10] – will have contributed to the success of her book, as did the conservatism of the opening chapters, which impelled erstwhile traditionalists like Margaret Oliphant to declare their unequivocal support for the heroine: one of the 'other revolutionaries' who gave voice to 'a great many thoughts of the moment', Ideala had, she asserted, inspired the 'mothers' to veer 'round in sympathy with [their daughters] to the new standing-point'.[11]

The particular allure of this 'new standing-point' was without doubt that it was inclusive of the entire range of attitudes on the Victorian woman question. This can be illustrated with reference to Margaret Atwood's concept of the four basic 'victim' positions available to colonised individuals or groups.[12] Atwood argues that responses to the collective condition of oppression can vary from denial (position one) through resigned acceptance of what is considered 'the inevitable' (position two) to protest and constructive action (position three). The last position is that of the 'creative non-victim',[13] the best position for a writer because it releases creative energies otherwise channelled into victimisation and protest, but also one ultimately impossible to attain unless the causes of oppression have been removed. In terms of Atwood's model, Victorian feminists could be said to be moving between positions three and four, whereas conservatives would be occupying positions one and two. In the case of *Ideala*, however, all positions are presented as valid by the heroine at some stage in the novel: an irresistible bait for the contemporary reader, in whatever camp she might be placed. The unreconstructed Ideala divulges starkly conventional views on the aspirations of women, is in denial of her marital subjection and seeks to conceal her nervous disorders – 'bursts of enthusiasm ... followed by fits of depression, and these again by periods of indifference' (*ID*, 25) – behind the cover of eccentricity. In a second phase, her husband's violence and its (by now fully acknowledged) impact on her mental state prompts her to seek medical advice, yet she still fails to relate her personal experience to the collective position of women in patriarchal society. It is through sexual desire rather than insight into the prevalence of oppressive social structures that Ideala becomes aware of her own subject condition; initially guided by the yearning for individual fulfilment, her protest takes on political dimensions only when her experience in a different culture opens her eyes to the extent of women's willing subjection at home.

Just as Ideala successively occupies each of Atwood's four victim positions, so she progresses through the three 'classes' of 'new' women she defines in her long speech. Starting off in 'class' three (general dis-ease: the condition of the hysteric), she moves through position two (decadence) and eventually ends her journey of self-development in position one (social and political activism). In Chapter XI, Ideala again attacks decadent women writers by berating the sentimental mood and immoral tone of 'The Passion of Delysle', a proto-*fin-de-siècle* poem much admired by her friends; later she confesses that the poem is, in actual fact, of her own making, her diatribe against the female 'sex writers' having been directed at none other than herself (*ID*, 78–9, 98). The text thus carefully undermines traditionalist preconceptions about women, morality and feminism. Ideala's speech constructs a contrast between the 'unnatural' suffragists and the 'noble devotion' of the social reformers (the anti-CD Acts campaigners), a division immediately exposed as artificial since we learn that the two groups of feminists 'worked together'. The next two sentences further develop this contrapuntal rhetoric by suggesting that feminist educationalists pursue a 'good' object, which, nonetheless, proves to be detrimental to women's health.

The confused logic of Ideala's argument can be read as another instance of Grand's strategy of dissimulation, and also as a reflection of the confusion and self-division of the author at the time of writing the first draft. By 1888, when the book was published, Grand had learnt to challenge patriarchal discourses, but the late 1870s, when *Ideala* was conceived and written, saw her articulating her emerging feminist vision through the language and concepts of the medical establishment, which fought demands for women's higher education with the notion of the biological and mental inadequacies of the female. In the early to mid-1870s the American and British doctors Edward Clarke and Henry Maudsley issued alarmist warnings about the ravages wreaked by female education; Ideala's image of the students who suffer hair loss as a result of their book-learning is clearly modelled on their ugly, hysterical and sterile 'race' of university-educated women,[14] while the idea that what 'true' women wanted was not equality, but a master to tame them, reflects what Mona Caird called the 'pray-knock-me-down-and-trample-upon-me' rhetoric of the anti-feminists.[15]

Drawing on medico-scientific discourse, Grand's book seems indebted to Naturalism, the very genre her later heroines Evadne and Beth so forcefully critique. With the apologetic tone and inflated medical vocabulary of its preface, even more so with its male narrator, the novel represents a transitional stage in Grand's writing; like her protagonist, she was struggling hard to find her own voice. Imitating the rhetoric of Naturalist writers and adopting the language of her husband's profession, she justified her choice of subject matter by ascribing to herself the role of a doctor and scientist intent on healing society of its ills: 'Doctors-spiritual must face the horrors of the dissecting-room, and learn before they can cure or teach' (*ID*, viii).[16] The use of the Naturalist metaphor of the dissecting room, with its uncomfortable under-tones of violent and repulsive procedures, by a writer who was to become a fervent anti-vivisectionist and would attack this practice in her later novels (most prominently in *The Beth Book*, where the protagonist discovers a dissected dog in her husband's study; *BB*, 436–7), is an indication of the ideological distance Grand travelled between the first and the last parts of her feminist trilogy.

In odd contrast to the conservative beginning with its echoes of masculinist discourse, the novel's cumulative flashes of feminist interrogation gradually guide the reader in the direction of a critique of patriarchal society. Ideala's 'awakening' programmatically revolves around her experience of marital abuse, which is generalised and politicised by means of the husband's dual role as adulterer and seducer of working-class women. This is a frequent feature of New Woman novels and can be traced in the work of other writers like Ella Hepworth Dixon (*The Story of a Modern Woman*, 1894) and Olive Schreiner (*From Man to Man*, 1926). What is noteworthy in this text about a social purity activist by a social purity writer is the space given to the exploration of the heroine's sexual desire; even if this desire is circumvented as often as it is expressed, and the heroine does her best to deny it, the fact that it forms an integral part of the narrative suggests that today's equation of social purity with sexual puritanism is too simplistic. Though a moralist, Grand neither ignored nor silenced desire in any of her works.

While introducing her heroine as an hysteric whose over-exuberant spirits hide deep despair, Grand takes pains to contextualise Ideala's condition as the direct outcome of her position as a woman and a wife, implying that the conjunction of these roles constitutes a mental health hazard. With 'no obligations of consequence', and therefore 'nothing in [her] life to inspire a sense of responsiblity', Ideala is literally and figuratively 'sick' of her pointless existence (*ID*, 41), a feeling which intensifies in the course of her unhappy marriage to an oppressive man, a 'low brute' (*ID*, 165), as he is called by his discarded working-class lover; indeed, Ideala bears the marks of his violence on her body. The sympathy she feels for her rival connects the two women as fellow-victims, while also foreshadowing Ideala's future as a rescue-worker among prostitutes. In conjunction with the dirty and run-down environment in which the woman lies dying, the sexual nature of her disease (scarlet fever) seems overdetermined; the veiled allusion to soldiers' uniforms[17] and to 'scarlet' women would not have been lost on contemporary readers. This is Grand's first tentative exploration of the syphilis theme; in her follow-on novel, the exact cause of death will be named.

Drawing further on the melodramatic script which shapes the encounter between wife and mistress, Grand has Ideala fall in love with the doctor she had previously consulted about her depression, resolving the problem of how to provide a glimpse of an emotionally fulfilling relationship while avoiding the risk of jeopardising reader sympathy for an unconventional heroine by highlighting Ideala's flawed attempt to ignore the sexual nature of her feelings. Although '[s]he move[s] like one in a dream' and 'all life [is] one delicious sensation' (*ID*, 147), the moment Lorrimer declares himself, she sidesteps the issue by pretending that it 'had not ... occurred to her' that 'there could be anything but friendship between men and women who must not marry' (*ID*, 158 – a self-deception replicated in *The Heavenly Twins* when Angelica denies ever having thought of the Tenor in 'that' way; *HT*, 483). Grand may have wanted to convince the reader of Ideala's purity of mind, but what is most striking about her heroine is her naive sophistry: in her dilemma, she wishes she were Lorrimer's mother (*ID*, 103, 189, 255), and even when on the point of entering a free-love relationship with him, she circumvents the open acknowledgement of sexual passion by talking about 'the delightful intellectual contest and communion' they share (*ID*, 206).

Only indirectly can Ideala acknowledge her desire, as when she comments, in near-Hardyesque and Lawrentian terms, on the sweltering heat of the summer and the 'pungent scent' of the flowers, which 'penetrate and glow through everything' (*ID*, 187). In fiction and in unsent letters, her passion finds the open expression it is otherwise denied: 'You come to me and kiss me, and it is night and I am dreaming, and not ashamed', she writes in a letter never posted (*ID*, 231). Both of her poems on the adulterous love between a married woman and a monk celebrate the sensual ecstasy of the forbidden relationship, a near-consummation which in each case culminates in an eroticised drowning of the couple. In 'The Passion of Delysle' (*ID*, 70–6) the characters emulate Dante's lovers by plunging into the abyss formed by the waves; in 'The Choice' (*ID*, 83–8) they are trapped by the incoming tide, in a scene which anticipates a similar incident with a less tragic outcome in *The Beth Book* (*BB*, 237–43). While the two poems have a contrasting emphasis, highlighting sensual abandonment in one case and dutiful self-abnegation in the other, they both end with the lovers' deaths, thus suggesting that the author's (Ideala's) hope for sexual and emotional fulfilment is ultimately futile. This is also reflected by Ideala's final version of the poem after her renunciation of Lorrimer and her return from China: the lovers part without even the consolation of a sexual embrace in death (*ID*, 270).

By making Ideala simultaneously espouse her sexual desire and abrogate it in the course of a discussion with the male narrator, who in this scene acquires the status of a super-ego, Grand is able to counter the arguments of free-love advocates with the voice of moral purity, whose spokesperson Ideala is in the process of becoming. 'I must obey my own conscience', the unreconstructed Ideala pleads at the outset of the conversation, anticipating Grant Allen's *The Woman Who Did* (1895), a text whose free-love ethic Grand condemned unequivocally;[18] '[t]here is no degradation in love … I owe nothing to society … I am free … to dispose of myself as I like – to give myself to whomsoever I please' (*ID*, 237, 239). This declaration of independence notwithstanding, the narrator succeeds in convincing her that personal fulfilment is of little importance and that individuals have a 'duty … to sacrifice themselves for the good of the community at large' since '[e]very act of [ours] has a meaning; it either helps or hinders what is being done to further … the object of life' (*ID*, 239–40). Not only would Ideala lose her honour and ruin Lorrimer's career, she would also set a bad example to other women.

Paradoxically, while Ideala is going to build her new feminist identity on an ethic of sexual self-denial and political separatism, her concurrence with what at this point is a male injunction repositions her, for the time being at least, within the patriarchal family: 'She was quite exhausted, and passively submitted when I led her to her room … She clung to me then as a little child clings to its father, and, like a father, I ministered to her, reverently, then left her, as I hoped, to sleep' (*ID*, 243). It is only the ending, with its apotheosis of Ideala as the 'grand heroic' and, crucially, single woman (*ID*, 267), which proves her decision to leave lover as well as husband to have been the right one. Grand clearly did not see divorce and remarriage as a solution to the problem posed by men's desire to possess women, suggesting that only if she withdrew from hetero-sexual relationships altogether could an 'ideal' feminist come into being.

Ideala's sacrifice of personal gratification to a higher morality is associated by the narrator with saintliness, and Ideala passes all the tests of a saint: temptation, mental and physical torment, renunciation and spiritual purifi-cation (catharsis). After a prolonged period of mental recuperation spent in China, where she meets indigenous women reformers, she returns to Britain and, impelled by a new political awareness, starts working with prostitutes. The book ends with a feminist manifesto: 'What I want to do is to make women discontented … They have … to learn to take a wider view of things, and to be shown that the only way to gain their end is by working for everybody else, with intent to make the whole world better, which means happier … It is to help in the direction of that force that I am going to devote my life' (*ID*, 296–7).

Ideala's renunciation of a personal life in favour of a public mission is identified with political and also, crucially, quasi-religious agency, a point that was not missed by conservative reviewers: 'For religion, we must look to Ideala', William Barry noted with disapprobation before dismissing her as a female Casaubon, if not worse: 'did we trust the witches in questions of divinity, we should find ourselves, at best, in a luminous cloud.'[19] Certainly Grand's narrator draws attention to Ideala's divine calling (*ID*, 39). In *The Heavenly Twins* Ideala explicitly associates (her) feminist activism with a new and better religion ready to replace the *ancien régime* of the established churches. The 'true spirit of God' is not to be found in the 'terrible clergy' with their 'dreadful cant of obedience', but

> It is in us *women*. *We* have preserved it, and handed it down from one generation to another of our own sex unsullied; and very soon we shall be called upon to prove the possession of it, for … already I – that is to say Woman – am a power in the land, while you – that is to say Priest – retain ever less and less even of the semblance of power. (*HT*, 266–7, emphases in original)

Generated and fuelled by the spiritual potential of women, this religion provides a synthesis of the philosophical insights of all faiths while discarding the paraphernalia of patriarchal power: 'The religion of the future will neither be a political institution, nor a means of livelihood, but an expression of the highest moral attribute, human or divine – disinterested love' (*HT*, 265). Its proactive support for the weaker members of society and faith in the perfectibility of humanity is reflected in the work Ideala takes up among female social outcasts; in both *Ideala* and *The Heavenly Twins* the new religion spearheaded by Ideala is equated with social purity feminism, in the same way as the next generation of feminists was to equate it with the suffragette movement.[20] By the late nineteenth century religious, especially spiritualist, discourses had become an established feminist vehicle for conveying political thought; a 'feminist spirituality', Joy Dixon points out, 'was a crucial component of much feminist politics, and it was one of the sites at which feminist politics … was constituted and transformed'.[21] As Rose Lovell-Smith notes, this new and alternative discourse 'often draws authority from science *and* religion'.[22] Social purity feminism's evolutionary-cum-spiritualist (and, as I will argue in the next chapter, theosophical)[23] dialectics were central to

Grand's political rhetoric. In her allusion to the Second Coming of Christ in the shape of a woman, she drew on the long-standing female tradition of deifying women reformers in order to invest feminism with spiritual, cultural and socio-political authority. In the seventeenth century radical women like Lady Eleanor Davies, Quakers like Katharine Chidley and fifth monarchists like Anna Trapnel claimed to speak for God (or even be God), and in the late eighteenth and early nineteenth centuries Mary Evans and Joanna Southcott, among others, had attracted a huge following in the wake of proclaiming themselves the 'bride of Christ' and the female Messiah respectively.[24] In the 1850s, Florence Nightingale, herself the emblem of female-led redemption, wrote that the 'next Christ will ... be a female Christ',[25] and at the end of the century Frances Swiney promoted women to divine status when she declared in her *Awakening of Women* (1899) that, in constituting 'the human embodiment' of God's love, they were to be considered 'the ultimate goal of all creation in the cosmic plan'.[26] The 'Divine Feminine' Swiney predicted was to be the next incarnation of Christ was represented by the militant suffragettes, as Christabel Pankhurst maintained in 1914, for it was these women 'in whom the spirit of Christ is living today'.[27] By glorifying her heroine not only as a redemptive figure but as a saviour of women in particular, Grand simultaneously invoked and problematised this tradition, for in *The Beth Book* a disillusioned Ideala warns Beth that if she wants to join the women's movement, she must steel herself against disappointment:

> Women who work for women in the present period of our progress ... must resign themselves to martyrdom. Only the martyr spirit will carry them through. Men will often help and respect them, but other women, especially the workers with methods of their own, will make their lives a burden to them with pin-pricks of criticism, and every petty hindrance they can put in their way. There is little union between women workers, and less tolerance. Each leader thinks her own idea the only good one, and disapproves of every other. They seldom see that many must be working in many ways to complete the work. And as to the bulk of women, those who will benefit by our devotion, they bespatter us with mud, stone us, slander us, calumniate us; and even in the very act of taking advantage of the changes we have brought about, ignore us, slight us, push us under, and step up on our bodies to secure the benefits which our endeavours have made it possible for them to enjoy. I know! I have worked for women these many years, and could I show you my heart, you would find it covered with scars – the scars of the wounds with which they reward me. (*BB*, 392)[28]

In the course of her narrative existence across three novels, Ideala thus moves from the position of the traditional woman to the feminist scarred by the traditionalist, from the idealist to the resigned pragmatist, and from a quasi-religious saviour to a female Christ-figure crucified by both feminists and anti-feminists – a multifaceted process which throws into relief the complexity and instability of *fin-de-siècle* feminist identities. This instability is further highlighted by the collision between (female and feminist) narrated and (male and masculinist) narrating voices. If she intended to present her protagonist's journey into independence, why did Grand structure her story around competing perspectives?

In the Preface Grand notes that she wants to describe the 'transitional state' (*ID*, vi) in which modern woman finds herself as she progresses from reactive victim to proactive agent of her fate. This trajectory takes her through three preliminary stages whose very names signal her self-alienation: 'the *vinous*, alcoholic, or excitable stage; the *acetous*, jaundiced, or embittered stage; and the *putrefactive*, or unwholesome stage' (*ID*, v; emphases in original). As long as Ideala allows herself to be defined and possessed by male (scientific) discourse, she remains an object, enacting the repression of the hysteric, the destructive rage of the 'madwoman', and the sensual abandon of the fallen woman. Only by breaking free from male structures can she attain the subject position of the 'ideal' woman. It is no accident, then, that this final stage has no name: it is beyond patriarchal control.

But *does* Ideala struggle free from male control? She may decide to live her life apart from men and in opposition to masculinist values, yet on the level of the narrative her character is circumscribed and appropriated by the narrative voice. By choosing a male narrator for her novel, who, as one of the men in love with Ideala, even though he is too high-principled to tell her about it, has a vested interest in her self-renunciation, Grand restricts the freedom Ideala can attain. It is manifestly because of the narrator's intervention that she breaks off her relationship with Lorrimer, just as it is his voice and point of view that dominate the story. Grand's utopia of sisterhood is ultimately only possible because a man inscribes sexual 'purity' on the woman he loves. God-like, he remains nameless, and it is only in the sequel to *Ideala* that we learn his identity: he is Lord Dawne, the uncle of the 'heavenly twins'.

As Mangum notes, Grand's choice of a male narrator problematises masculine narrative authority by 'playing out a woman's fantasy of a man's fantasy of a woman (character's) fantasies'.[29] Lord Dawne's authority is implicitly undercut by the 'revisionary readings' proffered by his widowed sister Claudia, who acts as a female 'corrective' to his pronouncements on Ideala's actions and frequently challenges his perspective,[30] highlighting the ambivalent nature of his friendship: 'It must be trying to have a friend who believes so little in one as you do in Ideala' (*ID*, 106). Though this has little impact on his ideological appropriation of Ideala, the disagreements between brother and sister function as authorial asides, alerting the reader to the degree to which the narrator constructs Ideala and shapes her story and opinions to his own liking. When, at the beginning of the novel, he reports her wish to be the mere passive reflection of beauty and harmony instead of actively inscribing these qualities on the world, the reader may wonder whether he merely projects his own wishful thinking into her words. 'My function is not to do, but to be,' she says (he says). 'I make no poetry. I am a poem – if you read me aright' (*ID*, 12). That Ideala might wish for nothing more than the pleasures of representing a beautiful still-life surely originates in the narrator's desire; in *The Heavenly Twins* Angelica takes up cross-dressing precisely because she feels stifled, exclaiming that she 'wanted to *do* as well as to *be*' (*HT*, 450). Significantly, the passage about Ideala's self-effacement is soon followed by one which draws pointed attention to her artistic output: 'She loved music, and painting, and poetry, and science, and none of her loves were barren. She embraced them each in turn with an ardour that resulted in the production of an offspring – a song, a picture, a poem, or book on some most serious subject, and all worthy of note' (*ID*, 42). Two of Ideala's poems, included in full in the novel, generate an extended discussion about the purpose of literature. Not only does all this belie her earlier words, as recorded by the narrator, but his use of the childbirth metaphor also implies that art, textual production, and social activism come naturally to Ideala, more naturally perhaps than actual child-rearing does (her only son who, at the age of six weeks, is taken away from her at the instigation of her husband, dies of diphtheria).

The female imperative to 'be' rather than to 'do' (attacked so passionately by Olive Schreiner's Lyndall)[31] reduces Ideala to a fetishised object painted, and possessed, by the gaze of the narrator and, implicitly, the reader:

> I have some pictures of her as she was then, dressed in a gown of some quaint blue and white Japanese material, with her white throat bare – I was just going to catalogue her charms, but it seems indelicate to describe a woman, point by point, like a horse that is for sale. I have some other pictures of her, too, as she appeared to me one hot summer when I was painting a picture by the river, and she used to come down the towing-path to watch me work, and sit beside me on the grass for hours together ... It was then I learnt to know her best. And I am always glad to think of her as I used to see her then, coming towards me in one particular grey frock she wore, tight-fitting and perfect, yet with no detail evident. It was like an expression of herself, that dress, so quiet to all seeming, and yet so rich in material, and so complex in design. The wonder and beauty of it grew upon you, and never failed of its effect. (*ID*, 27)

Lord Dawne's sexual desire transforms Ideala into a sequence of erotic stills, with her dress assuming subject character, while she herself, framed by the narrative, fades into a passive figure frozen on canvas. Small wonder that he learns to 'know her best' at moments of complete inaction, when she is content to sit next to him and watch *him* at work. If he begins his eulology with a disclaimer (that to praise her 'charms' would be tantamount to reducing her to a horse), he ends by turning her into a sexless, impersonal *objet d'art:* 'it ... grew upon you, and never failed of its effect'.

It is Ideala's function as an art object, as an image created and animated by him, rather than the prosaic possession of her body, that Lord Dawne sees threatened by her relationship with Lorrimer. Narcissistic and voyeuristic, his love demands not physical, but pictorial and specular consummation. When Ideala fails to turn up for a promised visit, pleading that she has too much work to do, he is disgruntled about being deprived of the opportunity to 'help' (control) her: 'I was half inclined to believe she had avoided me' (*ID*, 135–6). His injunction on her to sacrifice her love for the sake of society has a personally gratifying side-effect, in that Ideala's singleness assures him of permanent access to her. In *The Heavenly Twins* and *The Beth Book* he is shown to be closely allied to Ideala; in the innermost circle of her friends, he collaborates with her on social-reform projects. Ideala's decision to break with Lorrimer allows Lord Dawne to resume his surveillance of her. The penultimate chapter ends on an allegory he paints of her, the novel itself providing the most startling proof of the degree to which he has taken possession of her: he knows her most intimate thoughts and even prints a love letter to Lorrimer which she herself never posted. The narrator's evasive note that his knowledge is drawn 'from papers that have come into [his] possession' (*ID*, 137) suggests that Ideala is denied even an indirect agency in the telling of her own story (for how did he gain access to her papers unless she entrusted them to him, and why does he not tell us so?).

Anything but a reliable narrator, Lord Dawne constructs himself as a New Man intent on encouraging Ideala to 'work in a wider field', while all that Lorrimer has to offer are 'the natural joys of a woman', domestic life and a family; where Lorrimer 'would have limited intellectual pursuits of women', Lord Dawne strongly implies that he himself envisages a public life for them (*ID*, 251). However, in *The Heavenly Twins* his treatment of his niece Angelica falls substantially short of this egalitarian vision: reproving her for what he regards as unwomanly conduct, he exclaims that he would be 'ashamed to have [her] at [his] house', and reminds her sternly that she has to get used to behaving in a proper manner since she 'will marry eventually' (*HT*, 317–18). The idea that she might want to have an occupation and a public life of her own never occurs to him.

Surely the most puzzling question *Ideala* raises is how it was possible for Grand to choose such an untrustworthy and essentially autocratic male voice for a text intended to exalt female autonomy? With its tension between externalised feminist and internalised patriarchal structures, the novel might be seen to encapsulate the self-contradictory nature of Grand's feminism. Just as *Ideala* is preceded by a long quotation from Ruskin (who, unsurprisingly, disapproved of the novel),[32] Grand's works resound with the voices of male friends, husbands and doctors who superimpose their reality and perspectives on heroine and female reader alike. While Ideala recovers her independent voice beyond the framework of the story narrated by Lord Dawne, Grand's next novel, *The Heavenly Twins*, ends by silencing one of its two feminist heroines.

By directing the reader's attention to the collision between gendered points of view and the power differential between male and female voices, Grand was able to highlight the entrapment of women within male-identified symbolic (linguistic, conceptual) frameworks, pointing to the need for autonomous female subject-constitution as a necessary first step towards feminist liberation. In this context it is significant that Ideala does not remain permanently confined to the parameters of male narration and interpretation. In turning her back on men, she is also able to break away from Lord Dawne's authorial voice, which is limited to retelling her past story. Her metamorphosis from male-constructed object (hysteric and fallen woman)[33] to feminist subject and agent of her destiny takes place in a blank space beyond the narrator's control and even in the face of his manifest ignorance: unable to provide an account of her life outside his frame of reference, he can but record Ideala's abrupt disappearance. A year later her vision, shaped by her experience in a country the narrator has never visited, successfully competes with his voice, with extended space being given to her direct speech. If Ideala's coming-into-language destabilises the master discourse, her deification has an equally adverse effect on the narrator's God-like propensities. As Luce Irigaray argues in 'Divine Woman', a God made in man's image, figured as a holy trinity of father, son and spirit, not only excludes women from divinity but also disables them from constituting themselves as subjects and as women: 'as long as woman lacks a divine made in her image she cannot establish her subjectivity or achieve a goal of her own.'[34] Constrained by the patriarchal narrator's gaze and his constructions of the biblical ('fallen' versus 'ideal') feminine,[35] Ideala is able to start the process of 'becoming' a woman (an autonomous subject) only when she withdraws from his control. On her return from China (Grand's Eurocentric version of Christ's retreat into the wilderness?), Ideala assumes the 'occult' dimension of a female trinity: woman-mother-spirit (*ID*, 270).[36] As the Go(o)d-mother of women victimised by the law of the father she invokes Irigaray's choice of the 'perfect' woman '*positing new values* that would essentially be divine' by offering a 'possibility of our autonomy, our salvation, of a love that would not just redeem but glorify us in full self-awareness.'[37] If women, as Irigaray argues, need to be 'getting them*selves* together as a unit',[38] it is Ideala's express purpose to get women 'united to use their influence steadily and all together against that of which they disapprove' (*ID*, 296). The novel ends with a vignette of her achievement: 'Wherever she is you may be sure that another woman is there also' (*ID*, 305).

By mapping Ideala's coming-to-language as a coming into her own as a 'divine' woman, the novel metaphorically recreates the New Woman's assumption of spiritual, cultural and political authority. Evadne's loss of language in *The Heavenly Twins* encodes the opposite object lesson. There is no point, this novel suggests, in re-enacting the sign-language of the Victorian madwoman when the new dawn of women's linguistic empowerment has broken:

> 'You see, in the old days, women were so ignorant and subdued, they couldn't retaliate or fight for themselves in any way; they never thought of such a thing. But, now, if you hit a woman, she'll give you one back promptly,' [Diavolo] asseverated, rubbing a bump on his head suspiciously. 'She'll put you in *Punch*, or revile you in the Dailies; Magazine you; write you down an ass in a novel: blackguard you in choice language from a public platform; or paint a picture of you which will make you wish you had never been born ...' (*HT*, 273)

With their irrepressible volubility and wit, their anarchic games, and their high-spirited stagings of the fluidity of gender and identity, the 'heavenly twins' Diavolo and Angelica serve as a comic counter-weight to Evadne. Not only does their anarchic revelry undermine male authority more successfully than Evadne even when at her most determined, by exposing the defects of patriarchal religion they also affirm the expediency of Ideala's project of spearheading a new female-oriented social-spiritual movement.

Exploding/reincoding patriarchal script(ure)s: the limits of mimicry and masquerade

As identical but opposite-sex twins Angelica and Diavolo confound biological arguments about the inherent difference of the sexes, highlighting instead the performative nature of gender. Their pranks parody the issues raised by Evadne, but they also rearticulate them in a more palatable form. With her high seriousness and forbidding severity, Evadne is not, as George Meredith noted, a reader-friendly character.[39] In defusing her intimidating potential through comedy, the twins validate and also radicalise her concerns. The most subversive ideas are expressed by them, not by Evadne, who attempts to practise on a purely individual level what they enact in more general terms. Thus, while Evadne rejects a husband who does not come up to her standard, Angelica turns moral expectations and marital practice upside down by declaring her intention of 'buy[ing] a nice clean little boy, and bring[ing] him up to suit my own ideas. I needn't marry him, you know, if he doesn't turn out well' (*HT*, 250). Later she reverses traditional roles by proposing, in a peremptory manner (by 'stamping her foot at him'), to a much older man, not because she is in love with him but because she wants to be free to 'do as [she] like[s]' (*HT*, 321).

Despite her critical insight into patriarchal institutions, Evadne does not directly challenge religious authority; in fact she is a conventional church-goer who is 'genuinely shocked by a sign of irreverence' (*HT*, 558). By contrast, the twins launch a concerted attack on masculinist religion, poking fun at the Anglican and Roman Catholic habit of regarding their respective acolytes as either 'converts' or 'perverts' (*HT*, 153), exposing the naive credulity of their representatives by setting up a ghost hunt (*HT*, 309–15), and charging church leaders with reckless profiteering by calculating how much money they can make in a given period out of starving nuns by prescribing extensive fasting spells (*HT*, 268). They also explode biblical myths. Thus in conversation with his grandfather, the Duke of Morningquest, who, after a lifetime of entertaining himself with chorus girls has become concerned about his spiritual well-being in the after-world, Diavolo confutes both religious and general patriarchal clichés about women by reading the Bible literally:

> 'It was a woman, my boy,' the duke said solemnly, 'who compassed the fall of man.'
>
> 'Well,' Diavolo rejoined, with a calmly judicial air, 'I've thought a good deal about that story myself, and it doesn't seem to me to prove that women are weak, but rather the contrary. For you see, the woman could tempt the man easily enough: but it took the very old devil himself to tempt the woman.'
>
> 'Humph!' said the duke, looking hard at his grandson.
>
> 'And, at any rate,' Diavolo pursued, 'it happened a good while ago, that business, and it's just as likely as not that it was Adam whom the devil first put up to a thing or two, and Eve got it out of him – for I grant you that women are curious – and then they both came a cropper together, and it was a case of six of one and half a dozen of the other. It mostly is, I should think, in a business of that kind.'
>
> 'Well, yes,' said the duke. 'In my experience, I always found that we were just about one as bad as the other' – and he chuckled.
>
> 'Then, we may conclude that there is a doubt about that Garden of Eden story whichever way you look at it, and it's too old for an argument at any rate,' said Diavolo. 'But there is no doubt about the redemption. It was a woman who managed that little affair. And, altogether, it seems to me, in spite of the disadvantage of being classed by law with children, lunatics, beggars, and irresponsible people generally, that, in the matter of who have done most good in the world, women come out a long chalk ahead of us.'
>
> 'Why the devil don't you speak English, sir!' the duke burst out testily. (*HT*, 261)

Grand's rereading of biblical myths opposes an emerging feminist tradition to male-biased theological doctrine, suggesting, as Josephine Butler intimated in 1869, that religion had been institutionalised for patriarchal purposes.[40] The text echoes ideas articulated in the early seventeenth century by Emilia Lanyer ('surely Adam cannot be excused; … / What weakness offered, strength might have refused')[41] and in the late eighteenth by Joanna Southcott: 'A woman

Satan chose at first, to bring on man the fall / A woman God has chose at last, for to restore us all'[42] – words later to be reinvigorated by the African-American anti-slavery activist Sojourner Truth in her famous 'Ain't I a Woman?' speech held at the second National Woman's Suffrage Convention of 1852.[43] Grand also debunks gender stereotypes by associating lack of logic and irrationality with the strategic over-performance of 'masculinity' (at a loss for a counter-argument, the duke resorts to shouting, as does Evadne's father in similar situations).

Significantly it is Diavolo, not Angelica, who presents the feminist case, in a situation in which the 'man-to-man' intimacy with his grandfather could be misappropriated for the verbal abuse of women (indeed, this is precisely what the duke expects to happen, starting the conversation as he does with a scornful remark about women's minds). Through Diavolo Grand demonstrates that male bonding does not have to be premised on conspiratorial sexism, and that there is no (bio)logical reason why being a man should entail contempt for women. Diavolo's close association with his sister has generated a 'natural' rather than a patriarchal relationship with women; as a result he is neither impelled to prove his masculinity by treating them as a different species, nor does he feel the need to assume (as Lord Dawne and Dr Galbraith do) the self-appointed position of the 'champion of women': 'I haven't the conceit to suppose they would accept such a champion' (*HT*, 273). Feminists, the text suggests, have no need for male authorities who adopt the women's cause only to lecture them: in a meta-fictional sense, Diavolo's statement operates as an indictment of the authorial (and authoritarian) position Lord Dawne and Dr Galbraith espouse in their narrative appropriation (colonisation) of women's stories and lives.

Diavolo's support is crucial for Angelica's unrestrained childhood development. When the twins grow up, however, their lives divide along gender lines, with Angelica increasingly coming under the constraints to which Evadne has been exposed from the beginning. Although there is much to separate the two young women (one being as earnest and stubborn as the other is funny and provocative), they begin to share important experiences of gender discrimination. Despite their very different home environments (Evadne's choleric and narrow-minded father and cowed mother are the very opposite of Angelica's chaotic but congenial and liberal-minded parents), and notwithstanding their mothers' opposing views on the innocence/ignorance issue (*HT*, 39, 41), the two girls come up against the same barriers when they start challenging the subordinate role allocated to them in life. While Evadne, in keeping with her introverted temperament and in response to her more oppressive home environment, keeps her thoughts and increasing knowledge to herself, Angelica, with the help of her brother, rebels against their father's gender stereotyping. John Kucich comments usefully that by representing 'two competing models of "angelic" womanhood, an old-fashioned moral ideal represented by Evadne and a new, morally self-inventing womanhood represented by Angelica', the text engenders an 'implicit debate between Evadne's extended Victorian commitments to truth-telling and Angelica's cavalier explorations of perform-ance, disguise, and fabrication'.[44] However, as he points out, Angelica is not the only New Girl to economise with the principle of 'honesty' and to adopt duplicitous strategies in the interest of self-development. In actual fact both women embrace disguise as a form of self-expression – Angelica openly, Evadne indirectly – and both modes of resistance (silent disobedience and comical subversion) are, initially at least, successful. As Evadne appears to comply outwardly with parental expectations, her reading is not checked, as a result of which she is able to familiarise herself with the very literature that enlightens her on the venereal dangers of the law of the father. Ironically it is her father's sexism which first provides the stimulus for study:

> she once heard [her father] say to one of her brothers: 'Find out for yourself, and form your own opinions,' a lesson which she had laid to heart ... Not that her father would have approved of her putting it into practice. He was one of those men who believe emphatically that a woman should hold no opinion which is not of masculine origin, and the maxims he had for his boys differed materially in many respects from those which he gave to his girls. But these precepts of his were ... only matches to Evadne which fired whole trains of reflection, and lighted her to conclusions quite other than those at which he had arrived himself. In this way ... he became her principal instructor. She had attached herself to him from the time that she could toddle, and had acquired from his conversation a proper appreciation of masculine precision of thought ... As she grew up she became her father's constant companion in his walks, and, flattered by her close attention, he fell into the way of talking a good deal to her. He enjoyed the fine flavour of his own phrase-making, and so did she, but in such a silent way that nothing ever led him to suspect it was having any but the most desirable effect upon her mind. She never attempted to argue, and only spoke in order to ask a question on some point which was not clear to her, or to make some small comment when he seemed to expect her to do so. He often contradicted himself, and the fact never escaped her attention ... [Thus] he ... unconsciously made her a more logical, reasoning, reasonable being than he believed it possible for a woman to be. Poor papa! (*HT*, 5–6)

In her own quiet way, Evadne is engaged in the performance of gender just as much as the twins are, the only difference being that she mimics normative expectations whereas they explode them. Both Angelica (as the Boy) and Evadne have 'pretty ways' (*HT*, 504, 664) which help them trick men into believing what they are not. The irony of Evadne's enactment of her father's ideal of dumb femininity is that it leaves him entirely unprepared for the mental battle which follows in the wake of her wedding to Colonel Colquhoun.

If in Evadne's girlhood Mr Frayling had not applied a double standard or if he held women in less contempt, he might have discovered the unconventional bent of his daughter's thoughts long before her spirit had ripened into rebellion. With a more congenial-minded mentor, she might never have started questioning male authority, nor begun to see the relation between the sexes as one marked by conflict. His own powers of ratiocination could only have gained from discussion with her, since he would have had to develop arguments that stood up to logic, which in turn might have led him to reconsider some of his entrenched views. As interlocutor rather than silent listener, Evadne would have been less likely to notice his constant blunders. It is the clash between his pompous celebration of masculine superiority and his manifest personal shortcomings which triggers off her critical attitude towards men, just as it is his division of sexes into hierarchies which makes her aware of women's oppression. In this sense her gradual move towards feminism is a direct outcome of her father's misogyny, just as his disparagement of women's minds lays the foundation for her studies. Angelica's development is a result of similar experiences: 'I believe I could have satisfied them', she says about her parents and friends, 'if only they had not thwarted me' (*HT*, 450). No longer content to accept old truths unconditionally, these New Girls about to become New Women are propelled into the condition-of-women question by the daily demonstration of male prejudice and incompetence. Ultimately, the text suggests (and Grand will make the same point in *The Beth Book*; *BB*, 274), it is the patriarchs themselves who are responsible for the birth of feminism:

> It was that which set her mind off on a long and patient inquiry into the condition and capacity of women, and made her, in the end of the nineteenth century, essentially herself. But she did not begin her inquiry of set purpose; she was not even conscious of the particular attention she paid to the subject. She had no foregone conclusion to arrive at, no wish to find evidence in favour of the woman which would prove the man wrong. Only, coming across so many sneers at the incapacity of women, she fell insensibly into the habit of asking why. The question to begin with was always: 'Why are women such inferior beings?' But, by degrees, as her reading extended, it changed its form, and then she asked herself doubtfully: 'Are women such inferior beings?' a position which carried her in front of her father at once by a hundred years, and led her rapidly on to the final conclusion that women had originally no congenital defect of inferiority, and that, although they have still much way to make up, it now rests with themselves to be inferior or not, as they choose. (*HT*, 13)

Premised as it is on silent rebellion, Evadne's development remains unchecked until it comes in collision with her social role and therefore with men's status and power. When she draws practical conclusions from her reading, refusing to live with the man she has married in ignorance of his profligate past, she encounters iron opposition, and even though she agrees to a compromise

which saves Colonel Colquhoun's face, the paternal home remains permanently shut to her. Colquhoun himself, though accepting his sexless marriage
and his wife's unconventional views in private, imposes a ban on any public
activity (with disastrous consequences for Evadne's mental health) merely
because it might interfere with his image of military prowess: 'It would be too
deuced ridiculous for me, you know, to have my name appearing in the papers
in connection with measures of reform, and all that sort of thing' (*HT*, 345).

Likewise, the twins' cross-dressing escapades are tolerated as long as they are
children: viewed as harmless entertainment, their pre-pubescent androgyny is
not perceived as posing a threat to the patriarchal order. Their persistent
swapping of identities, for example at Evadne's wedding (*HT*, 60–1), is
considered a practical joke, not a way of debunking sex-role expectations. The
twins themselves, on the other hand, are quite explicit about their challenge to
the principle of gender segregation. As a result of a masquerade they manage
to be taught jointly by the male tutor, albeit not because their father has been
converted to the principle of co-education, but because, 'provided they
amused him, they could make him do anything' (*HT*, 126). In puberty, the
twins' anarchic games take on more ominous proportions in his eyes: no
longer an amusing spectacle, their actions now become a marker of transgression. Since this transgression is grounded in their symbiotic relationship –
so close is Diavolo to his sister that, at a time when it was synonymous with all
things unmentionable, he refers to menstruation in confidential conversation
(*HT*, 244) – the relationship itself must be curtailed. Consequently, Diavolo is
sent to Sandhurst, while Angelica is faced with the prospect of being 'brought
out' as a first step towards being married off to a suitable bidder.

This development pinpoints the parameters within which Angelica is
allowed to display deviant behaviour. First, it is only in play that she can divest
herself of socially imposed femininity, turn into Diavolo, whose gender (and
name) reflect her nature to a much greater extent than they do his. Not only
'the taller, stronger, and wickeder of the two' and the leading light in all their
pranks, she is also her brother's intellectual superior (*HT*, 126). Of the two, she
is the one who wants to lead a public life, whereas he would be content to stay
at home. Her transgressive impulses notwithstanding, she remains tied to a
name and an identity alien to her.

Secondly, even the playful subversion of gender roles is critically dependent
on male support. Without Diavolo's complicity, Angelica's defiance of paternal
injunctions is bound to fail, for as she realises at seventeen, 'Diavolo's indifference was putting an end to everything … in consequence of [his] attitude,
rebellion on her part would be both undignified and ineffectual' (*HT*, 321).
Prior to this psychological separation, there had been no checks on her
imagination; in a dream, she had envisioned herself as a modern Joan of Arc
bent upon liberating womankind: 'I am Judith. I am Jael. I am Vashti. I am

Godiva. I am all the heroic women of all the ages rolled into one' (*HT*, 296). After Diavolo's departure for Sandhurst her rebellion is toned down to an individualised bid for regaining her lost freedom: instead of turning herself into the heroic woman of her dreams (a feat Ideala is able to achieve), she impersonates her absent brother. Though conceived as an extension of their childhood androgyny, a carnivalesque space free from the restraints of gender and sex, Angelica's adult cross-dressing proves to have a grave and ultimately fatal impact on the man she befriends in the guise of Diavolo. A mysterious and melancholy stranger, whose feminine looks and manner, coupled with his nameless state (his illicit sexuality as unspeakable as his name),[45] hint at the nature of his 'affliction', the village tenor instantly and passionately falls in love with 'the Boy'. The active expression and enactment of homosexuality is narrowly circumvented by the breakdown of the relationship when Angelica's sex is revealed accidentally. Inevitably both characters are punished for their transgression, with the Tenor's death propelling Angelica into the resigned acceptance of her subject position as a woman.[46] By the end of her story (Book V) she has internalised the feminine imperative to the point of being 'grateful for the blessing of a good man's love' (*HT*, 551) – even if this man cannot bring himself to countenance the notion that a wife might have a right to enjoy a public career and an income of her own. Angelica's transformation from free spirit to tame child-wife cajoling her 'Daddy'-husband for some pin money carries unsettling echoes of Ibsen's *Doll's House*, but while Nora slams the door of her doll's house firmly behind her, Grand's heroine moves in the opposite direction: 'All this trouble was tending to unite them; it had brought her home' (*HT*, 551).

In different ways, then, Angelica's and Evadne's stories conjointly illustrate the need for women's active and continued resistance to gender-role expectations if they want to survive as individuals. As their stories also suggest, marriage, by eroding the will of all but the most determined of rebels, acts as a patriarchal corrective to female independence. Once married, none of the heroines in Grand's trilogy has much of a life left, and all of them experience phases of hysteria and depression. Evadne never recovers her ability to give expression to the rage boiling beneath her impassive surface, and even Angelica is reduced to helpless rage: 'inwardly she raged – raged at herself, raged at everybody, at everything' (*HT*, 478). Ideala and Beth, by contrast, are able to transform anger and despair into constructive action and political energy. The most successful characters in terms of achieving inner harmony and outer (public) fulfilment, they also leave their husbands. Ironically, the most prominent of the New Woman writers to defend the ideals of marriage and to oppose divorce in the periodical press was also the one whose novels consistently argued that marriage was the single most decisive factor in driving women mad.

While (in *The Beth Book*) Angelica recovers limited agency as a social purity campaigner, Evadne's potential is lost in hysteria. By ending the novel with the voice of her second husband, a doctor, Grand suggests that women's liberation must fail if they compromise their autonomy by devolving the responsibility for their lives to others. The text hints at the performative edge of Evadne's hysteria only to cast into doubt the effectiveness of such a strategy. By shifting the narrative perspective to her physician's point of view, the final part of *The Heavenly Twins* raises central questions about the limits of feminine mimicry and its capacity to disrupt medical discourse.

Overwriting the doctor's tale: the New Woman as newly born hysteric[47]

A synonym for femininity in nineteenth-century medical textbooks, hysteria was frequently associated with women's transgressive or rebellious desires in Victorian literature: Charles Dickens's Miss Havisham, Mary Braddon's Lady Audley and Charlotte Perkins Gilman's narrator in 'The Yellow Wallpaper' all draw energy from their rage, the hysterical *mise-en-scène* of which enables them to invert patriarchal power structures, albeit within tightly regulated parameters and for limited periods of time only. In paying equal attention to the subversive (liberating) and injurious (restraining) potential of female hysteria, New Woman writers such as Gilman and Grand problematised the equation of hysteria and feminism, a conceptual link that continues to exercise the imagination of feminist theorists today. Like Hélène Cixous conjuring up the hysteric's ability to confound patriarchal structures, they threw into relief the 'ambiguous, antiestablishment, [yet ultimately] conservative' impact of the hysteric. For as Catherine Clément argues, hysteria merely 'mimics, … metaphorizes destruction, but the [patriarchal] family [always] reconstitutes itself around it'.[48] Casting the hysteric, Evadne, as the embodiment of first-wave feminism (she is repeatedly associated with the notion of a 'seventh wave', a contemporary metaphor for the progressive force of feminism generated by individual women's martyrdom),[49] Grand challenged Victorian medicine's conceptualisation of hysteria while also taking issue with the literary and feminist conflation of hysteria and rebellion. Like Gilman she provided an account of female madness but chose to present it through the eyes of the physician-husband because this enabled her to draw on contemporary medical discourse in order to undermine its authority by exposing its destructive impact on female identity. Her strategy of disrupting the doctor's story with the voices of the female narrator/editor and heroine anticipated that other *fin-de-siècle* hysteric who exploded the narrative frame of her case study, Anna O. By ultimately relegating Evadne to the shadow land of the failed rebel, Grand suggested that, while hysteria dramatised the clash between patriarchal law and female experience, thus marking the transition from internalised conflict to externalised anger, its liberating potential was lost unless this externalisation did in fact take place. To a writer then in the process of becoming an activist, it was the commitment to organised political action, and not the earlier phase of hysterical self-absorption, that was the mark of the successful feminist.

If, as the Victorian medical establishment saw it, hysteria was 'the female malady',[50] *The Heavenly Twins* takes pains to attribute its aetiology to women's position in the patriarchal family and, in particular, in marriage. Even consensual marriages lack substance in Grand's text; Evadne is desperately unfulfilled and disenfranchised in her relationship with Dr Galbraith, and Angelica's marriage to Mr Kilroy, at best an arrangement for furthering her creative faculty to devise ever new methods of dispensing with his company ('she knew how to get rid of him', *HT*, 469), is gravely overshadowed by the Tenor's death. For both women marriage is closely related to punishment and death, and this message is sensationalised through the fate of Edith Beale, a bishop's daughter, who dies after contracting syphilis from her dissolute husband, Sir Mosley Menteith.

Although Edith (the Old Woman) is constructed as Evadne's (the New Woman's) opposite (she does not listen to Evadne's warnings, does not enquire into her fiancé's past life, and consequently becomes infected with disease, whereas Evadne retains her physical health), the two friends change dramatically as a result of their marital tragedies, with Edith becoming more like Evadne, and Evadne turning into a weak-spirited, submissive Edith. While still unmarried, Edith evades all knowledge of life, thus anticipating Evadne's later attitude (whose name already hints at her later spirit of evasion: Evad[n]e): 'She did not want to think. When any obtrusive thought presented itself she instantly strove to banish it' (*HT*, 168) – a mind-set Grand condemned in no uncertain terms elsewhere.[51] In the face of disease and death, however, Edith is suddenly inspired by a capacity for revolt previously inconceivable for her; metamorphosing into a mad Bertha Rochester, she dreams of stabbing her husband:

> I am quite, quite mad! … Do you know what I have been doing? I've been murdering him! I've been creeping, creeping, with bare feet, to surprise him in his sleep; and I had a tiny knife – very sharp – and I felt for the artery … and then stabbed quickly! and he awoke, and knew he must die – and cowered! and it was all a pleasure to me. Oh, yes! I am quite, quite mad! … I want to kill – I want to kill *him*. (*HT*, 304, emphasis in original)

The label and experience of 'madness' liberate Edith as decisively as they silence Evadne. Edith's dream of revenge is enacted, in a more moderate form, by Angelica who (in a further echo of *Jane Eyre*) attempts to elude harassment by Edith's husband by hiding behind the curtains of the bay window in the library, but then emerges to hurl a Bible at his face, literally putting his nose out of joint (*HT*, 361). Of the three women, Angelica alone is able to deal constructively with periods of intense anger or despair, which in the case of the other two inevitably result in 'mad' spells culminating in fantasies of violence (Edith) or pathological withdrawal (Evadne). Angelica's indifference to social decorum, her exuberance, extraversion and energy allow her to respond to problems constructively, through positive action and physical activity. Thus at the height of a crisis, when she mourns the Tenor, for whose death she feels partly responsible, she finds relief in putting on her brother's trousers and going for a proto-Lawrentian night-time run through the forest: 'She threw up her arms and stretched every limb in the joy of perfect freedom from restraint; and then with strong bounds she cleared the grassy space, dashed down a rocky step, and found herself a substance amongst the shadows out in the murmuring woods' (*HT*, 530). Being used, from childhood, to 'talk[ing] things out', she shares her grief with others, as a result of which 'she found herself the better in every way' (*HT*, 532, 128). Anticipating Anna O.'s 'talking cure', as theorised in Josef Breuer and Sigmund Freud's *Studies on Hysteria* (1895/ 1955),[52] and linking a treatment which was to revolutionise psychoanalysis to the contemporary feminist demand for healthy outdoor exercise and non-constricting clothes, Grand rewrote the old texts and rest cures of patriarchal medicine which insisted that women's desire for an active public life was itself a form of madness, and that sanity, for women, consisted in a return to domesticity.

While Angelica is saved from serious illness because of her proactive approach and her ability to play with, and thus invalidate, gender/sex imperatives, Edith and Evadne, unable to struggle free from the normative constraints of femininity, succumb to hysteria. Their different manifestations of madness reflect the female condition of being deprived either of vital knowledge or of an outlet for action: Edith goes mad as a result of sexual ignorance; Evadne's hysteria, rooted in the promise exacted by her first husband not to join any social or political movement during his lifetime, is compounded by her fear of the dimension her pent-up rage could take:

> I can be the most docile, the most obedient, the most loving of women as long as I forget my knowledge of life; but the moment I remember I become a raging fury; I have no patience with slow processes; 'Revolution' would be my cry, and I could preside with an awful joy at the execution of those who are making the misery now for succeeding generations. (*HT*, 672)

Too frightened of her anger and its destructive potential (Edith's madness), too conscious of social problems to banish them altogether from her mind, after Colquhoun's death trapped in a second marriage which allows for even less mental freedom than her first, while robbing her (sexually, in reproductive terms, and medically) of control over her body, Evadne withdraws into mental illness. The most disturbing reflection of her disintegration is the fact that her voice and perspective are filtered through a male consciousness, with the last book moving from a third-person narrative to a first-person account delivered by her doctor and second husband. Tragically, the more Evadne relinquishes her authority as a writer and reader of texts – she stops writing feminist appraisals of canonical literature and at the culmination point of her malady considers burning her books (*HT*, 672) – the more she is appropriated and embodied by male texts and masculinist discourses.

Though on the face of it cast as a positive character, Dr Galbraith's twin roles of physician and husband suggest grim analogies with Charlotte Perkins Gilman's 'The Yellow Wallpaper', published a year before *The Heavenly Twins*. Written from the opposite angle, the story provides chilling insights into a marriage in which the husband is so 'careful and loving' that he 'hardly lets [his wife] stir without special direction' ('YW', 12). Read in conjunction with Gilman's text, the patriarchal authority behind Galbraith's concern for Evadne becomes transparent, for even if he does not reduce her to his 'blessed little goose' ('YW', 15), he counts his 'little lady' (*HT*, 656) as one of his children (*HT*, 672, 675). In both texts, the doctor-husband's medical regimen (indoors incarceration and enforced passivity in Gilman's story, strenuous outdoor exercise and enforced activity in Evadne's case) contributes to his wife's condition. Both women experience pregnancy as particularly alienating because of the additional control their husbands gain over their bodies. But Gilman's narrator uses her madness to break free from her husband, hypnotising and paralysing him with her Medusa's gaze and crawling (walking) over him when he has fainted; Evadne, by contrast, directs her anger and despair against herself. Whereas 'The Yellow Wallpaper' ends with the wife's declaration of independence ('I've got out at last … so you can't put me back!', 'YW', 36), Evadne has grown so attached to her shadow existence that she no longer wants to 'get out', asking Galbraith to let her 'live on the surface of life, as most women do' (*HT*, 672). A comparative reading of the two texts throws into relief the different encodings of female madness in turn-of-the-century feminist fiction, subversion in Gilman's story contrasting with disempowerment in Grand's.

Faced with Galbraith's imperialist gaze, Evadne is frozen into a frame defined by his perspective, a position which echoes Ideala's appropriation by Lord Dawne. Yet Ideala finds her own voice at the end of Dawne's narrative and withdraws from his control, whereas Evadne's identity is lost in Galbraith's medical notes. Their first encounter, shortly after her aborted wedding, foreshadows the parameters of their later relationship. While visiting her aunt, he discovers a girl asleep in an armchair, and appraises her facial features with a mixture of voyeurism and scientific detachment:

'But tell me,' he exclaimed, catching sight of Evadne placidly sleeping in the high-backed chair, with her hat in her hand held up so as to conceal the lower part of her face; 'Are visions about? *Is* that one I see there before me? If I were Faust, I should love such a Marguerite. I wish she would let her hat drop. I want to see the lower part of her face. The upper part satisfies me. It is fine. The balance of brow and frontal development are perfect.'

Mrs. Orton Beg coloured with a momentary annoyance. She had forgotten that Evadne was there, but Dr. Galbraith had entered so abruptly that there would have been no time to warn her away in any case. (*HT*, 97, emphasis in original)

Galbraith's attitude anticipates the way in which he will later dissect Evadne's 'case' and seek to enter the recesses of her mind – an activity whose phallic symbolism was well established by the end of the nineteenth century when, as Elaine Showalter and Elisabeth Bronfen have pointed out, dominant images and metaphors in culture and art represented women as boxes ('cases'/case studies) whose mystery could only be lifted if they were opened and penetrated, with the writer's pen, the painter's brush, the doctor's knife or the psychoanalyst's gaze.[53]

Throughout the text, Galbraith keeps coming across Evadne's sleeping body, the object of his ever more intensified gaze; at one point he even watches her through a telescope and, convinced that 'her whole attitude ... appealed to [him] like a cry for help', sets off for her house in great agitation, only to find her 'perfectly tranquil ... with no trace of recent emotion' (*HT*, 587). His telescopic appropriation of Evadne echoes aspects of Jean-Martin Charcot's use of the camera at the Salpêtrière; like Charcot, Galbraith seeks dramatised external poses which reflect his patient's inner mysteries.[54] Eroticising his medical interest in Evadne, he constructs her as a Lady of Shalott figure because this image 'appeals' to him, just as the pictorial representation and dramatic performance of feminine hysteria appealed to the nineteenth-century medical establishment more generally.

However, since her discourse on female madness foregrounds the instability of, and changing power relations between, the figures of male doctor and female hysteric, Grand resists the temptation to construct Galbraith as a straightforward villain and Evadne as his passive victim. Both Galbraith and Sir Shadwell Rock, the medical celebrity he consults, earnestly wish for Evadne to recover, and their holistic treatment, with its emphasis on the stimulation of body *and* mind, represents a significant departure from real-life Victorian doctors' punitive and invasive medicine. Contemporary treatments meted out to the female hysteric, ranging from the rest cure to clitoridectomy, leave little doubt about the primarily disciplinary function of medical interventions on the female body; thus Silas Weir Mitchell noted that

The moral uses of enforced rest are readily estimated ... The result is always ... a remarkable and often a quite abrupt disappearance of many of the nervous symptoms ... [T]he physician ... should ... seize the proper occasions to direct the thoughts of his patients to the lapse from duties to others, and to the selfishness which a life of invalidism is apt to bring about.[55]

As a result of Mitchell's rest cure, Charlotte Perkins Gilman (whose depression was rooted in her loss of identity following her marriage and the birth of her daughter) 'came so near the border line of utter mental ruin that [she] could see over'.[56] Whereas Mitchell wanted to castigate the mind and destroy women's selfish will, Isaac Baker Brown, performing clitoridectomies in the 1860s, wanted to castigate the body and destroy women's sexual desire.[57] Hysteria was associated with unrestrained female sexuality as well as with sexual resistance to marital intercourse, both of which were thought to be injurious to men: the oversexed woman would, doctors warned, drain her husband of all his energy, while the undersexed and resistant wife left him in imminent danger of impotence.[58] Exceptionally well read in the medical literature of the time, Grand constructed *The Heavenly Twins* as a counter-narrative to the master discourses of Victorian medicine, suggesting that, while husbands' health was not impaired by their partners' sexual withdrawal, wives suffered grave damage to their mental health as a result of their husbands' prohibition of meaningful work. Colonel Colquhoun dies from a heart attack brought on by too much alcohol consumption, not from the after-effects of impotence, but Evadne falls permanently ill the moment she makes her fatal promise.

By encouraging Evadne to take an active interest in intellectual and socio-political matters, Galbraith sounds a new note in medical treatment, but ultimately Grand considers him unable to disengage himself from the dominant ideology. In a variant on the rest cure, Galbraith restricts Evadne's reading (*HT*, 662). Further echoes of real-life doctors and their patriarchal authority over their women patients surface in his belief that 'steady moral influence' is required to 'awaken the conscience' of hysterics to their 'depraved' ways (*HT*, 575). Although professing sympathy for the women's movement, he clings to the belief that it is only by first fulfilling their 'natural' role as wives and mothers that women can gain the mental equilibrium required to 'distinguish' themselves as feminists. Consequently, the moment Evadne becomes pregnant, her biological function as a mother takes precedence over anything else: 'a new interest in life was coming to cure her of all morbid moods for ever' (*HT*, 660). Even though his own experience flatly contradicts his medical diagnosis, he insists that '[n]othing could have been healthier or more natural than her pride and delight' in her maternal role (*HT*, 667). In reality, Evadne's mental state deteriorates considerably during pregnancy, culminating in an attempt to poison herself and her baby. Far from providing an incentive to take an interest in the outside world, motherhood encloses her once and for all within the domestic sphere. After the birth of their son, who even in his name ('Donino') reproduces the father ('Don') while their daugher remains nameless, the transformation from 'raging fury' to meek and dependent child-wife is complete. Like Edith at the beginning of her marital career, Evadne now sees her life's purpose in fulfilling an exclusively home-bound role: 'I will do nothing but attend to my household duties and the social duties of my position. I will read nothing that is not first weeded by you of every painful thought that might remind me. I will play with my baby by day, and curl up comfortably beside you at night, infinitely grateful and content to be so happily circumstanced myself' (*HT*, 672).

As Lyn Pykett has pointed out, Evadne's defiance of Galbraith's wish that she 'take her proper place with the *best* of her sex' (*HT*, 661, emphasis added) by insisting that all she wants and will do is to be like '*most* women' (*HT*, 672, emphasis added), her refusal to become the woman into which he wants to fashion her can be read as a form of passive resistance.[59] However, as a means of political or even only individual protest, Evadne's mimicry of hyper-femininity is singularly ineffective, given that her voice is lost and she fades into a simulacrum of ladyhood. While Angelica and Galbraith play an important role in *The Beth Book*, Evadne appears only in her official function, as 'Lady Galbraith', acting as a silent shadow to her husband during dinner parties, and failing to respond to the one rhetorical question addressed to her (*BB*, 415, 351). Instead of fulfilling her early promise of becoming what Galbraith calls a 'seventh wave' (a reformer and revolutionary who carries the tide of humanity on to its next evolutionary stage), Evadne validates his pessimistic prognosis that she 'will have the perception, the inclination; but [not] the power' (*HT*, 98), and concludes her narrative existence as a pre-decessor of Virginia Woolf's Lady Bradshaw: 'Fifteen years ago she had gone under. It was nothing you could put your finger on; there had been no scene, no snap; only the slow sinking, water-logged, of her will into his' (*MD*, 152). Ending *The Heavenly Twins* with Evadne's silence and Galbraith's acknow-ledgement of his failure, Grand reaffirms the impression that male medicine is detrimental to women's mental health.

This is further accentuated by the novel's dual narrative structure which pointedly draws attention to the competing discourses of women and men, and to the discrepancies between feminist and medical readings of female breakdown. Thus Galbraith's account is preceded, and undermined, by an editorial note which deploys the same textual strategy of hiding damning criticism behind ostensible praise which is used to such effect in 'The Yellow Wallpaper'. In the guise of commending Galbraith, the text points to the gaps in his knowledge, suggesting that his incomplete understanding of the case and his personal bias led to diagnostic errors, and advising readers to approach the first-person narrative with caution:

The fact that *Dr. Galbraith had not the advantage of knowing Evadne's early history* when they first became acquainted adds a certain *piquancy* to the *flavour* of his *impressions*, and *the reader, better informed* than himself with regard to the antecedents of his 'subject,' will find it interesting to note both the accuracy of his insight and the *curious mistakes* which it is possible even for a trained observer like himself to make by the *half light of such imperfect knowledge* as he was able to collect under the circumstances. His record, which is minute in all important particulars, is specially valuable for the way in which it makes apparent the changes of habit and opinion and the modifications of character that had been brought about in a very short time by *the restriction Colonel Colquhoun had imposed* upon her. In some respects it is hard to believe that she is the same person. But *more interesting still, perhaps, are the glimpses we get of Dr. Galbraith himself in the narrative*, throughout which it is easy to decipher the simple earnestness of the man, the cautious professionalism and integrity, the touches of tender sentiment held in check, the *dash of egotism*, the healthy-minded human nature, the capacity for enjoyment and sorrow, the love of life, and, above all, the perfect unconsciousness with which he shows himself to have been a man of fastidious refinement and exemplary moral strength and delicacy; of the highest possible character; and most lovable in spite of *a somewhat irascible temper and manner which were apt to be abrupt at times.* (*HT*, 554, emphases added)

The first sentence establishes the unreliability of the first-person narrator, highlighting the essentially constructed nature of his account by drawing on a vocabulary which pinpoints its sensory (emotional) rather than scientific basis ('piquancy', 'flavour', 'impressions'). By emphasising the reader's superior knowledge, Grand challenges the doctor's privileged status as a master narrator, alerting her readers to the need to scrutinise his 'performance' carefully with a view to detecting errors of judgment. She thus reverses the power dynamics, especially in the case of female readers, by encouraging them to study *his* 'case' while he is engaged on examining Evadne's.

That masculinist discourse is apt to be confounded when the subject of enquiry begins returning the male gaze is indicated by Galbraith's acute embarrassment when his psychoanalytic musings are mocked by Evadne. On one of their walks she picks a flower from a bush, debunking his quest for hidden meanings by commenting that

'You will want to know why I do that, I suppose,' she said. 'You will be looking for a motive, for some secret spring of action. The simple fact that I love the gorse won't satisfy you. You would like to know why I love it, when I first began to love it, and anything else about it that might enable you to measure my feeling for it.'

This was so exactly what I was in the habit of doing with regard to many matters that *I could not say a word.* But what struck me as significant about the observation was the obvious fact … that, *while I had been studying her, she had also been studying me*, and I had never suspected it. (*HT*, 605, emphases added)

Casting doubt on the accuracy of Galbraith's 'Impressions', Grand, in her editorial note and in between the lines of Galbraith's observations, carefully and cleverly directs readers to her own, feminist reading of Evadne's mental illness as a result of the promise of passivity exacted by her first husband. At the same time she implies that Evadne's second marriage contributed its part, signalling her disapproval of Galbraith's character by ending her exaggerated eulogy with a damning remark on his temper, and by framing her editorial comments with his professional and personal failings. What thus emerges is a complex multiple narrative whose surface structure is destabilised by the feminist editor's critique of male science. As the spokesman of nineteenth-century medicine Galbraith constructs marriage and motherhood as beneficial, whereas Grand exposes both as damaging to women.

In many ways Evadne's story is a mirror image of Ideala's. Both women have profligate first husbands, suffer from depression, and fall in love with their doctors. Social purists by temperament and as a result of their marital histories, they both have sensual predispositions held in check by their pronounced sense of morality. Both passionately desire and require an object in life and find it in feminism. The only difference is that Ideala remains true to her purpose, whereas Evadne, trapped in consecutive marriages, submits to the patriarchal order, with the result that one turns into 'a miserable type of a woman wasted' (*HT*, 645), while the other becomes a 'volcano, with wonderful force of fire working within' (*ID*, 302–3). Read in conjunction, their two stories carry a poignant message, the very opposite of Galbraith's cure by marriage.

Grand takes care to emphasise that neither Ideala nor Evadne are 'cold-blooded' women with no sexual desire. As a girl Evadne 'revel[s] in sensations' to the extent that, as the narrator informs us, 'she would have gone girl-stalking in earnest – *probably* – had she been a young man' (*HT*, 47, emphasis in original). Briefly attracted to a young priest, the teenage girl swiftly transfers her longing to dashing Major Colquhoun, in an effusion of emotion which has as much of the sensuous as of the romantic to it: 'Her heart bounded – her face flushed … she thrilled through the rest of the service to the consciousness that there … her future husband sat and sighed for her' (*HT*, 53). Years into her marriage, Sally Ledger notes, her senses are still 'troubled' by the close proximity of a husband with whom she has never shared sexual intimacy (*HT*, 344).[60] But even if, as adult women, Evadne and Ideala make a conscious decision to frustrate their sexual desire, Grand is at pains to stress that neither of them suffers any physical or mental harm because of it. Ideala's unbroken energy across the space of three novels is a case in point, and so is the fact that for years, Evadne is 'quite happy' (and of perfectly stable mind) in her sexless marriage to Colquhoun because 'he never interfered with [her] pursuits or endeavoured to restrict [her] liberty in any way' (*HT*, 341). Galbraith's assumption that Evadne's depression is caused by sexual frustration is not borne out by the text, since she so manifestly fails to recover as a result of her second marriage. The only time we see her in radiant health is when she is working as a nurse during a smallpox epidemic: 'She was the life of the camp, bright, cheerful, and active, never tired apparently, and never disheartened' (*HT*, 599). At a time of transition, when the medical establishment was moving from the doctrine of the non-existence of sexual pleasure, which criminalised sexually active women (William Acton),[61] to the opposite position, which pathologised spinsters (Sigmund Freud), feminists like Grand pointed out that what drove women mad was not the absence of sex, but the lack of a meaningful and fulfilling occupation.

The consequences of denying women a self-determined life are demonstrated by Evadne's retreat into fantasy. Prefiguring Anna O.'s 'private theatre' as described in Breuer's case study, Evadne takes to day-dreaming, only to find that, gradually, the dreams take over:

> I began to be intoxicated. My imagination ran away with me. Instead of indulging in a daydream now and then, when I liked, all my life became absorbed in delicious imaginings, whether I would or not ... I lived in my world apart. If people spoke to me, I awoke and answered them; but real life was a dull thing to offer, and the daylight very dim, compared with the movement and brightness of the land I lived in – while I was master of my dreams ... By degrees they mastered me; and now I am their puppet, and they are demons that torment me. (*HT*, 626–7)

As Laura Marcus notes,[62] day-dreaming was a complex and ambivalent concept for Freud and Breuer, associated as it was both with the creative imagination of the artist (constructive) and with feminine pathology (destructive). Profoundly influenced by male psychoanalytic discourse, while simultaneously aware of the way in which fantasy provided women with an outlet for their repressed desire for an active and/or creative life, female analysts like Anna Freud and Lou Andreas-Salomé constructed (their own) day-dreaming as a signifier of female sexuality (interiority) *and* a symptom of women's rebellious impulses (exteriority). It is against this background that day-dreaming, as a marker of autobiographical experience, became a metaphor for female resistance in *fin-de-siècle* feminist writing. Thus Gilman, who at the onset of puberty had been forbidden by her mother (the patriarchal substitute for the missing father) to indulge in the dream world which she had inhabited for years, drawing on this 'richer, more glorious life ... inside' at a time when she was increasingly coming to resent her brother's fuller life outside, in her writing later encoded madness as the outer sign of women's 'captive imagination', representing their withdrawal into an alternative, inner, reality as the inevitable outcome of their social confinement to the world within.[63]

What is striking in Grand's story are the similarities between Evadne's breakdown and Anna O.'s case study. Like Evadne, Anna O. has a 'powerful intellect' and 'great poetic and imaginative gifts', and as with Grand's character, her energy, will-power and craving for intellectual stimulation and an occupation, when frustrated, degenerate into 'suicidal impulses' and nervous symptoms, her amnesia (repression of memories) corresponding to Evadne's all-too-conscious repression of all painful knowledge.[64] With her sexuality 'undeveloped', Anna O., too, seeks relief in a fantasy world of the senses. Breuer writes that '[t]his girl, who was bubbling over with intellectual vitality' and who, like Evadne, briefly recovered from her depression while looking after the sick,

> embellished her life in a manner which probably influenced her decisively in the direction of her illness, by indulging in systematic day-dreaming, which she described as her 'private theatre'. While everyone thought she was attending, she was living through fairy tales in her imagination; but she was always on the spot when she was spoken to, so that no one was aware of it. She pursued this activity almost continuously while she was engaged on her household duties ...[65]

Although at first able to switch back and forth 'on the spot', Anna O. goes through a complex process of mental disintegration, with a gradual falling away of language, and the emergence of hallucinations and non-organic paralyses. Paradoxically, Anna O. and Evadne are simultaneously incapacitated *and* empowered by their hysteria, which enables them to 'abreact' (deal with, abject) their anger. Thus Evadne's somnambulistic immersion in a dream world and loss of a sense of reality provide her with an excuse for breaking the male-written codes of ladyhood, allowing her to walk through a disreputable part of London, unaccompanied and at night, to the great consternation of Galbraith, who follows her, ostensibly in order to protect her, but in reality to spy on her. Unable to rebuff Galbraith's advances in day-time reality, Evadne repulses a night-time pursuer while Galbraith looks on as if glancing into a mirror: for the man who propositions Evadne is also a gentleman, and as such the dark double of Galbraith, the honourable knight (Galbraith is knighted in *The Beth Book*). When questioned on her conduct the next day, Evadne resolutely challenges Galbraith's own motives, both in street-haunting London at night and in subjecting her to an interrogation: 'What were you doing there yourself? ... I don't recognise your right to question me at all ... what business have you to take me to task like this?' (*HT*, 620–1). In Hélène Cixous's terms, Evadne displays the hysteric's capacity of confounding patriarchy with a vengeance:

> if [the hysteric] succeeds in bringing down the men who surround her, it is by questioning them, by ceaselessly reflecting to them the image that truly castrates them, to the extent that the power they have wished to impose is an illegitimate power of rape and violence ... if woman begins to speak in [those] other ways, it would be a force capable of demolishing those structures.[66]

Indeed, just as Evadne's spirited response leaves the night-time stranger 'a considerably perplexed man', greatly discomfited by the indecent exposure of his sexual designs towards a 'lady' misrecognised as a street-walker, so Galbraith admits to being taken 'aback completely' by her questions – 'the more so' on realising that she is making light of him: '[she spoke] with an unmistakable flash of merriment ... her levity ... annoyed me' (*HT*, 619–20, 620–3). Like Evadne, Anna O. draws energy from her shadow existence, making it possible for her to give expression to and yet contain her inner resistance. An indefatigable nurse during her father's last illness and a paragon of domesticity, she unexpectedly takes to her bed, subverting the law of the father by refusing to speak his language, and reviving at night, under hypnosis, to give an uninhibited account of her 'real' feelings: 'in the day-time', Breuer writes, she was 'the irresponsible patient pursued by hallucinations, and at night the girl with her mind completely clear' who, '[a]fter giving ... energetic expression to the anger she had held back ... woke from her hypnosis ... [with] the disturbance vanished, never to return'.[67]

Certainly the subterfuges of hysteria enable Anna O. and Evadne to carve out a space of independence for themselves and to confound patriarchal authority even as they sustain the masquerade of femininity in their day-time capacity of dutiful daughters, wives or patients. Thus 'Anna O.' felt empowered enough to move from discursive object (patient, medical case) to subject (author/ity) in possession of discourse; Pappenheim's biographer, Melinda Given Guttmann, draws attention to Bertha's effusive story-telling ability which prompted Breuer to compare her to Scheherazade. In fact, Pappenheim used storytelling as a means of blackmail: if Breuer absented himself for a night, he would have to coax her back into narrative activity the next night, and she refused point-blank to 'perform' towards a colleague who replaced him during a holiday.[68] The effectiveness, as Cixous sees it, of the strategic deployment of hysterical performances in dismantling the institutional structures of patriarchy, however, is at best doubtful, for Pappenheim had to battle with debilitating illness when psychoanalysis had finished with her, while in her marriage to Galbraith Evadne loses her capacity to challenge authoritative discourses.

A creative work of mythological dimensions, *Studies on Hysteria* was first published in 1895, two years after the international success of *The Heavenly Twins*, and was not fully available in English until 1955.[69] Evadne's case study can therefore not be seen as a feminist response to a specific medical text; instead, Anna O.'s story constitutes Freud's (via Breuer's) literary (re)construction of female hysteria and transference through the medium of science at a time when this medium was increasingly being challenged by feminist writers deconstructing hysteria as failed rebellion and debunking medical case studies as the product of male doctors' counter-transference (as a result of their erotic fantasies of feminine frailty). In this instance at least, psychoanalysis reflected the themes, though not the political direction, of women's writing, with both cultural arenas creating powerful myths of female hysteria as subversion.

Bertha Pappenheim, the woman behind the sign (Anna O. – the Alpha and Omega of womanhood), was treated by Breuer in the early 1880s, half a decade before Charlotte Perkins Gilman consulted the less congenial Silas Weir Mitchell, and some fifteen years before Grand herself suffered a number of breakdowns and rest cures in the 1890s and early 1900s.[70] Though Breuer ended his case study on a cautious note of success, Pappenheim's recovery was not the foregone conclusion as which he presented it under pressure from Freud. In reality, Pappenheim continued to suffer from severe nervous symptoms and morphine addiction, with prolonged hospital stays considered necessary until 1887, five years after Breuer had 'officially' terminated his treatment, the year in which Gilman took up her rest cure, and a year before Grand started writing *The Heavenly Twins*.[71] Like Gilman, Pappenheim eventually cured herself; and like Grand, she developed into a feminist writer and activist with social purity proclivities, moving into journalism, political pamphleteering and narrative writing after a sustained career as a social worker. She translated Mary Wollstonecraft's *Vindication of the Rights of Woman* in 1899, founded the *Jüdischer Frauenbund* (Jewish Women's Union) in 1904, and, like Grand's Ideala, devoted herself to the rescue and rehabilitation of prostitutes.[72] Pappenheim and Gilman remained violently opposed to Freudian psychoanalysis for the rest of their lives.[73]

The mental breakdowns of these three feminist writers and their protagonists reflect the conditions and pressures under which the New Woman laboured towards the close of the nineteenth century. Infusing their narrative writing with autobiographical experience, and drawing strength from literature in living their political activism, they all suggest that it is the lack of intellectual and professional opportunities, compounded by medical and sexual oppression, which impairs women's physical and mental health, rather than the repression of their sexual desire. In *The Heavenly Twins*, Evadne's compliance with her first husband's prohibition of work imposes a rest cure which lasts a lifetime. Like the narrator in Gilman's 'The Yellow Wallpaper', and like Bertha Pappenheim in Breuer's study of Anna O., Evadne is driven mad by the images that take over her mind. A few years before the birth of psychoanalysis Grand was thus articulating a socio-political counter-narrative to the Freudian construction of hysteria as a quintessentially sexual neurosis. With each of her major novels engaging with the abuses of medicine and its spokesmen, Grand made a systematic and far-reaching contribution to the literary attack on medical patriarchy.

This chapter has traced Grand's complex authorial masquerades in two of her major novels, arguing that the conflict between patriarchal and feminist standpoints, so central to her plots, is also inscribed into the narrative structure of her works. Reading Grand thus became an exercise in decoding, probing and, ultimately, resisting hegemonic paradigms; for a female audience in particular, Grand's (play with) narrative impersonations raised fundamental questions about female identity and subjecthood in a patriarchal world order which persistently appropriated and (mis)represented women's voices. *Ideala*, Grand's 'coming-out' story as a feminist,[74] is marked by the sharpest friction between 'authoritative' and 'authentic' (internally persuasive) discourses, mapping the heroine's journey into feminist separatism through the eyes of a controlling male figure. The ideological tensions so ripe in the configuration between female protagonist and male narrator are exploded in *The Heavenly Twins*, which, by attributing Evadne's downward spiral into mental illness to her compliance with the law of the fathers, calls for the rejection of patriarchal authority. The novel's most subversive – and modern – aspects are its eponymous 'heavenly twins' whose gender-bending masquerades challenge and undercut sexual hegemonies. An expression of the author's self-division and cautious portrayal of feminist awakening in *Ideala*, the polyvocality and multiple perspectives of *The Heavenly Twins* signal a programmatical exploration of the clash between female consciousness and male point of view, feminist experience and patriarchal imperative.

The Heavenly Twins was praised by the contemporary critic W. T. Stead as 'the most distinctively characteristic of all the novels of the modern woman'.[75] The most highly acclaimed of Grand's books, it was also the most controversial and widely read.[76] Perhaps it derived its greatest appeal from the fact that it reassured female and male, feminist and conventional readers alike, by providing a vehicle for the expression of female discontent, while at the same time limiting the extent to which women could transform the patriarchal institutions of marriage, the family and medicine. Grand's next novel was to paint a more optimistic image of the possibility of independent female development. The unstable narrative structures of her earlier works (*Ideala*'s authorial male voice and female heroine; the competing male and female voices of *The Heavenly Twins*) were resolved in a text which privileged its heroine to the extent of calling her a 'genius' in the very subtitle, and which self-consciously addressed itself to a female audience.

3

New Woman jouissances: subversive spirits and the girl artist in *The Beth Book* (1897)

The tide was coming in. The water … was … bright dark sapphire blue, with crisp white crests to the waves, which were merry and tumbled. It was the sea for an active, not for a meditative mood; its voice called to play, rather than to that prayer of the whole being which comes of the contemplation of its calmness; it exhilarated instead of soothing, and made her joyous … She stood long on the rocks by the water's edge, retreating as the tide advanced, watching wave after wave curve and hollow itself and break, and curve and hollow itself and break again. The sweet sea-breeze sang in her ears, and braced her with its freshness, while the continuous sound of wind and water went from her consciousness and came again with the ebb and flow of her thoughts. But the strength and swirl of the water, its tireless force, its incessant voices … invited her, fascinated her, filled her with longing – longing to trust herself to the waves, to lie still and let them rock her, to be borne out by them a little way and brought back again, passive yet in ecstatic enjoyment of the dreamy motion. (Sarah Grand, *The Beth Book*, 1897)[1]

[W]hen male or female mystics speak of [jouissance], they all describe the same ocean. A flood; a torrent of waves; a delicious immersion; a feeling of drowning; arriving in a liquid that rolls, shakes, exhausts, and draws one up. Romain Rolland invented the image of 'oceanic feeling' … This is jouissance, *even without the sexual act*. Here is jouissance: falling, rolling, trembling inside. (Catherine Clément, *Syncope: The Philosophy of Rapture*, 1994)[2]

Her rising: is not erection. But diffusion. Not the shaft. The vessel. Let her write! And her text knows in seeking itself that it is more than flesh and blood, dough kneading itself, rising, uprising openly with resounding, perfumed ingredients, a turbulent compound of flying colors, leafy spaces, and rivers flowing to the sea we feed. … Seas and mothers … we ourselves are sea, sands, corals, seaweeds, beaches, tides, swimmers, children, waves … More or less vaguely swelling like wavesurge indistinctly sea-earth-naked, and what matter made of this naked sea-rth would deter us? We all know how to finger them, mouth them. Feel them, speak them. – Heterogeneous, yes, to her joyful benefit, she is erogenous; she is what is erogenous in the heterogeneous; she is not attached to herself, the airborne swimmer, the thieving flyer. (Hélène Cixous, 'Sorties', 1975)[3]

The 'oceanic feeling' that modern French feminists have (re)claimed for the woman writer – the woman who in writing at once creates and pleasures herself[4] – is central to Beth Caldwell Maclure's identity and trajectory. Like Cixous's paradigmatic woman-as-creatrice, Beth 'belongs to the race of waves'.[5] In childhood she is drawn to the sea, which in adolescence becomes the site of her first homosocial and heterosexual romances, and as an adult woman and writer she achieves a sense of completeness in a cottage with a sea view. The periods spent far from the sea correlate with the bleakest experiences of Beth's life: Uncle Jimmy's household, school and marriage all impose rigid bodily regimes which lead to the loss of Beth's 'further faculty' (*BB*, 16), her artistic gift. Patterned by cyclical returns to seascapes, *The Beth Book* constructs the girl artist as a 'wild creature' (*BB*, 107) in a manner which evokes the later theorised writing of Hélène Cixous: like Cixous's wild woman-writer, Beth the adult writer is the girl-woman returning 'from afar, from always: from "without," … from below, from beyond "culture"; from [her] childhood'.[6] When at its most active, her creative spirit infuses Beth with a sense of 'rapture' and a 'passion' illustrative of what poststructuralists today conceptualise as *jouissance*: writing was 'like love – love without the lover' (*BB*, 394). Called into being by sensual inspiration, this exquisite experience of 'falling, rolling, trembling inside', which subsequent cerebration shapes into art, is figuratively and literally associated with, and located within, a nature environment and aligned with the element of water. 'My idea of perfect bliss', Beth muses in the interval between the publication of her first, instantly acclaimed, novel and her rise into prominence as a feminist orator, 'is to lie my length upon a cliff above the sea, listening to the many-murmurous, soothed by it into a sense of oneness with Nature, till I seem to be mixed with the elements, a part of sky and sea and shore, and akin to the wandering winds' (*BB*, 521). Grand's early exploration of the libidinal economy of the feminine body in apprenticeship works like *Singularly Deluded* and *Babs the Impossible* is here organised into a systematic, sophisticated discourse that establishes a conceptual link between the heroine's libidinal body and the creative urges of her mind, suggesting that feminine writing – a writing recreative of the female body – is born from the dynamic fusion of the two within a natural setting. It is no accident that Beth's moment of revelation – in Lyn Pykett's terms, a 'quasi-religious conversion'[7] – should come about in her secluded cottage by the sea when, opening her window to the dawn illuminating the sky outside, she is struck by the insight that '*Love is God!*' (*BB*, 523, emphasis in original). The 'oceanic' sense of overflowing emotion and joyfulness with which the novel ends can be read both as an authorial attempt to reward the heroine for her private and public labours by granting her personal fulfilment (*jouissance*) in both spheres, and as a manifesto for a new aesthetics which couples social responsibility (expressed through political activism) with sensual gratification.

By encoding female creativity as natural (elemental) and spiritual, Grand came perilously close to underwriting the binary opposition between 'feminine' nature and 'masculine' culture, so often mobilised to exclude women from the realm of 'high' cultural production. One of the reasons why her female aesthetic had to be grounded in nature discourses was to dissociate it from what she considered to be the 'unnatural' (because affected and unreadable)[8] texts of Decadence (writing with which the New Woman was typically associated in the contemporary press). Grand's firm stand against male-dominated 'highbrow' culture was further signalled by her alignment of Beth's 'further faculty' with spiritualism, mysticism and the theological-philosophical concepts of theosophy, and thus with social and discursive formations which took account of women's visions and voices. Gauri Viswanathan's observation that theosophical writings constitute 'a composite of voices, actors, writers, and interpreters, all of whom combine to create a complex presence of spiritual authority, alternately accommodating and subversive',[9] can be applied to Grand's own textual practice. For not only is her version of the extraordinary woman – the 'genius' proclaimed in the novel's subtitle – constructed with reference to a composite number of discourses of a primarily subversive yet also authoritative nature, but with her multifaceted and often contradictory personality the heroine also comes to stand for a multiplicity of women, not least because as an artist she is also always giving voice to others: 'She was generally somebody else in these days, seldom herself ... she was ... speaking consistently in the character which she happened to be impersonating' (*BB*, 131). Beth's dual function as both an exemplary and a representative figure is encoded by the waves, an emblem of the shifting boundaries of the feminine self, whose cyclicity and fluidity are reflected in the sea's 'ebb and flow ... strength and swirl ... [and] dreamy motion', the object of her contemplative (self)speculation. Beth's consistently pleasurable immersion in seascapes implies that she succeeds where Evadne failed, in that she becomes the harbinger of the 'seventh wave' of New Women (*HT*, 99).

At the end of the last chapter I argued that in *The Beth Book* Grand was able to resolve the ideological tensions of her earlier works. Unlike Angelica, Evadne and Ideala, Beth is empowered to live her passion *and* to proceed with her career. Yet her achievement as one of the 'new', feisty 'race' of New Women stands in odd contrast with, and ultimately remains circumscribed by, her reliance on enlightened patriarchal figures. Ilverthorpe Cottage, the site of Beth's public and private consummation, is 'Daddy's' gift, a gesture of benevolence by Angelica's paternalistic husband. The clichéd Arthurian knight who arrives on horseback shortly after Beth's breakthrough as a feminist orator must have been something of an anticlimax even to contemporary feminist readers, not least because he turns out to be Arthur Brock, a writer Beth had previously nursed through serious illness at great personal expense.

By no means a flawless character, he proved entirely oblivious to her plight, abandoning her to dire poverty and semi-starvation on his convalescence. The self-satisfied pleasure he expressed when 'superintending her domestic duties' while she kept house for him (*BB*, 503), allied to his type-casting of feminists as 'the unsexed crew that shriek on platforms' (*BB*, 509), does not bode well for his suitability as the politically enlightened, egalitarian-minded and caring partner a feminist at the height of her success might be forgiven for fancying. To modern feminist critics like Rachel Blau Du Plessis, Terri Doughty and Lyn Pykett, the ending is indicative of Grand's 'tremendous ambivalence' towards the professional woman, particularly the woman artist.[10] They argue that, as Beth moves from self-affirmation to self-sacrifice, writing to nurturing, the feminist quest plot is superseded by a romance plot which 'offers the conciliations and closures demanded by the femaleness of the artist'.[11]

Before condemning Grand for her inability to 'break free of the discourse of the proper feminine',[12] it may be useful to consider her reasons for choosing this particular representation of virtue rewarded. By drawing attention to Beth's dreams of romantic love, she was able to counter the conservative stereotype of the feminist as frigid man-hater, a 'prig in petticoats' (as Grand herself was dubbed), afflicted with 'moral frostbite' and a manner as 'aggressive as that of a Sunday-school' teacher.[13] The ideal feminist, Grand suggests, is none of these things; if anything, her femininity is enhanced by the passion which propels her into political work. Wishing to appeal to the conventional woman as well as her more progressive sister, Grand presented readers with two final tableaux, Freedom and Fame coupled with Romance and Companionship. At the same time she pointed to the need for fantasy to make way for a more realistic attitude to life: this is why the figure of the 'knight' (the romantic image Beth conjured up during her marital depression and which helped her recover her mental balance) reveals a New Man with human blemishes, though with none of the serious moral failings of the Old Man. Through this character, Grand seeks to outline the potential that might be possible in the relations between women and men once both have passed the test of maturity and purity:

> It was all as congenial as it was new to her, this close association with a man of the highest character and the most perfect refinement. She had never before realised that there could be such men … and this discovery had stimulated her strangely – filled her with hope, strengthened her love of life, and made everything seem worth while. (*BB*, 504–5)

While most New Woman writers ended their novels with the defeat of their heroine in professional and/or personal terms, Grand, following the model of Elizabeth Barrett Browning's *Aurora Leigh* (1857), chose to posit the possibility of self-realisation in both spheres: as Penny Boumelha observes, Beth constitutes a 'rare instance of a surviving and fulfilled female genius' among New Woman heroines.[14] Olive Schreiner, by contrast, felt unable to take her own artist-novel, *From Man to Man*, beyond the point at which the New Woman Rebekah's love of a suitable specimen of the New Man might lead to an actual relationship. The instant, spiritual recognition of the 'soul partner' in each text[15] is followed by projected self-sacrifice in *From Man to Man*[16] and the prospect of emotional and sensual fulfilment in *The Beth Book*. Paradoxically, of the two writers it was the spokeswoman of social purity, not the sexual libertarian, who projected an ending which sanctioned adultery and free love: for Beth's husband is alive and divorce unobtainable (*BB*, 518). Behind the cover of romantic window-dressing Grand's text thus presents us with a forceful subversive message which brings together what appeared to be irreconcilable in Beth's mature life: passion and purpose, art and feminism, the contemplative life of the writer and the busy schedule of the political activist. If, like Ideala, Beth must pass through consecutive stages of suffering in order to achieve a sense of completion, this is a female Christ relieved from the martyrdom of the body. The spiritual illumination leading to Beth's recognition of the all-importance of love at the end of the novel is prompted by reading about the passion of Christ and a saintly trajectory marked by four phases: '*The communion of saints ... the forgiveness of sins ... the resurrection of the body ... and the life everlasting*' (*BB*, 523, emphasis in original). These stages correlate with Beth's experiences and apply in equal measure to her public (feminist) and private (emotional) careers. Beth recovers from her deep depression with the help of advanced friends (the New Woman 'saint' Ideala and the somewhat less saintly Angelica), learns to forgive herself for the degradation endured in her marriage, while also gaining public pardon for being the wife of a lock hospital doctor; after successfully 'resurrecting' herself as a writer, she finds her 'true' vocation ('life everlasting') in political oratory. This upward movement is replicated in her personal history of companionship with Arthur which, after a brief period of misrecognition, lays the foundations for a very literal 'resurrection' of Beth's body through a passionate relationship between equals.

It is ironic that because of Grand's critical engagement with marital abuse, prostitution and vivisection, contemporary critics overlooked the conciliatory, even celebratory note in the novel's conclusion. Though commended for its depiction of Beth's childhood, the book was heavily attacked for its feminist subject matter: 'she *must* preach her wonderful doctrine of the equality of the sexes', an exasperated Frank Danby (Julia Frankau) wrote in the *Saturday Review*, 'she *must* jumble up medical and moral questions ... she *must* ruin her own works of art and deface them ... by all the refuse of the controversies that raged twenty years ago around the dead C. D. Acts'. Her fellow reviewer, Frank Harris – who as the editor of the *Fortnightly Review* had supported advanced views on women's political rights in the late 1880s – responded with even greater sarcasm to the issues raised by Grand's text, dismissing it without further ado as so much 'irrelevant and foolish drivel'.[17]

In one sense the reviewers were right: *The Beth Book* is certainly a novel about the women's movement, more specifically about Grand's own shift of emphasis from writing to political activism. A particularly interesting aspect is that, while reflecting the major concerns of Grand's social purity feminism, the text provides central points of contact with Olive Schreiner's and Mona Caird's approaches. Like Schreiner's *From Man to Man* it allies the heroine's struggle to survive in an oppressive marriage to her self-genesis as an artist in the psycho-social space of a room-womb;[18] and like Caird's *The Daughters of Danaus* (1894) it analyses the way in which mother–daughter relationships serve to reproduce patriarchal power relations. Sharing the other two writers' concern with developing a female and feminist aesthetic, Grand was the only one to allow her artist-protagonist unqualified success in carrying out this project, thus mounting the most explicit challenge of the three to male art and the decadent movement of the 1890s. Whereas Caird's Hadria and Schreiner's Rebekah expend their energies in trying to recover a female tradition, Grand's Beth produces her own feminist art manifesto. Unlike Schreiner and Caird, who concentrate on the problems the artist faces as a woman, Grand plays with and comically subverts mainstream tradition. This is apparent from the outset of the book in her anti-heroic depiction of Beth's birth.

Tradition, subversion and the individual talent: the artist as a young girl

Like a traditional (fictional) (auto)biography, *The Beth Book* starts with the protagonist's birth; yet while seemingly conforming to traditional modes of writing, the text immediately and ironically sets out to explode these traditions: it is a grey day (not a particularly glorious background for the birth of a heroine), and if Beth's mother is dreading the new arrival, her father 'never wanted [her] at all' (*BB*, 73). To compound this sense of an anticlimax, Beth is born shortly after Mrs Caldwell has entertained herself with watching the butcher kill a lamb (an image which foreshadows the mother's later sacrificial attitude towards her daughter *vis-à-vis* her brothers), and while Mr Caldwell is presumably engaged on indulging his latest extra-marital affair. Grand's satirical mimicry of canonical deconstructions of the eponymous hero – Sterne's *Tristram Shandy*, Fielding's *Tom Jones* (a character she heartily detested), Dickens's *David Copperfield* and Thackeray's *Barry Lyndon* – go beyond the male literary model, for in the very act of conceiving the 'Grand' heroic woman the text calls itself into question by implying that if only Mrs Caldwell had been sharp-witted enough to practise birth control, the subject of the novel (and thus the novel itself) need never have seen the light of day: 'What she suffered she accepted as her "lot", or "The Will of God" … That … the misery was perfectly preventable never occurred to her, and if any one had suggested such a thing she would have been shocked' (*BB*, 1).

While radically destabilising the notion of 'the hero/ine', the first chapter introduces the central concerns of the book: women's socialisation into victim positions and their oppression within the patriarchal family, counter-balanced by the healing potential of art. The only harmonising factor in the otherwise broken marriage of Beth's parents, impaired as much by Mrs Caldwell's willing participation in her own subjection as by her husband's parental irresponsibility and marital despotism, is the couple's shared interest in literature. But even the consumption of art is fraught with difficulties for women. As she is nearing her confinement, Mrs Caldwell intensely yearns for the comfort of a day spent reading, a longing always frustrated because of the demands of her domestic role. Just as her active desire to read subsides into receptive passivity as she listens to her husband's reading, her response to life in general is reactive rather than guided by her own needs. In stark contrast to her mother, Beth proves to be an irrepressibly energetic and proactive agent of her destiny who, by literally and metaphorically writing her own story, is able to superimpose her imagined world on to the real one even in the consciousness of others. As in Angelica's case, however, Beth's power to shape and write life stories and change identities only lasts until adolescence and marriage, when an alien identity is imposed on her; like Evadne she falls ill, but like Ideala she undergoes an inner process of recuperation that enables her to refashion herself into a 'new' woman.

The principle of subversion, of exploding traditional ideologies alongside narrative structures and themes, is a determining feature of *The Beth Book* and particularly vibrant in the account of Beth's childhood and adolescence. Beth is like Angelica when deprived of Diavolo's support: unruly and apt to express strong feelings – joy as much as anger – without inhibition, an intense, imaginative and creative child craving for affection. In contradistinction to her older and younger sisters, she ignores all attempts undertaken to feminise her. As in *The Heavenly Twins*, femininity is deconstructed as an artifice, a masquerade women are trained to turn into their sole purpose in life as a means of preventing them from spending time on more contentious matters such as education. In puberty, when Beth's inner resistance is weakened by the changes in her body, her mother prevails on her to sacrifice to her privately educated brother's expensive tastes her aunt's inheritance expressly meant to provide for her schooling. In exchange for an education, Beth is to be rewarded with the paraphernalia of femininity:

> There is no hurry for your education. In fact, I think it would be better for your health if you were not taught too much at present … I should like to help you to make the best of yourself, Beth … You are a tall girl for your age, and are

beginning to hold yourself well already ... And you have the complexion of the Bench family, if you will take care of it. You should wash your face in buttermilk at night after being out in the sun. I'll get you some, and I'll get you a parasol for the summer. Your hands are not nearly so coarse as they used to be, and they would really be quite nice if you attended to them properly ... I must see to your gloves and boots. I don't know what your waist is going to be, but you shall have some good stays. A fine shape goes a long way. With your prospects you really ought to make a good match, so do not slouch about any more as if you had no self-respect at all. You can really do a great deal to make yourself attractive in appearance. (*BB*, 223, 225)

If in her journalism Grand was at pains to promote grace and beauty as a mark of feminist self-respect, her fiction consistently highlighted the detrimental effects of the beauty myth on girls' inner development. Determined to challenge the patriarchal binaries of boy versus girl, mind versus body, and substance versus surface, she railed against a system which deprived girls of intellectual and boys of moral training, turning the former into mentally atrophied half-creatures, and the latter into egotistic monsters. Her novels castigated the reduction of girls and women into feminine apparel (stays, gloves and boots), arguing that intellectual attainments and the pursuit of a purposeful life did not curtail but on the contrary often enhanced a woman's femininity because in strengthening her individuality they added to her personal magnetism, and that it was the imposition of artificial and restraining props, not education, which ruined women: 'It is fashion that unsexes women and unmakes men' (*BB*, 317). This is a lesson impressed on Grand's heroine Agatha Oldham (*A Domestic Experiment*, 1891), who, driven to masochistic acts of self-destruction at the height of her marital depression, assumes the 'unhealthy, degenerate' and deforming dress style favoured by her adulterous husband (*DE*, 64). Agatha later recovers her equilibrium and reverts to the healthy femininity of a woman unconfined by constricting garments, albeit one whose freedom of movement continues to be fatally circumscribed by the patriarchal structures of marriage.[19] Beth, too, falls victim to sex-role conditioning, with disastrous consequences in the shape of an unhappy, physically and mentally cramping marriage. If, unlike Grand's earlier heroines Agatha and Evadne, she is able to leave the confines of the patriarchal family for a counter-community of artists and feminists, this is primarily due to the fact that, despite an outer show of 'habitual docility', she never entirely loses her dissenting voice in marriage. Her husband feels duly 'sobered' and even 'staggered' when encountering her 'flash[es] of spirit': 'He tried to subdue her by staring her out of countenance; but Beth scornfully returned his gaze. Then suddenly she stamped her foot, and brought her clenched fist down on the dining-room table ... "Come, come, sir," she said, "we've had enough of this theatrical posing. You are wasting my time, explain yourself"' (*BB*, 377–8).

As a child, Beth is even less daunted by the prospect of conflictual situations. First puzzled, then exasperated and increasingly angry at the universal contempt poured on her sex, she challenges boys and young men when they try to uphold their own superiority by berating women. As in Evadne's case, her education in misogyny starts at home. In her verbal battles with her older brother Jim Beth uses the same strategy of literal interpretation that Diavolo employs in his discussion of religious myths in *The Heavenly Twins*: by taking sexist statements at face value, both expose the absurdity of such views. 'And when all the buttons are sewed on and all the socks mended, what is a girl to do with her time?' she asks Jim after he informs her that sewing is the only occupation available to girls:

> 'Oh, there's lots to be done,' Jim answered vaguely. 'There's the cooking. A man's life isn't worth having if the cooking's bad.'
> 'But a gentleman keeps a cook,' Beth observed.
> 'Oh yes, of course,' Jim answered irritably. 'You would see what I mean if you weren't a girl. Girls have no brains. They scream at a mouse.'
> '*We* never scream at mice,' Beth protested in surprise. 'Bernadine catches them in her hands.'
> 'Ah, but then you've had brothers, you see,' said Jim. 'It makes all the difference if you're taught not to be silly.'
> 'Then why aren't all girls taught, and why aren't we taught more things?'
> 'Because you've got no brains, I tell you.'
> 'But if we can be taught one thing, why can't we be taught another? How can you tell we've no brains if you never try to teach us?'
> 'Now look here, Miss Beth,' said brother Jim in a tone of exasperation, 'I know what you'll be when you grow up, if you don't mind. You'll be just the sort of long-tongued shrew, always arguing, that men hate.'
> 'Do you say "that men hate" or "whom men hate"?' Beth interrupted.
> 'There you are!' said Jim; 'devilish sharp at a nag. That's just what I'm telling you. Now, you take my advice, and hold your tongue. Then perhaps you'll get a husband; and if you do, make things comfortable for him. Men can't abide women who don't make things comfortable.'
> 'Well,' said Beth temperately, 'I don't think I could "abide" a man who didn't make things comfortable.'
> Jim grunted … (*BB*, 154–5)

When it comes to common sense, Beth has all the arguments on her side, whereas Jim, the self-appointed spokesman of patriarchy, can only resort to empty phrases, personal invective and inarticulate sounds; as Grand demonstrates, there is no logic to patriarchal dogma. In order to keep them subordinate, women must be indoctrinated with the ideology of the natural hegemony of man, and be denied an education that would allow them to challenge the views used as a justification for their subjection; the inherent flaws in the system are thus projected on to its victims. A century after Mary

Wollstonecraft's repudiation of the traditional model of female education in *Vindication of the Rights of Woman*, New Woman writers like Sarah Grand, who had themselves been deprived of academic schooling, drew attention to the fact that her demands were still waiting to be met.

The more Beth learns to call the prevalent gender relations into question, the less she is prepared to avoid conflict. When at 11 her first boyfriend, Sammy, tells her that women cannot write books, she is scandalised by his ignorance, referring him to Jane Austen, Maria Edgeworth and Fanny Burney, names all patently unknown to him. Since he persists in his refusal to believe that she herself is the author of the poem she has given him to read, she sees no other course of action left than to beat him up (*BB*, 172, 179). That Grand situates this comical role-reversal at pre-pubescence, before Beth becomes fully aware of her body's libidinality (explored in the course of sensuous sea baths with other girls and, later, a boy), is surely significant. According to Judith Butler, the sex/gender distinction on which much feminist theory is grounded is fundamentally flawed, in that not only gender but also sex are culturally and discursively constructed.[20] At a time when Beth has not yet 'discovered' a 'discrete' (in Butler's terms, fragmented) sexual identity (as evidenced by the sequence of reverse-heterosexual, libidinal-defused-into-companionate-heterosexual and homosocial relationships she enters into with Sammy, Alfred Cayley Pounce and Charlotte Hardy), she also flies in the face of Victorian gender paradigms. Grand hardly goes as far as Butler, who argues that sex is as problematic a concept as gender, but if her fiction consistently pokes fun at the idea of inborn gender traits reflecting anatomical differences, it also – albeit tentatively – destabilises the notion of fixed sexual identities. For like the masquerades of the 'heavenly twins', Beth's relationship with Sammy comically explodes all clichés about femininity, masculinity and 'natural', biological gender/sex equivalences. Beth is the active pursuer, Sammy the reluctant and frightened object of desire; it is she who initiates their relationship by presenting him with a love letter, then comes to get him when he is too shy to turn up for the meeting she has arranged, and finally escorts him home afterwards. It is the girl and not the boy who has the brains and whom 'love' inspires to write poetry, whereas the boy is reduced to the status of a muse:

> Beth felt on the subject of Sammy. The fact of his having a cherubic face made her feel nice inside her chest – set up a glow there which warmed and brightened her whole existence – a glow which never flickered day or night, except in Sammy's presence, when it went out altogether more often than not; only to revive, however, when the real Sammy had gone and the ideal Sammy returned to his place in her bosom. For Sammy adored at a distance and Sammy within range of criticism were two very different people. Sammy adored at a distance was allready response to Beth's fine flights of imagination; but Sammy on the spot was dull. He was seldom on the spot, however, so that Beth had ample leisure to live

on her love undisturbed, and her mind became extraordinarily active. Verse came to her like a recollection. (*BB*, 174)

If Beth is a satirical representation of the male writer and poet in love with being in love, projecting his enthusiasm on to a desirable female body, then Sammy, with his chubby face, golden curls, blue eyes and utterly deficient mind, represents the stereotypical dumb blonde: 'His pretty colouring was all that he had had to attract her, and that, alas! had lost its charm' (*BB*, 185). Comically but patently Grand deflated Victorian gender paradigms, and her readers did not miss the point: Beth, a reviewer wrote in the *Young Woman*, was 'the most virile specimen extant of the *enfant terrible*'.[21]

Jouissances: theosophy, auto/eroticism, and the seventh-wave New Woman

In *The Beth Book* as in *The Heavenly Twins*, parody serves to deconstruct the nature argument which underpins the hegemonic structures of gender relations. With his bad-tempered grunts and defective powers of ratiocination, Jim is as poor an advocate of the theory of the 'natural' superiority of the male sex as Sammy is with his excessive timidity and bland imbecility. As patriarchal logos is exposed in all its absurdity (Uncle Jimmy's penchant for adulterous amorous ululations reflecting the collapse of patriarchal language), Beth and her primarily sensory responses to the world, including her aggressive impulses, become signifiers of the 'natural' and 'authentic' as opposed to the artificial, affected and unbalanced which marks orthodox masculinity. Beth's spontaneous drives foster creative self-expression; the men, in contrast, are unable to move beyond imposture and self-pretence. As Patricia Murphy has pointed out, *The Beth Book* inverts scientific taxonomies of the time by promoting feminine intuition and sensory-based knowledge acquisition over more traditional, linear channels of cognition.[22] Sense and sensibility, cognitive and experiential susceptibilities, which in patriarchal culture are split into hierarchised gender binaries, are here reinterpreted as the joint prerogative of femininity, which thus appears closely aligned with both nature (body) *and* culture (mind). For notwithstanding Sammy's protestations that 'Men write books … not women, let alone gels' (*BB*, 172) – a statement later echoed by Alfred and Beth's husband – Beth is in facile command of language from early childhood, yet language is precisely what always eludes the men. Faced with her eloquence and the vibrancy of her outbursts, the torchbearers of patriarchy are reduced to a pantomime of linguistic prostration: 'Uncle James blinked his eyes several times running, rapidly, as if something had gone wrong with them' (*BB*, 98).

Indicative of her inherent 'genius', Beth's gift of oratory is linked to inspirational acts of 'writing' – songs, poems, fairytales, stories, romances –

undertaken from the age of 5. Day-dreaming, which has such damaging repercussions on Evadne's mental health because it acts as a substitute for rather than a stimulant of life, proves of great benefit to Beth, whose day-to-day interaction with other people is enriched by her imaginative ventures. A creative, potentially 'divine' force (*BB*, 213), Beth's 'further faculty' is associated with spiritual, supernatural energy: 'I sometimes feel as if I were listening, but not with my ears, and waiting for things to happen that I know about, but not with my head ... it [is] just as if there were two doors, and one ha[s] to be shut before I [can] look out of the other' (*BB*, 213). That this supernatural sense is explored as a sign of Beth's exceptional powers represents a conceptual break with *The Heavenly Twins*, where Grand ridiculed the belief in the supernatural as naive superstition compounded by religious indoctrination on the part of patriarchal institutions. By contrast, in *The Beth Book*, subsequent short stories and her late novels, the Gothic comes to play an important part, and supernatural experience is encoded as a reflection of the spiritual powers of exceptional women.[23]

From early childhood Beth has visions of past and future events. The supernatural theme links *The Beth Book* to earlier literary traditions, notably the female Gothic, and in particular to feminist precursors like Charlotte Brontë. In *The Beth Book* (and later in *Adnam's Orchard* and *The Winged Victory*), Grand also implicitly located herself within the contemporary cultures of spiritualism and Madame Blavatsky's Theosophical Society, both increasingly feminised arenas of cultural activity.

From the 1840s onwards through to the first two decades of the twentieth century spiritualism enjoyed particular popularity among women, including many women (as well as male) writers.[24] As patriarchal ideology constructed women as spiritual and other-worldly in order to justify their social and political confinement to the domestic world, a counter-religion which invoked women's spiritual powers in order to invest them with social and cultural authority, and which counter-poised the male-centred discourses of Church and Science with the concept of female agency (feminine mediumship) must have been singularly appealing even to women who did not consciously set out to challenge hegemonic structures. With different aims and for different reasons, feminists and female spiritualists, by simultaneously drawing on and subverting traditional concepts of femininity, were jointly engaged in redefining the role of women in society.[25] In Britain, the 1850s and 1880s marked the singular synchronicity of the two movements, which began and had their heyday at roughly the same time. Thus the 'golden age of English spiritualism' coincided with major legislation which extended women's rights, such as the Married Women's Property Act of 1882.[26]

Both movements were from their inception linked with social and political reform – socialism, social purism (temperance, sexual morality), health reform (rational dress, alternative medicine) and animal rights (vegetarian-ism, anti-vivisection) – and both implicitly and explicitly posed a challenge to, and therefore provoked a fierce backlash from, the male establishment. The newly coined synonym for hysteria, 'utromania', applied to the unruly female in her feminist or spiritualist configuration alike, reflecting the medical profession's conflation of women's agency, female sexual anatomy, monstrosity and insanity. The utromaniac, the American physican Frederic Marvin warned in 1874, 'becomes possessed by the idea that she has some startling mission in the world. She forsakes her home, her children, and her duty, to mount the rostrum and proclaim the peculiar virtues of free-love, elective affinity, or the reincarnation of souls.'[27] As medical scandals about patients' wrongful imprisonment in lunatic asylums began to rock late-Victorian society, it became increasingly clear that women were at particular risk, especially if, like Louisa Lowe, they combined spiritualist beliefs with marital rebellion, displayed an alarming indifference to bourgeois conventions in their self-confident promotion of philanthropic schemes like Georgina Weldon, or like Edith Lanchester demonstrated their commitment to socialism, feminism and free love.[28]

While in their struggle for personal justice and public enlightenment about medical misconduct, individual women like Lowe and Weldon skilfully turned to high melodrama, transforming traumatic experience into sensational narratives about wicked husbands, body-snatching mad-doctors, and plucky and ever resourceful heroines,[29] feminist writers like Grand validated women's spirituality by reconceptualising it as a sign, not as male medicine would have it of the unsettled female mind, but, on the contrary, of women's exceptional psychical powers, a fountain of their artistic energy. This undertaking was facilitated by the emergence of a new alternative philosophy, theosophy (literally 'divine wisdom'), founded in 1875 by Helena Petrovna Blavatsky and Henry S. Olcott. A Russian émigrée with flamboyant antecedents and notorious occult powers, whose intense vitality and enormous personal magnetism were allied to an extraordinary depth of philosophical knowledge, Blavatsky quickly became one of the most highly controversial figures in the world of English spiritualism when, after some years spent in the United States and extensive travels in India and Europe, she settled in Britain in 1887.[30] Although the last decade of her life was overshadowed by repeated accusations of fraud, her impact on *fin-de-siècle* and early twentieth-century writers and artists on both sides of the Atlantic was tremendous.[31]

Stressing the universal brotherhood of humanity and the organic unity of the universe, theosophy 'combined socialist and feminist ideals with a sophisticated esoteric philosophy', and held particular appeal for the women's movement because it celebrated the matriarchal principle: 'the great (female) producer, genitrix of the Sun', Blavatsky wrote in *The Secret Doctrine* (1888), 'is the first born, and ... is not begotten, but only brought forth, and hence is the fruit of an immaculate mother.'[32] Perhaps because its oppositional politics, like those of feminism, 'existed in an unstable relationship to the conventional distinctions of left and right',[33] the Theosophical Society was able to recruit considerable numbers of feminist activists, suffragists and later suffragettes to its ranks, counting among its most prominent devotees the free-thinker and erstwhile atheist Annie Besant, who after her conversion in 1889 emerged as a possible successor to Blavatsky, and Charlotte Despard, the leader of the militant Women's Freedom League.[34] Other members included the suffragists Eva Gore Booth and Esther Roper, the suffragettes Gertrude Colmore and Annie Kenney, the socialist free lover Edith Lanchester, the matrocentric evolutionary theorist Frances Swiney, and the editor of *Shafts*, Margaret Shurmer Sibthorpe. Dora Marsden, founder editor of the *Freewoman* (the first incarnation of what was later to become the modernist *Egoist*) and the *enfant terrible* of the suffrage movement, had a characteristically tempestuous relationship with theosophy.[35] In the three decades between the 1890s and 1930s Joy Dixon has estimated that roughly 10 per cent of feminist activists had some form of involvement with the Theosophical Society.[36]

Mysticism became such a major cultural force at the turn of the century that, even though she had not much time for theosophical circles and left the London 'Golden Dawn' in protest about its links with the Freemasons, Maud Gonne still devoted an entire chapter of her autobiographical account of her part in the struggle for Irish independence to 'Occult Experiences'.[37] For 'a world desperately in need of some kind of non-materialistic background', the New Woman writer Netta Syrett affirmed in her autobiography, the engagement with psychical research was of 'paramount importance'.[38] While, as Dixon points out, the 'spiritual was itself a site of struggle [and] feminist versions of theosophy ... existed in tension with one another',[39] female spirituality offered potent grounds for justification for women who engaged in oppositional public and political activity. The New Woman and *fin-de-siècle* feminism, if not exactly scripted into being by the 'curious alliance between literature and occultism', as Diana Basham has suggested,[40] were certainly energised by their dynamic relationship with spiritualism and particularly theosophy, which provided a far-reaching philosophical and theological framework for women's political demands. 'Theosophists are of necessity the friends of all movements in the world', Blavatsky noted in 1888. 'We are the friends of all those who fight against drunkenness, against cruelty to animals, against injustice to women, against corruption in society or in government.'[41]

As a metaphysics of humanity which gave philosophical clout to social purity reformism, Blavatsky's teachings and books, published at a time when she was finding her own voice as a writer and feminist,[42] could not but have appealed to Grand, and so would some of the coincidences in their lives. Born outside of England and widely travelled, both drew inspiration from the creative friction between 'outsider' and 'insider' knowledges; both had breached the barriers of a conventional female education to become prominent critics of institutionalised male discourses (the religious and medical establishments); unhappily married, each had left her husband; both saw in literature and writing primarily a didactic medium and conceived of themselves as teachers on a grand scale, signalling this sense of personal eminence by adopting the title 'Madame'. Both women took subversive delight in mimicking and subverting Victorian gender paradigms: Grand by juxtaposing a public persona resonant with exquisite femininity with the flamboyant gender impostures of her heroines, Blavatsky in sporting a preposterously unfeminine appearance coupled with an imposing masculine demeanour, while simultaneously drawing authority from the conventional claims of female spirituality.[43] In her work Blavatsky stressed the originally matrocentric but ultimately androgynous nature of the universe, arguing that as 'the Ego or Higher Self developed, [it passed] through numberless lives in both male and female bodies [and] began to manifest the highest qualities in both, culminating in the emergence of the spiritual androgyne or "Divine Hermaphrodite"'.[44] This is echoed in *The Heavenly Twins*, when Angelica asserts that true genius resides in 'the attributes of both minds, masculine and feminine, perfectly united in one person of either sex' (*HT*, 403). Blavatsky's Universal Divine Principle of double-gendered sexlessness as the origin of all cosmic development is recreated in a different form in Grand's 'Proem', which celebrates the union of 'the male and female principles which together created the universe, the infinite father and mother' as the foundation stone of good government (*HT*, ix).

Both Grand and Blavatsky ventriloquised authoritative discourses in order to superimpose oppositional ideologies on the public consciousness of their mass audiences. While Blavatsky played on the contradictions and discursive instabilities arising from invoking the masculine authority of sages feminised by their exotic eastern origins,[45] Grand manipulated patriarchal notions of domestic housekeeping into powerful feminist polemic about the need for social and political regeneration. Possessing something of a trickster persona herself, Grand could only have appreciated Blavatsky's grandiose project of self-fictionalisation, and as a writer must have admired her for the 'complicated narrative maneuvres' which went into buttressing her theosophical self-authentication.[46] Biographical sketches published during her lifetime and after her death may have provided further links between the two writers. Thus Vera Petrovna de Zhelihovsky's 1886 account of her sister's storytelling habits and the ease with which the child captivated juvenile and adult audiences is evocative of Grand's own life:

The marvellous and sensational stories that we, children and schoolgirls, heard from Helen ... were countless. I well remember when stretched at full length on the ground, her chin reclining on her two palms, and her two elbows buried deep in the soft sand, she used to dream aloud, and tell us of her visions, evidently clear, vivid, and as palpable as life to her! ... She had a strong power of carrying away her audiences with her, of making them see actually, if even vaguely, that which she herself saw ... It was her delight to gather around herself a party of us younger children at twilight, and ... to hold us ... spellbound ... with her weird stories ... [E]ven grown-up persons found themselves interested involuntarily in her narratives.[47]

Grand later recalled in interviews that in her childhood she too was 'much addicted to spinning yarns', holding listeners in suspense with terrifying stories 'of unlimited continuation'.[48] This magnetic-cum-diabolic energy is also typical of Beth who, like the young Helena, possesses mesmerist and clairvoyant faculties and is held in great awe by the servants for her ability to invoke curses on unfortunate subordinates. When the local Irish farrier responds to her unionist taunts by killing her magpie, Beth, at age 5, foretells the death of his horse (*BB*, 59–63) in much the same manner in which the 4-year-old Helena is reputed to have predicted the death of a boy who had displeased her and who was later found drowned.[49] While as a child Blavatsky conjured up chilling tales of death by water to enthrall her audience,[50] the adolescent Beth narrowly escapes drowning on two occasions (*BB*, 240–2, 324–5). The sheer energy of elemental forces seems to have held a similar fascination for both women. Like Blavatsky, Grand considered herself exceptional, inscribing this sense of uniqueness into an artist-heroine whose creative potency and leadership qualities are the result of her spiritual oneness with all organic and inorganic matter. Theosophy, Blavatsky explained in her *Theosophical Glossary* (1892), 'teaches that all which exists is animated or informed by the universal soul or spirit, and that not an atom in our universe can be outside of this omnipresent Principle'.[51] Reflecting such beliefs, Beth's further faculty develops and matures in communion with nature and particularly with elemental forces such as the sea, the wind and the waves. At 14, in a female-centred version of a proto-Lawrentian script, Beth becomes part of the sea's waves and is then joined and admired by a group of girls:

She sat a long time on the warm dry sand, with her chin resting on her knees, and her hands clasped round them, not gazing with seeing eyes nor listening with open ears, but apprehending through her further faculty the great harmony of Nature of which she herself was one of the most triumphant notes. At that moment she tasted life at its best and fullest – life all ease and grace and beauty, without regret or longing – perfect life in that she wanted nothing more. But she rose at last, and, still gazing at the sea, slowly unclasped her waistbelt, and let it fall on the sand at her feet; then she took her hat off, her dress, her boots and stockings, everything, and stood, ivory-white, with bright brown wavy hair, against the lilac greyness under the tall dark cliffs. The little waves had called her, coming up closer and closer, and fascinating her, until, yielding to their allurements, she went in amongst them, and floated on them, or lay her length in the shallows, letting them ripple over her, and make merry about her, the gladdest girl alive, yet with the wrapt impassive face of a devotee whose ecstasy is apart from all that acts on mere flesh and makes expression. All through life Beth had her moments, and they were generally such as this, when her higher self was near upon release from its fetters, and she arose an interval towards oneness with the Eternal.

... A troop of what Mrs Caldwell called 'common girls' came suddenly round the cliff into her sheltered nook, with shouts of laughter, also bent on bathing ... They undressed as they came along, and were very soon, all of them, playing about her, ducking and splashing each other, and Beth also, including her sociably in the game. And Beth ... responded so cordially that she was very soon heading the manoeuvres ...

'My!' one of them exclaimed, when they came to their clothes ... – 'My! ain't *she* nice!'

Then all the other girls stood and stared at Beth, whose fine limbs and satin-smooth white skin, so different in colour and texture from their own, drew from them the most candid expressions of admiration. (*BB*, 271)

By exalting Beth's mystic unity with natural and supernatural elements, and by linking the spiritual power she thus gains to her social authority among the other girls, Grand aligns Beth with theosophical teaching, in particular the idea of being 'In Tune with the Infinite' (the title of an influential theosophical text published in the same year and authored by Ralph Waldo Trine). According to Blavatsky, the coming together of physical body, soul and spirit forged a moment of immortality.[52] In light of such close encounters with eternity, it may not be surprising that the adult Beth will instantly be recognised by Ideala as representing 'the genius for whom we are waiting ... She sees what we have never seen, and never shall in this incarnation; hers are the vision and the dream that are denied to us' (*BB*, 390–1). Ideala's allusion to her present incarnation refers to the theosophical concept of Metempsychosis ('the progress of the soul from one stage of existence to another'),[53] a theory for which Blavatsky made evolutionary claims[54] in *Isis Unveiled* (1877), suggesting that in order to complete its 'grand cycle' and reach spiritual perfection, each human being passes through a series of (re)incarnations.[55] Beth, it is implied, has evolved into an even higher state of being than Ideala and is therefore predestined to become a spiritual leader of even greater potency and influence, a prediction that appears confirmed by the novel's ending. Her oratorical power to command words and inspire deeds has the potential to reach a wider audience with greater repercussions on social and political superstructures than does Ideala's largely local community-based welfare work (a conclusion that may have served to validate Grand's own trajectory from New Woman writer through feminist speaker to political activist).

If placed within the framework of Blavatsky's Anthropogenesis, both Ideala and Beth would occupy the higher stages of spiritual development as yet inaccessible to ordinary humankind (the 'common' village girls). In *The Secret Doctrine* (1888) Blavatsky traced human spiritual progress through seven stages or 'races', arguing that humanity in its present form (the fourth and fifth root 'races' who were firmly tied to their physicality) had developed from the 'third race' of androgynes, themselves the descendants of the astral-bodied, sexless or asexual first and second 'races'. The future of humanity resided with the coming sixth and seventh 'races' because these would be able to recover the spiritual powers of the first 'races'.[56] The theosophical concept of the 'seventh race' as the highest possible stage of perfection in some sense correlates with Grand's notion of the 'seventh wave'. Feminists at the time frequently invoked the elemental force of the waves as a signifier of feminist evolutionary advancement; prominent examples are Florence Nightingale's fragment 'Cassandra' (1852–9/1928), Frances Power Cobbe's *Duties of Women* (1881) and, after the turn of the century, Olive Schreiner's *Woman and Labour* (1911) and Gertrude Colmore's *Suffragette Sally* (1911).[57] Blavatsky's notion of 'Adepts' (superior beings closer to the next stage of 'racial' progress than their fellow humans) bears some analogies with Grand's conception of the New Woman. Adepts must possess three qualities: Intelligence, Conscience and Will.[58] Conscience is exactly what Babs lacks and Angelica only belatedly learns to prize, while Will is deficient in Evadne. Ideala and Beth, the only characters in Grand's work to boast all three virtues, emerge as successful New Women.

Beth's role as the harbinger of a new 'race' of seventh-wave women adepts is signalled early on in the course of vivid dream-memories of strangely luminous, torch-bearing 'ancestors ... [and] distant relations' – 'Ancestors' being Blavatasky's name for the first 'race' of ethereal '*Angels* ... possessed of the physical creative fire'[59] – who come to her in the 'dark space beneath a theatre' (the world at the eve of humanity's creation) and leave her 'alone in a cave full of smoke' (the temple of the earth-bound fourth and fifth 'races' left with only the smouldering ashes of the divine fire?). 'Was it recollection?' the narrator asks, 'Or is there some more perfect power to know than the intellect – a power lying latent in the whole race, which will eventually come into possession of it; but with which, at present, only some few rather rare beings are perfectly endowed' (*BB*, 27). Beth, it would appear, is one of the elect few, an intermediate being, indistinctly conscious of the splendour of the first 'race' through fragments of memory, and impelled forward in visionary antici-pation to the final stages of spiritual development:

She was with a large company in an indescribable, hollow space, bare of all furnishments because none were required; and into this space there came a great commotion, bright light and smoke, without heat or sense of suffocation. Then she was alone, making for an aperture; struggling and striving with pain of spirit to gain it; and when she had found it, she shot through, and awoke in the world. She awoke ... with the consciousness of having traversed infinite space at infinite speed in an interval of time which her mortal mind could not measure. (*BB*, 28)

So evocative as a memory of her own birth, this passage simultaneously marks the 'birth' of the human (fourth and fifth) 'races' in Blavatky's cosmology and the cyclical return to the origins by means of evolving towards the astrality of the seventh (and first) 'races'. Grand's celebration of the New Woman artist as the 'seventh wave' and thus implicitly also as the herald of the 'seventh race' of humanity is frequently coupled with lofty condescension towards the 'inferior' classes and races, as for example in Beth's encounter with the village girls. This dichotomy between visionary radicalism and socio-political conservatism reflects much feminist discourse of the time, and is a tension also inherent in theosophy, which promoted human equality (enshrining as its 'First Object' the principle of the Universal Brotherhood as being one that knows '[no] distinction of race, creed, sex, caste or color')[60] while retaining the register of a 'master' or super(wo)man class of 'Adepts' and conceptualising spiritual as racial advancement.[61] The Theosophical Society was self-consciously elitist, drawing support from and addressing a primarily educated Western middle- and upper-class clientele, while at the same time engaging in what Dixon calls a form of 'middle-brow orientalism ... which reinscribed divisions between eastern mysticism and western science'.[62] Similarly, Grand's text is under- pinned by race and class stereotypes that come to the fore in the juxtaposition of superior ivory-white goddess (Beth) and brown-skinned village 'commoners' (or 'natives', the social class of the girls being clearly aligned with racial deficiency),[63] a juxtaposition which echoes theosophist constructions of Blavatsky's white Western woman sage's ascendancy over 'native' (Indian) wisdom.[64] The experience of spiritual epiphany, it seems, is contingent on social and racial pre-eminence, with the result that even failed New Women like Evadne can boast of the biological marker of the sovereign race: a marble complexion (*HT*, 607).

If *The Beth Book*'s 'sea bath' passage exemplifies the discursive synergies between Grand's feminist and Blavatsky's theosophist taxonomies, it is also indicative of the difference in their approaches. *The Secret Doctrine* defines the highest stage of human development as one which transcends sex and desire. Theosophist teaching emphasised the need to curb and redirect sexual desire into other channels because too much desire was thought to 'disturb and agitate the astral body', thus circumscribing the use of occult energies.[65] Grand, by contrast, draws explicit attention to Beth's sexuality as a spontaneous, natural and healthy overflowing of physical, emotional and spiritual energy. Beth's merging with the waves is clearly of a sexual nature, as is her ecstasy. This particular incident is preceded, two chapters earlier, by a highly eroticised scene in which Beth and Alfred Cayley Pounce, a young man with whom she has exchanged meaningful glances at church, are both drawn to the beach in the hope of a chance meeting. Lying flat on an overhanging cliff, Beth watches Alfred sculpt the figure of a woman out of wet sand on the ground beneath her. In its celebration of female sexual desire the scene carries a subversive literal message: like the waves that frame her vision, Beth 'was all one sensation', a feeling the narrator takes pains to endorse as both perfectly 'natural and right' (*BB*, 236, 233). But Beth's adventure is even more significant when placed in the context of artistic production, for here the art discourse (a man's 'imaging' of his idea of 'woman' and a real woman's critical appreciation of his vision) is mediated by the sex discourse governed by 'the needs of nature' (*BB*, 233). If Alfred fails to shape his sexual longing into a satisfactory form – for displeased with his idealised sculpture, he 'fell upon the figure and demolished it' (*BB*, 237) – Beth is more constructively successful in giving expression to her desire and holding on to it: 'every inch of him was a joy to her' (*BB*, 237). When some time later he falls asleep and she attempts to wake him, her movements cause the cliff to crumble; as she slides into the sand next to him, she symbolically reconfigures herself as the object of his desire, but she also superimposes her concrete bodily reality and libidinality on to his vision. The waves of the incoming tide that almost submerge and drown them at this first physical encounter, and which orchestrate their embrace and kiss in the water, are a metaphorical representation of the sexual energy that draws them together, and ultimately signify sexual intercourse and orgasm itself:

> The steady gentle heave of the sea ... rose round them once more, up, up, over Beth's head. They clung closer to each other ... staggering and fighting for their foothold. Then it sank back from then, then slowly came again, rising in an irregular wavy line ... with a sobbing sound as if in its great heart it shrank from the cruel deed it was doing – rose and fell, rose and fell again ... Gently, gently the water came creeping up and up again. It had swelled so high the last time that Beth was all but gone; and now she held her breath, expecting for certain to be overwhelmed. But, after a pause, it went down once more, then rose again, and again subsided ...
>
> The tide had seemed to come in galloping like a racehorse, but now it crawled out like a snail and they were both so utterly worn, that ... at last ... they just sank down ... leaning against each other, and yearning for ... [the opportunity] to stretch themselves out and go to sleep. (*BB*, 242–3)

This erotic experience leaves Beth 'tingling in every nerve' (*BB*, 245), in a state of multiorgasmic exaltation that prompts her to withdraw to the privacy of her home. Significantly, the return to the female sphere is followed by

Alfred's proposal of marriage the next day, an enticing yet threatening offer of fulfilment within the seclusion of domestic life: 'now we shall never part', he declares after she has confessed her artistic aspirations, 'I don't want you to be anything, or to care to be anything, but just my wife' (*BB*, 247). Whereas Alfred literally and figuratively endeavours to mould, circumscribe and even undo ('demolish') female artistic desire, Beth's sea bath with the other girls fires her imagination, energising her into forming a secret (quasi-theosophical, proto-feminist) society and appointing herself its leader. Heterosexual relations close off the avenues for independent agency; by contrast, woman-to-woman contact fosters communal interaction and social commitment. Even more importantly, self-directed eroticism evidently furnishes the most constructive and creative context for artistic (self-)discovery. If water symbolism in *The Beth Book* is read as a marker of sexual energy, Beth's self-pleasuring abandonment to the waves prior to meeting the girls points to the auto-erotic potential of the female body in its dynamic interplay with the element of water:

> [S]he longed to be alone with the sea. The tide was going out, and she had a fancy for following it from rock to rock as it went. Some of the bigger rocks were flat-topped islands … and on these she would lie her length, peering down into the clear depths … where … seaweeds of wondrous colours waved in fantastic forms. The water lapped up and up and up the rocks, rising with a sobbing sound, and bringing fresh airs with it that … caused her to draw in her breath involuntarily, and inhale long deep draughts with delight. As the water went out, bright runnels were left … and miniature bays became sheltered coves, paved with polished pebbles or purple mussels, and every little sandy space was ribbed with solid waves … It was an exquisite scene … Her bosom heaved with the heaving water rhythmically, and she lost herself in contemplation of sea and sky scape. Before she had been many minutes prone upon the farthest rock, the vision and the dream were upon her. That other self of hers unfurled its wings, and she floated off, revelling in an ecstasy of gentle motion. (*BB*, 257)

Some seventy years later Hélène Cixous would define this process of erotic-cum-creative self-exploration as a 'world of searching, the elaboration of a knowledge … a passionate and precise interrogation of [woman's] erotogeneity', a process leading to the recognition that 'I, too, overflow' with 'these waves, these floods, these outbursts', thus enabling women to activate and give expression to their repressed artistic faculties.[66]

In stark contrast to auto-erotic and homoerotic gratification, Beth's heterosexual encounters prove to be life-threatening experiences. Thus one of her early meetings with her future husband is preceded by a scene which recaptures the moment of near-drowning with Alfred: 'the strength and the swirl of the water … filled her with longing – longing to trust herself to the waves … The longing became an impulse … Had she yielded to the attraction, she must have been drowned' (*BB*, 325). Heterosexual desire is thus constructed as both intoxicating *and* threatening for women since it submerges (literally drowns) female identity. Beth's encounter with the girls, on the other hand, exalts this female identity through the idea of sisterhood while also activating an ethic impulse, the utopian dream of collective social regeneration (*BB*, 272). Beth soon tires of her Secret Service of Humanity, but this teenage game is one step forward in the long process which leads to the cathartic – or karmic – moment at the novel's close when Beth discovers the purpose of her life.

Beth's further faculty thus emerges as an intensely *personal* gift which helps her articulate her artistic vision, while it is also figured as a *social* attribute; in both instances its free expression is linked to open spaces, nature and elemental forces. In conceptualising her portrait of the 'seventh wave' creatrice through theosophical paradigms, Grand aligned her vision of the New Woman with Blavatsky's new religion. Although there is no record of her ever having been a member of the Theosophical Society,[67] Grand attended at least one séance,[68] and her letters, personal reminiscences and friends' memoirs as well as her fiction testify to her life-long interest in spirituality and psychical phenomena.[69] While as hesitant about the concept of reincarnation as Helena Blavatsky herself,[70] she nevertheless experimented with the idea in *The Beth Book* and *The Winged Victory*. When Beth is trapped by the rising tide, she declares her belief in reincarnation when she assures Alfred that 'even if we were [drowned], it wouldn't be the end of us. We have been here in this world before, you and I, and we shall come again' (*BB*, 240). To emphasise this point, the text repeatedly draws attention to Beth's uncanny resemblance, in appearance, manner and temperament, to her rebel grandmother, an artist as well as an unhappy wife who, like Beth, found a refuge in a room of her own (*BB*, 93, 197–8, 200–1). Grand expressed a keen interest in her step-granddaughter (Eliza)Beth's psychic abilities and her espousal of Rudolf Steiner's version of theosophy, Anthroposophy,[71] and claimed to have had supernatural experiences herself,[72] some of which she said she had recreated in two ghost stories written from the perspective of a woman artist.[73] If, as Diana Burfield has argued, theosophy's celebration of the feminine principle had its 'secular analogue in the image of the New Woman',[74] Grand's New Womanism drew inspiration from Blavatsky's symbology.

The timing of Grand's creative revalidation and experimentation with Blavatsky's ideas is interesting. *The Beth Book* was written in 1895–6,[75] half a decade after Blavatsky's death in 1891 and following posthumous efforts to undermine the Theosophical Society by discrediting the authenticity of Blavatsky's work. In 1893 Max Müller published in the journal *Nineteenth Century* a scathing scholarly indictment of 'Esoteric Buddhism' in which Blavatsky was castigated as an hysteric and a trickster ignorant of the most basic tenets of Buddhism; she would have done better, Müller opined, if she had 'follow[ed] in the footsteps of Rider Haggard' and decided to 'make money by writing new *Arabian Nights*' rather than attempting to establish herself as the founder of a fraudulent faith.[76] This attack was followed, in 1894, by a number of articles published by Edmund Garrett in the *Westminster Gazette* which, as Joy Dixon recounts, called attention to the controversy raging within theosophical circles about letters received from the Mahatmas after Blavatsky's death. Though these were widely believed to have been forged by William Quan Judge in a successful bid to compete with Annie Besant for the leadership of the Esoteric Section, the ensuing scandal raised questions about Blavatsky's own authorial manipulations of the earlier Mahatma correspondence. It also, crucially, throws into relief concerted male efforts within the organisation to wrench power from women and redefine theosophy as a manly science.[77] Besant did not accede to the presidency of the Theo-sophical Society until 1907, when female members began to emerge as a dominant force. While prior to her taking office, women constituted one third of the membership, positions of power were firmly concentrated in the hands of men; at the time Grand was writing her novel, the Theosophical Society was, as Dixon has observed, the spiritual equivalent of male clubland.[78] The Blavatsky Lodge, formed in 1887, was largely established to counteract the masculinising influences within the organisation, which privileged the 'life of the mind [over] the inner life, intellect [over] intuition', study over devotion, and abstract principle over emotion and personal relationships.[79] A site of fierce gender/power contestation, the Theosophical Society thus presented a mirror image, in miniature, of wider developments in *fin-de-siècle* culture, where the same battles were fought across and within different literary factions and movements. The Mahatma controversy to some extent retraced the cultural debates of the 1880s and 1890s about women's changing role in society, in particular the (in)expediency of women's participation in ideo-logical formation-building. The same motive of policing patriarchal paradigms and keeping women confined to firmly controlled parameters which had spurred male intervention on the theosophical plane lay behind conservative critics' endeavour to bring New Woman writers into disrepute on the grounds of their decadent and degenerate obsession with the sex question, just as it animated male authors to jump to the defence of virile standards in literature by slighting women writers and readers for their lack of originality and moralising didacticism.[80] The fierce determination with which New Woman writers like Grand pursued their project of social and literary regeneration through large-scale feminisation of cultural values was paralleled by female theosophists like Blavatsky and especially Besant, the latter of whom shared many of Grand's feminist concerns, not least in her vocal opposition to the Contagious Diseases Acts.[81] In conceptualising her protagonist as a feminist artist whose inner development reflects the principles laid down by female theosophists, Grand, aiming to strike a blow at malestream attempts to invalidate women's achievements, asserted in no uncertain terms the authority and even 'genius' of female cultural, socio-political and philosophical activity. Eager as she was to release the New Woman from men's ideological and aesthetic frameworks, she could not but have felt apprehensive about the rising influence of clubby and scientifically minded middle- and upper-class males on a movement whose original emphasis on femininity, interiority, connectedness, psychic receptiveness and spiritual devotion had placed women and their voices centre-stage. Just as male theosophists were keen to push women to the sidelines, so male decadents, she believed, belittled the work of women, especially New Woman, writers and sought to impose their slipshod morals and writing styles as the ultimate in art. Her novel was an attempt to intervene on both cultural planes at once with the aim of reinserting women into their rightful place as arbiters of social, religious-spiritual and artistic genius.

Attacks/ways out/forays:[82] from the aesthetic doll's house to a room of one's own

The very title-page of *The Beth Book* announces and exalts the iconoclastic nature of female cultural agency, drawing inspiration from Emilia's momentous coming-into-language in *Othello* to proclaim the author's oppositional textual politics: 'Let heaven, and men, and devils, let them all, / All, all, cry shame against me, yet I'll speak' (Figure 9). At the same time, playing with the conventions of (auto)biography, Grand self-confidently (in the eyes of male reviewers, arrogantly)[83] declares her fictional *alter ego* 'a woman of genius' (Beth's three names, Elizabeth Caldwell Maclure, thinly veil the allusion to her own composite name, Frances Elizabeth Bellenden Clarke McFall). She thus affirms the centrality of what Cixous calls women's 'acquisition of speech' (an act of bodily self-imprimature which writes 'her story in[to] history')[84] to the cultural project of artistic-cum-social renovation that lay at the heart of the New Woman movement. This renovation is intrinsic to Beth's quest for creative self-expression in adulthood. Not only does she decide that she will 'write for women' (*BB*, 376), she also defines her writing practice in sharp opposition to masculine ('high') culture's aesthetic paradigms. The programmatic alliance, forged in the final chapter of the novel, between women's writing and women's oratory, female cultural and political self-articulation, ruptures the binaries of the logocentric order which condemns woman to silence. Like Cixous, Grand predicates 'femininity in writing' on 'a privilege of *voice*', for in Beth's dual vocation, as in her childhood and adolescent habit of interlacing storytelling with oration, '*writing and voice*

The Beth Book

Being a Study from the Life of

Elizabeth Caldwell Maclure

A Woman of Genius

By

Sarah Grand

Author of " The Heavenly Twins," etc.

IAGO. *Come, hold your peace.*
EMILIA. *'Twill out, 'twill out:—I hold my peace, Sir ? no;*
I'll be in speaking, liberal as the air:
Let heaven, and men, and devils, let them all,
All, all, cry shame against me, yet I'll speak.
SHAKESPEARE.

London
William Heinemann
1898

9 Original title page of *The Beth Book* (Heinemann, 1897)

are entwined and interwoven and writing's continuity/voice's rhythm take each other's breath away through interchanging'.[85] When, stunned by the enthusiastic response to her breakthrough speech at a feminist rally, Beth reflects on her achievement, her greatest sense of fulfilment and quasi-*jouissance* ('the success she had most desired', 'the fulfilment of a promise') derives from the knowledge that her words should carry weight with and offer sustenance to 'thousands' of other women (*BB*, 527).

In gaining resonance as a published writer and public speaker, Beth recovers the voice of her childhood, an unadulterated 'Voice' which, in Cixous's terms, 'sings from a time before law'.[86] Beth's first creative stirrings were indeed songs that, like her 'song of the sea in the shell' (*BB*, 68) conjured up a pre-Symbolic time evocative, as Lyn Pykett has noted, of the Kristevan concept of the semiotic.[87] In adulthood this potent feminine voice becomes muffled in marriage, but regains its vibrancy in proportion to Beth's reclamation of literal and literary breathing space. The resurgence of her muted voice is closely linked to her quest for and appropriation of a room of her own. Drawing on a rich tradition in women's writing which encoded the attic as a space of female interiority, and revising in particular Charlotte Brontë's and Charlotte Perkins Gilman's metaphors of the room as tomb (which, by confining and burying female sexuality and/or creativity, induces an implosion of madness), Grand turned Beth's secret garret into an emblem of the womb, the locus of individual and artistic rebirth.[88] In this symbolic space Beth moves from a state of subjection to independent subject status, progressing from consumed object to consumer (of male texts) in order to constitute herself as producer (creator) of art in her own right.

Just as Beth's room is located within the marital home, remaining part of the patriarchal superstructure even while representing an enclave of sedition within it, her initial course of study, which will eventually initiate her own writing and subsequent departure from both marriage and the house of male art, reflects male tradition at its most powerful: theology, the great (male) writers, mathematics and philosophy (*BB*, 357). As a feminist and writer, Beth comes into her own only after assimilating the law of the father which, subsequently, equips her with the tools to dismantle it. She is thus an ironic reflection of the author and her own strategy of ventriloquism for the purposes of subversion. Like Evadne, who learns to appreciate consistency of argument and rationality of manner through exposure to her father's polemics, Beth is taught the expediency of 'clear thought' (*BB*, 357) by careful perusal of the male canon, only to recognise the deficiency of 'academic' training, and to reject as 'artificial' and stultifying the modern male writer's preoccupation with style (*BB*, 371, 374). Decadent writing, which itself was a reaction to (male) conventions in art, literature and sexuality, and as trans-gressive in its own way as feminist writing, is thus associated with, and discredited as a mere variant of, stuffy institutionalised verbosity: 'vain, hollow, cynical, dyspeptic; they appeal to the head, but the heart goes empty away' (*BB*, 374). In *The Human Quest* (1900) Grand went even further, attacking aesthetes as a coterie of charlatans, insufferable snobs 'whose constant effort it is to avoid the Obvious', and who 'for want of ideas expend themselves in the search for *expressions* that shall not be obvious, and the consequence is that they ingeniously present us with our own familiar thoughts wrapped up with infinite pains in puzzling obscurity' (*THQ*, 3, emphasis in original).

Grand's hostility to 'male' aestheticism was partly grounded in her deep distrust of male sexuality, a sentiment not likely to have been eased by aestheticism's close association with sexual deviance (*The Beth Book* was published in the year of Wilde's release from prison, but even three years later Grand was still reluctant to name 'that now notorious person' directly; *THQ*, 3). More importantly, she repudiated what to her seemed an obsession with the superficialities of form and language at the cost of depth, authenticity and purpose. 'To be true to life', she stressed in the preface to *Our Manifold Nature* (1894), ought to be the 'noblest ambition' of a writer. She later reaffirmed her Realist credo in *Emotional Moments* (1908), where she pronounced artistic merit to be contingent, not on formal aspects, but on the degree to which a book embodied 'truth ... in fiction': 'A novel ... should be like life itself – an unfolding, and not a regular structure'.[89] In promoting truthfulness over stylistic innovation she was of course not alone; other New Woman writers like Olive Schreiner also came down on the side of the 'method of ... life' rather than the 'stage method',[90] and Emile Zola lamented that the 'exaggerated importance ... given to form' was bound to result in 'rotten ... lyricism'.[91] However, in her struggle to distance herself from the sexual/texual politics of male decadence, Grand paradoxically ventriloquised the aesthetics of literary Realism even as she was engaged in rupturing Realist narrative with her feminist metaphysics. She thus found herself in the equivocal position of defending, on moral and literary grounds, a movement which, having become appropriated by the bourgeois malestream and its institutions (conservative circulating libraries), objected to her own writing on these very grounds.

In Grand's eyes, the formal experimentation of the decadents would have appeared emblematic of their sexual anarchy: they disrupted the 'natural' and organic patterns of art and society while, perversely, dictating what she considered artificial rules of expression. In this sense the strictures which aestheticism applied to style seemed as stifling as those which patriarchy imposed on women. Small wonder, then, if there were few 'great' women artists: 'A subjugated race', Grand's New Woman figure Barbara Land pronounces in *Babs the Impossible*, produces no great work of art; why do you expect a subjugated sex to produce more than a subjugated race under similar circumstances? So far, woman has been the thrall of law and custom, and she has only been able to indicate the possession of power. But you will see that as soon as women begin to let themselves go in art, so soon as they cease to respect hampering laws, and try for the expression of fine ideas, they will succeed. (*B*, 147)

For a woman to become an artist, she needed 'to let [herself] go' (*B*, 147): she had to break the rules, challenge and unravel male structures – hence Beth's fusion of feminist art and political activism. Of equal importance for the woman artist's development was the uncovering of a female counter-tradition; Beth's interest in embroidery signals her awareness of traditional female art forms, and later she feels drawn to women writers and female (auto)biography (*BB*, 370). Moving from the 'cold polish' of cerebral artistry (*BB*, 376) to the 'more full-blooded' female tradition grounded in lived experience (*BB*, 374), Beth (the New Woman) begins to write.

In Grand's work the quintessential New Woman is an artist, more particularly a writer: a woman who has learnt to write herself into being. Ideala starts her career as a poet, and even in *The Beth Book*, at the height of her fame as a feminist reformer, she is busy writing what, in light of her discussion of character, style and verisimilitude, appears to be a narrative rather than political work (*BB*, 388–9). In *The Heavenly Twins* Evadne fails to develop her latent gift, the 'further faculty' (*HT*, 46) with which she, too, is endowed being crushed by the disappointment of her first marriage; and perhaps this frustrated creativity is a further reason for her hysteria, since art would provide an outlet for her tormented spirit. Like Ideala and Beth, Angelica is a feminist and artist, but her full potential as a musician is blocked by her paternalistic husband (who, nevertheless, holds no objection to her composing his parliamentary speeches). What is striking in Grand's trilogy of novels is that all three artist figures are also feminist activists, whereas characters like Evadne and Edith, who lose or lack a capacity for art, fail in their endeavours. As in her life, feminism and art were intricately connected in Grand's work, and this in itself is an indication of the way in which she privileged the social and political, rather than the aesthetic, function of art, which pitted the feminist writers of the *fin de siècle* against mainstream art and, mostly, malestream[92] decadence.

The competing aesthetics of feminist and decadent art or, in Teresa Mangum's words, the 'style wars of the 1890s'[93] inscribed into Grand's works are increasingly constructed as a clash between female and male art and artists, and between women's 'higher' moral values and men's sexual and social failings. Locating this conflict within the psyche of the woman artist, *Ideala* reveals the protagonist as the author of both a decadent and a moralistic poem about forbidden love ('The Passion of Delysle' and 'The Choice'). Significantly, though, Ideala conceals her authorship of the aesthetic piece, charging decadent writers, and women writers in particular, with merely 'stimulat[ing]' the senses but failing to 'nourish' the mind or heart (*ID*, 78–9, 90). Her move into feminism and social reformism is accompanied by her rejection of aestheticism on the grounds of political incorrectness.

In *The Heavenly Twins* the discussion of art and feminism is, as Rita Kranidis has shown, inscribed into the 'Proem', which draws on the metaphor of the chime of a bell and the changing responses it evokes from different people over the course of time, in order to throw into relief the 'material determinations of both art and aesthetic judgment', calling into question the validity and durability of 'the aesthetic standards of both "philistines" (such as Mudie and the growing number of booksellers) and antisocial figures (such as the aesthetes)'.[94] Starting with an implicit dig at aestheticism (the most absurd controversy inspired by the innocent bell is one about the 'question of expression'; *HT*, ix), the text moves on to a tentative exploration of early feminist literary criticism in the form of Evadne's Commonplace Book, the site of her emerging ethical and aesthetic vision. Here the late-century New Girl reviews canonical literature and in the process comes to locate herself on the side of the overtly political rather than sentimental writer: in response to Gaskell's *Ruth* (1853) she determines that the head as well as the heart 'should be satisfied by a work of fiction' (*HT*, 34). Mill's *Subjection of Women* (1869) introduces her to an intellectual 'world of thought in which she could breathe freely' (*HT*, 14), an experience which equips her with the confidence not only to challenge patriarchal paradigms in literature, but also, crucially, to apply her critical insight to her own life. Thus Goldsmith's *The Vicar of Wakefield*, when viewed from her newly enlightened perspective, reveals itself to be a case study of male prejudice and female educational deprivation (*HT*, 14, 16–17). Her critical rereading of this text – an act of feminist re-vision in Adrienne Rich's sense[95] – leads to the recognition of her mother's subject condition, sparking off the resolve that she, for one, will 'not give in' when under pressure from male authority (*HT*, 16). Years later she will put this determination to the test when she refuses to comply with her father's command to return to Major Colquhoun. Similarly, her unqualified indignation at Fielding's *Tom Jones* and *Roderick Random*, books glorifying 'the self-interest and injustice of men, [and] the ... ignorance and slavish apathy of women', and the resulting conviction that men with indifferent morals are a 'danger to the community at large', will shape her later attitude towards her fallen husband (*HT*, 20). Evadne's early writing exercises thus serve as an object lesson on the relevance of feminist literary criticism to women's lives. They also provide a context for Grand's feminist rewritings of *Tom Jones*, for if Evadne is cast in the role of a non-compliant Sophia who punishes Tom/Colquhoun where it hurts most (by withholding sex), Angelica's interaction with the Tenor – who, as a foundling with a highly placed mother[96] and a man with sexually transgressive, albeit frustrated desires, is cast as an androgynous, disempowered version of Tom Jones – illustrates the fatal consequences of reckless behaviour, especially when allied to double standards (Angelica deceives the Tenor and plays with his feelings, yet expects him to embrace her as a friend when her identity is revealed).

Although *The Heavenly Twins* thus appears to privilege feminist over masculinist readings, the introduction of the Lady of Shalott myth as a metaphor of femininity and gendered desire has the same destabilising effect as the juxtaposition of decadent and moralistic poetry in *Ideala*. At first Evadne regards Tennyson's poem and its many paintings as '[s]ingularly inappropriate' for modern life because they eroticise female passivity and self-sacrifice:

> When you first come across the poem or the picture which perpetuates the sentiment that slew the girl, and beautifies it, you feel a glow all over, and fancy you would like to imitate her, and think that you would deserve great credit for it if you did. But when you come to consider, there is nothing very noble, after all, in a hopeless passion for an elderly man of the world who is past being benefited by it, even if he could reciprocate it … I think it is a sin to make unwholesome sentiments attractive. (*HT*, 35)

To Evadne, the myth is reprehensible because it seduces women into subservience, turning them into all-too-willing objects of the male gaze by infusing them with the desire to become the girl in the poem/picture, and directing their thoughts and energies into fantasies of a *grande passion* instead of more useful channels. The irony of course is that Evadne ends up as precisely the kind of forlorn and crazed figure that she finds so unappealing. Not long afterwards she marries her own Lancelot, and is later constructed as a modern Lady of Shalott by her second husband-to-be. If, in *The Heavenly Twins* and *The Beth Book*, Grand wanted to make a point about the way in which male artists transform ('kill') women into beautiful objects when what is required is for women to refuse to be thus possessed, and to pass on from being mere consumers of and subjects for male art to becoming producers of feminist art, then her continued interest in the Lady of Shalott motif in these and later texts is puzzling. Lyn Pykett therefore reads Grand's domestication of the myth as a sign of her reluctant enthralment to the patriarchal mystique.[97]

In *Adnam's Orchard* (1912) the artist figure, a lace-maker, is again associated with the Lady of Shalott theme. In all instances the myth operates on two different levels in Grand's work. On the mythical plane, it carries a warning, signalling a crisis while also offering the potential of radical transformation in the life of the heroine. Evadne's woeful, directionless gaze from the window indicates her mental aporia, present and future; in Ella's case the Shalott motif points to a fatal (incestuous) attraction that must be resisted before she can come into her artistic own. Beth's impending mental breakdown, on the other hand, is averted by her sightings of an unknown rider who carries the promise of change (from immobility to life, suspension to agency) and direction (a purposeful and fulfilled existence): it is as a result of these 'visitations' that she recovers her equilibrium and leaves the house of patriarchy. In her next home, an attic with a difference in that it is located in a female-dominated counter-community, she falls captive to Shalott's romance of self-sacrifice, but is saved by female intervention and equipped with a room and then house of her own in which the artist gives birth to the orator.

On a secondary level Grand's use of the Lady of Shalott theme serves to exalt the specifically feminine craft of the female artist. Crucially, all three characters are engaged in needlework. Beth's embroidery and Ella's lace-making are arts which inscribe creative agency into the myth about a woman's confinement to the patriarchal world of mirror and web. Female craftwork, while also constituting a vital source of independent income, thus facilitates an explorative journey towards feminine art production. If Evadne allows herself to be locked into the shadow world of Shalott, Beth and Ella draw inspiration from the desire for agency encoded in the myth and are able to transform it, and themselves, in the process: Beth completes her book and Ella becomes a professional lace-maker and businesswoman. The recurrence of Shalott imagery in Grand's work, instead of pinpointing her conceptual entrapment within patriarchal myth-making, might then suggest a deliberate strategy of feminist re-vision analogous to her tragicomic rewriting of Fielding's *Tom Jones* plot.

The project of feminist revision is also reflected in the novel's emphasis on female genius. As Penny Boumelha, Teresa Mangum and Patricia Murphy have pointed out, in proclaiming her exceptional woman not simply an 'artist' but a 'genius', Grand affirmed the inherent rather than acquired nature of female creativity, undercutting Victorian scientific taxonomies which defined genius as a biological prerogative of masculinity.[98] 'Authentic' art is thus, once again, identified as quintessentially feminine, spiritual, natural, lifelike and organic, and contrasted with hegemonic (male) artifice, rejected for its contrived, hollow and essentially lifeless particularities. Through her figure of the woman artist, Grand promotes what Mangum calls 'an ethical aesthetics, an artistic vision grounded in female experience and devoted to the improvement of women's lives yet also capable of transforming male and female readers alike'.[99] Beth's decision to move from individual art production (writing) to communal political activism (oratory) denotes her commitment to the collective cause which, as Mangum observes, anticipates suffragette activism; Grand circumvents the 'facile dichotomy between art and politics with an alternative aesthetic that can encompass both. "Purpose" motivates art, language ceases to be art unless driven by purpose. Art without purpose – art for art's sake – thus ceases to be an aesthetic category.'[100] The 'literary battle of the sexes'[101] between woman-centred Ethics and male Aesthetics is satirised in Beth's encounter with a decadent journalist who turns out to be none other than the romantic hero of her girlhood, Alfred Cayley Pounce:[102]

> Beth noticed ... an old-looking young man whose face seemed familiar to her. He wore a pointed beard upon his chin, and a small moustache cut away from his upper lip, and waxed and turned up at the ends. His face was thin and narrow, his forehead high and bald; what hair he had grew in a fringe at the back of his head, and was curly, and of a non-descript brown colour. Had he worn the dress of the Elizabethan period, he might have passed for a bad attempt to look like Shakespeare; and Beth thought that perhaps might be the resemblance which puzzled her. (*BB*, 446)

Though he poses as a dandy and prides himself on his sexual conquests among fading female decadents (he unsuccessfully attempts to add Beth to his list), this is no longer the man whose erotic charisma electrified Beth when both were in their teens. Nor has he fulfilled his early promise of becoming a sculptor, having given up modelling during his 'Varsity' years because it was deemed unfashionable in his set, and reorientated himself towards French literature and style instead (*BB*, 475). A half-comic and half-pathetic figure of degeneration, he has refashioned himself into a decadent sculpture. With his pointed beard and aesthetic mannerisms a feeble imitation of *Dorian Gray*'s Lord Wotton,[103] Alfred is exposed as 'a ponce' (as Angelique Richardson points out, his initialled surname reads 'A. Pounce').[104] If his degeneracy appears congenital – as a boy he had 'long, delicate and nervous' hands and a 'sallow complexion' which 'looked smooth to effeminacy' (*BB*, 237) – it is, as Richardson notes, 'his encounter with the French novel that is his undoing'.[105] An obsessive name-dropper and intolerable snob with an entirely unoriginal cast of mind, he affects the manners of an aesthete whose 'pose is brains' (*BB*, 452). An amateur with but a few articles to his name, he presumes to superior knowledge of what is, and is not, Art. As he hastens to inform Beth, it certainly is not anything written by a woman and with a purpose to it. As an occasional contributor to a journal called *The Patriarch* (possibly Grand's version of the ultra-conservative *Athenaeum*),[106] he self-importantly offers Beth advice on her book, threatening her with a slating review in the eventuality of the break-down of their (non-existing) friendship, and interrupting her work so persis-tently with his continual visits that she is unable to concentrate on it for any length of time. Hiding his failure to undertake any kind of serious work behind endless talk about the seriousness of his work, he is only too eager to put her in her place when her creative output becomes too challenging: 'Why, it takes *me* a week to write five hundred words. But then, of course, my work is highly concentrated ... You can only produce poor thin stuff in that way' (*BB*, 457).

At the height of her fame as a writer, Grand had reached a position of authority which allowed her to debunk the condescending arrogance, complacency and misogynistic sneering to which she herself had been exposed by male critics and writers earlier on in her career. Thus Alfred professes, in words which put one in mind of Grant Allen, H. G. Wells and Arnold Bennett, to have 'the greatest respect for woman. I believe that her part in life is to fertilise the mind of man' (*BB*, 469). In fact Allen had written in 1889 that he was 'an enthusiast on the Woman Question ... Only [women's] emancipation must not interfere in any way with [the] prime natural necessity' of bearing at least four children each.[107] Twenty years later Wells was to 'confess [himself] altogether feminist [and] ... had no doubts in the matter', the matter in question mainly relating to women's social obligation to embrace multiple single motherhood as a mark of their willing 'subordinat[ion] ... to the collective purpose'.[108] Echoing Wells and Allen, Bennett declared in 1920 that he was 'a feminist to the point of passionateness', believing as he did that 'women as a sex love to be dominated'.[109] If Grand at the time of writing *The Beth Book* had been able to savour only Grant Allen's sophistry, she knew the anti-feminist mind of some self-appointed progressives only too well to resist the temptation of satirising it in her fictional portrait of a conceited critic. Ironically, *The Beth Book* itself attracted the kind of response she parodied, hence her tribute to a real-life Alfred Cayley Pounce:

> That you should insult Scott and Thackeray and Dickens with your approval pains me but little, since they will never hear of it; that you are so much cleverer than I am I must modestly accept your word for; that you strain yourself to be facetious and but prove yourself a dunce, I must attribute to your academic degree, and a course of the blighting wit of the common-room; that you should attack me with base misrepresentation I set down to some rag of chivalry that still clings to you; that you are of ancient lineage I am willing to admit, since your putting into my mouth words and sentiments which are not mine shows you infected with the blood of Ananias; that you should take yourself as a serious judge of art is a crime for which it is painful to think you must one day settle between you and your God; but that you should write yourself down an admirer of mine is the ugliest blow that my art has dealt me, and I take this opportunity to publicly apologise for it. – Believe me, yours in sorrow for your insincerity, Sarah Grand.[110]

In the novel, Alfred is greatly annoyed by Beth's presumption of citing Milton – male canonical culture and art being his prerogative, not hers – and tries to shut her up with Schopenhauer. Beth's reply reflects Grand's exasperation with the patriarchal establishment in art and elsewhere: 'If culture leaves us liable to be taken in by a false postulate of any man's, however well turned the postulate or able the man, then I have no respect for [it]' (*BB*, 467). Offended by her indifference and her persistent refusal to bow to his superior judgment, Alfred eventually decides to slate her book, but inadvertently ends by praising it when his intellectual dishonesty plays him a trick:

> Mr. Alfred Cayley Pounce had been looking out for Beth's book, and, while waiting for it to appear, he had, misled by his own suppositions, prepared an elaborate article upon the kind of thing he expected it to be. Nothing was wanting to complete the article but a summary of the story and quotations from it, for which he had left plenty of space. He condemned the book utterly from the point of view of art, and for the silly ignorance of life displayed in it, and the absurd caricatures which were supposed to be people; he ridiculed the writer for taking herself seriously (but without showing why exactly she should not take herself seriously if she chose); he pitied her for her disappointment when she should realise where in literature her place would be; and he ended with a bitter diatribe against the works of women generally, as being pretentious, amateur, without originality, and wanting in humour, like the wretched stuff it had been his painful duty to expose. Unfortunately for him, however, the book appeared anonymously, and immediately attracted attention enough to make him wish to discover it; and before he found out that Beth was the author, he had committed himself to a highly eulogistic article upon it in *The Patriarch*, which he took the precaution to sign, that the coming celebrity might know to whom gratitude was due, and in which he declared that there had arisen a new light of extraordinary promise on the literary horizon. The book, as it happened, was not a work of fiction at all. (*BB*, 517–18)

Angered by stereotypical responses to her problem novels, in particular by the equation of politics and purpose with artistic failure,[111] Grand must have enjoyed holding up a mirror to her conservative reviewers. Thus William Barry, writing in the *Quarterly Review*, had previously condemned *The Heavenly Twins* in terms similar to Alfred's intended review, as a 'violent and improbable story', whose 'absence of genuine humour, of wit and comedy, of refinement and ease' cast the artistic propensities of self-professed intellectual women in their true light: 'In mere shrieking who will look for a note of music?'[112] As in Alfred's case, reviews of feminist books often enabled conservatives to berate women's contribution to cultural production in more general terms: 'no one admires Falstaff in his borrowed petticoats, and a woman with the doctor's beard and spectacles was never winning', Barry wrote, and the *Spectator* lamented that, like 'so many novels with a purpose', Grand's book displayed a regrettable 'lack of proportion', in other words that it fell short of the qualities required for a work of art.[113] Judging by the near-hysterical response *The Beth Book* received from some quarters, Grand's message had struck home. In involuntary imitation of Alfred's *Patriarch*, the *Athenaeum* wrote that her men were 'ridiculous puppets which would be disgusting were they not so absurdly unreal',[114] and the *Saturday Review* even surmised that only a 'fanatic' could have written a novel with such a display of 'iconoclastic fervour'.[115]

The combative tone of some reviewers was, of course, as much a response to *fin-de-siècle* writing generally as to the feminist aspects of Grand's work – ironically, the ideological and artistic differences between New Woman writers, naturalists and aesthetes disappeared from view when judged by the standards of the conservative mainstream, which pathologised all three groups as 'literary degenerates' and 'erotomaniacs': 'they are all the offspring together of hysteria and Continental decadentism.'[116] This tendency in contemporary criticism to bracket together literary feminism and aestheticism was one of the reasons why Grand felt compelled to dissociate her own writing from a movement she considered to represent everything she most emphatically opposed. By joining in the chorus of outrage against male decadence,[117] she was able to repolarise the dichotomy between the New Woman's ethics and the Dandy's pleasure politics which the public debate threatened to erase, turning the feminist into an apostle of higher morality, a feminine force for the renovation of a society infected with male sexual and textual incontinence.

In this project Grand's strategic staging of her own persona as a standard-bearer of the new, socially regenerative femininity was undoubtedly some-thing of a master-stroke. In light of the author's 'womanly grace and charm, a very gentle, quiet manner, and a low, musical voice',[118] many a reviewer may have felt more generously disposed towards her work. Although few critics went to the lengths of the *Bookman*, which celebrated her as the 'Befreierin' (liberator) of her sex because '[h]er ideal women claim freedom for themselves ... and secure the fullest development',[119] Grand found herself applauded for breaking the 'conspiracy of silence ... on the serious side of marriage':[120] 'The authoress deserves the gratitude of all right-minded men and women', wrote the *Review of Reviews*, 'for her fearless handling of ... great ethical question[s]'.[121]

Ultimately, whatever the conservative press might say about her, Grand was 'immensely popular'[122] with her turn-of-the-century audience, a best-selling writer whose opinion was constantly sought by the fashionable magazine market for her aptitude in setting public trends. A subversive and independent thinker, she never lost touch with the mood of the day, just as in her capacity of spokeswoman of conventional middle-class femininity she always kept sight of her aim of generating contentious cultural and social debates about the roles, rights and responsibilities of women and men. At her ventriloquist best, she was at times able to adapt patriarchal discourses for feminist purposes. By incorporating the traditionally female crafts of embroidery and lace-making within her conception of art and by connecting art both with women's social and political activism and with alternative, female-centred religions like theosophy, she radically redefined aesthetic values from a female and feminist perspective, re(en)visioning male myth to generate new, feminised mytho-logies which celebrated women's cultural alterity. Most interestingly perhaps for a twenty-first-century readership, Grand effected a discursive slippage between women's creative and erotic sensibilities, anticipating French feminist discourse by suggesting that the woman artist constitutes herself through her immersion in natural cycles which orchestrate and regenerate her spiritual, sexual and artistic energies. Like Hélène Cixous a century later, she configured women's writing as 'the passageway' of the other in culture, thus 'affirm[ing] woman somewhere other than in silence',[123] giving expression to and exalting the New Woman's endless capacity for psycho-erotic and artistic *jouissance*.

Part II

Allegories:
Olive Schreiner

(1855–1920)

4

Transitions and transfigurations: *Dreams* (1890), *The Story of an African Farm* (1883) and *From Man to Man* (1926)

H: you see the stylised outline of a ladder. This is the ladder writing climbs ... Writing has as its horizon this possibility, prompting us to explore all ages. ... With the Bible, we climb up and down through generations. ... We are those who later on transform, displace, and canonize the Bible, paint and sculpt it another way. ... As I reread this dream [of Jacob's Ladder] I realized there is a sequel I always eliminate. I always stop my memory at the pure vision of the angels climbing up and down. ... The *dream scene* was always far more important to me than the scene of revelation. It is the first dream. In order for the ladder that enables us to pass from one place to another to be set up, we have to leave. Moreover, if we follow Jacob's path, it's through a system of permitted transgressions ... yet this is the way we must go, leaving home behind. Go toward foreign lands, toward the foreigner in ourselves. Traveling in the unconscious, that inner foreign country, foreign home, country of lost countries. (Hélène Cixous, 'The School of Dreams', *Three Steps on the Ladder of Writing*, 1993)[1]

Then we came out upon a lonely mountain-top. ... [F]ar off on a solitary peak I saw a lonely figure standing. Whether it were man or woman I could not tell; for partly it seemed the figure of a woman, but its limbs were the mighty limbs of a man. ... And I saw the figure bend over its work, and labour mightily ... I said to God, 'How came it here?' – God said, 'By a bloody stair. Step by step it mounted from the lowest Hell, and day by day as Hell grew farther and Heaven no nearer, it hung alone between two worlds. Hour by hour in that bitter struggle its limbs grew larger, till there fell from it rag by rag the garments which it started with. Drops fell from its eyes as it strained them; each step it climbed was wet with blood. Then it came out here.' (Olive Schreiner, 'The Sunlight Lay Across My Bed', *Dreams*, 1890)[2]

Most people have a prejudice against allegories ... The form is dangerous for the artist, and rarely acceptable to the public. ... But [Olive Schreiner's] allegories ... are something entirely new ... Written in exquisite prose ... they have the essential qualities of poetry; and are, indeed, poems in prose. ... [T]hey express, in the only form possible, that passion for abstract ideas which in her lies deeper than any other. ... Apprehended thus, the allegory may be considered the essence of art, all art being symbol, and allegories themselves pure symbols. ... [In her allegories] Schreiner ... has given us ... her most deeply-felt 'message'. (Arthur Symons, Review of *Dreams*, 1891)[3]

[My writing] is all poetry from the first to the last ... There are [many] allegories in it; I've tried to keep them out, but I can't. I have come to the conclusion that only poetry is truth. That other forms are *parts* of truth, but as soon as a representation has all parts, then it is poetry. As soon as there is the form and the spirit, the passion and the thought, then there is poetry, or the *living* reality. (Olive Schreiner to Havelock Ellis, 2 November 1888)[4]

In her conceptual slippage between religion and art Cixous invokes writing as a metaphysical quest for the self and the sacred at one and the same time: in both cases dreams act as the key to opening the doors of the unconscious through which the elusive/Elysian knowledge might be attained. Aligning this creative process of recovery and discovery with one of Western culture's first creation stories, the Bible, Cixous posits the writer as a creator with divine propensities: 'We are those who later on transform, displace, and canonize the Bible, paint and sculpt it another way.' If in her celebration of the artist as an agent (angel) of metaphysical insight Cixous draws on biblical allegory – the ladder in Jacob's Dream – in order to sanctify the creative process (dreaming as the first step towards writing), Schreiner (Figure 10) reconfigured dream-allegory as political poetry in her secular reclamation of biblical tropes and paradigms for her new religion of humanity. Singular as Schreiner was for her time 'in transforming the allegorical mode into political and social criticism, satire, and exhortation', Joyce Avrech Berkman notes that she secularised *Pilgrim's Progress*, 'emphasizing social redemption and propaganda among the aims of moral instruction'.[5] As she explained to Havelock Ellis, allegory was the purest, most cerebral form of poetry, and it therefore permitted the most 'truthful' rendering of her thought; 'while it is easy clearly to express abstract thoughts in argumentative prose', she wrote in *Woman and Labour* (1911), 'whatever emotions those thoughts awaken I have not felt myself able adequately to express except in the other form [allegory]' (*W&L*, 16). The direct appeal to 'emotion' – what Olive Renier called the 'Ancient Mariner character of her writing'[6] – made allegory the most effective medium for the transmission of 'abstract thought' (feminist theory) and concrete message: 'by throwing a thing into the form of an allegory', she found that she could 'condense five or six pages into one, with [...] a great gain to clearness'.[7] Carolyn Burdett has suggested another reason for Schreiner's preference of allegorical to 'argumentative prose': her 'increasing unease about the direction of European modernity, and about whether its "truth" language of evolutionary science could really help to call into being an emancipated womanhood'.[8] If, as Deborah Madsen observes, allegory is an essentially unstable category because of the conceptual confusion to which it gives rise 'of

10 Photograph of Olive Schreiner, Art Studio, Cape Town, 1910s?

"speaking other" in a figurative language and "speaking of the Other" in a spiritualising interpretation (whether discursive or narrative)',[9] it was this very ambivalence that would have appealed to Schreiner in her determination to speak of and for the Other in the act of speaking other. Just as her political vision challenged the 'truth' of new and old authoritative discourses, contesting the division of humanity into neatly demarcated categories of gender, race and class, so her 'aesthetics of literary miscegenation'[10] confounded textual and sexual boundaries by incorporating allegorical and visionary elements into her novels and other writings.

Interestingly, Schreiner and Cixous encode their allegory of spiritual-creative epiphany in analogous conceptual imagery. Like the ladder in Cixous's 'School of Dreams' passage, the stairs in 'The Sunlight Lay Across My Bed' and the 'Hunter' allegories (in *The Story of an African Farm* and *Dreams*)[11] denote the human subject's inner progress towards transcendence. Bodied forth in the letter H, the ladder for Cixous and the stairs for Schreiner are emblematic of androgyny, a world beyond binaried hegemonies: while Cixous reflects on the letter's semantic fluidity in the French language ('[i]n addition to this *hache* – a cutting instrument, an axe to clear new paths – the letter … is masculine, neuter, or feminine at will'),[12] Schreiner figures H(eaven) as a realm delivered from gender categories: 'In the least Heaven sex reigns supreme; in the higher it is not noticed; but in the highest it does not exist' (*D*, 175).

Schreiner's visionary resolution of the sex question might be correlated with the theosophist concept of the sexless first and last 'races' as construed in Blavatsky's cosmology, and Schreiner's pantheism indeed combined trans-cendentalist with mystic elements;[13] but her allegorical writing has little in common with Sarah Grand's invocation of theosophical metaphors, nor did she ever align herself with any particular organisation or cause – theological, social or political – to the exclusion of all others: she had, she wrote in 1912, 'never been able to bind [her]self to any one section of any great world movement, like socialism or the woman [movement]' because 'it seems to fetter me. It's not my function.'[14] Born of the struggle for personal survival, Schreiner's pioneering feminism was the outcome of her passionate quest for identity and moral-political integrity against the backdrop of intellectual, emotional and physical isolation. An independent and lonely fighter, she was always, like the enigmatic figure in her 'Sunlight' allegory, 'a party of one'.[15] The compelling conjunction of passion and poetry, politics and prophecy in her work, its lyrical quality and probing philosophy, its allegorical force palpable even in her most politically inspired writings, stirred the imagination of her time and had a more powerful and lasting, quasi-scriptural, impact than even Grand's or Caird's most incisive writings.

This chapter explores allegorical paradigms in two of Schreiner's 'Dreams', *The Story of an African Farm* and her unfinished and posthumously published novel-of-a-lifetime, *From Man to Man*, in order to explore what could be considered the 'transitional' aspects of her writing in the context of the parameters of my study, both in the sense of her mythic/mythopoeic construction of the feminist endeavour as one that finds completion only through dis/misembodied transfiguration in allegory and utopia, and in relation to the 'intermediary' position Schreiner occupied between Grand's and Caird's contrasting ideological and aesthetic positions. Like Grand, Schreiner felt painfully drawn to different and often opposing directions; her life and work embody the conflict between the need for (artistic, emotional and sexual) self-realisation and the moral imperative of altruistic self-sacrifice. Of British nationality, she was brought up in a colonised country, thus sharing the experience of imperialism with Grand; but unlike her, she politicised her troubled relationship with her nationhood and ethnicity, and was one of the few voices who unconditionally challenged British colonial, as well as Boer supremacist, politics. Her most notable contribution to first-wave feminism was her conceptualisation of the essential correlation between the imposition of gender, race and class hegemonies, an insight which resulted in her firm commitment to universal human rights.

Schreiner's transition from colonial missionary child to anti-imperialist visionary feminist was painful and full of contradictions. She frequently faced social and political isolation because of her uncompromisingly principled stance. Identifying with South Africa's struggle against British capitalist interests and siding with the Boers during the Anglo-Boer war, she also condemned the oppression of the black population by both British colonialists and Boers, and left the South African Women's Enfranchisement League she had helped found because no provision was made for the rights of black women; in her fiction, however, she tended to deal out stereotypically raced roles and, inevitably perhaps, wrote from a white perspective even as she gave voice to the racial Other.

Despite the fact that in embracing a wider human and animal rights stand Olive Schreiner and Mona Caird reached beyond Sarah Grand's more narrowly defined focus on white middle-class womanhood, and in spite of the radically different lives the three writers led, they form a singular synthesis of late-Victorian feminism, with each throwing light on the others' work and beliefs. United in their condemnation of the double sexual standard and its male beneficiaries, they drew radically different conclusions. While on the face of it Grand's moral purism made her a typical representative of the nineteenth century even as she was engaged in subverting established moral codes in her exploration of women's transgressive desires, Schreiner's free thought and in particular her advocacy of female sexual autonomy anticipated the attitudes of a later generation, yet her equation of femininity with the reproductive instinct and exaltation of female self-consecration reveal her residual allegiance to authoritative discourses, whose sanctification of woman-sacrifice was resolutely rejected by Caird.

Grand and Schreiner both resorted to utopian or dream modes to conjure up the idea of an equal partnership between the sexes that would allow for individual artistic development, while at the same time denying the feasibility of such a relationship in contemporary society and their own private lives. Grand persistently defended marriage and motherhood in the face of her own departure from both institutions, and could never bring herself to seek a divorce. Schreiner, by contrast, made her heroine Lyndall prefer death to marrying the father of her child. '[M]arriage is not and cannot be a right thing for a nature like mine,' she told Havelock Ellis in 1886. 'If I am to live I must be free.'[16] 'I regard marriage as other people regard death,' she wrote to Karl Pearson in 1887.[17] Seven years later she was married, yet most of her subsequent life was spent separate from her husband. Even as she transcended the sexual and matrimonial mores of her time, her ideal of feminine nurturing remained rooted in traditional gender-role expectations, just as her radical transformation of theological and scientific traditions into a religion of evolutionary humanity retained the Christian concept of redemption through self-abnegation. The fact that self-sacrifice was the keynote of her work is often seen as a reflection of a misspent life, of deep unhappiness and personal trauma – a reading which patently disregards the extent to which Schreiner constructed herself, and was constructed by others, as a tragic and neurotic personality.[18]

Apparently a constitutionally unhappy person, Schreiner's enjoyment of life and capacity for work were, it has been argued by feminist and non-feminist critics alike, severely impaired by her asthma; her early conditioning, with its deeply painful experience of maternal rejection and inherent personal guilt, is taken to have overshadowed her entire adult life.[19] The onset of her asthma in her late teens, after the breakup of her first sexual relationship, has been read as the external manifestation of internalised guilt, a subliminal attempt at punishing herself for the 'crime' of her sexuality,[20] possibly even for teenage abortion.[21] An alternative reading stresses the 'hysterical protest'[22] encoded by her troubled health, which allowed her to resist and repulse the maternal and matrimonial demands made on her: 'She fought for breath throughout her life,' her god-daughter Olive Renier claimed, 'for a breathing space from the tensions, oppressions, of her emotional conflicts.'[23] However, the conditions under which Schreiner lived and travelled (damp bedrooms and leaking coaches) must have played an important part in aggravating the health problems that had started in childhood, when she had contracted tuberculosis and frequently suffered from respiratory illnesses and angina spasms.[24]

Schreiner was neither the only writer experiencing parental intolerance and alienation from her environment, nor the first writer to have to contend with poverty and a health condition, or to respond physically to acute mental distress. What Liz Stanley has called Schreiner's 'asthmatic personality'[25] has almost assumed the iconic proportions of Sylvia Plath's suicidal madness, a myth which, by linking women's creativity to disease, reaffirms patriarchal assumptions about the essential anomaly of women's writing. Ironically, the critical trope which has superimposed Schreiner's physiology on to her textual 'body' has become an allegory in its own right (Schreiner as the prototypically dis-eased female genius). Already harnessed for contemporary satire in 'Gasps' (1892), as authored by 'Olph Schreion, author of *Screams, The Allegory of an Asian Ranche*' (see Figure 11),[26] the collapse between Schreiner's physiology, assumed mental instability and love of allegory is also inscribed into modern fictional representations such as Ann Harries' *Manly Pursuits* (1999), which figures Schreiner as a physically frail and unkempt, manically obsessive hysteric with strategically well-timed asthma attacks, dangerous oratory powers and a knack of tracking down enormous feathers shed by passing birds.[27]

G A S P S.*

By OLPH SCHREION,

Author of " Screams," " The Allegory of an Asian Ranche."

—•—

11 Satiric title and illustration, 'Tant' Sannie stewing Kraut', in R. C. Lehman,
Mr Punch's Prize Novels: New Series (Bradbury, Agnew & Co., 1892), pp. 134, 137.

If, as Symons observed, allegory was a 'dangerous' mode for the artist to engage an audience in – a supposition confirmed by Elaine Showalter's dismissal of *Dreams* as 'sentimental … in the most nauseating *fin-de-siècle* style'[28] – Schreiner's allegories far from alienated but rather electrified most of her contemporaries. The emotional immediacy and intensity of her 'dreams' may account for their popularity with a diverse audience: the essence of aestheticism to decadent readers at the *fin de siècle*,[29] they embodied the essence of feminism to suffragettes after the turn of the century. Schreiner's work more than that of any other writer, Constance Lytton declared in 1914, 'symbolised and immortalised' the women's movement.[30] One of the reasons for the impact of her allegorical writing was that it lent universal significance to the personal and political aspirations of her readers. Inspired by her archetypal language and biblical imagery, white women in particular were able to conceptualise their claim to equality and citizenship as a spiritual quest for human redemption. With her central Christian metaphor of self-sacrifice and the transfiguration of the material body into transcendental energy Schreiner tapped into the feminist unconscious of the time. For turn-of-the-century feminists on both sides of the Atlantic, her work assumed quasi-scriptural dimensions: in Britain Edith Lees (Ellis) compared *The Story of an African Farm* (1883) to a 'hymn' which had turned 'militancy into a heroism', and Vera Brittain recalled the 'clarion call' which *Woman and Labour* sounded to her generation, while in North America *Dreams* (1890) appeared a 'consecration' to Charlotte Perkins Gilman and her friends.[31]

As Olive Banks has noted,[32] first-wave feminism's marriage of women's liberation and Evangelical religion was not unproblematic, pointing as it does to the conceptual constraints of the movement. This begs the question of how much feminists like Schreiner remained caught in the trope of female self-immolation when they used religious symbolism as a political strategy to unlock the spiritual and physical energies of women. In theory the discourse of collective salvation through personal self-effacement was empowering to women; in practice it primarily addressed a constituency of white Western middle-class women, the only political group which could realistically expect to benefit materially from an extension of civil rights. In order to examine the residual exclusionary practices at play in the deployment of a universalist vision which, even in a writer who passionately defended the rights of all races and of black women in particular, was rooted in the centrality of whiteness, I shall first discuss the concept of self-sacrifice in relation to the *raced* female body in two of Schreiner's allegorical stories, 'Three Dreams in a Desert' and 'Dream Life and Real Life'. This will be followed by an analysis of the transfiguration of the *male* body in *The Story of an African Farm*. As I will argue, Gregory Rose's fluid gender identity suggests that femininity and the female body can become the sites of male self-reconstruction and even fulfilment if men are prepared to transcend their socially constructed masculinity. Yet bodily and spiritual transfiguration, while facilitating the birth of the New Man, here, too, remains firmly predicated on female self-immolation in the form of the death of the New Woman Lyndall. As in Schreiner's most influential allegory, 'Three Dreams in a Desert', the feminist's potential to 'make a track to the water's edge' ('TD', 83), to act as a catalyst for wider social change, is directly contingent on her willingness to embrace personal defeat and even annihilation.

Over our dead bodies: the transfiguration of the female body in 'Three Dreams in a Desert: Under a Mimosa-Tree' and 'Dream Life and Real Life: A Little African Story'[33]

'Three Dreams in a Desert' was originally intended for *Woman and Labour* (*W&L*, 16, n.1) but appeared instead in *Dreams* (1890), the first (and most popular)[34] of three collections written in Britain and on the Continent and published after Schreiner's return to South Africa after an eight years' residence in Britain and Europe. While primarily targeting the male establishment,[35] Schreiner also addressed the growing feminist constituency, with many of the allegories foregrounding the clash of duty and pleasure, sexual passion and spiritual freedom, personal ambition and collective advancement. As the most powerfully evocative encoding of woman's struggle for personhood, 'Three Dreams' held immediate appeal for the women's movement and proved so inspiring that it was often taken for the collection itself.[36]

The allegory pictures three different stages of female liberation, past, present and future. This monumental time scale is telescoped into the space of a single day in the course of which the narrator falls asleep under a tree in an African desert and in her sleep watches a sequence of scenes whose meaning is explained by a prophet-like figure. As Scott McCracken has pointed out, 'Three Dreams' is constructed around two frames, each of which contains figurative characters, thus creating a stage for the performance of New Woman-hood as an emerging subjectivity.[37] From their position on the outer frame, the narrator and the 'prophet' observe the changing parameters of the relationship between woman and man as it is being enacted in the inner frame. Though never clearly fixed, the narrator's gender can be presumed to be female:[38] her passionate empathy with the protagonist of the dreams suggests that this woman represents aspects of her own experience, and both women, by virtue of being juxtaposed with a male authority figure, are aligned with Emotion (the Heart) in a binary opposition which ascribes Reason (the Head) to an old man.

The beginning of the first dream establishes the analogies in the respective positions of the woman inside and outside the frame. Inside the dream sequence prototypical Woman is placed in a position of subjection, even abjection *vis-à-vis* paradigmatic Man, and although the narrator is not exposed to the same condition, she is nevertheless governed by the watchful, albeit benign, eye of patriarchy. 'And there stood one beside me watching' ('TD', 86). With its emphasis on vigilance, scrutiny and (in a more positive sense) protectiveness, this sentence conjures up the law of the father in its religious, social and familial dimensions. Yet just as the female object of their joint gaze, the woman inside the frame, struggles into subjecthood in the course of the three dreams, the narrator is gradually released from the tutoring voice of male authority, moving from the position of the bewildered child (the recipient of didactic instruction) to that of the self-reflexive adult as morning changes to midday and, finally, afternoon.

The narrator remains in the outer frame throughout, while the prophet merges with a white-bearded man representing Reason in the second dream sequence. In the third dream he is again located on the outside frame, but like the men in the dream who have learnt to embrace the idea of women's equality, he is placed alongside the narrator: there is no further reference to any scrutinising gaze, and his pedagogic influence is curtailed. Whereas he previously guided the narrator's vision (first dream), explaining while performing his understanding of woman's condition in the second dream, in the final dream sequence his role is limited to providing brief and pointed answers to the narrator's questions. It is she who moves the action on, his earlier injunctions for her to 'listen' and 'look' and be still ('TD', 69, 71, 72) now making way for her agency, markers of which frame the third dream: 'I thought I would go on my way now' ('TD', 83); 'And I walked towards my horse' ('TD', 85). In focusing on the increasing mobility and autonomy of the female subject both inside and outside the frame, the allegory enacts a programmatic passage from stasis to agency, solitary suffering to collective contentment, female self-sacrifice to self-realisation.

The first dream is a vision of woman's historic subjection. The inner frame depicts a generic man and woman tied together with the 'band of Inevitable Necessity'. With the 'burden of subjection' firmly fixed on her shoulders, where he placed it in the 'Age-of-dominion-of-muscular-force', the woman has no alternative but to lie in the sand, crushed and exhausted ('TD', 70). Because they are tied together, the man, though himself unburdened, has no more freedom of movement than the woman. Suggestive of the umbilical cord, the band holding the sexes together indicates an embryonic relationship in need of severance to enable adult growth. Its name notwithstanding, the band is not an 'Inevitable Necessity'. The *ide*ological as opposed to *bio*logical roots of the present, suffocating, relationship between the sexes are made clear when the prophet explains that in the pre-patriarchal era woman enjoyed equality and companionship with man: 'she who now lies there once wandered free over the rocks with him' ('TD', 69). It was only with the onset of the law of the father – the rule of the 'oldest man' underpinned by the authority of the 'oldest book' (the Old Testament, the Bible) – that the female came to be defined exclusively through her reproductive capacity: 'This is woman; she that bears men in her body ... [W]hen she stooped low to give suck to her young ... he put his burden of subjection on to it, and tied it on with the broad band of Inevitable Necessity' ('TD', 68, 70). However, it is not her body, but her resigned internalisation of her subject condition which is woman's worst predicament: when she became convinced that there was 'no hope' for her, 'she lay down on the sand' with the 'terrible patience of the centuries' ('TD', 70).

At this point it is the man who provides relief as, with the advent of the modern era, the 'Age-of-nervous-force' ('TD', 71), he employs technology – 'Mechanical Invention' ('TD', 72) – to cut the cord which holds the burden on her back. Released from the 'Inevitable Necessity' of subjection, the woman starts struggling up from the ground, a painfully slow and arduous process to which, on account of the involuntary tightening of the cord, the man responds with hostility. Even if he gained sufficient insight into her situation to wish to assist her in her struggle, he would be unable to do so: 'He cannot help her: *she must help herself* ('TD', 73, emphasis in original). Eventually, the woman raises herself to her knees: a mere 'creature' ('TD', 75) as yet, but with the 'light in her eyes' ('TD', 74) affording hope for her spiritual awakening, the theme of the second dream.

In the dream of the present, a woman reaches a river which she needs to cross to reach the 'land of Freedom'. An old man bearing (representing) 'Reason' advises her to shed all her garments (patriarchal traditions) save one which symbolises Truth, and he also persuades her to leave her baby (man) behind, as their separation will be beneficial to him too: 'put him down that he may grow' ('TD', 81). If this is the woman who in the previous dream struggled to her feet, the man who stood beside her has now regressed to infant status. Until the child screaming for passion grows into a man capable of partnership, there is no possibility of a mature and mutually sustaining relationship between the sexes: 'In the ideal condition for which we look men and women will walk close, hand in hand', Schreiner wrote elsewhere, 'but now the fight has … to be fought out alone by both'.[39] Not only must contemporary women sacrifice 'love' for 'freedom', given the absence of any existing path across the river, they must also be prepared to lay down their individual lives for the benefit of future generations. Rallied by the sound of the thousands of women following in her footsteps, the human bridge the woman in the allegory prepares to build with her body constitutes a significant variant on Cixous' ladder and Schreiner's stairs in the 'Sunlight' allegory, for here it is not the dreamer (writer, thinker, founder of a new creed or philosophy) her/himself, but the 'entire human race' ('TD', 83) who will be able to move on to a higher stage of spiritual existence. Like Grand, Schreiner presented the feminist pioneer as a redeemer, conceptualising the female Christ as a paradigmatic 'mother of the race' whose self-sacrificial act outlined, as she wrote in *From Man to Man*, 'the profound truth recognised everywhere that an almighty affection and the instinct for even self-immolation in the servicing of others is not merely one of the highest but one of the strongest forces modifying human life' (*FMTM*, 212).

The third dream of Schreiner's allegory shows the idealised outcome of the feminist pioneer's self-consecration: a harmonious fellowship of male–female and all-female groupings. The message of this allegory is, thus, that women's liberation can be achieved only by women's own efforts (a point reaffirmed in Schreiner's 'Spirit of the Age' allegory in *From Man to Man*, 223–5), with their ultimate success being predicated on the extent of their dedication to the political struggle and willingness to forgo personal fulfilment; and further, that a 'fellowship of the new life'[40] is contingent on men learning to prize companionship over sexual desire and on women overcoming their internal divisions.

With its emblematic moral encapsulating the contemporary feminist endeavour, 'Three Dreams' had an electrifying impact on the women's movement. In Constance Lytton's autobiography the chapter dealing with her prison experiences is entitled after Schreiner's story ('A Track to the Water's Edge'). Describing a scene in which Emmeline Pethick-Lawrence recited 'Three Dreams' to the other prisoners, Lytton suggested that what distinguished this allegory was the authenticity with which it captured the lived experience of suffragettes: 'this "Dream" seemed scarcely an allegory. The words hit out a bare literal description of the pilgrimage of women ... We ... went back to our hard beds, to the thought of our homes, to the depressing surroundings of our fellow prisoners, to the groans and cries of agonised women – content.'[41]

Schreiner's allegory also left a deep impression on the North American women's movement, with Charlotte Perkins Gilman basing the design of the front cover of her first book of poems, *In This Our World* (1893), on 'Three Dreams'[42] and circulating the allegory to her women friends. One of them, Harriet Howe, described a similarly intense response to Lytton's:

> And if I had been exalted before, over the poetry; here was vital truth, aspiration, reality for the whole human race, in so perfect a setting that no work of human hands could excel it. I cried incredulously, 'And this book is in the world, and still the women are asleep? Then what use is it to try further, for this cannot be surpassed.' In a reverent tone [Gilman] answered me, in the very words of the book, 'We make a path to the water's edge'. And I wept, unashamed, while she walked away a little distance, I think to conceal her own eyes ... From that hour I was dedicated to the work of lifting humanity by awakening women to a knowledge of their power and their responsibility.[43]

One of the reasons why Schreiner's message of self-sacrifice was so influential was that it drew on the combined reservoir of women's spiritual energy and physical desire by displacing *individual* passion for men, so fraught with problems and fears for many women at the time, into a *generalised* passion for women and 'the cause': a more compelling object of desire since it put the passionate woman centre-stage. A woman could now become the heroine of her own story rather than serve as a supporting actress in her husband's. Instead of being isolated in a domestic setting, she was encouraged to join a burgeoning female community whose members were energised by the same personal-and-political vision. 'It it this abiding consciousness of an end to be attained, reaching beyond her personal life and individual interests', Schreiner wrote in *Woman and Labour*, 'which constitutes the religious element of the Woman's Movement of our day, and binds with the common bond of an impersonal enthusiasm into one solid body the women of whatsoever race, class, and nation who are struggling after the readjustment of woman to life' (*W&L*, 128). A typological allegory with prophetic dimensions, 'Three Dreams' reconfigures biblical allegory in its most typical form[44] and abounds with biblical tropes which encode the woman's cause as the Christian salvation story *par excellence*. As indicated in the subtitle, the narrator falls asleep under a mimosa bush: the mimosa, whose golden flowers are associated with the sun (hence with eternal life), is a traditional symbol of resurrection.[45] In Jungian terms, the sun, or golden flower, is itself an archetypal image of wholeness which frequently appears in dreams.[46] The mimosa bush which gives shelter to the narrator's dreams might suggest that after her Passion (suffering), woman will be reborn into emotional, spiritual and political wholeness. The analogy between woman and Christ is reinforced by the frequent confusion, in symbology, of the mimosa with the acacia.[47] Christ's crown of thorns was made up of acacia; in the allegory the narrator is figuratively crowned with mimosa: like the woman in the dream sequence she, too, is offered the promise of rebirth. The mimosa as a symbol of Christian suffering and redemption is also invoked in *From Man to Man* (the first draft of which carried the title 'A Small Bit of Mimosa', and a novel which constitutes a site of further biblical rewritings),[48] where a thorny mimosa bush figures Bertie's expulsion from bourgeois 'paradise' and the beginning of her social crucifixion (*FMTM*, 136), and where in the 'Prelude' Rebekah's dream of her dead baby sister's resurrection as a pre-lapsarian New Eve is inspired by a mimosa pod (*FMTM*, 47).

Further biblical references are provided by the Christ-like mediator of the dreams when he makes an oblique reference to the 'oldest book' ('TD', 69), the Old Testament. The river which divides the land of bondage from the land of freedom connotes the Red Sea which provided a passage from Egypt to the promised land; like the Book of Exodus the second of the 'Three Dreams' constitutes a prototypically eschatological myth of deliverance, a myth which, as Laurence Coupe notes, is 'orientated forwards: though it assumes a hierarchy, in the form of a heaven above, it also assumes a horizon, in the form of a promised land or Messianic kingdom',[49] the land of 'heaven on earth' ('TD', 84) conjured up in the last dream. The Holy Trinity is reflected in the triangular structure of the allegory, where three central characters (the narrator, Reason, the woman) are juxtaposed with three signifiers of nature (the sun, the earth – sand – and the moon). Narrated at three different times of day, the dreams represent three evolutionary stages in the history of sexual relations across three different ages: the experience of past oppression, the present imperative of separation, the promise of future partnership. Not only does 'Three Dreams' invoke scriptural paradigms to define women's struggle for liberation, it also positions feminism in its troubled bond with evolutionary sexual relations in a relationship analogous to that of the New to the Old Testament. As Deborah Madsen points out, Christian allegorism, unlike its Classical predecessor, 'assumes a referent that is highly specific to the testaments – the Old prefigures the New and the New fulfils the Old Testament in a process of mutual reinterpretation'.[50] Schreiner problematises this allegorical relationship by positing the women's movement as the 'New Testament' of humanity emerging from a conflicted, archaic and anachronistic Old Testament patriarchy.

Some fifteen years before the emergence of militancy, Schreiner thus gauged with astute foresight the potency of the Christian iconography which was to become a standard motif in suffragette literature,[51] and which underpinned the political strategy of passive resistance through self-inflicted suffering (hunger-strike) and even more extreme cases of self-harming (Lytton's tattooing of her chest, Emily Wilding Davison's suicide).[52] Just as all 'New Testament ... situational allegory originated from a feeling that author and audience alike were participating in a new and extraordinary situation',[53] so Schreiner's radically reconstructed biblical allegories spoke directly and emphatically to an audience of contemporary feminist activists about the 'new and extraordinary situation' in which they found themselves. There was no doubt in Sylvia Pankhurst's mind that 'Three Dreams' reflected 'the aspirations of the women's movement'.[54] This was to a great extent due to the fact that it offered women a female-centred religious experience, transforming them from passive, reproductively receptive and mourning Marys into active, triumphant (albeit crucified) Christ figures. In revising 'Biblical images with subversive intention', Rose Lovell-Smith points out, Schreiner 'replace[d] Bible story with women's stories as a signal that ... women's history must be rewritten, and [that] this history ... has as great a mythic significance as scripture'.[55]

Significantly, however, this was a religious-political vision which marginalised black women, for just as the narrator's gender can be inferred, so can her race. The allegory foregrounds the colour white as a marker of both race and (age-related) wisdom: the undergarment indicative of Truth is white (purity), the old man in possession of Reason has a white beard (profundity, knowledge, insight), and the woman's hair turns white when she completes her journey towards political selfhood (experience and maturity); her baby has blond curls (ethnicity). Even the African setting – a moral as well as a geographically specific landscape[56] – underscores the invisibility of blackness by marginalising the colour brown (there is only one brief reference to the brown earth), instead emphasising redness (red heat, red sand), the hue of white skin exposed to the sun. Ultimately, then, this story which claims to carry universal significance turns out to be about white women only. Christian discourse, though typically pressed into the service of colonising forces, can be, and has been, used to represent the interests of the colonised (Sojourner Truth, Martin Luther King). In 'Three Dreams' it is mobilised for one colonised group at the price of ignoring another. As Chrisman has argued with reference to the sculpture and 'Hunter' episodes in *The Story of an African Farm*, the decoding of Schreiner's allegories relies on the shared cultural background of 'creator'/ mother (Waldo) and 'interpreter'/deliverer (the Stranger), and is thus premised on the exclusion or marginalisation of the African Other: the 'category of the "universal" is the province of the Western' subject.[57] Just as *Trooper Peter Halket of Mashonaland* reconfigures Christianity as Britishness,[58] so 'Three Dreams' represents Christ as a white woman. The fissures in Schreiner's ideological framework, in particular the dissonance between her committed anti-imperialist politics and her discursive practice which drew on the racist register common to her time, have been abundantly documented.[59] Read in conjunction with 'A Little African Story', 'Three Dreams in a Desert' marks out the tensions between Schreiner's vision of white women's journey towards freedom and black women's retreat into political marginality.

Written for and originally published in her brother Fred's *New College Magazine* in 1881,[60] 'A Little African Story' set the tone for Schreiner's second collection of allegories, *Dream Life and Real Life* (1893). It is a Christian tale of the martyrdom of an indentured girl who sacrifices her life to save her masters. The story begins with Jannita herding goats on an African plain. In her desolation, caused by the abuse she is suffering, she escapes into a day-dream in which she imagines a more congenial kind of race/class relations, yet even in her 'Dream Life' hegemonic dominance remains largely unchallenged. The most radical transformation she can conceive of is not a relationship of equality, but merely the absence of violence and the master race's appreciation of her services in which the master would stop beating her, the mistress would offer her food, the daughter would give her flowers and the son would thank her for pulling off his boots.

Unmediated by any vision of political liberation, the stark violence to which Jannita is subjected in 'Real Life' (where she suffers starvation and is repeatedly kicked, whipped and eventually killed) undercuts the expectation, evoked in the title, of a balance between 'Dream Life' and 'Real Life', highlighting the extent of Jannita's victimisation and sacrifical death (the goats with which she is associated from the outset function as markers of her role as scapegoat and, in coded allusion to William Holman Hunt's painting 'The Scapegoat' of 1854,[61] as Christ figure). In sharp contrast to 'Three Dreams in a Desert', where dreams provide the spiritual sustenance necessary to overcome the torments of lived experience, this story emphasises the destructive nature of day-dreaming. It is precisely because of her absorption in her dream that Jannita loses one of her goats, as a result of which she is brutally chastised. In both texts the fierce heat of the African sun causes the central character to fall asleep beside a bush in the *Karroo*, and in both cases the dreams are punctuated by the movement of ants in the sand, reminders of the evolutionary processes that have led from insect to human civilisation, and thus indicative of the potential for change in human relations. Given an almost identical setting, one of the 'Dreams' features a white woman so empowered by her vision of future freedom that she is able to make the dream come true, while the other shows a quasi-slave girl caught in a vicious cycle of violence which her dream is powerless to transform.

This sense of imbalance between the two allegorical texts is further compounded by instabilities in the representation of race. If 'Three Dreams' constructs the generic woman as white, 'A Little African Story' foregrounds an ambiguously raced girl. In her dream Jannita imagines her dead father coming to life again to tell her that 'they would go back to Denmark now' ('DL+RL', 16). Not only is the one figure who promises release from slavery cast as a white man, but, more importantly, the race of the child-slave is called into question, encouraging a reading which presumes on her whiteness.[62] With her identity tied to a Danish father and Spanish name (Juanita), Jannita herself seems confused over her ethnicity, and this confusion is reflected in the discrepancies between 'Real Life', which accentuates her 'brown curls', and 'Dream Life', in which her father compliments her on her 'long and silky' hair (16–17). The other black characters seem to be infected by a similar crisis, or collapse, of racial identity when they refer to Jannita as 'the little white girl' (40). The text fails to clarify whether Jannita is of mixed race, or whether she is a 'white' child whose fatherless (and motherless) state has turned her into a servant-slave, the working-class equivalent of the racial Other.

To make matters more complex still, the story, which seems to challenge reader expectations by blurring and confusing the protagonist's ethnicity, at the same time reaffirms racial prejudice by stigmatising those characters who are unambiguously identified as being black. Following her flight from the farm, Jannita's brief spell of freedom is brought to a violent conclusion when two black men invade the peaceful natural setting of the African *Karroo* to plot murder. For the slave-girl liberty is only possible beyond and outside of civilisation; ironically, the very people to represent hostile human civilisation, and to colonise the 'natural' (nobly savage) world in which she seeks refuge, are those classed as mere 'brutes' by white society. Dirk, who also works on the farm of Jannita's masters, conspires with two other men to set fire to the house. The black men are stereotyped along racial lines ('Dirk the Hottentot', 'the bushman'), and are further defined by their position within the slave economy, with Dirk's Dutch/Boer name reflecting his appropriation (naming) by the whites, while the 'bushman's' lack of a name and identity suggests that he is little more than an animal, an impression compounded by his stunted growth and monkey-like body (a 'tiny' and 'ragged' creature, he is no more than 'four feet high', 'DL+RL', 18). Denied any human individuality, these men have no sense of political solidarity. By stealing one of the goats, Dirk previously caused Jannita to be whipped, and neither of them recoils from killing her when she thwarts their plans. Nor does Jannita feel the slightest connection with them, even though she has every reason to share their hatred of the Boer family. Loyalty to her master prevails over the joint experience of subjection.

When her own life is at stake, she appeals to the black men's companion, a white navvy, imploring him to help her against the other two. The greatest danger and the most brutal violence is thus associated with the black, not the white men in the story.

By identifying the third criminal as a navvy and thus highlighting the class problematic underlying the story, Schreiner further destabilises reader expectations and sympathies. The three men are robbers and killers, but like Jannita they represent the oppressed Other in terms of class and race. Dirk becomes a thief because he is hungry; it is the instinct for survival, no inborn viciousness, which makes him take advantage of a fellow slave. His misrecognition of Jannita's essential sameness points to the master race's successful deployment of the 'divide and rule' strategy: as long as members of the subject race and class fight one another, white hegemony will remain unchallenged. Jannita's self-sacrificial impulse could thus be regarded as a retrograde reflex, a symptom of her indoctrination; the men's determination to deliver a blow at the master's house (the house of slavery, the Empire), at whatever cost, might then signal their emerging political consciousness. The navvy's wish to loot the farm is indicative of his desire to dismantle the master's economic power, just as the black men's attempt to burn down the master's house is motivated by their experience of white atrocities: 'I will set the roof alight in six places, for a Dutchman burnt my mother once alive in a hut, with three children' ('DL+RL', 38–39).

What ultimately makes this text into an 'African' story not of 'little' but of 'big' dimensions is the conflict it articulates between two opposing models of race and class liberation: a violent struggle against oppression, which, it is implied, can only lead to the further victimisation (Jannita) and brutalisation (the three men) of the oppressed; and, contrasted with this, the notion of Christian martyrdom and self-sacrifice, which may bring about a spiritual change in both coloniser and colonised and may thus offer an impetus for political transformation. However, it is difficult to see how Jannita's self-sacrificial death is to accomplish this. Alerted by her screams though unable to identify her voice, the white settler family is saved from being burnt alive, but in the face of their ignorance of her actions, her sacrifice can have no political ramifications. There is no possibility that it could work on their conscience in the way in which, in Schreiner's anti-Rhodes novel, Trooper Peter Halket's death leads to the conversion of his fellow-soldiers (*TPH*). Moreover, although her death leaves her murderers badly shaken, their escape into drink does not hold out much hope for a radical reconstruction of their lives, let alone for a redirection of their violent energies into constructive political action.

While in 'Three Dreams', female self-sacrifice is a powerful means of social and political transformation, in 'A Little African Story' it effectively reaffirms the racial *status quo*. In the first allegory the woman builds a bridge for other women; it is her single-minded focus on the cause of the oppressed group she represents, and her willingness to neglect the interests of the oppressor (man), which result in a more egalitarian world for all. By contrast, in 'A Little African Story' the subject group is internally divided: the possibility of effective resistance is fatally circumscribed by Jannita's identification with the master class and compounded by the three men's self-destructive violence; together, the oppressed break down the bridge that might have been built to achieve their joint liberation.

What point, then, was Schreiner's trying to make? By constructing Jannita as a martyr, she may have aimed at directing the sympathies of white readers towards the weakest member of human society, an ethnic girl-child, in order to draw attention to the pernicious effects which the oppression of marginalised groups had on all. The redemptive function assigned to the slave-girl as the trebly subjected (in terms of ethnicity, gender and age) points to her role as a boundary marker between atavistic reality and the potential of human progression – a potential crucially contingent on the principle of universal equality: 'Permanent human advance', Schreiner urged in *From Man to Man*, could only come about, and be maintained, if it was predicated on 'united advance' (*FMTM*, 192).

Jannita's impact and *raison d'être* are primarily spiritual, not political. If the woman in 'Three Dreams' represents Christ in a female configuration, then Jannita achieves the symbolical status of a girl Christ of indeterminate ethnicity. In conjunction with the lack of a surname which would ascribe her a distinct identity, the initial of her 'Christian' name points to Jesus, as does her dream of Heaven: 'She thought she was walking in a beautiful place, holding her father's hand, and they both had crowns on their head, crowns of wild asparagus. The people whom they passed smiled and kissed her; some gave her flowers, and some gave her food, and the sunlight was everywhere' ('DL+RL', 27–8). As a Christ-like figure she dies for all, black and white alike, hence her sacrifice for her white masters. Only in this sense could she be seen as making a track to the water's edge – but this is a track which remains firmly embedded in the cultural and religious 'ways' and superstructures of white society. For the slave-girl, the white woman's transformation of body into bridge (a feminist version, as it were, of transubstantiation) appears unattainable: instead of leaving behind a mark of her martyrdom (and therefore glory), she is returned to a state of nature, her only trace 'a little new-made heap of earth and round stones. Three men knew what was under it; and no one else ever will' ('DL+RL', 48). Bodily sacrifice, the necessary first step towards white women's liberation, becomes a purpose in itself, and is thus, when projected on to the 'black' woman martyr, divorced from the aim of enfranchisement. The absence of any utopian image of racial harmony is surely significant. There is no possible future in which Jannita could walk hand-in-hand with her master. While Schreiner programmatically resolved the sex question by imagining an egalitarian society in 'Three Dreams' and an androgynous one in 'The Sunlight Lay Across My Bed', the only resolution she could envisage to the race question was, paradoxically, one in which a female slave emerged as a Christ figure only to be written out of existence again by the males of her oppressed group.

A close reading of these two allegorical texts thus reveals an unresolved tension in Schreiner's work between the theme of liberation and its recontainment within patriarchal and colonial paradigms. In 'Three Dreams' the perspective of the female narrator is mediated by the male vision of Reason; in addition, just as the three stories are framed by the dreams of the narrator, her own story is framed by the shining and setting of a sun which, in the final sentence, is pointedly gendered. The story begins with a reference to the (ungendered) sun ('As I travelled across an African plain the sun shone down hotly') but ends with a masculine closure and a vision of male (not female) resurrection: 'Then the sun passed down behind the hills; but I knew that the next day *he* would arise again' ('TD', 67, 85, emphasis added). This collision between gender-neutral and masculine points of view is not untypical of feminist writing of the time. In Grand's *Ideala* the heroine's nascent feminism is also orchestrated by her male mentor's imposition of self-sacrifice for the future of the 'race'. Like *Ideala* and 'Three Dreams', 'A Little African Story' articulates a female perspective through the filter of a white male myth (redemption through crucifixion). While 'Three Dreams' ignores the black woman's point of view, 'A Little African Story' lends her a voice only to muffle it in a scream.

In her allegories, Schreiner's feminism and anti-imperialism appear haunted by the voices of patriarchy. Did her fiction offer a corrective to the troubled relationship, so conspicuous in the allegories, between visionary feminism and internalised hegemonic perspectives? In *From Man to Man* (1926) Schreiner indeed presents an alternative vision of black female self-consecration through the device of Rebekah's endeavour to teach her sons respect for racial alterity and engage their fraternal feelings for the mixed-race girl (the product of her husband's sexual exploitation of a black servant and thus a reminder of slavery[63]) whom she has adopted. In Chapter XII ('Fireflies in the Dark') two allegorical stories linked through an evolutionary account of the origin and development of species skilfully manipulate her sons' (white readers'?) identification processes, as the personal pronoun inhabited by the narrator and her audience assumes shifting racial identities. The shared subject position of the 'us' marks, first, the heroic struggle for survival, spiritual as much as physical, of white humanity after colonisation by a master-race of even whiter aliens equipped with advanced technological means of mass destruction. 'And we? What did we do then?' (*FMTM*, 422), asks one of

Rebekah's sons, his linguistic response signalling his sense of identification with the colonised. His mother's response – that the wisest determined 'not to die' but to 'grasp the new life, and live' by asserting their right to claim '[t]his world also [as] our home. We also are men' (*FMTM*, 423) – enjoins him to acknowledge the inviolability of the principle of equality and the need for peaceful cohabitation of all races; for '[y]ou see', Rebekah concludes her bedside story, 'when we talk of the dark peoples and the inferior races, it has often seemed to me, it is as with those terrible white faced strangers of my dream' (*FMTM*, 424). The second story substantiates this point by positioning the audience on the side of the oppressors. When she was 'a little girl', Rebekah admits, she 'could not bear' the indigenous population, until ultimately, in her imagination, she conjured up 'a high wall right across Africa and put all the black people on the other side, and … said, "Stay there, and the day you put one foot over, your heads will be cut off"' (*FMTM*, 435) – the very opposite of the human bridge which in 'Three Dreams' builds a future for human fellowship. The chilling reality that underlies racial division was brought home to her, Rebekah says, when she was told about a battle that had just taken place:

> It was a big fight. The white men had their cannon and all their soldiers on the top of a hill, and the Kaffirs came out below from the bush; there were hundreds of them; they had hardly any clothes or guns, only assegais, and they came on naked up the slope; but before them walked a young Kaffir woman. Her arms were full of assegais. As the men threw their assegais she gave them new ones; she called on them to come on and not to be afraid to die. … The guns fired and the dead lay in heaps. When she got close up to the mouth of the cannon she was blown away too with the others. … I felt I was suffocating … I saw the woman walking with her bare arms glistening in the sun and her red blanket tied across … with the assegais in her arms, calling the men to come on and not to be afraid to die … I lay down on the ground and cried. After that, often in the night when I lay awake I thought I was the young Kaffir woman, and I called the men to come on – and then the cannon fired. (*FMTM*, 435–6)

By placing a witness account of a real-life event sequentially after Rebekah's 'dream' of the noble struggle against colonisation from outer space, Schreiner collapses racial identifications, as the white soldiers with their superior technology ('us') turn into the genocidal aliens ('them'), while the black Africans whom Rebekah had wanted to see assigned to apartheid are reclaimed as the valiant warriors of the previous story. In this late text, Schreiner reconfigured her vision of the female Christ as an heroic African Boadicea who dies fighting for her race, and in dying wins the moral battle: 'I lay down … and cried … I thought I was the young Kaffir woman.' A bridge to cross-racial identification, her martyred body effectuates the transfiguration of the hegemonic gaze. Here, then, the African woman is ascribed a subject position far in excess of the function of 'boundary marker'[64] in Schreiner's work.

Not so, arguably, in *The Story of an African Farm* (1883). In contra-distinction to her late work, Schreiner's first published novel fails to provide a way out of white Western points of view, allegorical or otherwise. Black characters are relegated to the sidelines and treated with little or no sympathy: a toddler is reduced to a 'little animal' (*AF*, 273), a young mother stereotyped as 'a sullen, ill-looking woman, with lips hideously protruding' (*AF*, 71), and the African servants are cast as malicious, gleeful, inherently dishonest creatures. Nor do the Boer characters fare much better: Tant' Sannie is a monstrous travesty of European femininity, her domestic qualities grotes-quely perverted into marital cannibalism and (physical and emotional) child abuse. Uncouth and uncultured, she is violently oppressive of the overseer Otto's and his son Waldo's civilised (German) book-learning. The younger Boer women Trana and Em, though falling short of Tant' Sannie's propensity for sadism, approximate her physically in their oversized and forever swelling bodies, and mentally in their intellectual incuriosity and conventional outlook on life.

Clearly, then, if *African Farm* can claim to redress dominant orthodoxies, racial hegemony is not part of the equation. As in 'Three Dreams in a Desert', it is a white woman, and a woman of English extraction at that, who articulates the central feminist message. So irresistible was this vision, to its white audience at least, that it made the book and its author famous overnight. By capturing the *fin-de-siècle* mood and coupling it with the spiritual and socio-political imagination of late-Victorian social reform movements, the novel turned Schreiner into a key figure of the emerging New Woman movement, ensuring her lasting success with both the intellectual avant-garde and the general public to the end of the century and beyond.

What distinguishes *African Farm* from the two allegorical stories discussed earlier is that, while the feminist pioneer fails in her quest for freedom because of her inability to negotiate between the conflicting claims of self-develop-ment and self-sacrifice, female agency and empowerment are, paradoxically, represented by a white man. My concern here is not with the two protagonists of the novel and their struggles (Lyndall's feminism and Waldo's spiritual quest), but with this secondary character, the gentleman farmer Gregory Rose, whose capacity to explore and realise his feminine potential is central to his evolution towards New Manhood.

The parable of the ring: male femininity and the transfigured m/other in *The Story of an African Farm* (1883)

As Laura Stempel Mumford has pointed out, Gregory Rose inverts Schreiner's concept of the 'virile woman' as promoted in *Woman and Labour* by performing feminine manhood.[65] The story of 'Gregory's Womanhood' (as

Schreiner entitles her chapter) assumes the significance of what Ruth Parkin-Gounelas has called an 'allegory of androgyny'.[66] Introduced as an 'effeminate' man, Rose parades, and parodies, the feminine qualities of Edward Carpenter's 'intermediate sex', the sex which collapses binary categories. Like the male intermediate, Gregory Rose represents

> a distinctly effeminate type, sentimental, lackadaisical, mincing in gait and manners, something of a chatterbox, skilful at the needle and in women's work, sometimes taking pleasure in dressing in woman's clothes; his figure ... betraying a tendency towards the feminine, large at the hips, supple, not muscular, the face wanting in hair, the voice inclining to be high-pitched ... while his dwelling room is orderly in the extreme, even natty, and choice of decoration and perfume. His affection, too, is ... feminine in character, clinging, dependent and jealous, as of one desiring to be loved almost more than to love.[67]

In Lyndall's eyes he embodies the clichéd notion of 'a true woman': 'How happy he would be sewing frills into his little girls' frocks, and how pretty he would look sitting in a parlour, with a rough man making love to him!' (*AF*, 180). Gregory's conflicted gender identity is reflected in the domestic arrangements in his home:

> It was one tiny room, the whitewashed walls profusely covered with prints cut from the *Illustrated London News*, and in which there was a noticeable preponderance of female faces and figures. A stretcher filled one end of the hut, and a rack for a gun and a little hanging looking-glass diversified the gable opposite, while in the centre stood a chair and table. All was scrupulously neat and clean, for Gregory kept a little duster folded in the corner of his table-drawer, just as he had seen his mother do, and every morning before he went out he said his prayers, and made his bed, and dusted the table and the legs of the chairs, and even the pictures on the wall and the gun-rack. (*AF*, 156)

Already conspicuous in his names (the 'male' Gregory versus the 'female' Rose), the clash between his feminine self (modelled on his mother, whose every habit he imitates, beginning with the duster and ending with the fashion pictures) and his masculine role (the gun-rack, metaphorical reminder of his sex) is foregrounded by the mirror, the site of an endless narcissistic re-enactment of his double-genderedness: shaving masculinises him, yet the clean-shaven face in the mirror reflects the faces of the fashionable women on the wall. As if to inscribe an exemplary, glorious and inevitably white femininity on to their more deviant one, both the grotesque, man-eating Boer woman Tant' Sannie and the 'man-woman' Gregory Rose (*AF*, 181) have fashion pictures on the wall, she only the one – 'a gorgeous creature from a fashion-sheet ... pasted up at the foot of her bed' (*AF*, 30) – he the many, 'profusely covering' himself with images of his self-love. Small wonder, then, that he becomes instantly infatuated with Lyndall, for she is 'more like a princess, yes, far more like a princess, than the lady who still hung on the wall in Tant' Sannie's bedroom' (*AF*, 166).

With his love for Lyndall, Rose's warring genders merge to form an authentic and essentially female (no longer simply feminine) self. On discovering Lyndall in the last stages of a wasting disease, he turns himself into a woman in order to be employed as her nurse. In a sense, Lyndall's illness enables Schreiner to exonerate Rose from the charge of sexual deviance, but in fact his transvestite desire predates his discovery of Lyndall's critical condition. Significantly, it is in the paradigmatically female-gendered space of an attic reached by a ladder that his passage into womanhood is enacted:

> He ... proceeded to examine the contents of another [packing-case] ... He loosened one plank, and began to lift out various articles of female attire – old-fashioned caps, aprons, dresses with long pointed bodies such as he remembered to have seen his mother wear when he was a little child. He shook them out carefully to see there were no moths, and then sat down to fold them up again one by one. They had belonged to Em's mother, and the box, as packed at her death, had stood untouched and forgotten these long years. She must have been a tall woman, that mother of Em's, for when he stood up to shake out a dress the neck was on a level with his, and the skirt touched the ground. Gregory laid a night-cap out on his knee, and began rolling up the strings; but presently his fingers moved slower and slower, then his chin rested on his breast, and finally the imploring blue eyes were fixed on the frill abstractedly. When Em's voice called to him from the foot of the ladder he started, and threw the night-cap behind him.
> [...] [W]hen he could hear that she was gone, he picked up the night-cap again, and a great brown sun-kappje – just such a 'kappje' and such a dress as one of those he remembered to have seen a sister-of-mercy wear. Gregory's mind was very full of thought. He took down a fragment of an old looking-glass from behind a beam, and put the 'kappje' on. His beard looked somewhat grotesque under it; he put up his hand to hide it – that was better. The blue eyes looked out with the mild gentleness that became eyes looking out from under a 'kappje'. Next he took the brown dress, and looking round, furtively, slipped it over his head. He had just got his arms in the sleeves, and was trying to hook up at the back, when an increase in the patter of the rain at the window made him drag it off hastily. When he perceived there was no one coming he tumbled the things back into the box, and, covering it carefully, went down the ladder. (*AF*, 226–7)

In her satiric adaptation of the biblical parable of Jacob's ladder, Schreiner enables Gregory to accede to a higher spiritual, quasi-deified state. Adding a gender dimension to the feminist paradigm of the madwoman in the attic, Schreiner suggests that a man, when facing his 'true' feminine self, turns not into a 'madwoman' (a mad man who thinks himself a woman), but into a nurturing mother figure, the sister of mercy invoked by the nightcap. There is a distinct sense of saintliness, of Christian transfiguration almost.[68] This is already encapsulated in his full name, Gregory Nazianzen Rose, inspired by the fourth-century saint Gregory Nazianzen.[69] Furthermore, as Susan Casteras has argued, in Victorian painting the figure of Christ was frequently feminised (most prominently so in William Holman Hunt's 'The Light of the World', 1853).[70] In her novel Schreiner builds on this conceptual analogy by associating a man's femininity with Christ-like attributes. While the seclusion of the attic may allow a woman to release her anger, it helps the man achieve spiritual transcendence. As in his house, the tension between sex and gender, subject-identification and social role, selfhood and sainthood is encoded by a mirror: 'The blue eyes looked out with the mild gentleness that became eyes looking out from under a "kappje".' Assuming female dress, Rose feels less, not more, of an impostor, since this externalised femininity reflects his inner self and also his bodily materiality (soft blue eyes, stereotypically the eyes of a woman, and according to Lavater tell-tale signs of 'weakness, effeminacy' and a 'yielding' nature).[71] The act of covering himself with the attributes of femininity (the pictures on the wall, the lid on the box with clothes, the dress on his body) constitutes in reality an *un*covering of his 'real' gender; disguised, he is able to reveal his true self. What starts as a performance, a secret and guilty act of self-pleasuring, soon turns into an emotional, psychological and even, almost, physical sex change, as the distinction between gender and sex begins to blur. Rose does not just wear female clothing, but becomes in effect a 'woman'. With the shaving off of his beard (an all too obvious metaphor) this transformation, again enacted before a mirror, is complete:

> 'Am I, am I Gregory Nazianzen Rose?' he said.
>
> It was all so strange ... strange as the fantastic, changing shapes in a summer cloud. At last, tired out, he fell asleep ... When he woke ... [he] drew from his breast pocket a little sixpenny looking-glass, and hung it on one of the roots that stuck out from the bank. Then he dressed himself in one of the old-fashioned gowns and a great pinked-out collar. Then he took out a razor. Tuft by tuft the soft brown beard fell down into the sand ... Then the glass showed a face surrounded by a frilled cap, white as a woman's, with a little mouth, a very short upper lip, and a receding chin.
>
> Presently a rather tall woman's figure was making its way across the 'veld'. (*AF*, 251)

Again, femininity is associated with whiteness ('a face ... white as a woman's'); a black face, we may infer, is as incongruous with the notion of 'authentic' (divine) womanhood as a bearded (male) face. Furthermore, as Rose's example shows, while a beard can be shed, and a man attain womanly attributes, there seems little such hope for black women.

A 'true' woman, Rose also proves to be an exceptionally proficient nurse. The man who began his quest for femininity by mimicking his mother, and then assumed the guise of his mother-in-law, has now become a mother in his own right as he gently nurtures an infantile Lyndall. As her fatal malady makes abundantly clear, however, biological motherhood is dramatically different from its symbolic counterpart. For Lyndall pregnancy came as a shock and effectively terminated her struggle for autonomous selfhood, yet when her baby dies, she is prostrate with guilt and punishes herself with self-starvation. Originally subtitled 'A Series of Abortions',[72] Schreiner's novel paints a bleak picture of physical motherhood and its destructive potential, and Rose's maternal nursing of Lyndall is not an exception.

By the time Rose assumes care of Lyndall, her body has been devastated, and effectively defeminised, by anorexia. The loss of her long hair (the sign of her adult femininity, the equivalent of his beard) reflects not, as in his case, a change of gender positioning, but a loss of sex, even a mutilation: '"We had to cut if off," said the woman, touching [Lyndall's short hair] with her forefinger. "Soft as silk, like a wax-doll's"' (*AF*, 253). Unlike a child, Lyndall grows not 'up' but 'down', shrinking to the size of a 'small doll' (*AF*, 262), and all Rose's care cannot prevent her death. His regeneration as a woman is coincidental with her degeneration as a woman. Perhaps Lyndall never carries out her intention of giving her ring – as Helen Bradford argues, a symbol of the pregnant womb[73] – to the 'first man who tells me he would like to be a woman' (*AF*, 170), not because she fails to realise that Rose is this man, but because he, too, must ultimately fail in taking on the reproductive functions of woman-as-womb: like Lyndall's child, his baby (Lyndall) dies. Once his maternal experience, like Lyndall's biological motherhood, has run its fatal course, Rose reverts to Gregory.

Why does Schreiner make Lyndall fail so spectacularly in her quest for New Womanhood? 'Three Dreams in a Desert' may provide an answer here, for, as the allegorical woman learns from Reason, man has an easier and less existentially fraught passage into the 'land of freedom', whereas she herself risks drowning in the process – especially if she is burdened with a baby (or its ghost), which Lyndall is. (Lyndall's demise is associated with death by water since her illness starts with a cold contracted after sitting in the rain at her baby's grave.) In her allegorical writing Schreiner suggests that the 'successful' feminist is one who, irrespective of any personal cost, is able to concentrate on the political advancement of women: remorse about the neglect of maternal duties does not enter into the equation. The difference between an allegorical figure and a more fully fledged character in a realist novel is of course that the latter is more vulnerable to self-reproach. It is the agony of guilt about not having 'cared' enough for her child, and thus having precipitated its death, which is at the heart of Lyndall's suicidal self-erasure (*AF*, 259).[74]

Like female cross-dressing in other New Woman texts,[75] Rose's male trans-vestism offers no ultimate solution to the problems and pressures the woman protagonist has to contend with, although it does address, and transform, the nature of sexual relations. Unlike male cross-dressing in earlier women's writing, notably Charlotte Brontë's, the male crossing of gender boundaries no longer reaffirms, but serves to challenge and destabilise gender roles and hierarchies. Rochester's masquerade as a gypsy in *Jane Eyre* (1847) and the Comte de Hamal's imposture as the ghost of a nun in *Villette* (1853) work to reinforce the sexual and social hegemonies imposed on the heroine. Rochester wants a woman over whom he already exerts economic power to hand over her emotional autonomy and thus come under his sexual control, too, by acknowledging her love for him; Hamal's cross-dressing, staged in order to meet his lover undetected, has the effect of turning Lucy Snowe into an hysteric, the stereotypically feminine, disempowered woman.

In contrast to these earlier texts, *African Farm* suggests that for a man to masquerade as a woman invests him with a new, more humane quality. In embracing womanhood, Gregory Rose becomes an individual – albeit an individual who acquiesces in his feminine submission. After Lyndall's death he returns to the farm to marry Em, in compliance with Lyndall's last wish, which (in ironical invocation of her ring of bondage) he carries in a bag around his neck. Em, the woman he previously abandoned in his pursuit of Lyndall, cannot be said to have many illusions left about romantic love: an anti-climactic resolution to this story of multiple transgressions in which resigned pragmatism is coupled with maturity of vision. Like Gregory, Em has started to develop away from her former self, her naïve and unthinking Old Woman-hood, and has become more of an individual. In sharp contrast to the two idealists of the story, Lyndall and Waldo, Em and Gregory have demonstrated their capacity for survival by proving resilient in the face of personal misfortune; both have grown in moral stature through suffering and self-sacrifice. Schreiner, who in her 'Preface' noted her resistance to the 'stage method' on the grounds that its dénouement left the reader with 'a sense of satisfaction ... and of completeness'[76] so evidently at odds with 'real' life, subverts any expectations of a conventional happy ending by associating narrative closure with the death of the hero/ine (Lyndall and Waldo), while releasing her non-heroic characters into an open-ended story which refuses to pander to romantic tastes. In this sense, then, *African Farm* offers a pro-grammatically different resolution to the conflict between self-sacrifice and self-liberation explored in Schreiner's allegorical writings. If in 'A Little African Story' the black girl dies a pointless death, and in 'Three Dreams in a Desert' the feminist's death ensures a better life for (white) women (and men) in the future, *African Farm* sees a Boer woman and an Englishman achieve a measure of wisdom, albeit at the cost of their dreams.

Dreams, in *African Farm*, are intricately bound up not in the utopian vision of wider social regeneration, but in the desire for self-realisation through – or despite – motherhood. The impulse towards the experience of biological or metaphorical motherhood is central to the development, and failure, of the four characters in the text. The thought of motherhood transfigures Em as much as it paralyses Lyndall, while the men's espousal of symbolical forms of motherhood after a brief spell of epiphany invariably leads to mortification and the loss of the 'child': Lyndall dies; Waldo's 'first-born' (*AF*, 90), his sheep-shearing machine, is crushed by Bonaparte Blenkins, and his sculpture has an uncertain future with the Stranger. Of the four, those who attempt to 'mother' art fail most spectacularly. Waldo (both of whose creative offspring have a gestation period of nine months; *AF*, 91, 140) is consumed by his labour to the point of wasting away to an empty shell after delivery, and Lyndall, who aspires to become an actress 'bending men and things most unlikely to her purpose' (*AF*, 199), is trapped in her body and in a symbolic reversal of the birth process surrenders to the condition of a helpless infant. Like Caird, Schreiner encodes the troubled relationship between maternity and creativity in a heroine who fails both as a mother and as an artist.

None of the three writers discussed in this study create successful female artist figures who are also mothers. Ideala writes her poems only after the death of her child – Evadne cannot even bring herself to read after the birth of her children, and the only written text she produces is a suicide note; Angelica and Beth are artists but never become mothers, and Rebekah, who does, is inhibited in her creative output by her maternal and marital responsibilities; so is Hadria in Caird's *Daughters of Danaus*, while the two successful female artists in *One That Wins* are childless. Only in dreams and in allegory, such as 'The Child's Day' (the 'Prelude' to *From Man to Man*), can Schreiner conjure up the vision of a woman who is both a nurturing mother *and* a productive artist.

'Men's bodies are our woman's work of art':[77] art and the virile birth metaphor in *From Man to Man* (posth. 1926)

In 'The Child's Day' 5-year-old Rebekah responds to the shock of discovering her still-born baby sister – whom at first she assumes to be asleep – by turning her into the subject of an elaborate fairytale. The child's creative impulse to 'make up stories … she was always making stories' (*FMTM*, 44–5) is thus directed specifically at another girl, an imaginary daughter, in relation to whom she can define herself through the doubly creative and proactive subject positions of 'mother' and 'writer'. Falling asleep under a pear tree while reading her primer, Rebekah dreams of living on an island of her own, where on a bush overhanging the river she finds a long pod which, when cracked open, reveals a baby inside (*FMTM*, 46–7), whom after feeding and dressing she tells instructive stories about the world. Not only does reading act as a source of inspiration to Rebekah's dream of motherhood, books also play a central role within her story. Prior to her 'picking' her baby, Rebekah surveys her little kingdom and her house, the focal point of which is a 'room ... covered with books from the floor to the ceiling, with a little empty shelf for her own books ... and ... a microscope on the table' (*FMTM*, 46), an Alice-through-the-looking-glass version of the adult Rebekah's study both in her parental and her later marital homes (in each case her study will contain books, her own writings, a microscope and scientific memorabilia in the form of collections of insects and fossils). The empty shelf that the child Rebekah intends for her own published works, and even the entire room, fills out with the advent of motherhood: 'I am a person that makes stories! I write *books!*' she announces to her daughter, 'When I was little I used to scribble them in a copybook with a stick ... But when I grew up I learnt to write; – I wrote real books, a whole room full! I've written a book about birds, and about animals, and about the world; and one day I'm going to write a book something like the Bible' (*FMTM*, 53). The layered fairytale she invents for the didactic entertainment of her daughter serves as a further illustration of the perfect equilibrium that exists, in nature, between maternal and creative genius. When the little girl goes for a walk in the bush (so Rebekah's neo-Blakeian[78] tale goes), a beautiful bird shows her a blue egg from which, at the end of the story, a little bird will be hedged; a friendly tiger invites her to play with her cubs, after which an adder introduces her to her children, whom the girl promises to supply with milk, just as she previously fed cakes to a group of sociable monkeys and an amiable lion, and (in marked modification of the Old Testament paradigm) sang a male Cobra to sleep in her lap. Nurturing and storytelling are thus closely aligned; intensely personal, both are also eminently social activities, directed outwards to bridge the gap between self and other.

Emblematic of the happy marriage of artist and mother identities that an exemplary woman might achieve and as such an allegory of the 'ideal' woman artist of Schreiner's imagination, the 'Prelude' also, Schreiner claimed, represents 'a picture in small, a kind of allegory, of the life of the woman in the book'.[79] Just as Rebekah 'adopts' as her own child her dead sister, so she will devote herself to the surviving twin, Bertie, and at a later stage will parent Sartje, the mixed-race girl rejected by all. Similarly, the didactic stories she tells her fictive daughter will find their equivalent in her narrative instruction of her sons. However, as Tess Cosslett argues, the remainder of the novel starkly foregrounds the 'failure of female connectedness'[80] through the structural division of the sisters' stories into separate chapters, highlighting their inability to sustain the intimacy and communication established in childhood (the 'Prelude' closes with a vista of the older sister clasping the younger to her in deep sleep). Unlike Rebekah the girl dreamer, the adult woman will not be able to protect 'her' baby ('Baby'-Bertie) from the predatory impulses of the outside world, nor will the responsibilities of motherhood bear such easy congruence with the spatial and temporal needs of the artist.

A miniature picture of Schreiner's creative aspirations, 'The Child's Day' gives expression to Rebekah's desire to forge a work of quasi-scriptural eminence, 'something like the Bible' (an allusion to Schreiner's neo-biblical allegories; or to *Woman and Labour,* according to Brittain the 'Bible of the Women's Movement'; or even a reference to *From Man to Man* itself, in its dual configuration as 'both a new pseudo-Darwinian *Origins* and a new pseudo-Biblical "Genesis"'?).[81] Like 'Three Dreams', however, the young Rebekah's story reflects the instabilities of a universalist, 'sacred' vision communicated through ethnically exclusive paradigms. The central message of her fairytale – that an indissoluble concord exists between human, animal and natural worlds – is coincidental with the assertion of racial hegemony, reinforcing beliefs in the superiority of one 'world', or section of it, over another. Thus Rebekah envisages herself as 'the little Queen Victoria of South Africa' (*FMTM*, 45), imagining an encounter with the 'real' Queen Victoria who confers to her imperial rights over the island and its indigenous population. And even though, as Sally Ledger points out, the natural outdoor setting in which Rebekah imagines the 'birth' of her baby contrasts sharply with the closeted nature of her mother's delivery, thus pointing towards an identi-fication with '"black" childbirth and motherhood',[82] the racial markers of the 'pink' baby herself are unequivocal: emerging from a 'snow-white' pod hanging from a 'large white bush', she is instantly wrapped in a 'soft white shawl' (*FMTM*, 45–7). 'They are good angels, though they are black in the middle' (*FMTM*, 48), Rebekah reassures the infant, referring to a momentary trick of the eye. While she enjoys inventing an imaginary (white) play-fellow, Charles, 'live' boys, Rebekah states emphatically, are not to her liking because 'they are something like Kaffirs' (*FMTM*, 56). What Laura Chrisman calls Rebekah's 'missionary maternity'[83] is also reflected in the heroic tales of English martyrdom she has picked up from books, which position her dream of an Edenic fellowship of all creatures firmly within colonial parameters. 'What Hester Durham Lived For' (a narrative about an Englishwoman who, after losing her son, finds her life's purpose in India comforting fellow-missionaries during a Sepoy uprising in which they all lose their lives; *FMTM*, 53–4) extols the imperial female missionary as a Christian martyr, while Rebekah's enthusiastic account of Boadicea offers a counter-perspective ('The Romans were people who took other peoples' countries … I'm glad they burnt [Rome], aren't you?'; *FMTM*, 54–5) only to reaffirm the previous story's point about the sublimity of English femininity: 'she got into a chariot and her two daughters and her long hair flying in the wind' (*FMTM*, 54). The 'spasm of delight' (*FMTM*, 58) induced by the contiguity of creative and maternal faculties is thus intensified by the thrill of imperial martyrdom. As in 'Three

Dreams', the white woman pioneer's self-sacrifice for the sake of an impersonal, wider objective beyond her individual life-span elicits the greatest praise. The conflicted triad between creativity, motherhood and martyrdom, outlined and idealised in 'The Child's Day', is central to the adult Rebekah's failure as an artist.

If Grand used her artist-novel *The Beth Book* to articulate her views on purposeful (women's) as opposed to decadent (men's) art, *From Man to Man*, the novel of a failed artist, enabled Schreiner to conceptualise and allegorise her artistic vision. Both texts juxtapose a female and a male artist, but while Grand has the feminist triumph over the decadent writer, Schreiner brings a male and female writer together to highlight the reasons for the woman's failure. As the central metaphor of the 'virile' birthing processes of art implies, even from Rebekah's (and Schreiner's) perspective art is quintessentially a man's business, the equivalent to female reproduction and mothering.

The last chapter of the book, 'The Veranda', develops these ideas in the course of a long conversation between Rebekah and Mr Drummond (the estranged husband of her neighbour, Mrs Drummond, one of her own husband's ex-lovers). Rebekah and Drummond agree that, although the artist can create the conditions which are favourable to spark off an artistic impulse, for example by relaxing 'his' mental energies and turning them towards dreaming, and even by 'walk[ing] up and down' (as Schreiner did while telling stories to herself),[84] the artistic vision itself cannot be called up at will (*FMTM*, 468). In a 'sudden flash', a vision 'leaps out' of the artist's dreams, without 'him' knowing where it has come from (*FMTM*, 469–71). The notion of quasi-divine 'inspiration' sending a vision which is then consciously transcribed into art – a concept pointing back to Shelley's *Defence of Poetry* (1840) and at odds with the contemporary decadent ethic, especially Oscar Wilde's axiom of the exquisitely 'self-conscious and deliberate' artist[85] – was, Schreiner claimed, borne out by her own experience of conceiving the 'Prelude': it had, she wrote to Mrs Francis Smith in October 1909, '*flashed* on me … I hadn't thought of my novel for months, I hadn't looked at it for years. I'd never dreamed of writing a Prelude to it. – I just sat down and wrote it out' (*LOS*, 291).[86]

Only at the second stage, Rebekah (Schreiner's avatar of the woman writer) continues, that of transcribing 'his' vision into an 'external image' – the work-of-art-to-be – does the artist's consciousness come into play; but even now, the vision inside 'him' urges 'him' on: 'it is almost like the necessity of a woman to give birth to her child when the full time has come' (*FMTM*, 472–3). The third and last phase, that of 'the giving of art to the world', is the only one determined by the artist's free will. Now that the work is 'severed from him, the cord is cut … The child is weaned' (*FMTM*, 473), 'he' can do whatever 'he' wants with it. But for whatever reason the artist decides to publish, 'his' work was originally created by 'inborn necessity' (*FMTM*, 470), and thus not with the conscious thought of a public.

This is a surprising statement, coming as it does from a writer who had such a definitive sense of a mission, and whose works were always written with the thought of a particular audience in mind: 'it is to ... the great British public ... that my little book is addressed', she wrote about *Trooper Peter Halket of Mashonaland*. 'It is for them and not at all for the South African public (who would not understand it).'[87] *African Farm*, she said, was meant for 'working men', and *Dreams* was targeted at 'all Capitalists, Millionaires and Middlemen in England and America and all high and mighty persons'.[88]

Even more striking than her disavowal of any prior political purpose in her writing is the particular metaphor she uses to describe the creative act as a form of 'virile birth'. Her use of the birth metaphor is, in itself, not unusual, echoing as it does familiar male and female metaphors across the centuries.[89] Schreiner's fellow-writer George Moore also referred to the writing process as 'this terrible child-bearing': 'The artist, like the mother,' he wrote in *A Modern Lover* (1883), 'has to undergo the throes and labour of child-bearing, long months of solitude and suffering; whilst the amateur, like the father, unweighed by a struggling infant in the womb, is free to explain and criticise at ease' (*AML*, 157, 68). Nor does Schreiner's linguistic choice of the generic male form conflict with common usage of the time. Caird, too, conceptualised the artist as a man,[90] and almost a century later, at the onset of second-wave feminism, Susan Sontag still made reference to the artist in his male configuration.[91] What *is* extraordinary, however, is the curious aporia Schreiner forges between generically male language and generically female procreativity. Herself a woman artist and speaking from the vantage point of a female artist figure, she consistently employs a male pronoun to position the creative process in relation to conception, pregnancy, labour, childbirth and parturition, celebrating the artist as a 'virile' mother (*FMTM*, 469) in a manner evocative of her portrayal of the feminist as the vigorously masculine 'Teutonic' woman in *Woman and Labour*.

As Susan Stanford Friedman has suggested, male birth metaphors (meaning birth metaphors employed by male writers) reinscribe the patriarchal division of separate spheres by reinforcing the binary opposition between (male) creativity and (female) procreativity. By contrast, female birth metaphors subvert this dichotomy by establishing a 'symbolic reunion of mind and body', authorship and motherhood, thereby conferring authority on the woman artist.[92] However, the fact that Rebekah, who is both a mother and 'mothers' texts, uses a male metaphor, in other words, a conceptual framework that excludes her from this discourse even as she is engaged in shaping it, serves to foreground rather than resolve the tension she herself experiences between the conflicting roles of mother and artist. Not surprisingly, then, Schreiner's one successful artist – one who has not only given birth to his brain child but has also delivered it to the world – is a man, and a very active, adventurous one who has mastered the outer world, whereas the visions of her woman artist remain locked away in her study.

While in *The Beth Book* the protagonist's 'room of her own' provides a crucial space for self-creation and therefore leads to her 'birth' as an artist, the study to which Rebekah lays claim inside her husband's house is the site of radical ambivalence caused by the collision between her writer and woman selves, a conflict never successfully resolved. Rebekah's room differs from Beth's chamber in that she does not rediscover a female tradition[93] but, rather, tries to assure herself of the unbroken continuity of a life constantly disrupted by household tasks. Her study is a mirror-image of her own development: shelves of school books and cabinets full of insects and fossils collected since childhood, scientific and philosophical works, volumes on poetry, history and travel, her own literary and philosophical studies, and her diaries combine to form a rich personal atmosphere from which her husband is pointedly excluded.

The fact that Rebekah has five children where Beth has none introduces an important variation to the theme of private space and artistic voice.[94] Beth keeps her room secret from everybody; Rebekah poignantly incorporates her children in hers. They have direct access to it through their bedroom, of which it forms an extension; they know where she keeps the key and invite in a visitor in her absence. Both Beth and Rebekah perform traditional female tasks before assuming the persona of the writer, but while Beth's embroidery underscores her financial autonomy and at the same time enables Grand to valorise feminine art production, Rebekah carries out the unpaid work of the home-maker, sewing buttons on her children's clothes. Her love for her children puts limits to the independence she can achieve. This conflict between freedom and constraint is also reflected in the size, location and general outlook of her study, for whereas the window and an outside door allow her a view of, and access to, the garden – a view, however, circumscribed by rocks and a hedge – the claustrophobic interior and the circular footpath on her rug point to her sense of confinement, literal and figurative (the 'confinement' of the artist unable to progress to parturition). The mark on the floor – 'like a footpath where the nap had been worn off, running right round the desk' (*FMTM*, 175) – is chillingly suggestive of the mark against which, in Gilman's 'The Yellow Wallpaper', the unnamed narrator presses her body when under the onslaught of her psychotic condition she creeps around her nursery-prison:

> There is a very funny mark on this wall, low down, near the mopboard. A streak that runs round the room. It goes behind every piece of furniture, except the bed, a long, straight, even *smooch*, as if it had been rubbed over and over …
>
> But … I can creep smoothly on the floor, and my shoulder just fits in that long smooch around the wall, so I cannot lose my way. ('YW', 29, 35)

Significantly, Gilman's mad narrator's mark starts and ends at the side of her bed, the site of her marital and reproductive functions and the root cause of her insanity, while Rebekah's mark encircles the desk, the centre of her intellectual and artistic self-development. If Rebekah does not go mad, as Gilman's character does, then it is because her room remains a place of independent thought and literary production, albeit conducted intermittently. Even more importantly, Rebekah has a second home, a small farm acquired with money her father settled on her at her wedding (*FMTM*, 282). At a time when the disintegration of her marriage is undermining her health, confidence and belief in herself and life, she narrowly escapes a breakdown by buying and temporarily moving to this house. Later she employs two people to grow and sell cabbages on the land. Her 'hold on freedom and life' (*FMTM*, 182), this alternative home also provides a source of independent income and is one of the reasons perhaps why Rebekah, unlike Beth, feels little inner pressure to depart from the marital home.

Rebekah's failure to leave, however, has considerable repercussions on her intellectual life and therefore her creativity. Her room constitutes what Gillian Rose calls a 'paradoxical space', that is, a space which simultaneously positions women as prisoners and as exiles.[95] If she were deprived of this crucial space, she would be even more circumscribed than she already is by her role as wife and mother; but by withdrawing into her study, she exiles herself from the possibility of finding congenial companionship outside her husband's domain. Although she fantasises about being 'one of a company of men and women in a room together, all sharing ... the same outlook on life and therefore thinking ... the same thought', 'all the intellectual intercourse' she enjoys in real life are her books and, significantly, perhaps disconcertingly so, fossils and dead reptiles (*FMTM*, 174–5).

Indeed, much in Rebekah's room suggests that marriage and motherhood have taken a heavy toll of her creative energy. The notebooks which she keeps locked away in her desk and occasionally rereads – an image of creativity confined, curtailed, almost coffined as in *Undine* (1926)[96] – chart her intellectual and artistic development from childhood to adulthood, and record ample activity until that fatal turning-point in her life, marriage. While the child had produced verses, short stories, allegories, and even a novel, and the girl and young woman had worked on philosophy, kept a daily journal and entertained expansive plans 'for the life that was to be lived – countries to be visited – books to be written – scientific knowledge to be gained', the wife and mother seems to be permanently out of breath: 'there were only short scraps: outlines of stories never to be filled in ... short diary notes of a very practical nature ... [and] short notices ... in which dashes and letters took the place of words' (*FMTM*, 176). The repetition of the word 'short', in conjunction with the 'dashes and letters' which in Rebekah's diary have replaced longhand and the grammatically complete sentences that were previously required for the composition of novels, highlights the briefness and fragmented nature of her adult writing, as well as the speed with which it has to be accomplished. Under these circumstances it is hardly surprising that she seems to harbour doubts about her capacity as a 'real' artist. Her writing, to which, not unlike Schreiner herself, she invariably refers as 'scribbl[ing]' (*FMTM*, 182–6), is meant to soothe her inquisitive, always excitable mind rather than imprint her mark on the world. She does not write with an eye to publication, and her one attempt of reaching out to a private reader is futile: a long letter feverishly written to her philandering husband throughout the night is never even glanced at by him. The other project of considerable length that Rebekah undertakes, a philosophical study, is subject to constant interruptions prompted by her domestic and maternal responsibilities. In Rebekah's creative life rupture comes perilously close to determining structure. Schreiner's text systematically draws attention to the fact that, because of her household tasks, Rebekah's thoughts cannot follow a logical, linear sequence, but are forever marked by new beginnings:

> Here she had to go and make a poultice, and she had branched off on a side line when she came back. (*FMTM*, 177)

> Here she had been interrupted again. When she came back she had gone on to [consider the other side of the argument]. (178)

> Here she had had to leave off the first night. When she began the next night she went on to discuss [a new point]. (182)

> So far she had scribbled four weeks before, when she was sitting up to make poultices. Since then she had not thought of her discussion. (182–3)

Emblemised in the picture (a reproduction of Raphael's 'Madonna della Sedia'; *FMTM*, 90, 174) that connects her study with her children's bedroom, thus 'framing' her literary production, Rebekah's motherhood is so intricately bound up with her writing that it both sparks off her creative impulses and at other times interrupts them. An excursion with her children undertaken in the morning sets her mind wandering and makes her resume her writing in the evening, but the thought that her baby might be awake changes her back again from writer to mother, from the pen-wielding artist to the lady with the lamp: 'She threw the pen down on the table and took up the lamp, went into the next room and bent over his cot' (*FMTM*, 192).

Schreiner's novel brings to the fore the problems the artist faces when her creative space is colonised by a woman's marital and maternal 'duties'. A temporary, illusory escape from the confines of a marriage she never completely leaves behind, her study is refuge and prison-house in one. Ultimately, Rebekah remains stuck in it, so much so that Schreiner felt unable to complete the novel and left her protagonist forever suspended between her husband, the prospect of a lover and the option of single motherhood. Mothering, Carolyn Burdett has argued, is central to Schreiner's novel and serves as 'a means to express the values of patient creativity'.[97] In Schreiner's application of the 'virile birth' metaphor, however, the artist/mother paradigm worked in one direction only: the artist was like a mother, but a real-life mother could not be an artist. 'What has humanity not lost,' Rebekah muses in the course of one of her writing spells, 'what of the possible Shakespeares we might have had ... stifled out without one line written, simply because ... life gave no room for action and grasp on life?' (*FMTM*, 219). In that she herself comes to represent a Shakespearean promise unfulfilled, Rebekah's life neutralises the optimistic message of 'The Child's Day', illustrating as it does the incompatibility of writer and mother identities once the child has turned woman. Three pages from the end Rebekah admits to being haunted by the ghosts of her 'aborted' creativity:

> And then, when [the artist] is dying, they gather round him, the things he might have incarnated and given life to – and would not. All that might have lived, and now must never live for ever, look at him with their large reproachful eyes – his own dead visions reproaching him; as the children a woman has aborted and refused to give life to might gather about her at last, saying, 'We came to you; you, only you, could have given us life. Now we are dead for ever. Was it worth it? All the sense of duty you satisfied, the sense of necessity you laboured under: should you not have violated it and given us birth?' It has come upon me so vividly sometimes ... that I have almost leaped out of bed to gain air – that suffocating sense that all his life long a man or a woman might live striving to do their duty and then at the end find it all wrong. (*FMTM*, 478)

A vivid tableau of artistic failure, this vision contrasts sharply with Schreiner's allegory of creative consummation in 'The Artist's Secret' (1890, *D*, 117–21), where the artist dies having painted his greatest masterpiece with the blood drawn from his heart. The sacrifice that brings about the transfiguration, even transubstantiation, of the artist in *Dreams* (turning blood into paint and the artist's body into a work of unparalleled art) has no equivalent in *From Man to Man*. In her realist novels Schreiner eschewed the utopian or ideal solutions posited in her allegories,[98] resisting also and specifically the subversive romanticism of Sarah Grand's all-in-one dénouement of *The Beth Book* (reflected in the heroine's artistic, activist and emotional fulfilment with a New Man who is pointedly not her husband). In contradistinction to the allegories and even *African Farm*, Rebekah's ethic of self-renunciation (when in doubt, she 'would always choose' the path of 'most pain or least pleasure' to herself; *FMTM*, 479) serves no beneficiary and lacks a definitive objective: there is no prospect of creative completion as in 'The Artist's Secret', of human transcendence as in 'The Hunter', of women's liberation as in 'Three Dreams', of Christian martyrdom as in 'Dream Life and Real Life', or even of 'love-as-service'[99] as in *African Farm*. In the absence of any specific purpose, Rebekah's unshaken faith in the moral imperative of self-sacrifice appears pointless, her unquestioned submission to duty as resigned to patriarchal authority as in the 'The Gardens of Pleasure' (another of Schreiner's *Dreams* in which a woman is evicted from a beautiful garden by stern and relentless, significantly male-gendered Duty, and forced to relinquish even the flower she has hidden on her body). Small wonder if such a manifestation of unalleviated 'gloom, ... high ideals, [and]... self-sacrifice' proved 'an inspiration, a challenge, but also something of a burden' to aspiring feminists of the next generation; that Schreiner's books made for painful reading even her close friend Edward Carpenter was compelled to admit.[100] The impasse forged in a text about a feminist with no purpose overdetermines its abrupt termination. The final pages of Schreiner's last and most notable novel thus call into question the key concept of her overall *oeuvre*, suggesting that self-sacrifice might not be the solution to the woman question, after all; that it might barricade rather than build bridges: the bridge between New Woman and New Man; between the dreamer (writer) and her creative offspring; between Heaven (creative epiphany) and Hell (a life's energies spent on the pursuit of minor duties). The indictment of self-sacrifice tentatively mooted at the end of *From Man to Man* found its fullest, most passionate expression in Mona Caird's work.

Part III

Mythologies:
Mona Caird

(1854–1932)

5

Re-visioning myths: *The Morality of Marriage* (1897), *The Pathway of the Gods* (1898) and *The Stones of Sacrifice* (1915)

Re-vision – the act of looking back, of seeing with fresh eyes, of entering an old text from a new critical direction – is for us more than a chapter in cultural history: it is an act of survival. Until we can understand the assumptions in which we are drenched we cannot know ourselves. And this drive to self-knowledge, for woman, is more than a search for identity: it is part of her refusal of the self-destructiveness of male-dominated society. A radical critique of literature, feminist in its impulse, would take the work first of all as a clue to how we live, how we have been living, how our language has trapped as well as liberated us; and how we can begin to see – and therefore live – afresh. (Adrienne Rich, 'When We Dead Awaken: Writing as Re-Vision', 1971)[1]

[Myth] is history that is not over … The myth transmits itself making changes in accordance with historical and cultural evolution … If women begin to want their turn at telling this history, if they take the relay from men by putting myths into words (since that is how historical and cultural evolution will take place), even if it means rereading the most 'feminine' of them … it will necessarily be from other points of view. It will be a history read differently … (Catherine Clément, 'Sorceress and Hysteric', 1975/1986)[2]

I do not share your admiration for the woman who is 'sacrificial' … I do not agree with you in thinking that women have to prove themselves heroines and devotees of duty before they have a right to claim the fullest opportunity for development and life. They claim this right as human beings … Again you say 'take woman as she is meant to be': I deny that she is 'meant to be' anything in particular. She is as she makes herself, as the forces and conditions of life make her. The 'inspiration of humanity' she may still be, and in my opinion is much more likely to be, when she ceases to be afraid, ceases to worship morals, ceases to see the 'divine' only where she has been hitherto taught to see it in submission, sacrifice, 'duty' (so-called) and general self-destruction. (Mona Caird in a letter to Lady Wilde, 1889)[3]

'*Resistance is the secret of joy*': the central message of Alice Walker's troubling 1992 novel on women's psycho-sexual mutilation through internalisation of foundation myths (*PSJ*, 264, emphasis in original) was articulated a century earlier by Mona Caird. Rejecting other feminists' celebration of the 'ideal' feminist as one who saw her duty in acting as an 'inspiration to humanity' by embracing a self-sacrificial attitude (as illustrated, for example, in *Ideala*), Caird asserted, not only that women had every right to 'claim the fullest opportunity for development', but also that self-denial amounted to no less than self-destruction and was certain to inflict incalculable harm on the collectivity as it generated and fuelled an endless cycle of oppression sustained from one generation to the next. No free and egalitarian society could be built over the bodies of individuals, as Schreiner suggested so momentously in 'Three Dreams in a Desert'.

Notorious at the *fin de siècle* for her unorthodox views on sexual relations and the patriarchal family, Caird stimulated widespread discussion of such controversial subjects as coercive marital sex, contraception, unwanted pregnancy, single motherhood, wages for housework, public childcare and free love. With her shrewd insights into the social construction of marriage and motherhood and the politics of mother–daughter relations, she directly prefigured aspects of modern second-wave feminism.[4] What makes her case so remarkable is that, at a time when feminists like Grand and Schreiner invoked women's 'innate' maternal qualities as evidence of their moral superiority, Caird forged a critique of motherhood as an oppressive patriarchal institution. Where Schreiner looked to socialism and a (feminised) 'Christian' as opposed to social Darwinist version of evolutionary philosophy[5] as a means of re-defining the power imbalance between the sexes, and Grand appropriated eugenic ideas to validate the feminist call for a new sexual and societal morality, Caird exposed the patriarchal roots of all authoritative discourses, urging on her readers the recognition of the dangers inherent in imbuing the old mythologies of male-governed society with the new female-directed demands of the age. Her journalistic and narrative work reflects what Adrienne Rich, in 1971, conceptualised as the feminist project of 're-vision'. Caird 're-visioned' the law, language and literature of the 'fathers' in multiple and intersecting ways: historically, by tracing the emergence and impact of patriarchy on the condition of women in the family and society; discursively, by challenging dominant scientific taxonomies and models of interpretation; and intertextually, by rewriting Classical and modern myth in order to dismantle the foundation stories which defined women as objects of exchange (*The Morality of Marriage*), willing martyrs (*The Pathway of the Gods*) and bodies for slaughter (*The Stones of Sacrifice*), and which served to dampen insurgent spirits by hyperbolising the ghastly punishment meted out to the revolting daughter (*The Daughters of Danaus*).

For all three writers discussed in this study, reviving the past meant to establish an historical dimension to women's grievances, and thus to accomplish what Rich calls 'an act of [collective, feminist] survival'. In Grand this was underpinned by autobiographical experience, which assumed a prototypical character in her fictional work, with her own story reflecting and representing *her*story. In concentrating on women's most recent history (the Contagious Diseases Acts), she evoked a sense of injustice shared across different generations of readers. Caird's and Schreiner's writings sought to retrace the origins of patriarchy, interpolating visions of the ancient past with the depiction of contemporary social and sexual relations. The panoramic overview of centuries of female subjection was calculated to make readers aware of the continuity of oppression, reinforcing the message that it was not enough to address existing shortcomings in the system, but that a much more far-reaching overhaul of social and ideological structures was required. In Schreiner's work this programmatic rescription took the dual form of utopian allegory (*Dreams*) and anthropological-historical polemic (*Woman and Labour*); Caird's emphasis was on the feminist analysis of history, with the objective to examine the power of and then destabilise patriarchal discourse's all-too-close alliance with Classical mythology. As Catherine Clément argues in *The Newly Born Woman*, female/feminist revisions of mythological narratives do 'not [in themselves] compose a *true* history. To be that, it would have to pass through all the registers of the social structure, through its economic evolution, through analysis of the contradictions that have made and are making its history.'[6] Seeking to uncover the hidden history of women's 'true' sentiments, Caird anatomised the ideological and economic structure, evolution, and the inherent paradoxes within the institutions of marriage and motherhood.

Like Grand and Schreiner, Caird utilised the politicising potential of periodical literature to considerable effect. In her direct, explicit and unapologetic radicalism she differed from Grand, though not from Schreiner. Not for her the discursive contortions which Grand was inclined to suffer, journalistically at least, in her endeavour to appeal also to the more unenlightened of her middle-class readers. Caird's friend Elizabeth Sharp recorded that, 'disturbed and shocked by her plain statements', many of her contemporaries responded to her articles 'with acute hostility'.[7] Even the liberal journalist W. T. Stead, a staunch supporter of the more maternal version of the New Woman, felt called upon to protest that Caird was going 'far beyond the bounds of moderation' – after all, was motherhood 'not divine'?[8] The unequivocally strong language Caird used to attack the cliché of what Schreiner glorified as 'that crowning beatitude of the woman's existence' (*W&L*, 127) was bound to antagonise her Victorian readership: 'A woman with a child in her arms is, to me, the symbol of an abasement, an indignity, more complete, more disfiguring and terrible, than any form of humiliation that the world has ever seen', she wrote in *The Daughters of Danaus*, dismissing maternal 'instincts' as little more than 'acquired tricks' (*DD*, 341, 23). In *The Stones of Sacrifice* (1915) she derided the notion that every woman fulfilled her heart's desire of

'[s]omething helpless to love and tend' by means of 'the somewhat severe
condition of producing the helpless something out of one's own agonized
flesh and blood' (*SOS*, 76). She had a fierce delight in exploding the
euphemistic apologia of violence in the conventional conflation of woman
and Nature and compared institutionalised motherhood with rape: 'Nature in
her most maternal and uninspiring mood – Mother Earth submissive to the
dictatorship of man, permitting herself to be torn, and wounded, and
furrowed, and harrowed at his pleasure, yielding her substance and her life to
sustain the produce of his choosing, her body and her soul abandoned to his
caprice' (*DD*, 173). The shock content of Caird's association of motherhood
with mutilation might be compared to radical feminist Shulamith Firestone's
analogies in our own time between the pain of childbirth and the act of
'shitting a pumpkin'.[9] To both, motherhood was essentially oppressive,
biologically as much as culturally, and both protested the need for women to
seize control of the means of reproduction: by replacing male-imposed
(biological) motherhood with adoption (*The Daughters of Danaus*) or with
artificial means of reproduction (Firestone).[10]

By exposing the interrelationship between female 'honour' and men's
appropriation of the female body, Caird implicitly positioned Grand's celebration of female purity at the very centre of patriarchal ideology. Women
were compelled to possess virtue not for their own benefit, but so that men
could assume ownership of their bodies and their bodies' products. Deeply
indignant about the sexual double standard, Grand and other social purity
feminists demanded a levelling-up of male morals partly because they believed
that, ideally, women should be able to look up to and be guided by men. This
idea was dismissed by Schreiner and Caird, who stressed women's economic
and sexual independence as the precondition of any partnership with men.
However, whereas Schreiner espoused the concepts of self-sacrifice and the
'natural' instinct for motherhood, Caird saw them as deliberate stratagems
employed to keep women safely imprisoned within the narrow boundaries of
their sphere:

> Throughout history … children had been the unfailing means of bringing
> women into line with tradition. Who could stand against them? … An appeal to
> the maternal instinct had quenched the hardiest spirit of revolt. No wonder the
> instinct had been so trumpeted and exalted! Women might harbour dreams and
> plan insurrections; but their children – little ambassadors of the established and
> expected – were argument enough to convince the most hardened sceptics. Their
> helplessness was more powerful to suppress revolt than regiments of armed
> soldiers. (*DD*, 187)

In other words, women did not have children because they identified themselves primarily and exclusively as mothers – some might wish to be mothers

and many other things besides, and others might not want to be mothers at all. Rather, children and motherhood were imposed on women so that they could not define themselves in any other way. Once they were mothers, their love and sense of responsibility for their children combined with social expectations to stop them from protesting against the position of women, which, they could now be told, was a simple matter of biology, not of social and political conditions. Unable to realise their desire for personal development, and driven to sacrifice the most vital part of their identities for the sake of their children, women would unconsciously seek revenge by exacting self-sacrifice from the next generation of women, who would in turn instil this principle in their own female children, thus perpetuating the cycle of internalised oppression handed down from mother to daughter. In deromanticising motherhood as 'the means and method of a woman's bondage' (*DD*, 341), Caird has, as I have argued elsewhere, more in common with modern radical feminists like Adrienne Rich than with her feminist contemporaries.[11]

Not surprisingly, perhaps, Caird was felt to pose a challenge even to an advanced audience. According to Judith Walkowitz, Karl Pearson's Men and Women's Club regarded her as too much of a loose cannon to grant her full membership.[12] Caird attended a meeting on birth control in 1887, and remained loosely associated with the club, but as Lucy Bland notes, she was never formally invited to join.[13] Although evidently not prepared to accommodate her explosive views within their organisation, individual members had no qualms about crediting the club and its leader – hardly a model feminist – with her public success: the marriage debate in the *Daily Telegraph*, Maria Sharpe wrote in deference to her later husband, 'seemed in a way connected with our Club because Mrs. Caird's first article was so evidently founded on Mr. Pearson's first woman articles'.[14] Even Schreiner, who later corresponded with Caird on the debates conducted in the club,[15] initially considered her 'violently prejudiced against men',[16] though on closer acquaintance she adjusted her views, affirming that it gave her great 'hope to hear such free brave words from a woman'.[17]

Dubbed a 'priestess of revolt'[18] by Stead's *Review of Reviews*, Caird was held up as a 'pioneer of humanity'[19] by Margaret Shurmer Sibthorp's women's rights magazine *Shafts*. The journal's enthusiastic response to *The Daughters of Danaus* and *The Morality of Marriage* as 'the best books of the century'[20] resembles the impact *Woman and Labour* had on Vera Brittain's generation of feminists.[21] More moderate advocates of the New Woman, such as the trade unionist, suffragist and novelist Clementina Black and the critic Elizabeth Rachel Chapman, criticised Caird for alienating her readership,[22] expressing concern about the disrepute into which her articles brought the women's movement by aligning it with sexual licentiousness: her views, the *Review of Reviews* concurred, 'will be widely used as a kind of literary whitewash for adultery'.[23] Yet, as Elizabeth Sharp and Charlotte Perkins Gilman (who met Caird in the course of her British lecture tour in 1899) argued, the controversial nature of Caird's message was instrumental to prompting discussion of taboo subjects like adultery and compulsory motherhood, which ultimately had the effect of 'altering the attitude of the public mind in its approach to, and examination of, such questions'.[24]

Caird and Grand reflect opposite poles on the discursive spectrum of New Woman strategies. Both sought to further the public acceptance of feminism through socialising their readership(s) into New Woman thought, yet one operated on the principle of feminine subterfuge and seduction, while the other flaunted political shock tactics. Ernst Foerster, a contemporary German scholar, inferred that Caird deployed exaggeration strategically in order to provoke strong reactions in her readers.[25] She certainly appeared more consistent in her feminism than Grand. As members of the Pioneer Club Grand and Caird sometimes shared the same platform,[26] but there was little love lost between them. *Ideala* had been 'quoted against [her]', Caird wrote in 'Ideal Marriage' (1888), remarking with uncharacteristic understatement that 'the general drift' of the novel was not 'favourable to [her] view'.[27] Neither would Caird's uncompromising views on motherhood have endeared her to Grand who, in 'Marriage Questions in Fiction' (1898), asserted that '[t]he woman whose heart does not melt with tenderness merely at the thought of little arms stretched out to her in the first dumb recognition of her love should be spoken of compassionately, as one who is grievously afflicted, one who has been deprived of the greatest good in life'.[28] Caird's point, in 'The Morality of Marriage', that '[m]ore liberty would mean less licence' (*MOM*, 148) – an attitude George Moore mocked as 'morality without marriage'[29] – must have smacked of the 'customs of the poultry yard' to the advocate of self-restraint in both sexes.[30] Caird, on the other hand, expressed her horror of the 'deadly tyranny' of 'the highly moral person … The bravest of us flinch before Virtue on the war-path.'[31]

With all their political differences, Caird and Grand nonetheless shared some common ground. Caird's rhetorical preferences were for the straightforwardly iconoclastic, but like Grand she courted a distinctly feminine image. Thus on her 1888 visit to Britain Elizabeth Cady Stanton found her 'a very graceful, pleasing woman, so gentle in manner and appearance that no one would dream her capable of hurling such thunderbolts at the long-suffering Saxon people'.[32] A portrait painted in the 1880s appears to substantiate this impression of calm and self-possessed elegance (Figure 12). If Grand ventriloquised authoritative (scientific) discourses in order to subvert them for her conservative model of femininity, Caird, as Angelique Richardson points out, 'co-opted' the language of evolutionary biology with the aim to construct 'an alternative narrative' with which to undermine it.[33] Where Grand

12 Portrait painting of Mona Caird in young adulthood (mid- to late 1880s?)

advanced a collective feminist vision through the eyes of an exemplary individual (Ideala; Beth), Caird defended the rights of the individual with the narrative device of multiple perspectives (*The Stones of Sacrifice*). Both employed male points of view because they wanted to school women readers in what Judith Fetterley has called 'the process of exorcizing the male mind that has been implanted in us'.[34] Richardson has noted further analogies in their rhetorical use of medicinal metaphors: 'While Grand conceived of her fiction as having an allopathic effect on her readers, Caird conceived of hers as working on a homeopathic principle … cure through imitation.'[35] Politically opposed on the issue of eugenics, both took an active part in the anti-vivisection[36] and suffrage movements. A member of a number of feminist and suffragist organisations, Caird was loosely involved with the Women's Social and Political Union in 1907–8.[37] Grand, on the other hand, strongly disapproved of the militant methods of the WSPU and was, she told Gladys Singers-Bigger in 1931, 'not too pleased' to find herself mentioned in Sylvia Pankhurst's *The Suffragette Movement*, where she was listed as one of the 'notable people' heading the big WSPU procession on 21 June 1908.[38] Ironically, Pankhurst may have mixed Grand up with Caird, who, though attending the event (in fact she shared a cab with Mrs Pankhurst), did not receive a mention.[39] In her article on 'Militant Tactics and Woman's Suffrage', published the same year, Caird defended militancy, arguing that 'When women possess full human and civic rights, they may justly be called upon to confine themselves to constitutional measures, but since quiet appeals of 40 or 50 years' duration failed to obtain a hearing, it can hardly be said that constitutional measures of any efficacy are really open to them'.[40]

Like Schreiner's, Caird's feminism was embedded in a larger framework of human rights, to which Caird added a passionate commitment to animal rights. President of the Independent Anti-Vivisection League,[41] she published a number of tracts on the subject, and like Grand conceptually linked violence towards animals with women's oppression in her novels. An egalitarian and humanitarian with moderate social-democratic sympathies, she dismissed the idea of state socialism as beset with the peril of totalitarianism. While abhorring male violence against women and children and using her novels as a platform to draw attention to domestic violence, she nevertheless condemned populist calls for violent punishment.[42] After the Boer War, she expressed her hope that there was an end to 'warfare and stupid retaliation', so that 'a final … peace' would be possible.[43] A year before the outbreak of the First World War, she delivered the presidential address to the forty-first annual meeting of the Personal Rights Association, passionately upholding the rights of the individual against the new 'arithmetical morality' – the sacrifice of the few to the many.[44] After the war, she was one of those who warned against the dangers of jingoism and hostility to former enemy states, urging united international efforts to find ways of preventing the eternal regression to 'primitive brutality'. Contrasting nationalistic 'manliness' with the idea of 'a great international brotherhood, the Greater Community', she suggested an extensive programme of international cooperation and educational measures to tackle the problem of chauvinism and racial prejudice.[45]

Like Schreiner, Caird drew analogies between international relations and the condition of women in society. She provided an historical analysis of the emergence of the modern family and linked the subjection of women to other forms of oppression in society (organised cruelty to animals and 'lesser' humans in peacetime, organised brutality to all humans in war). Defining women's status in patriarchy as that of a subject-class, she compared the position of women with that of the working class, but was deeply suspicious of male-engendered visions of socialism. She held dysfunctional, male-identified mothering responsible for conditioning young women into a self-destructive mindset, and blamed marriage, with its imposition of non-consensual sex and expectation of female self-sacrifice, for the mental and physical maladies afflicting women in patriarchal society.

'A degrading bondage':[46] *The Morality of Marriage* (1897)

Male social-problem writers like Thomas Hardy also thematised the failures of marriage and the need for a radical overhaul of the institution. Others pointed to the success of the reformed legislation: in George Gissing's *New Grub Street* (1891) Amy Reardon is greatly relieved to find that the recent Married Women's Property Act safeguards her inheritance, which previously would have been transferred to her estranged husband (*NGS*, 323). In contrast, feminists tended to foreground issues of sexual exploitation and violence in order to suggest, not only that the existing legislation did not go far enough, but that it had not even begun to touch on the central question of consent and women's essential right to own their bodies. This was addressed in shocking clarity by Caird's article on 'Marriage', published in the *Westminster Review* in 1888 (revised version in *MOM*, 63–111). Preceding Charlotte Perkins Gilman's *Women and Economics* (1898) and *The Man-Made World* (1911), Cicely Hamilton's *Marriage as a Trade* (1909) and Olive Schreiner's *Woman and Labour* (1911) by a more than a decade, and Elizabeth Robins's *Ancilla's Share* (1924) by a quarter of a century,[47] Caird undertook a radical critique of patriarchy and its history by locating marriage and prostitution at the heart of a religious, economic and political system based on maintaining male rule by exploiting women as private or public property. At present, she argued, marriage was little better than sexual slavery; a physically, morally and psychologically sound *partnership* between women and men could only come about under conditions of legal equality, when women could enjoy the certainty of bodily autonomy and the absence of any form of coercion. This point was dramatised in *The Wing of Azrael*, published the following year, which poignantly captures the young Viola Sedley's traumatised response to her first experience of sexual harassment, an act of violence to which she will later be exposed in all legality as a wife:[48]

> Her grief was all the bitterer because she could not express it in words even to herself; she could only feel over and over again, with all a child's intensity, that she had been treated with insolence, as a being whose will was of no moment, whose very person was not her own; who might be kissed or struck or played with exactly as people pleased, as if she were a thing without life or personality. (*WOA*, I: 50)

That Caird's arguments hit the raw nerve of the age is illustrated by the extraordinary resonance her 1888 article found among the late-Victorian

MARRIAGE EVIDENTLY NOT A FAILURE.

Joan (to Darby, who is getting stout). "LET ME TIE IT FOR YOU, DARLING."

13 'Marriage evidently not a failure', *Punch*, 15 September 1888, 130.

public. Within six weeks, some 27,000 readers had taken up the *Daily Telegraph*'s invitation to respond to the issues raised by Caird; a selection of letters was subsequently published under the title *Is Marriage a Failure?*[49] In the United States a similar debate unravelled in the *Cosmopolitan*.[50] Inevitably, *Punch* poked fun at the events by figuring a happily subjected Old Woman blissfully engaged on tying her spouse's shoelaces (Figure 13), while its Cockney reveller sang the praises of men's naturally polygamous appetites.[51] In 'Donna Quixote' (1894)[52] Caird's insurgent writings on marriage hold pride of place with Ibsen and Tolstoy as the foundation texts of the paradigmatic New Woman figured in the cartoon.

This and subsequent essays on marriage were later collected in *The Morality of Marriage and Other Essays on the Status and Destiny of Women* (1897). However radical her conclusions, with her presupposition that legal, social and political equality would effect change from within Caird reflected the central tenets of Victorian feminism. Her belief that '[e]qual rights for the two sexes; the economic independence of women' and the 'establishment ... of real freedom in the home' were the preconditions for ending 'the patriarchal system' correlates with mainstream feminist thought.[53] Mary Maynard has listed four key issues which exercised nineteenth-century feminists: equal rights; employment and the need for women's economic independence; women's position in the family; and sexuality.[54] Focusing on precisely these issues, Caird's work explores the themes most characteristic of the time, adding a radical edge to feminist reform activism: rights (of citizenship) versus duties (morality, rationality); the nature of womanhood (equal or different?); the sexual division of labour; and independence versus protection (relating to employment laws). With her defence of the rights of the individual, Caird positioned herself in a tradition of Enlightenment thought and, drawing extensively on John Stuart Mill,[55] grounded women's claim to full citizenship on their essential equality with men. Equal by nature, women had become disabled by culture; their artificial and debilitating difference resulted from the separation of spheres and their enforced dependency on and subordination to men.

In order to contextualise the psycho-social condition of women in Victorian Britain, much of *The Morality of Marriage and Other Essays* is given over to an historical analysis of different forms of society ruled by varying degrees of physical force, and of the emergence of the current system. Exceptionally well versed in the historiography and anthropology of her time, and influenced by Friedrich Engels's *The Origin of the Family* (1884),[56] Caird explored the factors that had turned matriarchal into patriarchal societies. Her comparison of the changing, often contradictory, and by no means ever more progressive laws and customs of different patriarchal societies at various times in history enabled her to argue that gender roles were never 'natural', but were always the product of a given society ('The Emancipation of the Family', *MOM*, 21–40), and that patriarchy, with its changing economies of brute force (woman-capture) and capital (woman-purchase) firmly in the hands of men, was based on sex-slavery. As women's bodies ceased to belong to their rightful owners and were appropriated by men, so were their children. Men's paternal rights did not derive from biological fatherhood, but from their ownership of women:

> whether in the matriarchal or patriarchal era … there has prevailed one and one only idea as to the rights of parenthood, and that idea is: That the children belong absolutely *either to the mother, or to the owner of the mother*, whoever he may be, and quite irrespective of whether or not he happens also to be their father. The right to the children has always been *enjoyed by or derived from their mother*.
> ('Emancipation of the Family', *MOM*, 50, emphases in original)

In other words, the fact that women had been granted some degree of parental rights had not changed the property basis on which men's superior claims were thought to rest. A further problem arose from the coexistence of, and therefore conflict between, this patriarchal notion of property (the pater-

familias-system) and the new system of capitalism which heavily relied on
social Darwinism ('The Emancipation of the Family', *MOM*, 23). In an
increasingly individualistic state where women had to fend for themselves,
they continued to be treated as minors ('Emancipation of the Family', *MOM*,
54). As both patriarchy and capitalism were ruled by the imperative need to
maintain the status quo and protect property, they were static systems
impeding progress. In their stead Caird suggested a dual system of modern
state intervention (childcare provision, wages for housework) and private
negotiation (marriage contract, family size). Marriage, she argued, should be
an 'entirely private' matter, with the two partners drawing up their own
contract suited to their individual needs. Once relieved from the burden of
coercion, duty and self-sacrifice, marriage might develop into a partnership
between equals, a friendship based on mutual respect of two separate
individualities.[57] Caird's idea of a private marriage contract reflected not so
much her lack of awareness with regard to the dangers that the privacy of the
home held out for women, as her belief that state-governed marriage was an
even more unsafe option for them because it was predicated on their
willingness to surrender their personhood. A private contract would at least
ensure that every woman had a voice in shaping her destiny.

To enable women to leave uncongenial marriages, to which under the
present system they remained tied for existential reasons, Caird suggested the
introduction of wages for housework. Only if their work in the domestic and
childcare sector was remunerated could women achieve full public recognition and economic independence.[58] Yet just as fatherhood did not disqualify
men from full participation in public life, there was no reason why women
should be compelled to choose between domesticity and a career. To protect
women against the imposition of a double workload, traditional notions of
family structure had to be revised in light of modern lifestyles. As women
assumed an increasingly active role in both the private and public arenas, a
reduction in the average family size was essential.[59] The absence of women's
reproductive choice (what Caird called the 'duty to reproduce'), and implicitly
the lack of contraception, were 'the curse of our marriages, of our homes, and
of our children' ('The Morality of Marriage', *MOM*, 134, 138). Unlike Grand,
who toyed with the notion of professional childminders when it suited her
rhetoric but otherwise stigmatised state nurseries,[60] Caird promoted public
childcare, arguing that

> There is not sufficient ground in experience for believing that the mother and
> father are certain, or even likely, to be the best trainers for their children.
> Parenthood does *not* miraculously bestow the genius for education, nor the wide
> knowledge necessary for the task … Surely [children] have a claim to enjoy the
> best training that the conditions of their century can offer. And such training can

only be provided by those who have a natural gift for the work. ('The Morality of Marriage', *MOM*, 154–5, emphasis in original)

In subversion of the ideology of separate spheres, Caird suggested that it was only 'by this extension of the principle of the division of labour' that 'really excellent work [was] possible'.[61] She was thus articulating ideas similar to those held by Charlotte Perkins Gilman, in whose utopian state Herland (1915) only especially gifted and trained members are entrusted with child rearing. But while in Gilman's novel this is a collective decision, Caird's emphasis lies, as always, on individual choice.

In answer to the hypothetical question as to what she would suggest implementing in exchange for the current system that had proved so inadequate, Caird presented readers with two different responses: a reformist agenda (equal divorce and custody rights, the criminalisation of marital rape; the suspension of the principle of enforced cohabitation; and a gradual reduction in state intervention in what was essentially a private affair), and a more complex philosophical reflection on her discursive method: to engage with this question, she said, 'would lead the mind of the inquirer over the widest fields of history, of sociology, of science, of psychology; it would take him back into a far and legendary past, wherein he would find disproof of many a cherished preconception which, in his wildest dreams, he had never doubted' ('Introduction' to *MOM*, 5). History, sociology, science and psychology: these are four of the discursive frameworks with which Caird set out to deconstruct patriarchal ideology in her journalistic and narrative work. Concentrating on the history and sociology of marriage in her journalism, in her fiction she highlighted the role of science in buttressing oppressive regimes, like Schreiner[62] contrasting evolutionary biology and in particular eugenics with the concept of a humanistic, ethically oriented science, and atomising the psychology of gender through shifting and multiple points of view. In positioning the New Woman within an historical setting highly evocative of human sacrifice and exploring the sociology and psychology of moral conflict in interaction with gendered subjectivities, *The Pathway of the Gods* offers a particularly interesting study in discursive instability.

Caird's 'new voice': myth, multivocality and morality in *The Pathway of the Gods* (1898)

In the closing years of the nineteenth century, at a time when the New Woman novel had constituted itself in the public mind, pace W. T. Stead, as 'a novel written by a woman about women from the standpoint of Woman',[63] Caird constructed her fourth novel around the perspective of a New Man in order to take stock of the New Woman movement, repositioning herself in relation to some of its central discursive paradigms, while also interrogating the New Woman's cultural and ideological alignment with other *fin-de-siècle* movements. If in the 1880s her iconoclastic articles had paved the way for the New Woman debates of the 1890s, at the end of the decade her novel's channelling of a female identity crisis represented through the lens of male subjectivity served both to reflect critically on contemporary feminist discourses and to highlight neo-patriarchal attitudes among the proponents of avantgardist and alternative movements that defined themselves in opposition to the patriarchal mainstream and were therefore often seen to make common cause with the New Woman. Caird was thus engaged on a similar project of revisionism as Grand, but drew characteristically different conclusions.

The Pathway of the Gods offers four interpretive paradigms with which to capture the 'essence' of the New Woman, casting this figure in various guises – narcissist, Christian martyr, victim of male myth-making, and theosophist aesthete – only to deconstruct each in turn. Imputing narcissism to Anna Carrington's actions – a woman 'incessantly looking at herself in the glass (morally) to see if her appearance is correct' (*POG*, 203) – Caird ironicised the feminist navel-gazing of much New Woman fiction, especially of the social purist kind spearheaded by *Ideala*. Deeply critical as she was of Grand's celebration of the exceptional ('ideal') woman, she mocked the sententious moralising of such a heroine, problematising the tendency among contemporary feminists to sanctify the New Woman as a quasi-religious saviour. Anna is consistently constructed as a Christian martyr, yet always fails to live up to the heroic dimensions of this role. Importantly, however, myth-making of this kind is undertaken primarily by the male characters in the novel. In establishing a male surface perspective unable to respond to the New Woman other than through mythologisation (idealisation or demonisation), Caird articulated a feminist critique of the patriarchal strategy to contain the New Woman in and through myth, even as she was engaged in expanding the mythical scope of her own writing. Finally, the New Woman is juxtaposed with, and defeated by, an even 'newer' kind of woman, the female theosophist-cum-paganist-turned-aesthete. In her alignment of theosophy with aestheticism and anti-feminism, Caird positioned herself in opposition to both *fin-de-siècle* decadence and its feminine counterpart, female spiritualism, calling attention to the moot aspects of 'alternative' discourses which remained grounded in the metaphorical and mythological paradigms of patriarchy.

The radical instability of the central protagonist enabled Caird to pre-empt any attempt, on the reader's or critic's part, to 'make sense of', and thus stabilise, the New Woman. This figure is presented to us in all her ambiguity not 'from within' but from the angle of a biased observer, the expatriate painter Julian Ford, whose initial empathy turns into consternation and finally into disapproval, pity and even abhorrence. From this perspective, which was adopted by contemporary reviewers such as the *Athenaeum's*,[64] Anna's character and life are emblematic of the *fin de siècle* that has produced her: at war with herself and her environment, she represents 'the spirit of the modern world ... creedless, searching, restless, ravenous, egotistical, sick and sorry' (*POG*, 104; 316). In her urgency to maintain points of reference as she struggles to emerge into New Womanhood, Anna clings to the values she regards as obsolete. Having turned her back on her religious background, she remains enthralled by its rigid notions of morality and its privileging of appearances over the essence of things. In anticipation of Woolf's satiric deflation of Victorian sentimentalism in *Orlando* (1928), Caird describes 'a young woman who thinks the universe is about to collapse, if she decides a little wrongly on some nice point of conduct –: a dreadful product of the Christian religion, as interpreted by anaemic ecclesiastics and sentimental human fungi, born of twilight cities, and sopping climates' (*POG*, 202–3). Unless Caird was targeting social purity feminism and Grand's Ideala, to whose 'fussy sort of virtue' she would have objected (*POG*, 203), the fact that Anna has as many different faces as facets to her personality, as a result of which she eludes the grasp of Julian's painter friends who fail to capture her in a picture, may indicate that Caird thought of her more as a representative of the phenomenon of the New Woman than of a particular 'type' within that category: 'I *can't* get at the face', one of the painters complains, 'The woman seems to be a perfect *crowd!*', and another, equally unable to stabilise, on canvas at least, her mutable and shifting character, calls her a 'fugitive personality'. When the two compare notes, they find that one has created an image of a woman 'in her most modern aspect', while the other has painted a Christian martyr (*POG*, 251–2, emphases in original).

Martyr and sacrificial victim: this is the iconography associated with and superimposed on Anna from the first pages of the novel. When in the Roman Coliseum Julian first becomes aware of her, she emerges directly from his waking dream, which vividly conjures up the slaughter of the Christians in the amphitheatre, a vision culminating in the 'familiar dream' of an Anna-lookalike in religious ecstasy being devoured by wild beasts (*POG*, 32). Although this concept of martyrdom correlates with Anna's view of herself, it is an odd fantasy to indulge in on the part of a one-time lover. Fifteen years previously he had been dismissed as an intellectual lightweight, an insult from which he clearly has not recovered, given that he is still haunted by visions of Anna. Irresistible yet terrifying, her strong personality and towering intellect then held him in a Medusa-like grasp with an at once mesmerising and emasculating force:

> Her brain seemed to seize the average instrument that goes by that courtesy-title, and wring it out in two minutes, leaving it dry as tinder. And she would not only

thus summarily dispose of one's martyred brain (a poor one, but mine own,) but she seemed to fling it aside with a contemptuous shrug, as much as to say: 'So much for *that!* now bring me something more worth the wringing (*POG*, 56, emphasis in original).

On their re-encounter Julian finds, not without satisfaction, that their roles are reversed. His bohemian lifestyle has boosted his confidence in his ability to shape his experience according to his needs, whereas her departure from conventional modes of life has resulted in premature burnout (*POG*, 168, 98). Like Julian, Anna braved her parents' opposition in order to strike out on an independent existence, but the double strain of struggling to forge a career for herself in the face of professional competition while at the same time bearing the full brunt of parental disapproval brought on a nervous crisis which fatally weakened her resilience to the moral onslaught of familial demands. In the end she gave up her dreams of independence for that most feminine of occupations, a governess-chaperone, and now lives at the whim of her employer, a rich but shallow widow, under conditions which mirror conventional marriage.

While on the surface Anna appears a victim of circumstances, the credibility of her story, told in retrospective by herself, is undermined by an increasing sense of dishonesty, of staged effects. Thus we learn that she was a successful public speaker, but the specific cause or educational campaign in which she was engaged remains open to speculation (her brief reference to Russia might hint at an involvement with anarchism, and her anger at women's condition in society implies a feminist consciousness). In the absence of a clearly defined political or other contextual grounding, Anna's oratory appears to have served primarily performative ends; indeed she admits that what she loved most about her career was the opportunity it wielded to 'hold sway over the emotions of men and women' (*POG*, 97) – another implicit dig at Grand, perhaps, whose Beth is not entirely immune to Anna's enthusiasm when after her breakthrough lecture she opens her fan-letters. Once the epic role of heroic rebel and political agitator has proved unworkable, Anna switches to a different genre, social drama, and, playing to an audience of one, Julian, casts herself in rapid succession as imperious mistress, highly strung lover and jealous fiancée. In order to probe the depth of his attachment, she assumes a 'pathetic coquetry of sorrow' (*POG*, 125), revelling in a show of self-inflicted masochism that barely conceals the triumphant exaltation of the successful actress who holds her audience enthralled: 'This was a moment such as she had dreamt of: the issues of two lives hung in the balance, and *her* hand held the balance … She had power at this moment to choose unfathomable joy; to win the chance to pursue her ambitions … But [these chances] must be foregone – for the present at least' (*POG*, 196, emphasis in original).

Self-sacrifice, in Schreiner an essentially altruistic and life-affirming principle which serves to liberate others, is here turned into a narcissistic weapon of mind-control, a life-denying principle whose purpose it is to enslave others. After initially rejecting Julian's offer of marriage, Anna accepts him only to pursue him with her jealousy and incessant demands for attention, utterly incapable as she is of putting into practice her intellectual ideal of a partnership of equals predicated upon freedom and spontaneity of feeling. As his work and health become infected by her violent mood swings, 'creeping in and in, and drawing out and out, by some subtle process, all that was most vital in his nature' (*POG*, 270), his friends begin to regard her in the light of a 'vampire': 'She seems literally to take the life out of people … She exhausts, in the most appalling way. She must absorb other people's vitality … and use it afterwards to make them her slaves!' (*POG*, 260). Anna's vampirism is singularly self-destructive, however, for her craving to possess Julian absolutely leads to the breakdown of their relationship.

The gloating tone, barely disguised, with which Julian's friends welcome her demise, and the punitive message of the dénouement, coupled with the conceptual shift in Anna's narrative construction from Christian martyr to Gothic bloodsucker, seem to suggest that the New Woman, however much she may protest to the contrary, is a destructive rather than reconstructive force in society, and that her union with modern, egalitarian man leaves him prostrate with hysteria and 'deadly fatigue' (*POG*, 268). This is the very opposite of Grand's and Schreiner's scripts, where 'pure' women find their mental as well as emotional resources drained by their too close association with unregenerate males. A bundle of nerves, like Thomas Hardy's Sue Bridehead whose consuming energy takes a heavy toll on her lover, Anna appears the intellectual counterpart of the nymphomaniac, the sexually voracious woman against whom doctors of the time warned men to guard themselves. Such a woman, they affirmed, constituted 'a great danger to the health and even the very life of her husband … Just as the vampire sucks the blood of its victims in their sleep while they are alive, so does the woman vampire suck the life and exhaust the vitality of her male partner – or victim. And some of them – the pronounced type – are utterly without pity or consideration.'[65]

Anna, too, is a 'pronounced type' and (though not in any sexual sense) 'without pity or consideration'. By associating her New Woman character with that other image of deviant femininity which exercised the cultural imagination of the *fin de siècle* and beyond (in the early twentieth century Virginia Woolf, too, felt accused of consuming men with 'vampire like suction'),[66] Caird invoked anti-feminist discourses, in particular Bram Stoker's *Dracula* (1897). In *Dracula* the New Woman who threatens civilised (male) society and science is split into a sexual monster (the nymphomaniac Lucy who, in her fully vampirised state, even exhibits paedophilic proclivities) and an intellectual monster (Mina). While Lucy Westenra can be contained by the stake, which brutally reinscribes the power of the phallus onto the rebellious female body, it is Mina Harker, the less overtly transgressive of the two women, who poses the greater threat to the male unconscious: armed with 'a man's brain … and a woman's heart' (*DR*, 234), she exerts a profoundly vampirising (emasculating) influence on the men as opposed to Lucy's sexually reconstructive one. This is evidenced by the sobbing fits to which all of Lucy's suitors succumb (even Van Helsing at one point collapses weeping in Mina's arms), as well as by her husband's increasing mental exhaustion, galloping depression and fatal penchant for all-absorbing rest cures. Dracula's embrace, in releasing Lucy's restrained sexual energies, prompts his counterpart Van Helsing's frantic violence to restore the hegemonic order between the sexes disturbed by her libidinal deviance from the Victorian ideal of the chaste maiden; the Count's action thus sets in motion a development that requires a reaction in the upholders of the patriarchal system. Dracula's assault on Mina, on the other hand, no longer represents a challenge to but in fact buttresses the patriarchal order, for both his assault and Van Helsing's earlier decision to expulse her from the Crew of Light serve to discipline and ultimately destroy female mental powers perceived to be too challenging by all the men, vampire and non-vampires alike: 'And so you … would play your brains against mine', Mina is taunted by Dracula, '[b]ut you are to be punished for what you have done' (*DR*, 287–8). This follows shortly after Van Helsing, the spokesperson of Victorian medicine, has warned her that if she fails to adjust to her merely representative function as the men's 'star and … hope' (*DR*, 235), she will be condemned to 'suffer – both in waking, from her nerves, and in sleep, from her dreams' (*DR*, 242). Mina obliges, dutifully transforming herself first into an hysteric swayed by the hypnotist's will, and then into a submissive Old Woman, a model of self-immolation who goes so far as requesting her own decapitation (intellectual and social disempowerment), should a situation arise in which the men felt that she was moving out of bounds again.

Anna's experience in some measure reflects what happens to Mina. She too unsettles and destabilises her male environment, much more so in fact than Mina, demanding, rebellious and utterly self-centred as she is, where Mina proves accommodating, maternal and willing to embrace a servile role as the men's amanuensis, moving from the position of the 'type-writer girl' to that of the communal womb. Like Mina (a school-teacher aspiring to journalism), Anna is torn between domesticity (in her case, taking responsibility for her sister's family) and her professional ambitions, but unlike Mina she cannot accept the collapse of her dreams and settle happily into the life of conventional femininity (a governess and then a wife). Both Mina and Anna are subjected to male vampirism, the one literally, the other metaphorically (in having the image of a vampire superimposed on her by Julian's friends). An angry, aggressive hysteric to Mina's self-deprecating one, Anna is punished with the loss of her fiancé, whereas Mina is rewarded with a happy marriage of sorts and the birth of an heir, the symbolic product of the men's homoerotic and hegemonic couplings.[67]

By establishing a surface perspective filtered through male eyes (Julian and his friends) which approaches and constructs Anna through myth, Caird articulated a feminist critique of male mythopoeia. It is the men in the story who insist on mythologising Anna, first by romanticising her as a martyr, then by demonising her as a vampire. The oddly interlacing patterns in the piece of embroidery Julian presents to Anna are emblematic of the way in which patriarchal myth-making is as if woven into the tapestry of gender relations:

> Julian had bought for Anna a piece of old silken embroidery ... It reminded [one] of those compositions in which a secondary melody underlying the dominant theme, serves to support and enrich the latter, while remaining itself distinct and complete.
>
> In the embroidery, the themes were similar, though diversely treated, so that the forms and tints perpetually echoed one another, while the under pattern retained its leading tone of dull, mysterious gold.
>
> Curves repeated curves, in intricate order. The under pattern, more complex, was composed of a multiplicity of parts and branches, forming a rich tracery, whereon the simpler lines of the upper scrolls stood out in contrast. It was a design drawn by simplicity on complexity. And the upper pattern seemed as if it had grown out of the under one, as the Present from the Past. ...
>
> ... Julian and Anna lived an enchanted life, which the embroidery itself might have symbolised. Against the dim complexity of the great historic background, their own small but vivid drama stood forth, in its relative simplicity ... (*POG*, 196–7)

However much they may struggle to establish new and independent identities for themselves, women are forever defined by and rewritten into the patterns and historical structures of patriarchy. Caird here makes a similar point to Gilman's 'Yellow Wallpaper', in which the female artist-narrator feels strangled by the maddening arabesques of the wallpaper in the nursery room to which she is confined by her physician-husband. On closer examination she begins to perceive an outside and an inside pattern, the latter representing a woman – herself, Everywoman – trapped within the overlaying pattern. Release from the superstructures of patriarchy is, however, possible only at the price of sanity. With a vested interest in keeping intact the hegemonic patterns which ensure their privileged position, the men in both texts engage in myth-making, Gilman's 'John' by imprisoning his wife both literally and linguistically within the myth of woman-as-infant, Julian and his friends by locking Anna into the binaries of victim and vampire. The other women, by contrast, instead of imposing mythological paradigms, attempt to gauge the psychological springs of the individual. Thus the spiritualist Mrs Charnley, one of her antagonists, has considerably greater insight than Julian into Anna's behaviour, which she attributes to her intense sense of frustration: 'She has great powers, greater than she has scope for; and, like all such forces, they turn inwards and work destruction there, if they cannot go out harmlessly, in their natural direction' (*POG*, 260). The need for a female corrective to the men's construction of Anna is further emphasised when the narrative voice, shifting from Julian to an unspecified female point of view, intervenes to criticise him for his lack of empathy:

> Julian did not understand a woman's difficulties. He spoke as one to whom life has been a sort of experimental journey. All very well for those who run the race without a handicap, who belong to the sex who have no artificial disabilities to drag them back – the sex on whom other people's burden may not be laid, without so much as a 'by your leave.' (*POG*, 148)

Like Grand in *The Heavenly Twins* Caird thus introduces and sustains a counter-narrative, a voice that disrupts and destabilises the surface narrative, encouraging the reader to respond with greater critical alertness to Julian's biased point of view, perhaps even to call his account into question. Anna's dramatic performances of incongruous selves and stereotypical feminine roles – the hapless victim, the *femme fatale*, the jilted bride – suggest that she is aware of Julian's and the other men's attempts to contain her within fictional frameworks and deliberately sets out to mimic their expectations in order to gain control of and undermine their narratives. In meta-fictional terms, Caird was highlighting the constructionism to which the New Woman was subject on the part of the periodical press and narrative fiction. Like Julian and his painter friends, contemporary critics and writers were eager to arrive at the definitive interpretation of this social phenomenon, and just as the men mythologise Anna, while the women approach her from a psychological point of view, so Caird drew implicit attention to male writers' tendency to weave fantasies around the New Woman, whereas female and feminist writers like herself attempted to place her in her social and psychological context. In her stagings of multiple female selves, Anna the character would then be a counterpart of Caird the author, engaged on exploding the master discourse.

The critical reader may begin to wonder just how trustworthy this self-declared New Man is who only seems interested in the New Woman as long as she provides a foil for his inner vision, a Woolfian mirror whose surface reflects back to him his own subjectivity at twice its original size:[68] 'It was strange', he muses, 'that he should be able to recognise her increased attractions without any personal feeling in the matter. Here was an opportunity of observing himself objectively – *himself*, the majestic creature of will and intention, of sentiment and passion' (*POG*, 47, emphasis in original). As soon as Anna ceases to perform her specular function, Julian shifts his attention to another, less challenging woman only too happy to act out his fantasies. Ostensibly a caring, emotionally responsive man supportive of the New Woman and thus at first glance a prototype of the New Man, Julian turns out to be as ambivalent and unstable a character as Anna herself. His subjugation to Anna's regime is an ironic inversion of his original intention of punishing her for her one-time indifference to him: 'And then a little ambition seized him – : to take a sort of generous revenge; to lay her under some spiritual obligation to him, to be the arbiter of her impressions ... and to make life seem a little duller and emptier because of his absence' (*POG*, 80). Even in the grips of romantic passion he is not oblivious to other charms, using the occasion of a nocturnal *tête-à-tête* with his proclaimed lover to praise the owner of a disembodied female voice as 'the noblest woman in the world' and go off into the night in search for her (*POG*, 100). Female readers may find that it is not altogether surprising if poor Anna is consumed with jealousy.

The 'vernal promise' (*POG*, 222) of Clutha Lawrenson's beauty and general comportment is so singularly un-feminist, her whole person, though presented as the ideal born out of a tumultuous past much like Anna's, so lifeless and pliable when contrasted with Anna's explosiveness, that any straightforward reading of the ending as an invocation of a new dawn in human relations becomes destabilised. In this text, which consistently casts itself into doubt by undermining the credibility of its central characters, Caird aimed to unsettle reader expectations of narrative and ideological closure: for what appears to offer a resolution to the conflict explored in the novel only serves to raise further questions about the main actors. Anna is abandoned to her neurotic obsessions, while Julian, Clutha and their artist friends celebrate a neo-pagan festival which culminates in Clutha's crowning as the 'Queen of the Beautiful Past, and Prophetess of the Beautiful Future' (*POG*, 335); in the final scene the new Superman and his anima are joined together by the last rays of the sun. If this is to be the ideal couple of the future, their relationship hardly constitutes a new venture, resonant as it is with male fantasies. Clutha could have sprung from Ruskin's 'Queen's Garden' lectures,[69] and she also has more than a tinge of the Lawrentian woman (to modern readers, her name – Lawrenson – already acts as an involuntary reminder of Lawrence). As Lyn Pykett points out, the ritual dance to the sun-god with which the novel ends 'anticipates Lawrence's use of dance-like ritual in *The Rainbow*'.[70] By embedding her feminist message (the tragic demise of the New Woman) in a 'self-consciously aesthetic' form, Pykett argues, Caird 'blends formal renovation and innovation with a radical New Woman rhetoric'.[71] However, by contrasting her feminist with an aesthetic, patently non-feminist character, Caird calls either aestheticism or feminism into question. In her next novel, *The Stones of Sacrifice*, she was to expose the aesthetic woman as a reincarnation of the Old Woman. With her sweetly feminine – unchallenging, non-argumentative, soft-spoken, placidly passive – ways, Clutha is considerably closer to a revamped Angel of the House than to the feminist iconoclast.

While in her other novels, Caird makes her New Men suffer for their infatuation with Old Women,[72] here she provides an ostensibly happy ending with a mature, worldly wise, but still recognisably angelic Old Woman. Why did Caird choose to end her novel with a neo-pagan ritual and the union between New Man and Old Woman/New Aesthete? Paganism, coupled with human sacrifice, is the central metaphor of *The Stones of Sacrifice*, and this later text constitutes an unequivocal indictment of patriarchal traditions predicated on ancient myth and the sacrifice of human life, in particular the sacrifice of women. *The Pathway of the Gods* concludes with Clutha's crowning, but this crowning of the aesthetic woman coincides with the metaphorical crucifixion of the feminist. Significantly, the celebrations take place in what is described as a 'sort of natural amphitheatre' (*POG*, 332), a rural setting strongly reminiscent of the Coliseum which at the outset of the story inspired Julian's fantasy of Anna's martyrdom. The story of the modern woman's demise is thus framed by visions of the blood-games and the tearing asunder of female flesh. Just as in Roman times the Christian apostates were offered up to spectacular consumption by the beasts of a fiercely patriarchal state, so now the New Woman and her embryonic feminism are sacrificed on the altar of a new faith which is complicit with modern patriarchal society. The 'ancient processional dance' that Clutha and her friends perform quickly disintegrates into a frenzy of 'whirling figures' (*POG*, 332, 334) singularly evocative of the tarantella dance of the hysteric, described by Catherine Clément in *The Newly Born Woman* as a dance whose origins lie in rural southern Italy and which enacts the 'repetition of a distant past',[73] in Caird's case the slaughter of humans: 'The dance came and went, like a vivid thought. It was as if a dead century had turned in its grave' (*POG*, 334). As I discussed in Chapter 1, the tarantella is a ritual of inversion in which social roles are turned upside down, culminating sometimes, as Clément notes, in the 'elect[ion of] a mad-mother … those excluded from society, are thus promoted to function as prophets'.[74] Clutha's deification as the prophetess-goddess of the new dawn would then signal nothing more than a temporary reversal of hegemonic structures: if her crowning marks the inevitable reinstatement of patriarchal rule, her call on her worshippers to contribute to 'the making of a new world' (*POG*, 335) can only serve as a reminder of the necessity of paying allegiance to the old world order to be restored as soon as the dance comes to its close.

As this is a text which consistently deconstructs its own ideological and discursive parameters, Clutha and her mysterious mentor Mrs Charnley are presented with characteristic ambiguity. New paganistic aesthetes and Old Women, they lend resonance to views synergic with those expressed in Caird's journalistic writings, above all the need for independence in personal relationships (*POG*, 226–8), while at the same time professing to principles which run counter to Caird's feminism. Both are spiritualists who believe in the power of the soul as the only real fact in life, a conviction which makes Mrs Charnley indifferent towards material suffering such as the domestic violence endured by Anna's landlady: 'Real freedom comes from within. Why stir up revolt in our homes? ... You would but destroy the patience in suffering, through which the soul grows, and tempers, and frees itself' (*POG*, 155). Mrs Charnley is also an expert schemer, whose romantic intrigue – to make Julian fall out of love with Anna and in love with Clutha – quickly comes to fruition. Interestingly, she materialises as the self-appointed spokeswoman of the 'Brotherhood' of painters with which Julian is loosely associated. Her condemnation of 'purposeful' art puts her at odds with Julian and, between the lines, with Caird herself: 'The one unforgivable sin in painting a picture was to make it tell a story, or express an idea. An idea was an utterly damnable thing, in the eyes of the initiates. Art was art, said the Brotherhood, convincingly. It was not religion or morality ... What business, therefore had morality or religion, or anything else, in a work of art?' (*POG*, 161). Just as Julian transfers his feelings from the New Woman to the Old/newly Aesthetic Woman, so he also revises his artistic conception, from a belief in art as purpose, to one that celebrates art as beautiful conjuring: 'The artist', Mrs Charnley impresses on him, 'is the high priest of Illusion' (*POG*, 162–3). If in this intellectual and aesthetic transformation Mrs Charnley acts as Julian's guru, Clutha is the ideal vehicle of her teachings: she is beautiful, and instead of an authentic woman she appears more as an illusion. Rather than adopting an aesthetic and proto-modernist framework, then, this text enters the contemporary debate between feminism and decadence by contrasting feminism, in its alliance with purposeful art, to an aestheticism which draws on patriarchal myth and paganistic tradition, and by associating both paganism and aestheticism with anti-feminism and woman-sacrifice (since the union between Julian and Clutha is premised on Anna's demise).

Where Grand and other feminists invoked spiritualism and in particular theosophy as an ethic-cum-erotic counter-aesthetic to *fin-de-siècle* male decadence in art and life, Caird repositioned women's spiritualist and specifically theosophist discourses within the ideological superstructures of patriarchal culture. Anna's Mephistophelian antagonist, Mrs Charnley, is strongly evocative of Madame Blavatsky. Thus, on first encountering her in a church, Julian

found fixed upon him a pair of large, steady, deep blue eyes ... The owner of the eyes was ... a woman of somewhat matronly appearance, yet still young; with a round, smooth face which might have been commonplace but for the curious expression of the eyes. There was a quality of coolness mingled with their benevolence that was very singular. In spite of her benevolence, this woman gave the impression that she might have looked on at tragedies without any great emotion. She would believe that they were all for the best. She would sit out a performance, and watch a scene of carnage in the arena of this, our modern life, without a protest or a sigh. Julian found himself regarding her with a feeling of antipathy … he resented her calmness. (*POG*, 76)

A charismatic, dynamic character with steely blue eyes, a mesmerist's pene-trating gaze, a stocky figure, and an enigmatic and unwieldy personality, who believes in reincarnation and the primacy of the inner life, and who possesses the uncanny capacity to appear out of nowhere and shape the most dramatic moments of the plot according to her will, Mrs Charnley represents a Gothic caricature of the theosophist leader (Figure 14). The claims she makes for her religion, a faith originating in the East, as one which 'penetrates to the truth that underlies [all creeds] – so combines what is true in them all' (*POG*, 177), correlate with Blavatsky's and Annie Besant's teachings, which defined theosophy as 'the origin and basis of all religions'.[75] Despite his initial dislike, Julian quickly falls under her Svengali-like spell as she plots to draw him closer towards her friend: the desire for a 'profounder comradeship than Anna could give … had overcome him with unaccountable strength and suddenness, as if he had been the victim of a rush of external influences from unknown sources' (*POG*, 211). When they are not pressed into the service of personal motives, Mrs Charnley's hypnotic powers and magnetic passes can also exert a more constructive, healing influence, as Anna finds at the end of the novel: 'My head is so much better … I feel as if some intolerable tension had been relaxed. You must have some magic influence in the tips of your fingers, Mrs Charnley' (*POG*, 323). Anna's rival, Clutha, constitutes a less sinister, erotically more high-powered version of the theosophist. An enchantress, she appeals to Julian's senses when he is at his most vulnerable, in moments of romantic abandon or in his sleep, taunting him with her disembodied voice or fleeting visions of her enticing beauty. Like Grand's Beth, Clutha is associated with the sea; the 'deep sea-blue' of her aesthetic-styled gown in tune with her rhythmic motion, she 'seemed to wave along like a breeze, or a field of corn, or a river' (*POG*, 119–20), and even Anna 'seemed to hear the sound of those lapping waves on the sand, and to have before her eyes the solitary coast, and the crying sea-birds' (*POG*, 230).

Published a year after *The Beth Book*, Caird's novel offers a distinctly different perspective on theosophy's potential for subversion, suggesting that Grand's solution to the woman question did not constitute a feminist's best 'pathway to the gods'; significantly, Beth's final destiny (political oratory) correlates with Anna's point of departure (her failed career as a public speaker). While theosophy, because it lacked 'a stable political valence', was mobilised by movements with contrasting political agendas, Joy Dixon points out that it lent itself most forcefully to the 'critique of liberal individualism. … In place of

14 H. P. Blavatsky in 1889, London.

the liberal model, theosophists offered a vision of spiritual community.'[76] It is
this very idea of a spiritual collective which is conjured up, and then called into
question, on the final pages of Caird's novel. Like Anna, Caird may have felt
that the New Woman 'had escaped too recently from a spiritual prison-house
to sympathise with any definite form of religious feeling. It suggested to her
nothing but mental captivity and gloom' (*POG*, 92).

In light of the incrimination of the theosophist in *The Pathway of the Gods*,
Caird's later membership of the Theosophical Society, from 1904 until 1909,[77]
is intriguing. Her shift in spiritual politics may have reflected the momentum
women had gained in the movement since the turn of the century, when men
had constituted the dominant force.[78] Before 1898, however, her deep scepti-
cism towards any form of religion that drew its strength from ancient myth
and was complicit with patriarchal traditions would have counteracted any

such interest. In *The Wing of Azrael* (1889), written a decade earlier, her heroine's 'metaphysical consciousness of the Infinite and the Unknown' acts as a self-destructive 'curse', the very opposite of the liberating force it represents in Grand's novel (*WOA*, I:11). Here, too, the protagonist's essential 'otherness' is encoded in sea and wave metaphors, but instead of renewal and resurgent energy the waves signal her suicidal urge towards extinction:

> With awful tumult and distraction, the waters rushed to their doom, boiling, seething, rebelling in vain against the power that drew them with ever accelerating speed, onwards to the inevitable verge. And then once more, with a bound like that of some wild creature hunted to his death, they leapt over the brink, pouring down and down and down, in one smooth mighty stream, into the infinite darkness and infinite silence for ever. (*WOA*, III:172)

As a child Viola Sedley dreams of entering into mythical communion with the elements: 'if only she could reach the sea she would not be lonely any more' (*WOA*, I:5). In sharp contradistinction to *The Beth Book*, however, the sea – religion, myth, theosophy – fails to provide a solution to the social problem of female oppression. The pleasurable sensations (*jouissance*) evoked by 'the scent of the earth' and 'the breath of the sea' are disrupted by the threatening proximity of the seagulls, 'cold, able, finished creatures' with 'no feeling', whose sharp and 'utterly pitiless' beaks remind the young Viola of her assailant, Philip Dendraith (*WOA*, I:71). Only at rare moments do the waves serve as markers of female desire (as when a 'gigantic wave' breaking against the cliffs accompanies a 'long never-satisfied kiss'; *WOA*, III:145); more typically they denote failure: the wasted energy of women condemned, like 'dead waves, broken and gone, [to lose] the fever of their short lives in a gentle annihilation' (*WOA*, II:107). Primarily signifiers of the inescapability of fate, the waves reflect a world bereft of any metaphysical purpose: 'the movements of human destiny, the restless everlasting labour without aim or hope. What was this ceaseless turmoil of the ocean but a weary response to the perpetual stimulus of a blind necessity?' (*WOA*, II:184). Significantly, this is Viola's perspective, and the text repeatedly hints at the psychologically harmful effects of her over-identification with the elements: 'Her intense love of the sea ... [left] an indelible mark upon her character. Her instinctive fatalism might have been the lesson of unresting tides, of the waves, for ever advancing and retreating, blindly obedient, in spite of their resistless power and their vast dominion' (*WOA*, III:156). Akin to Anna Carrington in her overbearing sense of responsibility towards her family, yet too brow-beaten and demoralised to attempt Anna's bid for self-liberation, Viola seeks refuge in deterministic reincarnation fantasies woven around a tragic ancestress.[79] Like the waves rushing to her nemesis, she disappears into the depths of the night, presumably bent on throwing herself off the cliffs, after killing her violent husband in an act of self-defence: 'the solitary figure, with one last look over the moonlit country and the sea ... passed over the brow of the hill and out of sight, while a second later the sombre procession swept over the face of the moon and plunged the whole landscape in darkness' (*WOA*, III:224). As in *The Pathway of the Gods*, supernaturalism, because of its uncritical assimilation of nature discourses and its homage to human sacrifice (*WOA*, I:57), is revealed as constituting but the Janus face of patriarchal religion: 'Viola characteristically took all things connected with religion in grim earnest' (*WOA*, I:53). To Caird, religion, old or new, did not offer a resolution to the woman problem.[80]

Like Grand suspicious of male agendas, whether they related to the spiritual, political or aesthetic planes, Caird did not adopt her strategy of constructing a feminine counter-discourse from within, but attacked the patriarchal system more directly by drawing attention to the injurious impact it had on women, dramatising the way in which it worked to underpin the dominant sexual hegemonies and sustain woman-to-woman antagonisms, even when it was represented by women themselves. Instead of the prophetess Clutha, it would then appear to be the struggling, and failing, New Woman Anna who holds the key to women's past and future. Ironically, while the theosophists of the novel construct Clutha as the past purified and future reincarnate, it is Anna, Julian's ideal of the martyr, who more adequately reflects theosophical concepts of reincarnation. As Gauri Viswanathan explains, reincarnation, as outlined in Annie Besant's *The Ancient Wisdom* (1897), represented

> a return to a moment frozen in the past, whose recovery is possible only by connecting with prior forms of consciousness inculcated by morally evolved beings. Such persons hold the accumulated tracks of past experience and memory, which Besant terms 'ancient wisdom' ... the recovery of the past is a moment of new secular transformation, inviting all that has been suppressed to engage the construction of the present.[81]

In her transitional position of the no-longer Old and not-yet New Woman, Anna embodies such 'an expression of the past's ongoing relationship with the present'.[82] She is also emblematic of women's age-old rage, an anger which proves all-consuming in its white heat (*POG*, 337).

If Anna holds the ideological key to *The Pathway of the Gods*, why did Caird cast her in such an ambiguous and unsympathetic light? Rita Kranidis argues that in their exploration of 'new' female subjectivities New Woman writers frequently sought to problematise the inadequacy of all available roles and therefore presented their readers with 'a composite of a traditional type and an enlightened, rebellious nonconformist, a feminist'.[83] Yet even contemporary feminists would have found it difficult, if not impossible, to identify with an uninspiring, plaintive and psychologically self-harming heroine. Perhaps it is precisely this lack of identification, sustained as it is by the primarily male narrative perspective through which we perceive Anna always from the outside, that heightens the reader's awareness of the tragic conflict between rights and responsibilities from which result Anna's apparently inexplicable inconsistencies: her inability to refuse to sacrifice herself to her sister's family and her rage about this decision, her longing to break free from all obligations and her unfailing circumvention of anything that would release her.

This tragically flawed heroine enabled Caird to shed light on a central contradiction in the moral code into which women are socialised in patriarchal society, a contradiction that pervades the New Woman genre as a whole and can be traced in the biographies of many of the writers. All of Caird's narratives focus on the conflict between female self-sacrifice and female self-development. Much of her significance as a feminist writer and New Woman theorist resides in the fact that she constructed a feminist theory of the female self and of female and male conceptions of self and morality. Her insights into the stringency with which women internalise the moral imperative of selflessness anticipate some of the conclusions posited in Carol Gilligan's *In a Different Voice* (1982).

In her study of gender differences in the response to moral dilemma, Gilligan draws on Nancy Chodorow's *The Reproduction of Mothering* (1978), which links the emergence of gendered selves to children's experience of an exclusively female mothering, resulting in a 'feminine' sense of self orientated towards connectedness, and a 'masculine' sense of self marked by separateness.[84] When presenting her subjects with hypothetical moral problems, Gilligan found that, while the boys and men in the sample tended towards what she calls a 'morality of rights', the girls and women were more likely to respond in accordance with an 'ethic of responsibility'.[85] This led to her controversial claim that men define moral behaviour through the principle of personal rights (in a conflictual situation the rights of individuals and institutions would have to be assessed carefully in order to determine a 'just' hierarchy of rights), whereas women understand morality primarily as an obligation towards others because they define themselves in relation to them. The vast majority of girls in this study felt torn between their own needs and an inflated sense of loyalty particularly towards family members; the most important consideration in any conflict was how to avoid causing hurt. Faced with the impossibility of mediating between the different, often mutually exclusive claims of self and other, Gilligan argues, many women feel under an obligation to adopt a self-sacrificial attitude, which then results in resentment and bitterness. Full adulthood can only be achieved by means of a careful balancing act between self-assertive and socially responsive behavioural codes. Both are essential to society, and our social training and education should aim to integrate the concepts of rights and responsibilities into a single moral code mandatory for both sexes.[86]

Gilligan's interpretative model is of obvious relevance to *The Pathway of the Gods*. Anna's reluctance to make choices, her exaggerated sense of familial duty, the morbid pleasure she takes in self-mortification, even her emotional insecurity illustrate her imprisonment within the 'ethic of responsibility'. The fierce parental opposition and emotional blackmail that accompanied her struggle to find employment 'shattered [her] nerves': 'You can't conceive', she tells Julian, himself none the worse for his breakup with his father, not least because he enjoyed the full, if clandestine, support of his mother and siblings, 'what it is … to feel that you are causing incurable grief to your parents … what I went through … has weakened me permanently' (*POG*, 98). Caird had already outlined the Victorian middle-class daughter's 'problem with no name'[87] in her 1890 essay on 'The Emancipation of the Family'. In its alliance with capitalism, modern patriarchy, she argues in this piece, puts a double burden on women by forcing them to conform both to the old and new roles:

> the woman of the nineteenth century finds the old shells and sheaths of a decaying patriarchal system drawn away from her; while at the same time she is exposed … to the full blast of the competitive tempest in which modern life is passed … She sees her brothers going forth into the world with a thousand advantages, to her denied … For her, there is nothing but discouragement, opposition, eternal admonitions and reminders as to duty … Thus the woman must struggle with other women for the … means of livelihood … the family claims from her duty and obedience, as of old, but it expects her to provide for herself. (*MOM*, 51–2)

In the stranglehold of old and new pressures, Anna remains 'captive to herself' (*POG*, 192), mentally locked into the morality of responsibility, able to conceptualise but not exercise her rights. This is the case for many of Caird's heroines, all of whom are caught between the desire for personal-professional advancement and the socially imposed duty of self-sacrifice – the latter line of action usually carries the day, always with adverse consequences. A century before Gilligan, Caird atomised the damage inflicted on women's individual lives by the double standards inherent in a moral code which accorded men rights and women responsibilities. Grand, too, was aware of the self-destructive impact of a 'duty' falsely understood to comprehend a moral obligation towards oppressive parents or reprobate husbands and felt no qualms about enjoining her female readers to cultivate a spirit of rebellion,[88] but whereas she concentrated on exemplary individuals who braved all opposition and realised their potential whatever the obstacle, Caird focused readers' attention on the lesser individual, the weaker will, the failing New Woman. At a time when the Victorian and Edwardian women's movements held a heavy investment in the idea of individual self-abnegation for the sake of the cause, Grand and particularly Schreiner invoked women's self-sacrificial spirit as a potent metaphor of the political struggle for women's liberation as a quasi-religious project for human redemption. Caird, by contrast, always prioritised the rights of the individual over the rights of the collective. Where *Ideala* and 'Three Dreams in a Desert' posited the duty of self-sacrifice for the common good, Caird condemned the appeal to the greater benefit of the 'Community' as but 'another collective-term fetish', arguing that it was 'perilous to try to purchase social benefits at the expense of individuals' – 'What in fact, *exists*, but individuals?'[89]

This point is explored most potently in *The Stones of Sacrifice*, published at the beginning of the First World War, whose central symbol, a site of ancient ritual, modelled on the Standing Stones of Cairnholy close to her husband James Alexander Henryson-Caird's mansion, Cassencary, near Creetown, in Dumfries and Galloway (Figure 15),[90] serves as a reminder of the continuity of the age-old 'religion' of sacrifice: a crime against humanity always perpetrated on the defenceless (animals, women, 'lesser' humans like criminals and the 'unfit') – and always glossed over euphemistically with the invocation of the greater 'interests of the community'. Caird was not the only critical voice to raise objections to this concept: Charlotte Perkins Gilman, too, attacked patriarchal religion's imposition of the idea of sacrifice,[91] and Oscar Wilde came even closer to Caird's historicising approach when he stated that '[s]elf-denial is simply a method by which man arrests his progress, and self-sacrifice a survival of the mutilation of the savage, part of that old worship of pain which is so terrible a factor in the history of the world, and which even now makes its victims day by day, and has its altars in the land'.[92] But where Gilman saw no problem in depriving those she considered 'unfit' on eugenic and ethnic grounds of the benefits of her socially and racially purist society,[93] and Wilde was less bothered about the impact of the dominant moral code on women, Caird pronounced her unequivocal opposition to the cult of sacrifice in any shape or form as it affected all those deemed to be 'lower in the [evolutionary] scale of being'.[94] If *The Pathway of the Gods* exploded the Christian myth of deliverance employed to such tremendous effect in Schreiner's 'Three Dreams in a Desert' by throwing into relief the individual casualties suffered in the process of constructing what could only ever constitute a flawed utopia, *The Stones of Sacrifice* demythologised the concept of progressive modernity in its stark indictment of the contemporary alliance between Socialism and Science.

'Disobedience ... is woman's first duty':[95] rights versus responsibilities and *The Stones of Sacrifice* (1915)

Her fiction, Caird said, was intended 'to show the different effects upon various types of women of certain uniform conditions to which all are subject', exploring a range of possible responses to the experience of gender oppression:

'[cheerful] acceptance', 'tearful resignation', the use of 'cunning ... artifice and womanly wiles', or 'life-long revolt'.[96] In *The Stones of Sacrifice*, which ascribes the root cause of women's oppression to the patriarchal imperative of female self-sacrifice, these responses are reflected in the development of the four unmarried Galbraith sisters.

The Galbraith regime – whose name carries an intriguing echo of Evadne's domestic-cum-medical regime in Grand's *The Heavenly Twins*[97] – is intro- duced in detail in the third chapter of *The Stones of Sacrifice*, following closely on a discussion between the 15-year-old orphaned Alpin Dalrymple and his mentor Professor Owen, who acts as the voice of reason and wisdom throughout the novel. The Professor urges Alpin to reject the idea of human sacrifice wherever he may find it as 'one of the most ancient and deep-seated' negative principles of human history and society (*SOS*, 6–7). Shortly afterwards Alpin rescues the youngest Galbraith daughter, Graine, from a bonfire which symbolically sets the scene for her and her sister Leah's diametrically different fates. 'Cheerfully accepting' patriarchal rule, Graine is predestined to become a sacrificial victim of parental doctrines, and only escapes this fate by chance, while Leah, a female counter-model to Freud's paradigm of the 'child [that] is being beaten', develops into a wild and (self)- destructive rebel ('lifelong revolt'). In contradistinction to Freud's emphasis on fantasy and perverted desire,[98] Caird, like Grand in *The Beth Book*, draws attention to the lasting repercussions of childhood physical abuse on the female psyche and woman-to-woman interaction. Literally beaten into girlhood, Leah is driven to exact revenge on female fellow-sufferers who, like Graine, appear to carry a lighter load, and is unable to conceive of 'sisterhood' in any other sense than that of the socially ostracised, the 'odd' and 'fallen' women. Where the adolescent Beth explores an alternative to the patriarchal order through theosophical-libidinal fusion with the elements and membership of a feminist counter-community, Leah seeks relief from her overpowering rage in occult ritual with the village 'witch' Madge and in fellowship with prostitutes.

Doctor Galbraith operates a rigid system of repression which has already cost three children their lives and blighted those of the remaining four. The depressing, pervasive greyness of their existence on the 'Grey Ridge', the house symbolically overcast with the gloomy shadow of a dying tree, with their only purpose in life consisting in an endless production of superfluous anti- macassars, has turned the eldest daughter, Ruth, into a bigoted ('cunning') younger version of her parents, while pushing the next in line, Maggie, into neurotic invalidism ('tearful resignation'). Only when Graine, who effectively runs the household, falls seriously ill, are her sisters suddenly stirred into life and, released into meaningful action, find themselves temporarily roused from their paralysis (*SOS*, 278). By then it is too late; only Graine is fortunate enough to escape into a career of sorts (a happy marriage), while Ruth and

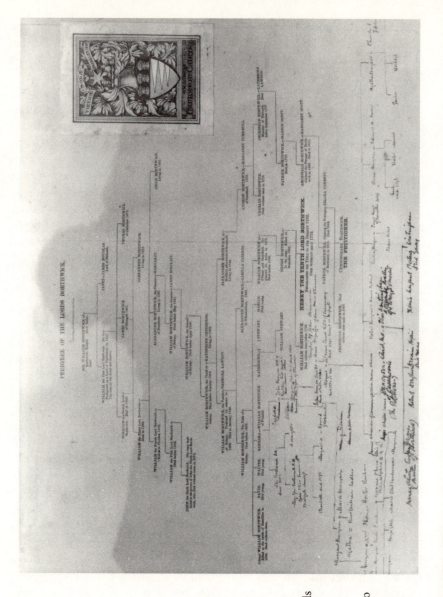

15 Pedigree of the Lords Borthwich (family tree which includes James Alexander of Cassencary's marriage to Alice Mona Alison and their son Alister James Henryson-Caird.

PEDIGREE OF THE LORDS BORTHWICK

[Section]

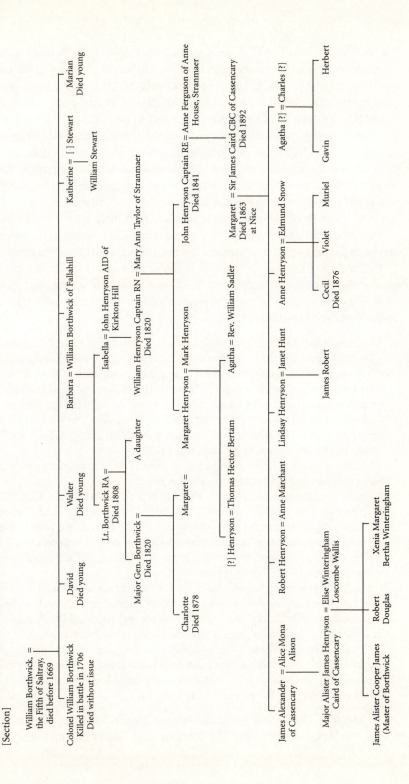

Maggie subside into the bleak vacuum of respectable women's death-in-life, an existence which their sister Leah compares to 'living … under gravestones and never stir[ing]' (*SOS*, 105). The text suggests that even Leah's drastic plunge into prostitution is preferable to this state of nothingness: at least it is, as the New Woman Claudia asserts, '*some* sort of life', offering the additional privilege of being spared the sickly sentimentality which marks domesticated femininity (*SOS*, 105). Leah's initiative in leaving her home, even for such a desperate choice of profession, provides her with the necessary energy to move on to a life more congenial to her nature; the end of the novel sees her married to a gypsy and relatively content in her alternative community.

Caird made the provocative point that, while all three female conditions – domesticity, marriage, and prostitution – were artificially imposed by men and served to degrade women, prostitution was, in effect, a cut above the other two in that it spared women the pain of humiliating hypocrisy, offering them a greater degree of bodily autonomy (Leah, as Claudia points out, can choose with whom to spend the night; the respectable wife cannot), and releasing them from their breeding function:

> '[A]t least *she* has some choice and freedom … A ghastly freedom, of course – ' [Claudia] paused, and then … a glint of fire came into the depths of her eyes. 'But at least she is not bound by a hundred thousand paltry conventions; above all, she is not bound to bear children as part of her official function – to provide an heir, for instance; and she can't be hounded by the eternal cry of "duty"! … And,' the iconoclast went on with rising warmth, 'and people don't talk to her about her Sphere … than which nothing can be happier or holier; and they don't sentimentalize over her "crowning joy" till she is sick!'
>
> Mrs. Duncan gave a little bursting laugh … 'Part of the ornament, my dear. Far better to accept and indeed make the most of it.'
>
> 'Yes, we *must* sentimentalize to enable us to bear it,' assented Claudia … 'Just imagine our dear familiar epithets - the "holys" and "crowns" and "sacred missions" – transferred to the *other* profession – (Sophy gasped). Suppose people *did* talk to Leah about her "Sphere", than-which-what, and so on; don't you see how it would soon come to be felt all that is virtuous and self-sacrificing? Heavens, it must be self-sacrificing any way!'
>
> Mrs. Duncan contemplatively smiled. 'Well, as a matter of fact, that fat volume over there gives an account of a state of affairs almost precisely such as you audaciously describe. "Holy" and "sacred" were the very terms used to character-ize the *metier* of the good women of the temples of certain ancient cults …'
>
> 'Of course they were,' said Claudia calmly, 'whatever men want women to be, they call "holy"; and whatever they want them to avoid like the plague, they call "shameful" – rewards and punishments being meted out accordingly. It's beautifully simple.' (*SOS*, 343, emphases in original)

Like Lyndall in *The Story of an African Farm*, Claudia challenges conventional moral templates, demythologising 'honour' and 'shame' as male-imposed, entirely arbitrary values whose only purpose it is to socialise women into internalising their oppression. In Schreiner's novel Lyndall declares that only 'when love is no more bought or sold, when it is not a means of making bread, when each woman's life is filled with earnest, independent labour, then love will come to her' (*AF*, 178). In having her heroine refuse to marry the man she desires and with whose child she is pregnant because she is materially dependent on him, Schreiner radically redefines sexual relations and marriage, extending the argument that to mix love and livelihoods leads to women's sexual degradation by cutting the link between sex and marriage. Sex *within* marriage is tantamount to prostitution unless the woman has paid work; without it she is not free to refuse sexual access to her body. Sex *outside* of marriage (conventionally regarded as prostitution) has no economic correlation: there is nothing to make it immoral, since the woman *is* free to dispose of her body as she wishes (Lyndall later refuses to accept any money from her lover, even though the birth of their baby leaves her prostrate with illness). While, untroubled by economic, social or institutional pressures, a free-love relationship ends as soon as it ceases to be based on sexual attraction and affection, marriage imposes continued sexual relations where affection may be wanting. Consequently, free love is essentially moral, while marriage, unless permanency of affection and sexual autonomy can be ensured, is not.

Caird and Schreiner concurred in condemning conventional marriage, but instead of separating sexuality from marriage, Caird defined a woman's bodily autonomy – her inalienable right 'to *possess herself* body and soul, to give or withhold herself body and soul exactly as she wills'[99] – as the prerequisite of any sexual relationship, and disengaged marriage from compulsory reproduction. Ironically, despite her radical reputation, in this novel she did not advocate free love as a practicable alternative to marriage. For, much to the disappointment of their more iconoclastically inclined friend Harriet Kirkpatrick, her New Woman/New Man couple Claudia and Alpin enter a reconstructed 'individualistic marriage' (*SOS*, 383) instead of, as Harriet expected, circulating 'cards announcing that they were going to live together': 'Now *that* would be consistent with your professed repudiation of the tyranny of marriage. But no – Oh it's heart-breaking!' (*SOS*, 374). Claudia's development and lifestyle are thus set off both against images of traditional, self-effacing womanhood (unhappily married women like her sister-in-law Sophy, self-sacrificial spinsters like the two elder Galbraith sisters) and against the individualised politics of feminine complicity and feminist rebellion adopted by her older mentor Mrs. Duncan and her friend Harriet Kirkpatrick. While these two characters provide Claudia with alternative female life-scripts, their attitudes are shown to fall short of the two basic moral principles advocated by the novel, personal integrity (Gilligan's morality of rights) and actively caring sympathy (Gilligan's ethic of responsibility).

In juxtaposing Claudia, the successful rebel, with an array of failing female characters, whose ultimate destinies are the direct or indirect outcome of their wavering or colluding attitudes towards the patriarchal system, Caird's novel, like Grand's *Ideala*, outlines Margaret Atwood's four 'basic victim positions'. If placed within the context of Atwood's model, Claudia starts her narrative existence at the juncture between positions two (resigned acceptance, or 'tearful resignation' in Caird's terms) and three (constructive protest, or 'lifelong revolt'): she is aware both of her condition and of the means to overcome it, but cannot at this stage bring herself to exert her rights at the expense of the responsibility she feels for others. The end of the novel charts her gradual move into the final position (the 'creative non-victim').[100] By contrast, Mrs Duncan's advice to Claudia not to 'fight against existing institutions ... [but to] *use* them' by subverting patriarchy from within reflects Atwood's second position (equivalent to Caird's 'cunning ... artifice and womanly wiles') and proves a futile compromise (*SOS*, 129, emphasis in original). Mrs Duncan herself does not derive much satisfaction from having sacrificed her emotional and intellectual aspirations for prudent marital considerations (financial security, social status, the semblance of a family). Although she gives Claudia crucial moral support and helps to alleviate the problems caused by the sexual exploits of Claudia's brother Stephen, her actions are purely remedial, and never pose a challenge to the system as such. At the other end of the spectrum, Harriet Kirkpatrick, a comical representative of Atwood's third position, is so busy upsetting the conventions that she becomes oblivious to the human tragedies closest to home, and ignores her sister's prolonged depression until it culminates in suicide. Intent on demolishing the old belief structures for the sake of destruction, she makes common cause with the eugenic socialists whose totalitarian vision is even more barbaric than the ideology she struggles to overthrow. In creating this eccentric character, Caird breathes new life into the late-Victorian *cliché* of the mannish New Woman, equipping her with positive attributes such as whirlwind dynamics and a 'devastating' yet admirable honesty (*SOS*, 40), but at the same time she advertises to her Edwardian readers, who by 1915 would have been familiar with New Woman discourses, that Harriet *is* a cliché, not the real thing:

> In appearance, Miss Kirkpatrick was precisely what, at that date, the New Woman was supposed to be: large and angular and masculine-looking. A black skimpy coat and skirt, and a manly shirt and tie constituted her attire; and she had wrung her hair, by dint of virile force, into a tight button and pulled down on the top of the button a black bowler hat ... She went on her cheerful way, careless of criticism, half attracting and altogether alarming the county by ... the explosive nature of her opinions. (*SOS*, 39–40; compare with Figure 16)

16 Caricature of the mannish New Woman: 'Disappointed Cabman: "What's this? Garn! Call Yerself a Gentelman, do yer?"'. *The New Budget*, 11 July 1895, 23.

Harriet's 'virile force' and flamboyant advocacy of personal rights at all costs empower herself and others, notably Claudia, who with her assistance steels herself against the domestic claims of her mother; but unlike Claudia, Harriet seems totally unencumbered with any authentic, deeper feeling: she is 'a kind-hearted woman without a heart' (*SOS*, 436). An incompletely individualised character, Harriet remains something of a caricature, and as a caricature she enabled Caird to explode anti-feminist images of the New Woman by contrasting the cliché with a 'real' New Woman. In sharp contradistinction to Harriet, Claudia struggles heroically to reconcile her rights with her responsibilities, striking out on an independent existence in the face of relentless maternal opposition, yet disrupting her career when her sister requires psychological support. Like Beth's mother, the Temples have neglected their daughters' most essential needs to the point of recklessness, killing two of them in the process, while turning their son into a monster of selfish irresponsibility. Undermined and 'paralysed' (*SOS*, 36) by her mother even on to her deathbed, Claudia's move towards independence follows a long and painful route. Her pursuit of basic professional training and plans to establish herself as an English teacher abroad take years to materialise because of Mrs Temple's unceasing efforts to sacrifice her daughter in the 'temple' of 'the Higher Life' (marriage to the highest bidder). It is by sheer force of will that Claudia finally prevails – but independence costs her dear in human terms; she is, we are told, 'fighting for dear life … and there was no time to consider the enemy's wounds' (*SOS*, 72). Significantly, this 'fight for life' between mother and daughter is only resolved through the death of either one or other; whereas Harriet's mother, Mrs Kirkpatrick, drives her daughter Mary to suicide, Claudia 'kills [her] mother by refusing to be so driven' (*SOS*, 326). Although at one stage Claudia professes to '*hate* men' (*SOS*, 130, emphasis in original) for their crimes against women, the most injurious private crimes in the novel are committed by mothers.

If, in the words of a David Lodge character, 'all the Victorian novelist could offer as a solution to the problems of industrial capitalism were: a legacy, marriage, emigration, or death',[101] Caird's post-Victorian novel thematised and subverted these conventions in its quest for a solution to the woman question. Mrs Temple dies, Claudia inherits money, *and* she marries – but she uses her inheritance to finance the founding of an anti-militaristic, pro-humanitarian group of political radicals called the Alternatives, while by virtue of its unconventional nature, her 'individualistic marriage' explodes rather than reaffirms the patriarchal institution.

As in *The Beth Book*, it is only after the New Woman and New Man have achieved full independence that they are allowed to come together as a couple. Their relationship serves to demonstrate Caird's theories of the free and equal partnership which would supersede conventional marriage. First and foremost Claudia and Alpin are friends who share an elective affinity premised upon a 'fellow-traveller element' (*SOS*, 126). When their close friendship develops into love, it is a mature feeling strengthened by the experience of prior attachments; Alpin was previously in love with two women, and the narrator hints at Claudia's equally 'absorbing and tumultuous' love-life in France. It is precisely because of their prior experience that Claudia and Alpin have no wish to possess and circumscribe the other: 'The real person can't be caught and put into a bottle', Claudia tells Graine (*SOS*, 397–8), and the narrator comments that 'if love meant jealousy, Claudia did not love' (*SOS*, 169). Aware of Graine's feelings for Alpin, they even contemplate the possibility of offering her a *ménage à trois*: 'If only one could annihilate the traditions and conventions, there might be a possibility of scrambling out of the mess … for there was deep love between the three of them' (*SOS*, 322). In the end Graine finds a more suitable partner and the other two settle into marriage, yet their unorthodox arrangements are met with stern disapproval by conservatives and progressives alike, both groups feeling equally disconcerted, albeit for different reasons, by the idea that the institution of marriage might successfully be reconstructed (*SOS*, 368). Clearly, Caird could not suppress an ironic dig at the incipient conservatism of 'advanced' circles like the Men and Women's Club which, while priding themselves on the daring nature of their discursive radicalism, shrank back in horror when faced with actual transformations in the relationship between the sexes. Any social revolution, if it was to be taken seriously, Caird implied between the lines, had to start at home, with a radical reconstruction of domestic life: 'Socialism, syndicalism, anarchism, any sort of "ism" that proposed the entire reconstruction of society, by all means; but when it came to a slight modification in the customs of domestic life, there was an instinctive feeling that something fundamental was giving way. It meant a loosening of the marriage bond' (*SOS*, 378).

Entering a formal union only to explode it, Claudia and Alpin assure themselves of individual living and working space by moving into two adjoining flats connected by one central sitting-room. Activities and meals are shared only insofar as this 'suit[s] the respective requirements of the occupants' (*SOS*, 377); both continue to pursue their individual projects and, though having mutual friends, keep in touch with separate sets: 'The marriage had made no difference to former relationships. Old friends could still see either of the pair freely ... No confidence leaked through with the usual sentimental treachery of married couples who "tell each other everything"' (*SOS*, 382–3). Their example not only creates a precedent for a growing number of followers, but also 'infects' traditional couples, much to their benefit, as the ensuing changes help to save the stifling marriage of Claudia's brother. Caird's novel thus outlines in practical and realistic terms what Grand and Schreiner were able to envisage only in utopia or fantasy: a successful day-to-day partnership between New Woman and New Man which safeguards the individuality and intellectual life of each, and, by allowing room for personal development, ensures the permanency of mutual affection.

One important aspect, however, appears to be absent from this exemplary marriage. Just as Claudia and Alpin move into the flats formerly rented by two women friends, so their relationship appears to be based on intellectual companionship and emotional affinity to the exclusion of any more dangerous element which might destabilise this harmonious balance. With the only shared space being the living-room, their marriage seems to be circumventing sex. Probably Caird wanted to make the point that more than any other room, the bedroom needed to be the site of radical independence and absolute freedom of choice. Crucially, Caird's ideal marriage is, at this point at least, a childless one, so that one of the central dilemmas explored in her work – of how to combine motherhood with full individual development – remains unanswered.

Despite these gaps, Caird's novel offers a fuller programmatic vision than Schreiner's and Grand's fiction of the potential of a radical revision and trans-formation of patriarchy through the reconstruction of its central institution, marriage. It is significant that Claudia's and Alpin's individual life choice has immediate repercussions on the Alternatives, as the new individualistic model is adopted as part of the group's broader programme for social change, and placed in sharp contrast with the reactionary sexual/marital politics of the socialist eugenicists. A passionate indictment of the ideology of inhumanity in all its forms, Claudia's story of personal and domestic liberation serves to expose the inhuman face of 'private' patriarchy (the reproduction of ideology in the family), while Alpin's story of political liberation attacks its 'public' side (the production of ideology in political organisations). Attracted to socialist ideas, Alpin sets up a Guild of the New Order (*SOS*, 102), a radical group probably modelled on the Fellowship of the New Life, founded in 1883 to 'promote the general social renovation of the world on the broadest and highest lines, seeking inspiration in its Goethean motto: "Im Ganzen, Guten, Schönen resolut zu leben"'.[102] Edward Carpenter, Havelock Ellis, Edith Lees (Ellis) and Olive Schreiner were all prominent members of the Fellowship, and stayed with the organisation when, in 1884, the progressives pushing for greater political commitment, among others Sidney Webb and George Bernard Shaw, split away to form the Fabian Society.[103] Both the Fellowship and the Fabian Society became deeply entrenched in the new 'religion of humanity', the eugenics movement founded by Francis Galton.[104] Havelock Ellis rejected 'eugenic fanaticism' and warned against establishing racial hierarchies, yet all the while approved of both 'positive' and 'negative' eugenics as a means of improving the 'human race'; positive eugenics consisted in encouraging only the 'best' to breed, while negative eugenics aimed to 'eliminate' the 'unfit'.[105] H. G. Wells advocated the compulsory 'sterilisation of failures', Sidney Webb expressed concerns about the danger that the decline of the birth rate might lead to the English nation 'fall[ing] to the Irish and the Jews', and Marie Stopes promoted birth control not least in order to contain the reproductive capabilities of the working classes.[106]

In Caird's text, the Guild quickly becomes a hotbed of eugenic thought, with Alpin challenged on both political and personal fronts by the socialist vivisectionist Gilbert Thorne. Alpin loses Elsie Bonner (an Old Girl revamped as aesthetic socialist) as well as the majority of the group to Thorne's politics, resigns from his position as vice president and founds the Alternatives. The ideological clash between Alpin and Thorne enabled Caird to denounce the unholy alliance of turn-of-the-century socialism with social Darwinism and the eugenics movement, and to advocate her vision of a society founded on the principles of individual freedom, altruistic fellowship, 'voluntary co-operation' aided by state subsidies and (non-compulsory) birth control to ensure general prosperity (*SOS*, 201).

Caird was hardly a political economist, and her novel offers at most a utopian sketch of the alternative society she envisaged. Her main objective was to expose the 'new Religion' of eugenics as merely another patriarchal institution behind whose pseudo-humanitarian discourse lurked 'primitive savagery' (*SOS*, 236). In the name of civilisation and science, the 'Triumvirate' led by Thorne advocate the vivisection of animals and 'lower' humans such as criminals (*SOS*, 176–77). As women are to be functionalised for reproductive purposes, marriage in this brave new world will be arranged and policed towards racially profitable ends; the multiplying family of golden-haired, eugenically sound clones of Swainson Stubbs, the Guild's skilful yet intellectually circumscribed propagandist, evoke the breeding policies of the Third Reich, as does the 'true woman' rhetoric: women fit for survival 'worshipped the strong man who knew how to master them … It was a matter of racial history' (*SOS*, 151). Science and socialism, Caird suggests, have replaced paganism and Christianity: the names may have changed, but the misogynist concepts and arguments are identical, the only difference being the insatiability of the new masters in leading new victims to the sacrificial altar: 'An endless perspective of victims of Humanity, running up the scale of fitness and importance; each group busily engaged in immolating members of the less important group immediately below, till, finally, at the summit, sat a cluster of Men of Science, who alone escaped the common lot in virtue of their stupendous importance' (*SOS*, 232).

To contemporaries familiar with the eugenics debate, Caird's novel must have read like a *roman à clef*, exposing as it did the virulent misogyny and totalitarian politics which shaped the views of its leading proponents. Thus Thorne's 'proposal to regulate marriages scientifically in the interests of the race, and to decide the vexed question of woman's position in strict accordance with her function of producing the largest number of healthy children for the State' (*SOS*, 154) carries uncanny echoes of H. G. Wells's *The New Macchiavelli*, published four years earlier, which proclaimed that women 'must become … subordinated … to the collective purpose … [A] conscious, deliberate motherhood and mothering is their special function in the State'.[107] Karl Pearson, Galton's 'closest disciple', wrote in 1885 that '[i]f child-bearing women must be intellectually handicapped, then the penalty to be paid for race predominance is the subjection of women'.[108] Caird's primary objective was to confute male science, but contemporary feminism's flirtation with eugenics is not spared criticism: Harriet Kirkpatrick who, though enjoying the fullest liberty herself and proudly single, takes over the vice-presidency of the Guild after Alpin's departure, is a singularly contradictory figure and loses her credibility as a feminist when she presides over discussions about women's innate desire to be trampled underfoot by virile men for the sake of their unborn children. Through this figure Caird drew attention to the ideological inconsistencies of writers like Schreiner, who glorified Teutonic virility, albeit in women (*W&L*, 90, 92), and attacked eugenic feminists like Grand, Gilman and Christabel Pankhurst – with the outbreak of the war the latter espoused patriotism, militarism and fascist beliefs.[109]

Despite the Triumvirate's barely concealed bid for tyranny and their overt misogyny, the slogan-like simplicity of their discourse quickly catches on among the members of the Guild, so that in a travesty of the Roman gladiatorial contests Alpin receives the sign of a thumb turned downwards when challenging Thorne. As in *The Pathway of the Gods*, Caird invokes the image of the bloodstained amphitheatre to direct reader sympathies; this time, however, the new creed is granted a visionary victory. While, unsurprisingly, the Triumvirate's model union between Thorne and Elsie proves a consummate disaster, the sexual politics of the Alternatives yield immediate positive results, and the novel ends with Alpin's rainbow-inspired epiphany and vision of a society in which human, animal and natural worlds are at peace.

In her last novel, *The Great Wave*, published a year before her death in 1932, Caird was no longer optimistic about the likely outcome of the collision between science and human rights. The wave metaphor, in Grand and Schreiner a positive image for the progressive force of the women's movement, here turns into the apocalyptic vision of a wave of war and destruction in a post-atomic world. In the wake of the First World War, Caird's idealistic hero Grierson Elliot, partly modelled on the British nuclear physicist Ernest Rutherford, finds a way to control radioactivity. When his discovery, conceived as a means of eradicating poverty and exploitation through automatisation, threatens to fall into unscrupulous hands, Grierson destroys all his records. Caird's mistrust of the eugenic socialist scientist comes to a head in the sinister character of the German fascist Ludwig Waldheim. A cynical demagogue who manipulates working-class sentiments by preaching destructionism under a pseudo-socialist banner, a ruthless follower of the Nietzschean Superman idea, and a warmongering nationalist whose dreams of world conquest involve the extermination of all lower races, this figure represents the rise of Nazi ideology; his celebration of brute force as the only truly virtuous and 'manly' principle anticipates the religion of fascism as described in Katharine Burdekin's dystopia *Swastika Night*, published five years after *The Great Wave*.[110] The figure of the fascist scientist also reflects the ideological trajectory of British eugenicists like Karl Pearson, who in 1934 praised Hitler's 'proposals to regenerate the German people' as the 'culmination' of an evolutionary process towards statistical-biological perfection which led from mathematics to biometrics, and thence to eugenics and global racial cleansing; if the 'experiment' currently 'in hand' in Germany failed, he noted, it would 'not be for want of enthusiasm, but rather because the Germans are only just starting the study of mathematical statistics in the modern sense'.[111]

Characters like Waldheim and Thorne served Caird as chilling examples to spectacularise the threat which contemporary scientific discourses and the ideological pace they had gained posed to international human rights. By interlacing 'domestic' with 'political' plots, her fiction consistently drew attention to the close interrelationship between sex/gender discourses and the prevailing ideological structures of the system. If marriage as it was currently practised was barbaric, so was the society which drew its strength from sheer rule of force. Only if society were to adopt a radically different system of ethics could the woman question be resolved. Whoever wanted to address the anomalies in the relation of the sexes had to work towards uncovering and rewriting the foundational myths that underpinned all social, sexual and political hegemonies: in Clément's words, had to 'read history differently'[112] and thereby help create a different history for humanity. At a time when most socialists and feminists were seduced by the idea of social advancement through 'race regeneration', Caird was one of the few critical thinkers to demythologise the truth claims of evolutionary biology and expose the contempt for human and women's rights that was so integral to eugenic taxonomies.

Caird's work is not marked by the discursive instability of Grand's and Schreiner's approaches. Intriguingly, the most radical feminist of the three, and a direct precursor of modern radical feminism in her deconstruction of marriage and motherhood, she was the only one to envisage the possibility of heterosexual partnership in the present. More optimistic than Schreiner, she allowed for the New Woman's success and personal happiness – provided she persevered on the narrow path between altruistic sympathy (responsibility for others) and self-realisation (personal rights). It is, however, significant that none of Caird's successful New Women (Algitha Fullerton in *The Daughters of Danaus*, Claudia Temple in *The Stones of Sacrifice*, Nora Geddon in *The Great Wave*) is an artist, while her most appealing artist-figure (Hadria Fullerton) is a tragic failure.

6

Re/membrance: mythical mothers and art/ists in *One That Wins* (1887) and *The Daughters of Danaus* (1894)

Radical feminism is not reconciliation with the father. Rather it is affirming our original birth, our original source, movement, surge of living. This finding of our original integrity is re-membering our Selves. Athena remembers her mother and consequently re-members her Self. Radical feminism releases the inherent dynamic in the mother–daughter relationship toward friendship, which is strangled in the male-mastered system. Radical feminism means that mothers do *not* demand Self-sacrifice of daughters, and that daughters do not demand this of their mothers, as do sons in patriarchy. What both demand of each other is courageous moving which is mythic in its depths, which is spell-breaking and myth-making process. The 'sacrifice' that is required is not mutilation by men, but the discipline needed for acting/creating together on a planet which is under the Reign of Terror, the reign of the fathers and sons. (Mary Daly, *Gyn/Ecology: The Metaethics of Radical Feminism*, 1979)[1]

I *believe* that we are called to the making of the world … we who have our heads a little above water – beginning to catch glimpses … Why, even now, we are, in some sort, the Fates – blind sisters no longer, but open-eyed, blundering little creators: yes, *creators, creators* …! (Mona Caird, *The Stones of Sacrifice*, 1915)[2]

There could be no half-measures with art … It was the affair of a lifetime. He had known many women with great talent, but, alas! they had not persistence. … how many brilliant careers had he not seen ruined by this fatal instinct [for motherhood]! … The instinct was terrible; a demoniacal possession. It was for women a veritable curse, a disease … This 'reproductive rage' held them – in spite of all their fine intuitions and astonishing ability – after all on the animal plane; cut them off from the little band of those who could break up new ground in human knowledge, and explore new heights of Art and Nature. (Mona Caird, *The Daughters of Danaus*, 1894)[3]

In defining female biology as 'the scourge of genius' (*DD*, 319), M. Jouffroy, Hadria Fullerton's Parisian music mentor in *The Daughters of Danaus*, attests to the conflation of woman and womb with which the Victorian medical and legal establishments sought to justify women's exclusion from professional and political life. Hadria is a mother, but her failure to realise her artistic potential is a matter of psychological and environmental rather than biological imperatives; it is rooted not so much in the dictates of her body as in the enormous familial pressures that are brought to bear on her. Socialised into the morality of responsibility, Hadria is unable to assert her rights under the moral onslaught of her traditionally minded and hostile mother. Patently aware of the destructive impact on women of an antagonistic mother–daughter relationship, Hadria attempts to set an example of supportive mothering by adopting the illegitimate daughter of a school-teacher driven to an early death by social ostracism. Caird thus anatomised the injurious consequences of maternal self-sacrifice for the daughter's generation (a prototypical feature of New Woman fiction), while simultaneously casting the daughter as a resisting mother in order to confound essentialist discourses. Like Adrienne Rich's and Luce Irigaray's paradigmatic daughters,[4] Hadria, in the absence of a constructive relationship with her mother, is drawn towards identification with the father, here figured as the well-meaning mentors Professor Fortescue and M. Jouffroy. But as Mary Daly argues, the assimilation of the law of the father has the effect of further displacing ('dis-membering') the daughter from her female origins. In *The Daughters of Danaus* Hadria's orientation towards paternal authority leads to her association with the not-so-benign father/lover Professor Theobald, a liaison which entails the loss of her adoptive daughter, severing the only supportive mother–daughter relationship in the text. Only when a reconciliation between ('re-membrance' of) mother and daughter is possible, can either accede to that knowledge of herself/the other which, through its 'spell-breaking' and 'myth-making' power, allows for a joint movement towards female-centred 'acting/creating': the creative remaking of the world envisioned by Claudia in the passage from *The Stones of Sacrifice* cited above. If *The Daughters of Danaus* enacts both the biological (Mrs Fullerton's) and the surrogate (Valeria du Prel's) mother's failure to proffer a positive role model that would release, or at the least cease to circumscribe, the daughter's creative energy, Caird's earlier novel *One That Wins* (1887) represents the recovery and 'reassemblance' of the artist-mother by her elective artist-daughter as a mythological act of female re/creative *jouissance*: 'What miracle you are working!', the older tells the younger woman. 'Child, as you were speaking, something so sweet crept into my heart that I could almost think it was a ray of hope. What is the power in you that seems – if one will but yield to it – to still the pain … and make one almost dare to believe that life … has promises of joy to such as I?' (*OTW*, II:221–2).

Re-membering the artist/mother: *One That Wins:*
The Story of a Holiday in Italy (1887)

One That Wins, like *The Pathway of the Gods*, is set against the mythological, historical and artistic background of Italy, and is again structured around a love triangle, but here all three actors are artists, and each perspective is given extended narrative space. Now it is the woman of experience, the acclaimed painter Oenone Evelyn, who loses the man she loves to a younger, more feminine rival untainted by a past. Disillusioned with Oenone's revelations of her earlier involvement with a Russian anarchist executed for high treason and her subsequent unhappy and sexually exploitative marriage, Launcelot Sumner (ironically named after the Arthurian knight) wishes petulantly 'that she had not had quite so much experience; it *did* … alter one's point of view. He wished that she had not given out so much feeling before he met her … above all, that she had not been married. The thought of it all hurt and annoyed him more than he could have expressed' (*OTW*, I:90, emphasis in original). With her alluring beauty and poetic name inherited from an enigmatic ancestress who stabbed her unfaithful lover's bride, Oenone appeals to Launcelot primarily as a work of art, 'one of Nature's masterpieces' (*OTW*, I:25). Aware of the aesthetic rather than erotic nature of Launcelot's affection, Oenone rejects his suit: 'it is not the woman, it is the art that you worship' (*OTW*, I:62). In her paintings she explodes aesthetic objectifications of the feminine by invoking her foremother's violence in the artistic style of the Pre-Raphaelites and aesthetes, mimicking the 'Brotherhood' of self-important male painters and critics led by the long-haired and pale-faced Coates and Clutterbuck (modelled on Ruskin and Whistler in their partiality for 'Mysteries in Monotone' and 'After-dark Studies Among the Shadows'), whom she takes delight in exasperating with her 'unorthodox' choice of 'breath', 'tone' and colour (*OTW*, I:82–3, 79, 18). In response to the question why the woman in the artistic looking-glass, the 'other' Oenone figured on canvas, should direct her rage against her innocent rival rather than her faithless lover, Oenone refers to the greater impact of striking at the roots of male desire. As Virginia Woolf was to point out some thirty years later, it was only by 'killing' the idealised product of male fantasy – the 'fair-haired and gentle' Angel in the House (*OTW*, I:83–4) – that the woman artist was able to constitute herself.[5] Just as Oenone confounds the male painters' and in particular Launcelot's desire to lay claim to and possess the 'essence' of woman, so the 'singular character or expression' of her high-vaulted, 'palatial' and 'majestic' studio mystifies Launcelot because it eludes all his efforts to define and inhabit it (*OTW*, I:39–40). Yet in the very act of confuting the male aesthetic, Oenone remains captive to its mythological dimensions. For though the perfect equipoise manifested in her 'beautiful form and beautiful expression', 'graceful, well-proportioned figure and fine carriage' (*OTW*, I:25) points to an exquisite balance of mind and body, a harmony mirrored in her working environment, which combines 'beaut[y] in form and proportion' (*OTW*, I:39), her conflicted interiority becomes apparent in the odd juxtaposition of interior decorations, where oracular detachment collides with traditional invocations of the patriarchal family romance: on one side of her studio she has placed, like markers of her transgression, 'two strange Egyptian figures, half human and half beast, which sat with wise, inscrutable faces, like two Fates, gazing into the Past and the Future', while on the other, in involuntary figuration of her split personality, hangs 'a picture of a virgin and child, lighted dimly by the flame of a lamp, such as hangs before the altar in Catholic cathedrals' (*OTW*, I:40). Ironically it is this allegiance to the feminine mystique, particularly in its biblical polarities (the virgin mother, the chaste lover), which will prevent her from recognising the potential of mother–daughter love until it is almost too late. The destructive energy of the golden serpent with which she adorns her hair, a signifier of the 'other' role accorded to women in Christianity, that of Eve the temptress – perhaps even of Lilith, imaged as a 'tortuous serpent' in the Kabbalistic tradition, the scourge of mothers and children[6] – will haunt Oenone to the very end, signalling the fatal hold that patriarchal icono-graphies of femininity have over her. As an artist Oenone subverts patriarchal mythologies; as a woman she remains enthralled by them.

When Launcelot, the object of her undeclared passion, turns his attention to the blonde-haired, blue-eyed English tourist Nelly Erskine, Oenone suffers a prolonged identity crisis which prompts thoughts of suicide and even murder. But the suspended expectation of a sensational reproduction of her predecessor's crime is not fulfilled. Far from being a nonentity, Nelly turns out to be an aspiring young artist herself, as well as a thoroughly modern woman eager to lead an unconventional marriage of the kind Caird was to describe in more detail in *The Stones of Sacrifice*.[7] Her most intense desire is to meet Oenone and be mentored by her: 'I want a woman to help me to learn my new lesson; a woman who has learnt it before me, and who has both suffered and enjoyed deeply' (*OTW*, II:171). When they finally meet, it is Oenone the 'mother' who learns to appreciate the ethical code of the New Woman daughter: that rather than fight each other as rivals, '[w]e should stand – we women – hand in hand, like comrades and fellow-soldiers in the battle' (*OTW*, II:221).

Nelly's conviction that 'it would be worth while being Oenone at almost any cost' (*OTW*, II:168) and her determination 'never [to] rest till I know her and make her call me friend' (*OTW*, II:170), when coupled with Oenone's intense sense of Nelly's presence ('I have felt her presence in the very air', *OTW*, I:191) even in the face of her misapprehension of Nelly as merely a younger version of Mrs Erskine (Nelly's cold, autocratic, self-serving and shallow mother) point to the urgency of both women's need to discover/recover the 'good' mother. Both carry the psychological wounds of dysfunctional mothering, the scars of which cut deepest for Oenone, for whom the death of the biological mother coincided with the ascendancy of an oppressive step-mother. Oenone's passionate indictment of her surrogate mother's stifling regime as one that produces a steady flow of 'phantoms of humanity, endowed with the framework of existence, but mindless as that log of pine-wood in the fender, soulless as this crystal in my bracelet' (*OTW*, I:42) is evocative of Elizabeth Barrett Browning's *Aurora Leigh* (1857), as is Oenone's memory of her affectionate artist-father, her desolation after his death, her contemptuous horror of England – 'my "home" (as we English women call our prisons)' (*OTW*, I:42) – her agonising choice between art and love, and her overwhelming sense of loneliness and emotional barrenness. In invoking Barrett Browning's epic of the victorious woman artist and motherly friend of a younger woman (Marian Erle), Caird contrasts Oenone's and Nelly's shared experience of mother–daughter antagonism with the positive model of an empowering literary artist-'mother'. Like Hadria (and also like Aurora), Oenone and Nelly are oriented towards their fathers because, fellow-victims of the regimen of the Old Woman, they endorse their daughters' ambitions. Both women fall in love with Launcelot, a version of the benevolent father in the guise of the romantic artist: for Oenone the reincarnation of her lost painter-father, the object of her adolescent desire, he represents the bohemian variant of Nelly's eccentric and warm-hearted father-brother. As in *The Daughters of Danaus*, however, female identification with the father obstructs processes of feminist individuation and circumvents the reconciliation with and recovery of the mother.

Significantly, Nelly's mythical (re)encounter with the m/other (in herself as much as in Oenone) becomes possible only in the absence of her husband. From the outset drawn to the older woman, Nelly's 'ever-increasing interest' in and fascination with Oenone (*OTW*, I:27) is gradually displaced into what Adrienne Rich calls compulsory heterosexuality,[8] while Oenone for her part is consistently misled about the identity of Launcelot's fiancée (whom she takes to be Nelly's dreaded older and colder sister Sylvia) and thus encouraged in her antagonism. It is Nelly who, after her marriage to Launcelot persistently probing him on the subject of Oenone, prompts their prolonged residence in a remote Italian mountain village because of its presumed proximity to Oenone's secret retreat. As Nelly's quest for the artist-mother gains pace, she begins to resemble Oenone in her playful deployment of feminine mimicry. During Launcelot's courtship she displays Oenone's tendency towards mockery and delights in presenting herself as an 'enigma! She said acute little things in an innocent way that was hopelessly puzzling' (*OTW*, I:93). Launcelot's patronising statements about her primarily inspirational role in 'brightening and beautifying existence, not by a picture or a poem, but by yourself' (*OTW*, I:140) – at best a double-edged compliment, reminiscent of Ideala's treatment at the hands of Grand's male narrator – backfire when Nelly copies his habits with such disconcerting determination that he starts suspecting her of 'an intended caricature of himself and his artist friends' (*OTW*, I:159):

> She had established a note-book, wherein she said she liked to jot down a peasant, a picturesque mule, or any charming object that chanced to cross her path. This was one of Launcelot's constant habits. She would stop, as he did, suddenly in the road, and make some grotesque-looking memoranda which she declared would come in usefully for some future work.
>
> On one occasion she told him that she thought she would give up wasting her time on puny subjects such as mules and peasants, and meant to work in the style of the old masters; in fact, she had resolved to paint a Holy Family. (*OTW*, I:159)

Nelly's flamboyant subversion of the master discourse – 'She was in her wildest moods, and would do nothing but talk artistic slang about "tone" and "breath," about realism and idealism, and always with an air of innocence impossible to overcome' (*OTW*, I:164) – reflects back to Launcelot his 'Pygmalion passion' (*OTW*, I:187) with a vengeance: 'That manner of hers was the most baffling thing he had ever encountered' (*OTW*, I:164). Reassured by the successful establishment of a working partnership, however, Nelly dispenses with her habits of mimicry and starts experimenting with a style of her own – so much so that Launcelot, for the first time, recognises the artist in the wife and begins considering her more of an equal:

> Her progress had been surprising of late. Perhaps the spirit of the place had penetrated and inspired her; anyhow her sketches were alive with it, and its strange poetry.
>
> Launcelot himself, with all the advantage of his technical skill, could not give more truly that look of melancholy to his fortress-villages, that abandonment and tumult to the hills that lay between them and the outposts of the Apennines. (*OTW*, II:164–5)

Yet, as if apprehensive of the disruptive consequences of Nelly's yearning for her artistic m/other, upon being recalled to Rome, he enjoins her not, 'on any account, [to] make an attempt to meet Oenone' (*OTW*, II:175): an inversion of Bluebeard's injunction not to enter the forbidden room. Inevitably, as soon as Nelly finds herself '[d]eprived of the inspiration of Launcelot's society', she is unable to withstand the appeal of her desire. Irresistibly drawn to the fleeting glimpses caught of a distant village, whose 'romantic and beautiful' aspect inspires her to paint sketch after sketch, she finally sets off in search of this enigmatic place:

> From a particular spot, and from there only, it could be seen, perched upon its high hill-top, far up and up against the serene and dreamy blue of the sky.

It did not appear to be very distant, but its position was very lofty.

She sketched it in the morning light, when the sun glared down upon it, and made it look arid and desolate; she sketched it in the afternoon, when the shadows fell upon the piled-up, hustling dwellings, and a veil of softness crept over the grey old stones; she sketched it when the evening sank dreaming over it, and wide across the sky and mountains, a pair of great soft wings seemed stretched to north and south from the heart of the peaceful sunset.

And then, when she had sketched it in all its phases, a strong desire assailed her to visit her high-born village. (*OTW*, II:176–7)

In its 'high-born' yet 'fallen' ('desolate' and decaying) state, the mysterious village embodies Oenone, and it is indeed here that Nelly will 'find' her 'mother' and herself. A signifier of the return of Nelly's repressed desire for the 'good' mother (as opposed to the uncongenial, emotionally and intellectually inadequate Mrs Erskine), the village (the outer shell of the mother/the self) is visible only from forever shifting angles, and Nelly is compelled again and again to attempt to 'draw' (closer to) the maternal bodyscape, a desire invariably frustrated until she sets out on her journey to the heart of darkness (the destination of the sunset, the sight of which foreshadows Oenone's and Nelly's later contemplation of the scene from the opposite direction and their subsequent reconciliation). That the village, despite its appearance of physical proximity ('not very distant'), is described as 'lofty' points ahead to the complicated psychological and emotional processes of negotiation that Nelly will have to undergo in her endeavour to obtain Oenone's love. Before any affective rapprochement between the two women is possible, even from Nelly's side, Nelly must retrace Oenone's most excruciating moments of despair. After Launcelot's departure Oenone had suffered a near-death experience on Capri:

Like a goddess she stood upon the shore of that blue sea, resplendent in beauty, in power, in every good gift of life; while the fire of an unspeakable anguish made heavy and desolate her beautiful eyes … [A]t the sight of [the island] Oenone fell upon her knees, careless of the hard stones that had rolled down from the hills above, and stretched her arms in desperate invocation towards the sea, towards the island. But the sea smiled on, and the island seemed to slumber …

Oenone turned her eyes away from it. Her whole desolate future lay before her, like some lorn and lonely place unvisited save by mourning winds.

Mile upon mile, league after league, she saw its bare length stretching boundlessly away. She had so vast a region to be alone in – and – merciful Heaven! – that endless road went on and on and into the here-after! …

She let herself fall from her kneeling posture upon the strand, lying with her arm crushed ruthlessly against the hard stones on the beach. They hurt her, but she moved not. … She lay thus, quite motionless upon the shore, her head lying upon her outstretched arm, her hand bruised and bleeding from contact with a sharp-edged fragment of fallen rock. The long red-gold hair had become loosened, and fell about her shoulders like a radiant veil; the serpent, shaken from its stronghold, lay with it upon her heart, like an evil spirit that had come to claim dominion over her.

And the minutes or the hours flew by … the hot sun ran victoriously upon his course, altering the shadow-lines, and throwing delicate changes over the sea and hills … Still Oenone lay there grief-stricken and heedless … She wished that she might lie here and die; she prayed to the gentle spirit of Death to come to her, and bend over her and close her eyes. How glad, how thankful to be spared the empty-hearted toil of living out her life! … But this cruel tideless sea would not flow up, however long she waited, to release her. … Oh, the insolent splendour of the scene! … With a suppressed cry she rose to her feet, and moved away towards the steep path by which she had wound her way downwards from the heights. (*OTW*, II:134–7)

In its explicit problematisation of the expectation of a psycho-mythological dimension to landscape and its quasi-naturalist exploration of the radical disjuncture between natural phenomena and human emotion, this scene starkly dramatises the rejection of Grand's theosophist mythopoeia. The 'goddess', her 'face and figure blended, as if by original affinity, with her surroundings' (*OTW*, II:134), is able to find neither solace nor a sense of universality in her encounter with the elements, but is instead faced with the recognition of her bleakest solitude and the horror (not, as in Beth's case, ecstasy) of the infinite in nature. As in *The Wing of Azrael*, published two years later, and *The Romance of the Moors*, which appeared in 1891, this is a universe bereft of any metaphysical presence or meaning: a 'great black gulf' 'appalling' in its 'ghastly silence' which 'seemed to put all human hopes to shame. The fragmentary scraps of religious faith … unprepared for the fierce encounter … quailed and sank' (*ROM*, 45). This scene of anguish correlates with Olive Schreiner's *Undine* (published posthumously in 1926, but written in the 1870s),[9] where the heroine's moment of greatest despair coincides with the brightest sunshine: the sun 'seemed a great, laughing, cruel human eye, looking down at her from the clear blue sky' (*U*, 114). Similarly, in *The Story of an African Farm* Waldo's endeavour to gain metaphysical reassurance fails spectacularly: 'Above him was the quiet, blue sky, about him the red earth; there were the clumps of silent ewes and his altar – that was all. He looked up – nothing broke the intense stillness of the blue overhead' (*AF*, 24). Like the first part of Schreiner's 'Three Dreams in a Desert', whose allegorical configurations are prefigured in Oenone's prostration in the sand, hope resides, not in nature, but in women's agency and the healing potential of human interaction: like Schreiner's mythical Woman, Oenone rises to her feet unaided, struggling to (re)gain control of her destiny, and later is guided back into the realm of human company with the help, ironically, of one of her would-be lovers (*OTW*, II:153).

In order to succeed in her quest for the mother, Nelly must undergo a similarly epiphanic moment of utter desolation and disorientation in the mountain desert where, literally as well as metaphorically, she 'loses her way', her sense of self, and therefore her metaphysical certainty of future deliverance:

> It was very lonely. A sunny benediction lay upon the hushed land; not a bird's note was to be heard; the winds went voiceless by, for there were no trees to whisper, no long grass to sigh at their too rapid passing. A quiet desolation lay around, expressive, as it seemed to the awed wanderer, of an eternal sadness. Fascinated as by some spell, she hastened onwards through the solitude. The way grew more intricate as she penetrated into unfamiliar regions ... The track, which was almost obliterated, led through an upland valley ... her trusted landmarks had vanished ... the country looked strange, and ten times more wild and desolate than she had ever thought it before. Her heart beat tumultuously. Could it be that she had been so mad as to lose her way? With a sickening qualm, she tried to gather together her energies and steady her thoughts for the problem before her. ...
>
> Marking her present position with a large stone, so that at least *that* should not be lost, she reconnoitred on every side, hoping to notice some familiar object. But there was nothing to be seen but hill after hill, shoulder above shoulder ... The loneliness and the silence were terrible.
>
> All idea of reaching the ideal village was given up; home had now become the goal of her ambition ...
>
> ... Nelly stood still and gazed at the dreadful loveliness of the scene ... An unspeakable dread possessed her, as of approaching death. Great gulfs of loneliness separated her from her beloved one ...
>
> ... As she peered wildly through the dusk, she became aware, with a violent heart-throb, of a human figure. It looked grey and spectral in the twilight, but after more careful scrutiny she saw, to her intense joy, that it was one of the peasant women, in the picturesque costume of the district.
>
> Help had come at last! (*OTW*, II:178–9, 181, 182, emphasis in original)

In her subtle re-vision of the Ariadne myth, Caird captures Nelly's sense of abjection towards the horrible sublimity of the maternal womb. In Greek mythology Ariadne enabled Theseus to negotiate his way through the deadly labyrinth and slay the Minotaur (the signifier of the mother, the hideous product of Pasiphae's monstrous union with a white bull);[10] in Caird's version, Nelly/Ariadne/Theseus, however many stones s/he may mark, is powerless to proceed until rescued (figuratively 'reborn' into life) by the female 'native' who leads her to the Minotaur (Montebello/Oenone/the mother). Nelly's mission is not to destroy the monstrous mother who threatens to devour (literally, kill) her, but to love her, and through love heal her from the paralysing self-loathing displaced into the hatred of the other woman/'daughter'. In mapping the difficult and painful process of reconciliation between artist-'mother' (Oenone) and artist-'daughter' (Nelly), Caird draws attention to the complex negotiation of subject positions which modern theorists like Julia Kristeva regard as essential to the successful reconstruction of the mother–daughter relationship. In 'Stabat Mater' Kristeva describes the unreconstructed relationship between mother and daughter as one driven by hostility, even hatred: feelings rooted in the fear of the other where once there was only one. If she is able to overcome her sense of antagonism, the mother conceives a new body language which carries the potential of releasing both her and her daughter into feminine *jouissance* and a 'woman's discourse':

> when the other woman posits herself as such, that is, as singular and inevitably in opposition, 'I' am startled, so much that 'I' no longer know what is going on. There are then two paths left open to the rejection that bespeaks the recognition of the other woman as such. Either, not wanting to experience her, I ignore her and, 'alone of my sex,' I turn my back on her … It is a hatred that, lacking a recipient worthy enough of its power, changes to unconcerned complacency. Or else, outraged by her own stubbornness, by that other's belief that she is singular, I unrelentingly let go at her claim to address me and find respite only in the eternal return of power strokes, bursts of hatred – blind and dull but obstinate. … Within this strange feminine see-saw that makes 'me' swing from the unnameable community of women over to the war of individual singularities, it is unsettling to say 'I'. The languages of the great formerly matriarchal civilizations must avoid, do avoid, personal pronouns: they leave to the context the burden of distinguishing protagonists and take refuge in tones to recover an underwater, transverbal communication between bodies. It is a music from which so-called oriental civility tears away suddenly through violence, murder, blood baths. A woman's discourse, would that be it? [11]

Like Kristeva's mother, Oenone is 'startled', even 'terrified' (*OTW*, II:197) by Nelly's assertion of a separate identity, a subjectivity distinctly different from the one Oenone had assigned to her. After a lengthy lecture intended to chasten Nelly into paying tribute to her immeasurably greater insight, Oenone is faced with the unsettling discovery that she is dealing with a personality not only equal but in fact superior to hers in maturity and critical self-reflexivity: 'there *are* exceptions, and I am one of them', Nelly affirms, a statement of authenticity that Oenone is reluctantly forced to confirm (*OTW*, II:198). Mortified, Oenone is initially unable to respond to Nelly other than with the fierce hatred she directed towards her step-mother, the woman who robbed her of the exclusive possession of the father. At once motherless and mother-oppressed, she was then precipitated towards a conflictual love–hate relationship with the law of the father (a struggle embodied in her anarchist lover), but this did not bring her any closer to a reconciliation with the mother. Now, for the first time, this reconciliation appears possible as a result of the inversion of mother/daughter positions prompted by Oenone's illness, which functions as the outer manifestation of her inner conflict. As Nelly assumes the role of companion, nurse and mother, Oenone begins to be affectively drawn towards her erstwhile adversary: the peaceful 'long hours' the two women 'spend ... together sketching among the mountains' (*OTW*, II:207) figures an emotional closeness that approximates the earlier working partnership of Nelly and Launcelot. The 'woman's discourse' invoked by Kristeva, however, cannot be born as long as Oenone remains captive to patriarchal conceptualisations of Woman, as encapsulated by her serpent-jewellery. A terrifying proto-Freudian snake dream marks the beginning of her transition from Eve to Ruth, *femme fatale* to woman-identified woman, as she struggles free from the horror of her murderous desires (*OTW*, II:48):

> She dreamt one night that a long black serpent was pursuing her wherever she went, and that, in spite of her terrified efforts to escape, it touched her and coiled round her, twisting its strong slimy body all round her body, its neck round her neck, till the creature's face was raised to hers with a venomous hiss, and she felt its fangs upon her cheek. With a wild cry she awoke – and then she realized that she had been acting out her waking nightmare in another form during her sleep. (*OTW*, II:210)

If, as I suggested earlier, serpent imagery in this novel points to the mythical figure of Lilith, Oenone's nightmare encapsulates the 'deadly conflict' of her intense emotions towards the 'other' in herself (*OTW*, II:48). As Raphael Patai notes, Kabbalists frequently 'split the person of Lilith ... into two and ... distinguish[ed] between an Elder and a Younger Lilith' locked into bitter enmity and combat.[12] Oenone's dream might then reflect her dawning recognition of the myth's stifling grasp, her identification with the younger 'Lilith' and desire to overcome the 'battle royal' between them, indicating a wish to transform the murderous serpent into a figure of maternal affection: 'She *could* not, *would* not love this girl, and yet, O strange necessity! She felt at moments that she *must!*' (*OTW*, II:218, emphases in original). Painfully released into the acceptance of their love for each other ('Will you hate me always, when I love you so?', Nelly pleads, *OTW*, II:221), Oenone gains the capacity for 'mothering' Nelly and protecting her from rather than causing her harm. This is signalled by her response to Nelly's desire to eat berries which Oenone knows are poisonous. At this juncture Caird again conjures up Greek myth, here inverting the Demeter/Core (Persephone) and, in the filicidal dimension, implicitly also Medea myths. As Luce Irigaray posits in 'The Forgotten Mystery of Female Ancestry', the Demeter/Core myth maps the displacement of mother–daughter attachment into heterosexual desire, symbolised through Core/Persephone's consumption of the fruit of the dead: forced to release her to Demeter, Hades 'induces Persephone to eat a pomegranate seed, which, unknown to her, makes her a hostage of the Underworld'.[13] In *One That Wins* Nelly's plea – 'Why should we not – we two –

by force of will and force of love, turn aside this threatening misfortune?' (*OTW*, II:220) – is carried into action by Oenone, who intervenes to prevent Nelly's involuntary self-poisoning (*OTW*, II:217), thus prompting their final embrace: 'Oenone drew her towards her, held her close in her strong arms, and kissed her long and tenderly' (*OTW*, II:222). By breaking the spell of alienation between mother and daughter, Oenone enables each of them fully to embrace herself: for a woman 'to be able to love herself and return in love the body that was "born" to her', Hélène Cixous argues, '[i]t is necessary that the best of herself be given to [her] by another woman ... Touch me, caress me, you the living no-name, give me myself as myself.'[14] Unlike Irigaray's paradigmatic figures in 'And the One Doesn't Stir without the Other', this mother/daughter pair does begin to speak. 'We have never spoken to each other', Irigaray's daughter laments, '[a]nd such an abyss now separates us that I never leave you whole, for I am always held back in your womb ... And what I wanted from you, Mother, was this: that in giving me life, you still remain alive.'[15]

Caird's closing vignette, which figures Launcelot's reappearance at the very point at which the two women embrace, carries a curious ambivalence. In the context of the novel's exploration of mother–daughter relationships the scene signals Oenone's successful resolution of the conflict, for by literally and symbolically embracing Nelly's and Launcelot's love, she 'remains alive' in the sense of ensuring her participation in their gratification: 'the spell was potent – I could resist no longer. Thank Heaven, I can rejoice now in his happiness and yours' (*OTW*, II:222). One might then visualise a utopian sequel in the form of a counter-family or, even, a counter-marriage of three artists bonded together in creative collaboration and affective intercommunication: the experimental arrangement Claudia briefly envisages in *The Stones of Sacrifice*.[16] On the other hand, the lesbian undertones of a desire which culminates in a passionate embrace on the last page of the novel, only to be foreclosed again by the intruding presence of masculinity, may suggest a different reading: 'A slight sound caused them to look towards the door, and there upon the threshold stood Launcelot' (*OTW*, II:222). The instability of the novel's moment of closure which invokes a new opening is also present in the title, for who exactly is the 'one that wins': Nelly (by gaining an artist-lover – but which? – or a supportive mother) – Oenone (by overcoming her demons and re/discovering herself in her love of Nelly?) – or Launcelot (whose name concludes the text)? Caird's *The Romance of the Moors* (1891) ends with two women, one of whom is an older artist, going off together, though both are ostensibly in love with the same man. 'Of all vulgar error, that is the vulgarest', Caird wrote in *The Wing of Azrael* in 1889, 'which supposes young women to be interested and attracted solely and chiefly by young men. There is no feeling more intense and romantic, in its own way, than the devotion of a girl to a woman a little older than herself. No lover ever admired more enthusiastically or worshipped more devoutly' (*WOA*, II:128). The novel hints at same-sex affection (between Viola and Sibella) being redirected towards heterosexual outlets (as Viola's abusive husband, Philip Dendraith, becomes the object of Sibella's desire). Here, too, the severed bond between women and their reorientation towards masculinity and marriage is encoded through (in this case, biblical) myth: Azrael (or Azazel), Caird explains in her introduction, denotes the 'Angel of Death, of Fate, of Destruction' who 'separates the soul from the body' (*WOA*, I:xiii). Fragmentation and alienation was the prize women had to pay in marriage; the 'wing of Azrael' was the fatal shadow marriage cast over women's lives.

When Caird invoked the emotional potential of woman-to-woman friendship, she was not so much exploring alternative female libidinalities as valorising the feminist concept of sisterhood. Whereas heterosexual love and marriage obstructed women's self-development as it reduced them to functional objects within the patriarchal family, turning them into objects of consumption, 'bodies' alienated from their 'souls' (their sense of selfhood), female friendship fostered a sense of identity and community which bolstered women's confidence and encouraged them in their efforts for self-improvement. The New Woman trope of the female community frequently served to offer readers a constructive alternative to the marriage plot even as it circumvented lesbian desire.[17] Like Grand and Schreiner, Caird was concerned with the detrimental impact of marriage on women's creativity, and argued that women's channelling of emotional energy towards heterosexual relationships interfered with their artistic agency. The incompatibility, for women, between 'art' and (heterosexual) 'love' and marriage is already pinpointed in Caird's first novel, *Whom Nature Leadeth* (1883), a sensation novel with a tortuous plot involving fraud, murder and various attempted abductions. Its gifted but self-sacrificing heroine, Leonore Ravenhill, fails in her ambition to be an 'agreeable and satisfactory wife … *and* a thorough and conscientious artist' (*WNL*, II:189; emphasis added). After only five years of marriage one of her allegorical paintings reflects her acute sense of resignation: deserted by Youth, Hope, Power, Genius, Talent and Strength, she is left with the images of Failure and Decay (*WNL*, III:251–2). An unhappy wife and a failed artist, she is, like Poe's Lenore, 'nameless here for evermore'.

This is a destiny pointedly not shared by Caird's unmarried women artists: Oenone Evelyn is 'the topic of conversation in every Roman studio' (*OTW*, I:18); 'one hears her name everywhere in Rome' (*OTW*, I:7). Similarly, in *The Daughters of Danaus* Hadria assures her scandalised mother that, as the author of advanced novels, Valeria du Prel 'has been heard of throughout the English-speaking world' (*DD*, 55). In 'The Yellow Drawing-Room' (1891) Vanora Haydon leaves her 'radiant' imprint not only on the drawing-room of the title but also, crucially, on the psyche of the male narrator, St Vincent, who begins his tale with the confession that 'I've never been the same man since I met

Vanora' ('YDR', 30, 22). Like Grand's *The Beth Book*, Caird's story, published a year before Charlotte Perkins Gilman's 'The Yellow Wallpaper', encodes the battle between female and male aesthetics as an erotic 'duel' ('YDR', 27) between a New Woman and an Old Man, from which the former emerges victorious only because she resists the appeal of heterosexual desire. Like Gilman's narrator, and like Anna in *The Pathway of the Gods*, Vanora defies the attempt to confine her to a masculine aesthetic, but whereas Anna and Gilman's character act out the rage and anguish of the hysteric, Vanora self-confidently creates a room of her own in the house of male aesthetics. As in Oenone's case, her artistic project is supported by a benign but absent paternal figure. Having gained her father's consent to the idea of redecorating the drawing-room, Vanora transforms this paradigmatic space of circumscribed and retiring ladyhood into a site of spectacularly subversive femininity by painting it a startlingly 'brilliant yellow': 'The colour had been washed out of the very daffodils ... the sunshine was confronted in a spirit of respectful independence, brotherhood being acknowledged, but the principle of equality uncompromisingly asserted' ('YDR', 22). '[B]old, unapologetic, unabashed' ('YDR', 22), the wallpaper embodies Vanora's iconoclastic personality: 'She was vital ... In the human colour-spectrum, she took the place of the yellow ray' ('YDR', 23). Like Oenone's paintings, Vanora's flaunting of herself in her art challenges male definitions of femininity: 'It was not the room that my ideal woman would have created. My ideal woman would unfailingly choose a nice tone of grey-blue' ('YDR', 22).

St Vincent's colour-coded objectification of women recalls Launcelot Sumner's conceptual collapse of female artists into male-engendered artefacts: 'Nelly had none of [Oenone's] quality of an "old master;" she was like a clear, clean water-colour drawing, by a practised hand-subject' (*OTW*, I:92). In both cases the male gaze struggles but patently fails to assume control over the woman artist. Launcelot's disconcerting sense of disorientation when confronted with Oenone's radical self-sufficiency and Nelly's perplexing mimicry is replicated in St Vincent's bewildered dismay when he attempts to disentangle the paradox of a 'distinctly unwomanly' environment inhabited by a 'supremely, overpoweringly womanly' woman whose 'exuberant feminine quality' eclipses her more conventional sisters: 'This was all out of keeping. According to my doctrines it was even impossible ... Everything was wrong and contradictory' ('YDR', 23). The 'optic horror' and self-alienation Gilman's female narrator experiences when exposed to the baffling, 'infuriating', even 'torturing' patterns of male aestheticism (the Morris-inspired wallpaper of her nursery prison; 'YW', 25)[18] are here inverted and redirected at a patriarchal subject. Unlike Grand's and Gilman's artist figures, Vanora does not repudiate but rather subverts contemporary aestheticism by reclaiming the colour of decadence as an emblem of women's liberation.[19] Vanora's appropriation of aesthetic paradigms for feminist purposes transforms the 'repellent, almost revolting ... smouldering unclean yellow' of Gilman's wallpaper ('YW', 13) into a potent symbol of life and resplendent female vitality. So irresistible is Vanora's 'absurd spell' ('YDR', 21) that despite his outrage St Vincent finds himself enthralled; in a sense, Vanora enthralls precisely because she outrages his ideal of femininity and his aesthetic sense. Invoking Ruskin as the arbiter of true femininity, he admonishes her that 'you may have a brilliant career in the future, but the more brilliant, the more complete will be your failure [as a woman]' ('YDR', 26): a futile attempt to recover his equilibrium in the face of his intense crisis of masculinity. Painfully aware of his foolishness, exacerbated by his inability to shake off a 'supercilious peacock' ('YDW', 25–6), he admits that his encounter with Vanora has permanently 'deprived me of myself, unhinged me, destroyed the balance of my character' ('YDR', 21). While Vanora, herself the victim of a politically incorrect attraction, rejects his suit and disappears from his life when she discovers his dishonourable conduct towards her sister, he becomes, and remains, an unwilling captive to her revolting aesthetic: 'I hate the whole subject, but I can't leave it alone' ('YDR', 21). Ultimately, Vanora's vision is able to enter the bloodstream of Old Manhood and endure only because her reason overrules her desire: 'to the end of time I should continue to shock and irritate you, and you would stifle, depress and perhaps utterly unhinge me' ('YDR', 29).

If Vanora resists the appeal of passion, *The Daughters of Danaus* explores the opposite scenario of a woman artist less immured to the spell of the moment. When Hadria marries Hubert, Vanora's prediction comes true: 'Hubert's instincts were scholastic and lawful, Hadria was disposed to daring innovation. Her bizarre compositions shocked him painfully. The two jarred on one another, in great things and in small ... She must have been mad!' (*DD*, 166–7)

'Under a singular spell': the artist and the minotaur in *The Daughters of Danaus* (1894)[20]

The Daughters of Danaus draws on Classical myth in order to problematise the condition of women in the late-Victorian family. 'Private' variants of prostitution, marriage and motherhood are presented as conditions more degrading and devastating in their psycho-social impact than women's public slavery. Socialised into abjection by their mothers, daughters are offered up to the Minotaur – the patriarchal family and its cult of woman sacrifice – to emerge from their ordeal as the willing executioners of the next generation of women. If these are the conditions that underpin female individuation, what are the consequences for the woman possessed of the qualities that constitute an artist? Conjured up in the title, the tragic inescapability of Greek myth and its particular repercussions on women serves to posit a challenge to the Emersonian belief, discussed in the opening chapter, in character overcoming circumstances; for as the novel illustrates, it is the '*relation* between character and conditions ... that determines Fate' (*DD*, 10, emphasis added), and the woman artist is all the more vulnerable to the general conditions precisely because of her greater sensibility.

In Greek mythology, the fifty daughters of Danaus, after whom Caird entitled her novel, were ordered by their father, who was afraid of being deposed, to kill their cousins to whom they had been promised in marriage. One sister disobeyed and saved her husband, yet she, too, was condemned with the others forever to fill with water a vessel full of holes.[21] In his play *Hiketides* ('The Suppliants'), Aeschylus introduced some changes which heighten the sense of injustice intrinsic to the fate meted out to the Danaides. Coerced into marriage after a failed attempt at flight, the women kill their husbands, thus incurring the savage revenge of the gods who engineered the nuptials.[22] Robert Graves presents a different version of the story; here, Hypermnestra, who saved her husband Lyncea because he did not force her to consummate the marriage, is spared the sentence passed on her sisters. Graves also notes that the Danaides later came to be seen 'as undergoing eternal punishment for matricide';[23] violent rebellion against patriarchal injunctions is thus displaced into the concept of daughter–mother aggression. *The Daughters of Danaus* reflects central aspects of the myth: compulsory marriage imposed by the gods (patriarchal society); frantic attempts at liberation resulting in the further tightening of oppressive conditions; the eternity of a life wasted on futile tasks. Like the Hypermnestra of the later versions, Hadria is doubly victimised in being punished for a crime she did not commit (matricide); to add to the tragic force of her novel, Caird inverts the positions and shows a daughter being crushed by her mother. 'I grudge them to the monster who will not spare us even one' (*DD*, 319), M. Jouffroy grimly declares when contemplating the endless procession of female disciples devoured by the Minotaur: the traditionalist mother who, with 'the claims of a nature unfulfilled', exacts 'the unconscious thirst for the sacrifice of others ... the groping instinct to bring the balance of renunciation to the level and indemnify oneself for the loss suffered and the spirit offered up' (*DD*, 363).

In her adaptation of the Greek myth, Caird replaces the wrath of the gods with the forces of environment, heredity and temperament. Like Viola Sedley and Hardy's Tess, Hadria is 'doomed by fate, by circumstance, by temperament' (*WOA*, III:222). The mood in which she accepts Hubert Temperley is reminiscent of Tess's perilous dream-states. Entranced by the magic of a Scottish dance, she responds to his urgent entreaties with careless fatalism, and as in Hardy's novel this mood recurs at critical points in the plot, suggesting that Hadria's personality (depth of feeling coupled with impulsive recklessness) and the circumstances of her life combine to push her to the brink of self-obliteration: 'Hadria might almost have accepted him in sheer absence of mind ... The bizarre old music smote still upon her ear. She felt as if she was in the thrall of some dream whose events followed one another' (*DD*, 137).

Unlike Hardy's intellectually undeveloped Tess, however, Hadria is fully aware of the nature of her predicament: either to '[cut] through prejudices that are twined in with the very heart-strings of those one loves' or 'like some wretched insect [be] pinned alive to a board throughout a miserable lifetime' (*DD*, 15). Her life oscillates between these two states. 'We are conscious of an ability to *choose*,' Caird wrote elsewhere, 'but our choice is, after all, an affair of temperament, and our temperament a matter of inherited inclinations ... modified from infancy by outward conditions' (*WOA*, I:78, emphasis in original). Introduced as a brilliant dancer, spirited speaker and gifted pianist, Hadria is able to stake a claim on the time and space required to practise her art only in the congenial context of the Preposterous Society, a debating club founded by her siblings. Outside this enchanted room, which like Beth's 'secret chamber' is located in an attic, her talents go to waste: her extraordinary powers as a musician and composer fail to be recognised other than by the select few, while the sensibility so essential to her artistic temperament is pressed into the service of parental expectations. As an unmarried daughter, she spends all her energies on fending off the incessant demands that her mother makes on her time: 'If Hadria yielded the point on any particular occasion, her mood and her work were destroyed; if she resisted, they were equally destroyed, through the nervous disturbance and the intense depression which followed the winning of a liberty too dearly bought' (*DD*, 109). In 'Cassandra' Florence Nightingale described middle-class daughters' predicament of 'never hav[ing] half an hour in all their lives (excepting before or after anybody is up in the house) that they can call their own, without fear of offending or hurting someone' – a system which 'dooms some minds to incurable infancy, others to silent misery'; this and only this, she asserted, was the reason why there were no female Murillos, Michael Angelos (sic) or Pascals.[24]

As Patricia Murphy suggests, the 'temporal regulation' of Victorian women constituted a Foucauldian regime of power analogous to the containment of prisoners, soldiers or workers: 'Time in all of these cases served as a disciplinary mechanism whereby the dominant culture could exercise its authority.'[25] In *The Daughters of Danaus* Caird details the repercussions of this disciplinary regime on the artistically inspired daughter who, as in 'Cassandra', is forced to forgo sleep in order to carve out time for her work and, with her erstwhile 'splendid constitution' severely 'weaken[ed] and unbalance[ed]' (*DD*, 109), turns to day-dreaming ('Dreaming always – never accomplishing; thus women live'),[26] finally to seek escape in marriage: 'the only chance (and it is but a chance)', Nightingale wrote, for a woman to 'escape from this death; and how eagerly and how ignorantly it is embraced!'[27] The unguarded moment in which Hadria gives in to Hubert's pressure entails a lifetime of interruptions anticipated in her composition 'Futility':

> She dreamt an absurd dream: That she was … one of those girls with the high pattering accents, playing tennis without ceasing and with apparent cheerfulness … and all the time, a vast circle of shadowy forms stood watching, beckoning, and exhorting, and warning, and turning away, at last, in sorrowful contempt, because she preferred to spend her youth eternally in futilities. And then they all slowly drifted by with sad eyes fixed on her, and she was still left playing, playing. And it seemed as if whole weeks passed in that way, and she grew morally tired, but some power prevented her from resting. The evil spell held her enthralled. Always cheerful, always polite and agreeable, she continued her task, finding herself growing accustomed to it at last, and duly resigned to the necessity, wearisome though it was. Then all hope that the game would ever cease went away, and she played on, mechanically, but always with that same polite cheerfulness, as of afternoon calls. She would not for the world admit that she was tired. But she was so tired that existence became a torture to her, and her heart seemed about to break with the intolerable strain – when she woke up with a start, and found herself lying in a constrained attitude, half-choked by the bed-clothes. (*DD*, 46–7)

Like Rebekah in *From Man to Man*, Hadria pictures the failed artist as a mother grievously neglectful of her imaginative offspring, whose spectral presence acts as a ghastly reminder of her wasted creative powers. However, by shaping this vision into art, she transcends Rebekah's position of the artist in limbo, while also rejecting Rebekah's maternal ethic when she abandons her sons in pursuit of her artistic career. In transposing her nightmare into a musical composition, Hadria authenticates her experience as a woman through the medium of art, just as she authenticates her aesthetic vision by grounding it in her lived experience. She thus becomes an avatar of the New Woman writer, a feminist artist for whom the personal resonates with the political in her exploration of a new aesthetic form in which 'art and ethic [would be] united' (*DD*, 21). When many years later Hadria rediscovers the forgotten composition, her recognition of its artistic value spurs her on to resume her piano practice: 'She knew that the music was good, and that now she could compose music infinitely better. The sharpness of longing for her lost art cut through her. She half turned from the piano and then went back' (*DD*, 467).

'Futility' is an apt *leitmotiv* of Hadria's marriage, whose tragic dimension resides in its banality. Hadria does not suffer the savage indemnities of a Greek heroine or the neo-Gothic, ancestral doom of a Viola Sedley or Tess d'Urberville, for the Temperley *ménage* is merely a marriage of incompatible temperaments and uncongenial daily grinds; and yet it is the very ordinariness of the pressures that, as Caird suggests, proves most destructive of the artistic impetus. Only by escaping to a Parisian counter-community of artists does Hadria recover a sense of personal identity which prompts a resurgence of creativity. Her mentor, M. Jouffroy, predicts a glorious future, even inter-national fame for her – but this cannot be achieved without 'steady, *uninterrupted* work' (*DD*, 318, emphasis added). Impressing on her that '[e]verything must be subservient' to her art, M. Jouffrey cautions Hadria in particular to withstand the demands of 'the fetish *la famille*' to which he has lost many earlier disciples (*DD*, 318, emphasis in original). For him, Hadria is a test case: it is on her single-mindedness, or lack of it, that his final judgment of the female sex will depend (*DD*, 319). The device of a supportive male mentor serves to invalidate the male cliché of female artistic inferiority (since an experienced male professional states that women's talents are 'astonishing' [*DD*, 319]), while at the same time enabling Caird to address the mis-conception on which male dismissal of female talent was so often based. What Jouffrey mistakenly interprets as weakness of character proves in reality to be an overwhelming omnipresence of social pressures to which men would not be subject to the same degree. As the market value of her musical composi-tions is in reverse proportion to their innovative character, Hadria shares the vicissitudes of many male artists in having to spend valuable time on Grub Street journalism in order to make a living. The primary interruptions to her work are, however, of a more personal nature:

> friends … pressed her to visit them, to accompany them hither and thither … Even here, where she seemed so free, the peculiar claims that are made, by common consent, on a woman's time and strength began to weave their tiny cords around her … To give pain or offence for the sake of an hour or two … seemed cruel and selfish, yet Hadria often longed for the privilege that every man enjoys, of quietly pursuing his work without giving either. (*DD*, 322)

The text suggests that even if women escape from the ties of marriage, they remain subject to the obligations of their socially circumscribed feminine role (people's demands on their time) or their own internalised response to it (the fear of giving pain or offence). Exhausted by the onslaught of conflicting pressures, Hadria is all the more susceptible to the ultimate invasion of her space and time in the form of her mother's life-threatening illness. She returns home and, told that her mother's survival depends on her compliance, resigns herself to a life of 'ornamental womanhood' (*DD*, 382); where previously she strove to live for art, she now freezes into a lifeless statue, one of the 'beautiful objects' collected by her acquaintances (*DD*, 380).

If the circumstances that shape and circumscribe a woman's life are obstructive to artistic development, Hadria's recurrent Sisyphus dream, in which 'hands without bodies' keep 'placing stones in the path, so that they rolled down and had to be evaded at the peril of her life ... amid thin, scarcely audible laughter' (*DD*, 319–20) indicates wilful human sabotage as a major factor in the demise of female genius. Though stuck in an unhappy marriage and later, briefly, an ill-advised affair, Hadria suffers most severely and lastingly from the interventions of Old Women: her mother and her sister-in-law Henriette Temperley, both of whom belong to the category of 'destroyers' which in her opening speech to the Preposterous Society Hadria defined as the opponents of society's 'organizers' (*DD*, 9). Even Valeria du Prel, Hadria's role model of a 'free' woman and successful artist, contributes to her downfall by joining in the chorus of female voices urging her on towards the fulfilment of what she, too, believes to be women's 'natural' instincts: 'Had only Valeria been on her side, she would have felt secure, but Valeria was dead against her' (*DD*, 142). The New Woman theme of woman-to-woman antagonism is countered with the vision of constructive sisterhood as it is reflected in the relationship between Hadria and Algitha and invoked programmatically at the end of the novel (*DD*, 473). Significantly, the Sisyphus metaphor here makes way for a different image, hardly less gruesome, yet evocative of Schreiner's vision in 'Three Dreams in a Desert':

> She recalled a strange and grotesque vision, or waking-dream, that she had dreamt a few nights before: of a vast abyss, black and silent, which had to be filled up to the top with the bodies of women, hurled down to the depths of the pit of darkness, in order that the survivors might, at last, walk over in safety ... Hadria knew, in her dream, that some day it would have claimed its last victim, and the surface would be level and solid, so that people would come and go, scarcely remembering that beneath their feet was once a chasm into which throbbing lives had to descend, to darkness and a living death. (*DD*, 451)

The symbol of the sieve which can never be filled, and the mountain path made inaccessible by other women's obstructively placed stones, is transformed into the image of a living tomb which carries the potential of metamorphosing into a womb regenerative of future women with improved opportunities. Like Schreiner, Caird suggests that, if the present generation of women has little chance of escaping with their skins, the next one may enjoy a measure of freedom because of their predecessors' struggle. Less programmatic than Schreiner, Caird foregrounds the absolute lack of choice and the abject violence involved in this process of involuntary redemption: her women do not nobly decide to sacrifice themselves, but are 'hurled down' into a 'pit of darkness'; nor does the later generation remember and celebrate their foremothers, as is implied by the triadic structure of the dream memories of Schreiner's feminist Pilgrim's Progress.

The image of the tomb-womb anticipates Hadria's later portrayal of herself as a living deterrent, a 'scarecrow' whose example might help younger women avoid the 'pitfalls' in their quest for a life of their own (*DD*, 473–4). That individual failure does not necessarily denote a wasted life but carries the potential of aiding the collective effort towards creating better conditions for everybody is a notion strongly supported by Professor Fortescue, Caird's spokesperson of compassionate humanity and universal brotherhood (later reconfigured as Professor Owen in *The Stones of Sacrifice*). A prematurely aged New Man whose own efforts to forge a new relationship between the sexes have remained fruitless, he enjoins Hadria to consider 'the lives that never fulfil themselves; the apparent failure' as forming part of an evolutionary process 'in the upward movement of the race' (*DD*, 488–9). His death on a 'glorious morning' in spring, in a room resplendent with sunshine and alive with 'sweet air' and the colours of cherry blossom, daffodils, azaleas and wallflowers, culminating as it does in a metaphorical 'requiem' sung by a tame robin, an emblem of the soul (*DD*, 490–1), invokes a transcendentalist vision of renewal and rebirth in a manner reminiscent of Schreiner's *Story of an African Farm*, which concludes with a similar image (Waldo's death in the 'yellow sunshine' of Em's farm in the midst of chickens 'climb[ing] about him and perching on him' [*AF*, 281]). While presenting a feminist critique of Emerson's concept of the always-victorious genius – 'Emerson never was a girl', protests Hadria in the opening discussion; '[i]f he had been a girl, he would have known that conditions *do* count hideously in one's life' (*DD*, 14, emphasis in original) – Caird validates Emersonian transcendentalist beliefs in her final tableau, precisely because they offer a mystic space for the recuperation of the failing female artist.

With its abrupt swerve towards mysticism this otherwise fiercely realistic and iconoclastic text gains a curious ambivalence, which Sally Ledger attributes to the unresolved tension inherent in Caird's use of evolutionary discourse in order to 'negotiat[e its] implications for women'.[28] In fact the novel gestures towards two different endings, one offering the vista of Hadria's cynical assumption of her new 'rôle of scarecrow' (*DD*, 474), the other transcendental and open-ended. The bird which used to be fed by the now dead Fortescue fills Hadria with new hope when it settles in his room, its male gendering perhaps suggesting that, to Hadria at least, the spirit of the man who shortly before his death expressed his new-found belief in the immortality of the soul has somehow passed into its living frame. If material death might be overcome, then, one may assume, Hadria may yet have a life too. Birds as mythological harbingers of rebirth and emblems of the unity between animal and human life are a recurrent motif in Caird (in *One That Wins* Oenone also recovers from her depression with the help of a bird's song [*OTW*, II:70]). In *The Daughters of Danaus* Caird thus at one and the same time translates the visitations of fate and the wrath of the gods in Classical myth into contemporary reality, and remythologises this reality in order to configure Hadria as both a tragic heroine and a feminist rebel, the one Danaid different from the rest whose example might put an end to what Valeria calls the 'curse that has been laid upon our mothers through so many ages' (*DD*, 450).

This 'curse' evokes another paradigmatic myth of women's tragic doom which gained cultural currency specifically in the later Victorian age, the Lady of Shalott (*DD*, 287, see also *OTW*, II:52–3). As I argued in my discussion of this motif in Grand's work, New Woman writers were often drawn to the Pre-Raphaelite mystique of the Lady of Shalott, even as they challenged the aesthetisation of the beautiful as the invariably passive and death-stricken woman. Hadria's decision to act the 'scarecrow' may not be without its compensations, since throughout the text she embraces satirical roles, all the more parodic as her performances are usually taken at face value by her audience. Hadria particularly delights in mimicking orthodoxy and thus exploding the cult of femininity. Presented with the spectacle of their own absurdity, her Old Men and Women rarely get the joke, encouraging the reader to side with the trickster figure. Hadria's mockery of Henriette Temperley may serve as a case in point. Shortly before her as yet unannounced departure to Paris, Hadria resolves to ensure her sister-in-law's unwitting assistance by parodying her own maternal incompetence and the absurdity of the established notion that women, by virtue of being mothers, are possessed with instinctual child-rearing expertise: 'It amused Hadria to reproduce, for Henriette's benefit, the theories regarding the treatment and training of children that she had found current among the mothers of the district' (*DD*, 277). Neither a mother nor a woman of advanced views, Henriette turns out to hold considerably more sensible opinions than the multiple and multiplying mothers of Hadria's acquaintance. Playing the part of the mother who poses a health hazard to her children, Hadria gains Henriette's ready consent to take charge of domestic affairs during what she intends to be her permanent absence. Throughout the scene Hadria makes a show of working on and bending over a piece of embroidery – an ironic marker of her performance, since what on the face of it appears to be the quintessential prop of the superfluous lady, implicitly points to the intricate 'art' involved in enacting ladyhood. By underpinning her act of the inept mother with embroidery work, the central motif of the Lady of Shalott and Penelope myths, Hadria undermines the biological and aesthetic constructions of femininity:

Hadria had brought out a piece of embroidery (about ten years old), and was working peacefully ... (*DD*, 279)

Hadria bent low over her embroidery ... (*DD*, 280)

Hadria carefully selected a shade of silk, went to the light to reassure herself of its correctness, and returned to her easy chair by the fire. (*DD*, 281)

Hadria's game of embroidery is substantially different from Rebekah's domestic needlework in Schreiner's *From Man to Man* in that what for Rebekah symbolises her children and her body's creativity is a mere (im)posture for Hadria. The implication for Caird's reader is that patriarchal theories of women, however much they may be internalised by the target recipients themselves, don't pass muster (they literally don't hold up to the light). Whereas the Lady of Shalott meets her doom the moment she steps beyond the frame of her loom, Hadria recovers her 'magic' gifts as soon as she leaves the marital and maternal enclosures behind; and just as Penelope weaves and unravels her tapestry to maintain her independence, so Hadria literally and figuratively embroiders her tale to gain hers. It is only when her project of artistic self-realisation has failed that she has recourse to the darker sides of the Shalott myth, inverting its sexually cautionary message by turning herself into one of the 'beautiful objects of art' consumed by, but significantly also consumptive of, men. Unable to dedicate herself to the healing spell of art, she exults instead in the 'evil' spell of feminine sensuality and invests herself with the deadly quality of the *femme fatale*. After turning the heart-strings of most of the men in her circle, she embarks upon an adulterous affair with Professor Theobald, the cruel, immoral but passionate Hyde to Fortescue's impersonal and asensual Jekyll. Before her marriage Hadria had impressed on Temperley her unconditional agreement with her sister Algitha's view that adultery is defensible when it reflects authentic feeling, which by definition could then no longer be directed towards the legal partner, as a result of which their marriage ceases to be morally binding (*DD*, 125–7, 142). As a wife, she reiterates these convictions in her defence of Helen of Troy, who in Hadria's feminist re-vision of Classical myth emerges as a rebel with a cause:

> a slave break[ing her] chains … a wife throw[ing] off her bondage and def[ying] the law that insults her … She revolted against the tyranny that held her shut in, enslaved, body and soul … I am charmed to think that she gave her countrymen so much trouble to assert her husband's right of ownership. It was at *his* door that the siege of Troy ought to be laid. (*DD*, 290–1, emphasis in original)

However, when Hadria puts her theories to the test, she suffers an 'agony of shame' on realising that, far from representing authentic emotion, her conduct, initially shaped by the desire to take hostages in the war of the sexes (*DD*, 393), was guided by 'mere excitement' and the longing for sensual distraction (*DD*, 418): 'she had fallen below her own standard … she had been hypocritical with herself, played herself false, and acted contemptibly, hatefully!' (*DD*, 419). As a result of her self-loathing, she again assumes the role of the Lady of Shalott, although this time involuntarily, in the guise of an hysteric driven with unfulfilled desire – desire not for any knight but for her *art*: 'It was this craving to fill the place of her lost art' (*DD*, 419). Once again,

Caird revises the myth, suggesting that the lovelorn, foredoomed lady is in reality a frustrated artist.

Caird's adaptation of the Medea myth represents an even more forceful example of the way in which the trope of thwarted love serves to cover up the rage and despair of the thwarted artist. Already evoked in *One That Wins* in Oenone's murderous desires, as well as in *The Morality of Marriage*,[29] the myth of Medea, developed in full metaphorical force in *The Daughters of Danaus*, serves to pinpoint the relentless tragedy that awaits the exceptional woman who aspires to be an artist. Euripides' play and a replica Greek temple form the backdrop of two scenes in the early part of the text (*DD*, 19–22, 95) which, together with characters' frequent invocation of Classical myth, establish a link between Hadria's dreamy, artistic nature and the figure and tragic fate of Medea. As in her revision of the Lady of Shalott myth, Caird here also radicalised a Victorian cultural traditon. For although Euripides' *Medea* was not performed in Britain in full translation before 1907 – when both the play and its vision of the wrathful woman warrior became identfied with suffragette drama and iconography – Victorian drama and fiction were, from the 1830s through to the 1890s, suffused with representations of (infanticidal) Medeas. Edith Hall and Fiona Macintosh have drawn attention to the popularity of early to mid-Victorian burlesques which contextualised the Classical myth within emerging nineteeth-century legislation that established women's rights as mothers (Infant Custody Act, 1839) and wives (Divorce and Matrimonial Causes Act, 1857; Married Women's Property Act, 1882).[30] At the same time, as Josephine McDonagh has shown,[31] Victorian Realist literature (George Eliot's *Adam Bede*, 1859; *Felix Holt*, 1865; and *Daniel Deronda*, 1876) and late-century Naturalist explorations of eugenic child murder (Elizabeth Robins's and Florence Bell's *Alan's Wife*, 1893; Thomas Hardy's *Jude the Obscure*, 1895) as well as New Woman fictions of working-class women's desperate condition (George Egerton, 'Wedlock', *Discords*, 1894) reflected rising public concern with infanticidal women throughout the Victorian period. In contradistinction to this tradition, Caird shifted the emphasis from Medea's violent transgression to her artistic aspirations, revalidating the aberrant woman as a tragic artist: an aspect that, while later eclipsed by the trope of infanticide, was inherent in the original myth.

A sorceress, healer, and like Hadria a musician,[32] the mythical Medea was equipped with the 'art of snake-charming' and was frequently, as in Sophocles and Seneca, represented in the close proximity of snakes.[33] In Euripides she triumphantly exits into freedom and a new life on a dragon-powered chariot. Also known as 'Hecate's Witch-Priestess',[34] Medea helped the leader of the Argonauts, Jason, steal the golden fleece and undertook other outstanding acts of great bravery but also perfidy, including, possibly, the gruesome murder of her own brother, but not originally infanticide, the crime with which she later

came to be identified.[35] Jason 'swore by all the Gods of the Olympus to keep
faith with Medea for ever',[36] but eventually broke his oath. Euripides' fifth-
century BC play begins with the news of Jason's imminent wedding to Glauce
(the daughter of Corinth's ruler Creon), in the wake of which Medea and her
sons are to be banished from their adoptive home, and paints a vivid portrayal
of the depth of Medea's devastation. A woman not to be crossed with
impunity, she swears revenge and dispatches her sons to her rival, bearing a
poisoned gift whose deadly acid consumes Glauce and her father Creon.[37] In
her dual configuration as witch and healer, destroyer and creator (mother),
Medea is sometimes conflated with other mythical women, and can be figured
'in [a] triad ... as Persephone-Demeter-Hecate: the three daughters of Pelias
dismembering their father'.[38] Impelled by the fiery and indomitable spirit of an
immortal, Medea was celebrated as both Earth Goddess (Demeter) and Moon
Goddess (a cosmic inversion of Persephone's underworld?).[39] The Medea
myth also correlates with the Danaides, because here, too, the children are
made to atone for the sins of the parents. In some versions of the myth Medea's
sons fall victim to acts of retribution, either in consequence of their mother's
murder of Glauce or (as in Christa Wolf's early twenty-first-century version)
in an outburst of abject hatred against the banished Medea. '[T]his crime',
Graves notes, originated a ritual which consisted in selecting, every seventh
year, 'seven girls and seven boys ... [who would] spend a whole year in the
temple of Hera ... where the murder was committed'.[40] Sarah Iles Johnston
offers a further interpretation of this rite of atonement: the death of Medea's
children resulted from a broken promise by Hera to protect them, and in order
to avert further infant casualties in the community, fourteen children were
assigned the task of appeasing the goddess by devoting a year of their lives to
her. Johnston also draws attention to the ancient Mediterranean custom of
erecting an apotropaic statue of an ugly woman in order for 'like [to] avert
like'; this statue she interprets as a symbol of the 'reproductive demon' (the
woman who has 'failed the reproductive cyle'; Medea would be such a demon
in that her children died, irrespective of whether she was the agent of their
death).[41] Medea's role as a 'reproductive demon' may place Hadria's 'scarecrow'
function in a new light: having failed the *artistic* reproductive cycle, she casts
herself in the part of a cautionary figure to aspiring women artists.

Like Medea, Hadria is a tragic artist whose potential for 'good' (self-
realisation as a composer) turns to 'evil' (the squander and misuse of her gifts)
because of the treachery of others. Jason's betrayal here translates into
Temperley's deliberate deception (aware that Hadria would reject his suit, he
claims to share her radical views on marriage) and is also reflected in the
disloyalty of other women, above all Hadria's mother and sister-in-law.
Transgressive women, Medea and Hadria are both stigmatised as bad mothers,
Medea dramatically so (in that she is held responsible for her sons' deaths,

Euripides representing her as a literal child-killer), Hadria because she sacrifices her sons to her career. If Medea provokes divine anger by resisting the advances of Zeus,[42] Hadria suffers recriminations when she ends her brief relationship with the demonic Professor Theobald, who retaliates by withdrawing Hadria's custody rights over his daughter. In some versions of the myth Medea later confers her kingdom on Sisyphus,[43] the figure whose tragic fate pursues Hadria into her dreams. Like Medea, who acts as a frequent 'symbol of the freedom fighter' in modern adapations of the Classical myth,[44] Hadria engages in 'guerrilla warfare' (*DD*, 18) after her life's purpose has been thwarted. 'I am not trying to do good,' she assures her sister Algitha; 'I am merely refusing to obey these rules for our guidance, which are obviously drawn up to safeguard man's property and privilege. Whenever I can find a man-made precept, that I will carefully disobey; whenever the ruling powers seek to guide me through my conscience, there shall they fail!' (*DD*, 396). Medea's choice of 'a golden crown and a long white robe'[45] as the vehicles of Glauce's destruction spectacularises Hadria's indictment of motherhood as the 'crowning glory' of a woman's life, while incriminating marriage (emblemised in the white robe) as the funeral-pyre of women's aspirations.

Most significantly, in her feminist adaptation of the Medea myth Caird follows both earlier and contemporary women writers such as Christine de Pizan, Amy Levy and Vernon Lee in reclaiming the wronged artist in the patriarchal trope of the monstrous mother, while also foreshadowing the complex meanings of the figure in twentieth- and twenty-first-century women's art such as Christa Wolf's *Medea*.[46] In *The Book of the City of Ladies* (1405) Pizan celebrated Medea as an 'extremely beautiful lady with a tall, slim body and a very lovely face' (*BCL*, 63), a magnificent artist-priestess and white witch, and pointedly neither wife and mother, nor murderess. Associating her creative powers with the sublime in nature, Pizan wrote:

> In learning she surpassed all other women … Indeed no art had been invented that she hadn't mastered. Intoning a song that she alone knew, Medea could make the sky go cloudy and black, draw the wind out of the dark caverns in the depths of the earth, stir up storms, cause rivers to stop flowing, brew up all kinds of poisons, create fire out of nowhere to burn whatever she wished, and perform many other marvels besides. (*BCL*, 63)

Hadria resembles Pizan's Medea in her desire to become 'a priestess in the temple of art' devoting herself to 'the religion of the artist' (*DD*, 335). Like Pizan, Caird thus drew attention to a quality present in the Classical myth but which was marginalised by the focus on Medea's monstrosity. In Euripides' version – generally considered the first instance in which Medea was ascribed direct culpability for the death of her children[47] – Medea is honoured as an artist, one of the few outstanding women to possess the gift of poetry:

> Should woman find
> No inspiration thrill her breast,
> Nor welcome ever that sweet guest
> Of Song, that uttereth Wisdom's mind?
>
> Alas! not all! Few, few are they, –
> Perchance amid a thousand one
> Thou shouldest find, – for whom the sun
> Of poesy makes an inner day.[48]

Coinciding as it does with the grisly death of Glauce and Medea's agonising indecision over whether she will or will not kill her sons, the Chorus's ovation stands as a singular tribute to the extraordinary woman who in art as in life violates the boundaries of femininity, aligning the female artist's transgressive energy with the grievances, even the violence of the feminist, and vindicating both. 'Surely, of creatures that have life and wit', Medea rages in the early part of the play,

> We women are all unhappiest,
> Who, first, must buy, as buys the highest bidder,
> A husband – nay, we do but win for our lives
> A master! Deeper depth of wrong is this.
> Here too is dire risk – will the lord we gain
> Be evil or good? Divorce? – 'tis infamy
> To us: we may not even reject a suitor![49]

Medea's explosive proto-feminist self-affirmation would have held strong appeal for a writer like Caird. It certainly appears to have inspired Caird's contemporary Amy Levy, in whose verse drama 'Medea' ('After Euripides', *Cameo Series*, 1891) the protagonist's murderous actions are preceded by a passionate indictment of the patriarchal order:

> You never knew Medea. ...
> She was not born to serfdom ...
> ... Now behold me free,
> Ungyved by any chains of this man wrought;
> ... Freer, freer than the air or wingèd birds;
> Strong, stronger than the blast of wintry storms;
> And lifted up into an awful realm
> Where is nor love, nor pity, nor remorse,
> Nor dread, but only purpose. ('M', 48)

Interpreted differently by Levy and Caird, this 'purpose' was promoted by both as the only possible way in which a woman could attempt to overcome the female condition, which 'poured the sap / Of all [her] being, [her] life's very life, / Before a thankless godhead', making her realise that she was 'grown / No woman, but a monster' ('M', 42–3). Monstrosity was thus the result of women's subjection, not of feminist rebellion.

In both Caird and Levy, the extraordinary woman finds herself burdened with faculties which set her above all others but by their very nature weaken her in her struggle towards selfhood. 'O gods, gods,' Levy's heroine laments, 'ye have cursed me in this gift! / More should ye have withhold or more have giv'n' ('M', 43). Likewise, Caird draws attention to Hadria's 'exceptional ... power and insight' only to emphasise that these 'bear upon [her more than] her sisters, since in all directions she sees and feels and thinks more than they do'.[50] By contrast, in 'Amour Dure', Vernon Lee's 1890 adaptation of the myth, it is the lasting quality of her magic powers which enable the 'learned', 'scholarly' and altogether 'splendid' figure who out-medeas Medea (known as '"la pessima Medea" – worse than her namesake of Colchis') to withstand death and the weight of centuries in order to wreak dreadful revenge on patriarchy's beneficiaries, men ('AD', 109, 103). As the text reveals, Medea Da Carpi, too, is a thwarted artist and wise woman who, 'forced to play a merely sexual role in men's power games', sought to shift the balance of power by virtue of this very sexuality.[51] Lee takes care to stress that male myth got it all wrong: 'To suppose Medea a cruel woman is as grotesque as to call her an immoral woman. Her fate is, sooner or later, to triumph over her enemies, at all events to make their victory almost a defeat' ('AD', 102). The 'imbecile' figure of a fossilised professor who pronounces 'such a woman' as being 'psychologically and physiologically impossible' ('AD', 106) serves to pour scorn on patriarchal mythopoeia which fantasises about exceptional women only to deny their existence or demonise them. Like Levy's and Caird's revisionary texts, Lee's story serves to explode patriarchal iconographies of femininity and to illustrate that, as Christa Zorn has argued, 'historical circumstances, rather than her innate evilness, have created [Medea's] image as *femme fatale*'.[52]

In their reclamation of the ancient myth, Lee, Levy and Caird thus sought to regenerate and revalidate the magnetism of the outstanding woman who, because she defied the law of the father, had become monstrified by patriarchal culture. The motif of regeneration is already inscribed into the myth itself. Thus Robert Graves draws attention to the Celtic origins of Medea's 'cauldron of regeneration',[53] the emblem of a magic rite of creative renewal and rebirth through incantation and conjuration. This image is invoked at the beginning of Caird's novel, when Hadria watches Algitha and their brother Ernest light a bonfire in a cavern in the Scottish Highlands, close to the Greek temple where Valeria later bemoans women's fate (*DD*, 95). In Hadria's fertile imagination, Algitha assumes the aspect of a sorceress weaving spells over her cauldron:

> They collected the withered harvest of the winds upon the cavern floor, in a big brown heap, and then Ernest struck a match and set light to it. Algitha, in a large black cloak, stood over it with a hazel stick – like a wand – stirring and heaping

on the fuel, as the mass began to smoulder and to send forth a thick white smoke that gradually filled the cavern, curling up into the rocky roof and swirling round and out by the square-cut mouth, to be caught there by the slight wind and illumined by the sun, which poured down upon the soft coils of the smoke, in so strange a fashion, as to call forth a cry of wonder from the onlookers. Standing in the interval of open pathway between the two rock-passages, and looking back at the fire-lit cavern, with its black shadows and flickering flame-colours, Hadria was bewildered by what appeared to her a veritable magic vision, beautiful beyond anything that she had ever met in dream.

The figures, stooping over the burning heap, moved occasionally across the darkness, looking like a witch and her familiar spirit, who were conjuring, by uncanny arts, a vision of life, on the strange, white, clean-cut patch of smoke that was defined by the sunlit entrance to the tunnel. (*DD*, 20)

In her subversion of Pre-Raphaelite iconographies, Caird represents the sorceress not as a distraught figure of destruction (as Anthony Frederick Sandys did in his 'Medea' of 1868),[54] but as an agent of life, whose smoky visions conceived in the cavern are born(e) into the 'rosy light' (*DD*, 18) of the sunrise outside: the opposite of the transience and mortality emblemised in John Everett Millais' 'Autumn Leaves' (1856).[55] That here it is Algitha, not Hadria, who is associated with Medea suggests that in Caird's re-vision of the Classical prototype the mythical figure is split in two, with Algitha representing the active, self-assertive and resourceful rebel-sorceress, while Hadria constitutes her introspective counterpart, the visionary and priestess of the imagination. Hadria's positioning in the open space between two pathways is indicative of the perennial 'in-betweenness' of the woman artist as she is defined by Hélène Cixous;[56] but what Cixous exalts as the dynamic interplay of creative bisexuality and multitextuality is much more problematic in Caird's novel, pinpointing as it does Hadria's suspension between states of dreaming and waking. Algitha, who is not afflicted with her sister's artistic temperament, has already cast her spell and made her choice, which she will pursue with robust determination (she will become a modern 'healer' of sorts, a charity worker), whereas Hadria will be condemned forever to conjure up in her mind's eye the ideal always beyond her reach, transfixed by 'a memory and a longing that never died' (*DD*, 423), Medea's vision of the time before, a paradise lost never to be regained:

a marvellous vision of distant lands, purple mountains, fair white cities, and wide kingdoms, so many, so great, that the imagination staggered at the vastness revealed, and offered, as it seemed, to him who could grasp and perceive it. Among those blue deeps and faint innumerable mountain-tops ... all the secrets, all the hopes, all the powers and splendours, of life lay hidden; and the beauty of the vision was as the essence of poetry and of music – of all that is lovely in the world of art, and in the world of the emotions. (*DD*, 20–1)

Like Coleridge's vision of Kubla Khan's Xanadu, Hadria's poetic epiphanies emerge from moments of spellbound reverie. These arise both in situations in which she occupies the position of the passive onlooker, as in the rock-passage and cavern scene with Algitha, and in communal dance sequences like that described in the opening pages of the novel. In the frantic 'revelry' of spectral shapes gyrating in the moonlight to the rhythm of an 'intoxicating primitive music', disrupted 'now and again [by] that wild Celtic shout or cry that sets the nerves athrill' (*DD*, 5), Hadria emerges as the central figure: 'Among the dancers was one who danced with peculiar spirit and brilliance, and her little cry had a ring and a wildness that never failed to set the others going with new inspiration' (*DD*, 6). As soon as she breaks from the magic circle, the dance 'flag[s]' (*DD*, 6). A riveting storyteller (*DD*, 7) and skilled orator as well as a musician and dancer, Hadria has the same electrifying impact as Grand's Beth: 'It seemed as if Hadria was exercising some influence of a magnetic quality. She was always the point of attraction, whether she created a spell with her music, or her speech, or her mere personality' (*DD*, 383). Significantly, however, where Grand's magician of words bends others to her will, Hadria, the conjuress of rhythms, is invariably, and fatally, carried away by the *jouissance* of her gift: 'Some mad spirit seemed to possess her. It would appear almost as if she had passed into a different phase of character. She lost caution and care and the sense of external events. When the dance was ended … [s]he went as if in a dream' (*DD*, 136). Like Beth one of Cixous's wild women 'from the heath where witches are kept alive',[57] the Hadria of the early parts of the text crucially differs from Beth in her ecstatic self-surrender: though mesmerised by the waves of the sea, Beth ultimately always disengages herself from the temptation of self-annihilation which Hadria embraces. As in *The Pathway of the Gods*, the wildness of pagan (here Celtic) dance resembles Clément's tarantella; but while abandoning oneself to the tarantella means to recover submerged memories of the past, it also substantially weakens a dancer's (woman's) resistance to the 'evil spell' of patriarchal pressures: Hadria accepts Temperley's offer of marriage because 'her will refused to issue a vigorous command. Even had he been hateful to her … she felt that she would have been unable to wake out of the nightmare' (*DD*, 137).

It is in and through dance that Hadria retrieves memories of her forebears, perhaps also flashbacks of a past even further removed than her Celtic heritage, that of the ancient Greek fertility rites and masked dance dramas which provided the original setting for Classical tragedy:[58] 'It fills me with bewildering memories … It seems to recall … some wild, primitive experiences – mountains, mists … It seems almost as if I had lived before, among some ancient Celtic people, and now, when I hear their music … Gusts of something intensely familiar return to me, and I cannot grasp it. It is very bewildering' (*DD*, 136–7). Whereas Beth draws personal strength from her link with the mythical past, Hadria, suspended between the *heimlich* and *unheimlich* aspects of the uncanny[59] and swayed by the fatalistic mood of Greek myth, loses her sense of a personal identity: 'Her sense of the importance of personal events had entirely disappeared. What did it all matter?' (*DD*, 137); 'All had been pre-arranged. Nothing could avert it. She seemed to be waiting rather than acting' (*DD*, 139). With no independent means of livelihood, Hadria can exercise her art (dance, piano performance, composition) only within the constraints of the parental home, and within this framework waiting is indeed an imperative (Hadria must wait for the round of social calls to be over, wait for everybody to go to bed, wait for her time to be her own). In this context *jouissance* (creative self-pleasuring) is possible only in brief moments of hysterical explosion, such as the tarantella. Women like her, Hadria realises, 'were all spinning round, in a dizzy little circle, all whirling and toiling and troubling to no purpose' (*DD*, 467), reeling in a mad carnivalesque spiral towards oblivion in the style of Jean Rhys's heroine Anna Morgan: '"I'm giddy," I said. *I'm awfully giddy – but we went on dancing forwards and backwards backwards and forwards whirling round and round*' (*VID*, 157, emphasis in original).

Once Hadria delivers herself into constructive action by embarking on a life and career of her own, her creativity finds inspiration in a new, life-affirming rhythm. This is no longer the tarantella of hysteria but a feast of sensory impressions conveyed through the rhythmic motion of a train. On the journey to Paris the swiftly changing vistas provide the backdrop to Hadria's 'trains' of thought, orchestrating her ecstatic sense of release from stasis to speed, mythic and pre-ordained past to open-ended future:

> The speed was glorious. Back flashed field and hill and copse ... Back flew iterative telegraph posts with Herculean swing, into the Past, looped together in rhythmic movement, marking the pulses of old Time. On, with rack and roar, into the mysterious Future. One could sit at the window and watch the machinery of Time's foundry at work; the hammers of his forge beating, beating, the wild sparks flying, the din and chaos whirling round one's bewildered brain; – Past becoming Present, Present melting into Future, before one's eyes ... Thoughts ran on rhythmically, in the steady, flashing movement through verdant England. (*DD*, 294)

In her progression through different geographic locations, not only does she become aware of her (own individual and women's collective) passage through time, she also gains a sense of place and, indirectly, of her identity ('England, England with her gentle homesteads, her people of the gentle voices', *DD*, 294). Where the tarantella induced dreamy apathy and self-oblivion, her journey into her new life generates a self-meditative mood affirmative of the force of will-power: 'Was this the response of the genius of the ring, the magic ring that we call *will?'* (*DD*, 294, emphasis in original). With the recognition that will, hence personality, does, after all, have the capacity to shape destiny (the Emersonian formula), an exquisite sense of reality takes the place of the dreams: 'The Real! *that* was ... the truly great, the true realm of the imagination!' (*DD*, 294, emphasis in original). Whereas previously, when stirred into enthusiasm, her imagination was propelled into flights of fantasy (such as that which transmogrified smoke into a city of dreams), now that she is equipped with a sense of the plasticity of the real, she responds to her experience impressionistically and self-reflexively. This is reflected meta-textually in the narrative move away from the mythical towards the repre-sentation of a modern(ist) consciousness which manifests itself in interior monologue:

> A rattle under a bridge, a roar through a tunnel, and on again, through Kentish orchards. A time of blossoming. Disjointed, delicious impressions followed one another in swift succession, often superficially incoherent, but threaded deep, in the stirred consciousness, on a silver cord: – the unity of the creation was as obvious as its multiplicity ... The rattle and roar grew into a symphony – full, rich, magnificent, and then, with a rush, came a stirring musical conception: it seized the imagination. (*DD*, 295)

This 'symphony' of life and resurgent energy takes the place of the 'death chime' which marked the futility of Hadria's married life. The first glimpse the reader was accorded of Hadria after her marriage was on the cemetery of her new home village, talking to the local gravedigger about the death of a young single mother (the schoolmistress, whose thwarted life parallels Hadria's) against the backdrop of a clock striking the eleventh hour from the church tower: 'One might have fancied that clock and pickaxe iterated in turn, "Time, Death! Time, Death! Time, Death!" till the clock had come to the end of its tale, and then the pickaxe went on alone in the stillness – "Death! Death! Death! Death!" (*DD*, 149). As Patricia Murphy points out, the 'syncopation' established by the cadence of sounds carries similarly portentous connota-tions as the chime of the Morningquest clock in Grand's *The Heavenly Twins*, suggesting that 'women are both controlled by and separated from the masculine temporality that the chimes mark'.[60] Significantly, as Hadria speeds away from the constraints of wifehood, this masculine temporality makes way for an impressionist synchronicity of 'unity' and 'multiplicity', setting the scene for her Parisian experimentation with a plurality of roles (flâneuse, student, composer, journalist) grounded by a unifying female counter-family consti-tuted of herself, the nurse Hannah, and the toddler Martha: a female trinity composed of the artist-mother, the 'professional' mother (the childminder and housekeeper) and the girl-child. On crossing the border to France – a location symbolically constitutive of the magical place envisioned in her rock-

and-cave epiphany – Hadria's transformation from wife to artist, mythical subject to modern woman, dreamer to creator is complete: 'One felt oneself in the land of artists' (*DD*, 300); here the '*other* [life] was the dream; it seemed to be drifting away already' (*DD*, 297). Energised by her new identity and invigorated by an experimental aesthetic grounded in sensory impressions, she forges 'a new language' of sound, rhythm and symphonic composition (*DD*, 321) – a language which reflects the quality that Caird, in her preface to *The Wing of Azrael*, defined as the principal attribute of art: the 'faithful rendering of an impression' (WOA, I:vii). As Murphy notes, this is a language which challenges the masculine order in its vocalisation of the female semiotic.[61] Hadria's music 'invaded fresh territory … [and] added to the range of expression'; inevitably, it is perceived as 'rebel music, offensive to the orthodox' (*DD*, 321).

Hadria's symphonic disruption of linguistic and artistic hegemonies is accompanied by an equally iconoclastic reconfiguration of the mother–daughter relationship. When embarking on her new career, Hadria has not a moment's hesitation in leaving her biological sons behind (a reminder of her unhappy marriage, they are possibly the product of coercive marital sex and therefore, as she declares to a shocked Valeria, her 'own private and particular insult'; *DD*, 190), but she pointedly includes her adoptive daughter in her reconstructed life. Conceived out of wedlock, Martha represents a challenge to the system of sexual and procreative impositions (enforced marital relations with the purpose of breeding the next generation of patriarchs); Hadria hopes to turn her into a strong, healthy and self-confident individual ready to fight for women's rights (*DD*, 246). A miniature iconoclast, Martha delights Hadria, not least because she loves demolishing fanciful constructions and (in anticipation of Toni Morrison's Claudia in *The Bluest Eye*) particularly relishes the dissection of dolls: iconographic femininity (*DD*, 329–30). That Hadria is ultimately unable to realise her vision because of the interventions of a patriarchal mother and hostile father (Professor Theobald) in its very failure validates her project of reconstructing the artist (as) rebel mother.

Caird's exploration of the mother/daughter/artist nexus is informed by the desire to fashion new models of female creativity out of the old mythologies of patriarchy. Just as she provided a narrative matrix for the successful reconfiguration of marriage, so she gestured towards a constructive resolution of the mother–daughter conflict in her neo-mythopoeic representations of the feminist artist. In her compelling reading of *The Daughters of Danaus* Patricia Murphy contends that Caird conceptualised history as 'debilitating destiny rather than vibrant change, exercising a firm hold over the present and foreclosing opportunities for reconfiguring the female role'.[62] As I have argued in this chapter, however, a different picture emerges when Caird's artist-novels are placed in the context of her subversive (de- and re)mythologisations of the patriarchal binaries of mother and daughter, wife and artist, woman and genius. If *The Daughters of Danaus* serves the purpose of a cautionary tale, anatomising the conditions which prevent the exceptional woman from being either, *One That Wins* constitutes its programmatic counterpoint in remoulding and transforming these roles in the dual configuration of two women artists acting both mother and daughter to one another. 'The cathexis between mother and daughter – essential, distorted, misused – is the great unwritten story', declared Adrienne Rich in *Of Woman Born*.[63] It is a story that Mona Caird sought to uncover and revitalise in her mythological and psychological reworkings of the processes which made and unmade the woman artist. In its feminist emphasis Caird's mythopoeia historicised the contemporary condition of women by revealing the ancient rites of woman-sacrifice on which dominant cultural discourses of turn-of-the-century Britain were predicated. Ultimately Caird anticipated even as she feminised the modernist project. In 1923 T. S. Eliot remarked of James Joyce's *Ulysses* that

> In using the myth, in manipulating a continuous parallel between contemporaneity and antiquity, Mr Joyce is pursuing a method which others might pursue after him. They will not be imitators, any more than the scientist who uses the discoveries of Einstein in pursuing his own, independent investigations. It is simply a way of controlling, of ordering, of giving a shape and a significance to the immense panorama of futility and anarchy which is contemporary history. ... Instead of the narrative method, we may now use the mythical method. It is, I seriously believe, a step toward making the modern world possible for art ... And only those who have won their own discipline in secret and without aid, in a world which offers very little assistance to that end, can be of any use in furthering this advance.[64]

The high-modernist experiment of 'manipulating a continuous parallel between contemporaneity and antiquity' through the use of the 'mythical method' was a central feature of the work of all three writers discussed in this book. Like Schreiner's use of biblical allegory and Grand's expert manipulations of the feminine mystique, Caird's mythopoeia reflects the turn-of-the-century feminist endeavour of revising and revolutionising patriarchal script(ure)s. Subverting Western discourses of religion, art and culture with a woman-centred aesthetics whose 'rebel music offensive to the orthodox' was calculated to prove irresistible to contemporary readers by virtue of its alluringly familiar and seductive rhythms of historical discursive paradigms, Grand, Schreiner and Caird conceived of the New Woman's struggle for self-realisation and social regeneration as the new epic which would ring in the new age of women's liberation in which 'to be born a woman will not be to be born branded' (*AF*, 171).

Sorties:
New Women, new myths?

> It ... is extremely difficult to vanquish myth from the inside: for the very effort one makes in order to escape its stranglehold becomes in its turn the prey of myth: myth can always, as a last resort, signify the resistance which is brought to bear against it. Truth to tell, the best weapon against myth is perhaps to mythify it in its turn, and to produce an *artificial* myth: and this reconstituted myth will in fact be a mythology. (Roland Barthes, *Mythologies*, 1957)[1]

Myth, Barthes argues, is such an essential paradigm of culture – bourgeois culture as he defines it, gendered culture we might add from a feminist perspective – that in the very act of deconstruction the mythologist (the critic of myth) is susceptible to becoming entangled within its seductive web of significations. Applicable to academic exegesis more generally, this has a bearing also on New Woman criticism. Since the rediscovery of the genre in the 1970s and particularly since what can be called the New Woman 'renaissance' of the 1990s critical taxonomies have provided the backdrop for the emergence of new feminist mythologies: of the New Woman as daughter of decadence or mother of modernism, as handmaiden of eugenic re-education, or as a feminist forerunner. In their contestation of patriarchal myths in literary criticism, critical and theoretical appraisals of the New Woman have generated potent reinscriptions of turn-of-the-century culture and literature which in themselves correlate to the strategy of resistance through remythification that distinguishes the discursive practices of New Woman writers.

As a semiological 'system of communication ... adapted to a certain type of consumption, laden with ... a type of social *usage*', Barthes writes, myth serves primarily ideological purposes.[2] This ideological function of myth is realised in its tripartite structure of signifier (form and meaning), signified (concept) and sign (signification): a pattern frequently present in the work of New Woman writers, most notably in Olive Schreiner's allegories. In 'Three Dreams in a Desert' the allegorical form lends meaning to the narrator's dream visions (signifier), which conceptualise the condition of women through history (signified) in order to posit the utopian signification of collective female liberation as being conditional on individual self-sacrifice. Grand's dynamic interplay of photographic, journalistic and narrative self-(de/re)constructions offers a more complex and ambivalent example of Barthes's model of myth-as-(counter)ideology. The 'constant game of hide-and-seek between the meaning and the form which defines myth' in his eyes[3] manifests itself in the apparently seamless slippage Grand's writing enacts between feminine mimicry and feminist militancy. Caird's *Daughters of Danaus* and Schreiner's use of the mimosa symbol illustrate Barthes's contention that '[a] whole book may be the signifier of a single concept' (can the woman artist assert herself irrespective of external circumstances?); and conversely, that 'a minute form ... can serve as signifier to a concept filled with a very rich history'[4] (the mimosa as a marker of deified female martyrdom).

Similarly, Grand, Schreiner and Caird variously embraced and provoked the three responses that Barthes considers constitutive of myth reception.[5] In reaffirming traditional concepts of femininity in her more conservative journalistic pieces, Grand exemplifies Barthes's 'producer of myth' who reinforces established mythological constructions, just as Schreiner's mythopeia remains heavily indebted to Christian iconography and its conceptual and discursive frameworks. Yet in her photographic self-stagings Grand debunked even as she glamorised the feminine mystique; like Caird's revisionary radicalism *vis-à-vis* Classical myth, her over-performance of femininity reveals the 'mythologiser' who aims to uncover, atomise and explode traditional mythologies. Barthes's third category, the 'reader of myths' who consumes the myth and 'lives [it] as a story at once true and unreal',[6] is reflected in the tremendous impact Grand's, Schreiner's and Caird's writings had on their contemporary audience. All three writers were able to draw advantage from the political effectiveness of mythological constructs that had already been harnessed for feminist social reform. Thus the Minotaur myth, lent spectacular prominence in W. T. Stead's spade of 'Maiden Tribute' articles on girl sexual abuse in 1885, was invoked in Grand's narrative warfare on the Contagious Diseases Act and its male beneficiaries, while furnishing the heroic context of Schreiner's iconography of feminist martyrdom, and resurfacing in its original force in Caird's indictment of patriarchal society's practice of woman-sacrifice.

In sensitising and radicalising their readers' perception of traditional mythical constructions, the three writers potently politicised myth, a discursive mode Barthes identifies as an essentially 'depoliticized speech'.[7] If 'myth has the task of giving an historical intention a natural justification, and making contingency appear eternal',[8] Grand, Schreiner and especially Caird exposed the contradictions and spectacularised the wrongs to which patriarchal mythology subjected women, specifically women artists. Barthes's contention that there is no such thing as revolutionary myth[9] might be qualified when applied to feminist activism: the successor to the New Woman, the suffragette movement, for example, was heavily invested in revisionist myth-making, drawing on the very same Christian symbology which was deployed to such effect in Schreiner's work. Both suffragette and New Woman activism reconciled revolutionary ardour with a reformist vision which sought to radicalise gender relations through the reconstruction, not the demolition, of established social institutions such as marriage. In the context of their determined push for social renovation which, however anti-patriarchal in essence, remained predicated on middle-class values, myth proved a particularly compelling tool of counter-hegemonic agency.

The ambivalent nature of the ideological positionings of New Woman writers may account for the fact that of the seven rhetorical figures Barthes lists as indicative of bourgeois myth,[10] Grand, Schreiner and Caird display only two: 'identification' (a strategy of obvious relevance to any politically motivated writer targeting a mass audience) and 'inoculation', which, Barthes postulates, consists in 'admitting the accidental evil of a class-bound institution the better to conceal its principial evil'.[11] Thus, while inculpating patriarchy and its institutions for the injurious repercussions of women's social and functional division into wives and prostitutes, none of the three writers argued for the wholesale abolition of marriage or a classless society. Like Grand's, Caird's feminism was firmly embedded in a middle-class position, and although she shared Schreiner's wider commitment to human rights, she was not concerned with racial inequality. Like Grand and Schreiner laying open the foundation myths of marriage, she went further than the other two in unravelling the conceptual frameworks to which they retained allegiance: female self-sacrifice, the biologistic model of motherhood, the project of social regeneration under the banner of eugenics. Caird thus mounted the most consistent challenge to patriarchal ideology and mythology of her time.

Caird was also the writer most systematically engaged in deconstructing the historical underpinnings of patriarchal myth. Whereas, as Barthes suggests, orthodox myth typically 'deprives the object of which it speaks of all History',[12] Grand, Schreiner and particularly Caird exposed the history of misogynist mythologies to a broad community of primarily women readers. Barthes postulates that 'when a myth reaches the entire community, it is from the latter that the mythologist must become estranged if he wants to liberate the myth';[13] however, the extraordinary resonance their writings had with their contemporaries and especially female readers indicates that through their creative use of myth, their deconstruction of patriarchal mythologies, and their remythifications of the woman artist, Grand, Schreiner and Caird not only did not alienate their communities but in fact went a long way towards reconciling these communities to New Woman mythologies. Above all, they were eminently successful in constructing what a century later one of Fatima Mernissi's autobiographical characters, speaking to a different community of women, would describe as 'the magic inside, woven of our dreams':

When you happen to be trapped powerless behind walls ... you dream of escape. And magic flourishes when you spell out that dream and make the frontiers vanish. Dreams can change your life, and eventually the world. Liberation starts with images dancing in your little head, and you can translate those images in words.[14]

In translating their dream visions into potent feminist counter-mythologies of the woman of genius, Grand, Schreiner and Caird anticipated Catherine Clément's project of forging, for a female community, 'a history arranged the way tale-telling women tell it. And from the standpoint of conveying the mythic models that powerfully structure the Imaginary ..., this history will be true. On the level of fantasy, it will be fantastically true: It is still acting on us. In telling it, in developing it, even in plotting it, [they sought] to undo it, to overturn it, to reveal it, to *expose* it.'[15]

Notes

In all bibliographical references the place of publication is London unless otherwise stated. Places of publication are omitted for university publishers listed under the following abbreviations:

BUP Birmingham University Press
CUP Cambridge University Press
EUP Edinburgh University Press
MUP Manchester University Press
OUP Oxford University Press

Notes to Introduction

1 Elizabeth Robins, 'To the Women Writers' Suffrage League', 4 May 1909, speech at the Waldorf Hotel, *Way Stations* (Hodder and Stoughton, 1913), p. 110.

2 Sandra M. Gilbert and Susan Gubar, *The Madwoman in the Attic: The Woman Writer and the Nineteenth-Century Literary Imagination* (1979; New Haven: Yale University Press, 1984), p. 80.

3 Sarah Grand to Professor Viëtor, 15 December 1896, in Ernst Foerster, *Die Frauenfrage in den Romanen Englischer Schriftstellerinnen der Gegenwart* (Marburg: N. G. Elwert'sche Verlagsbuchhandlung, 1907), p. 56, repr. in *LVMQ*, V.

4 See Ann Ardis, *New Women, New Novels: Feminism and Early Modernism* (New Brunswick: Rutgers University Press, 1990), p. 42.

5 Tania Modleski, *Loving with a Vengeance: Mass-Produced Fantasies for Women* (Routledge, 1988), p. 28.

6 Mary Daly, *Beyond God the Father* (1974), cited in Ursula King, *Women and Spirituality: Voices of Protest and Promise*, 2nd edn (Basingstoke: Macmillan, 1993), p. 6.

7 For details of the conceptual synergies between New Woman fiction and second-wave theory see my book *New Woman Fiction: Women Writing First-Wave Feminism* (Basingstoke: Macmillan, 2000), in particular pp. 10–13.

8 Adrienne Rich, 'When We Dead Awaken: Writing as Re-Vision' (1971), in Barbara Charlesworth Gelpi and Albert Gelpi (eds), *Adrienne Rich's Poetry* (New York: Norton, 1975), p. 90. For full quotation see epigraph to Chapter 5.

9 M. M. Bakhtin, *The Dialogic Imagination: Four Essays* (1981), in Pam Morris (ed.), *The Bakhtin Reader: Selected Writings of Bakhtin, Medvedev and Voloshinov*

(Edward Arnold, 1994), p. 78. For a more detailed application of Bakhtin's concept to New Woman discourse see Chapter 1.

10 Elaine Showalter, *Inventing Herself: Claiming a Feminist Intellectual Heritage* (Picador, 2001), p. 89.

11 See Elaine Showalter, *A Literature of Their Own: British Women Novelists from Brontë to Lessing* (1977; Virago, 1984); Lloyd Fernando, *'New Women' in the Late-Victorian Novel* (University Park: Pennsylvania State University Press, 1977); Gail Cunningham, *The New Woman and the Victorian Novel* (Macmillan, 1978); Patricia Stubbs, *Women and Fiction: Feminism and the Novel 1880–1920* (Brighton: Harvester, 1979); Penny Boumelha, 'Women and the New Fiction 1880–1900', *Thomas Hardy and Women: Sexual Ideology and Narrative Form* (Brighton: Harvester, 1982), pp. 63–97.

12 See Patricia Marks, *Bicycles, Bangs, and Bloomers: The New Woman in the Popular Press* (Lexington: University Press of Kentucky, 1990); Elaine Showalter, *Sexual Anarchy: Gender and Culture at the Fin de Siècle* (Bloomsbury, 1991); Lyn Pykett, *The 'Improper' Feminine: The Women's Sensation Novel and the New Woman Writing* (Routledge, 1992) and *Engendering Fictions: The English Novel in the Early Twentieth Century* (Edward Arnold, 1995); Rita Kranidis, *Subversive Discourse: The Cultural Production of Late Victorian Feminist Novels* (Basingstoke: Macmillan, 1995).

13 Sally Ledger, *The New Woman: Fiction and Feminism at the Fin de Siècle* (MUP, 1997).

14 See Ardis, *New Women, New Novels*; Jane Eldridge Miller, *Rebel Women: Feminism, Modernism and the Edwardian Novel* (Virago, 1994); Patricia Murphy, *Time is of the Essence: Temporality, Gender, and the New Woman* (Albany: State University of New York Press, 2001).

15 See Angelique Richardson, *Love and Eugenics in the Late Nineteenth Century: Rational Reproduction and the New Woman* (OUP, 2003).

16 See Gerd Bjørhovde, *Rebellious Structures: Women Writers and the Crisis of the Novel 1880–1900* (Oslo: Norwegian University Press, 1987); Teresa Mangum, *Married, Middlebrow, and Militant: Sarah Grand and the New Woman Novel* (Ann Arbor: University of Michigan Press, 1998); and Carolyn Burdett, *Olive Schreiner and the Progress of Feminism* (Basingstoke: Palgrave, 2001).

17 Sarah Grand was born Frances Elizabeth Bellenden Clarke in 1854 in County Down, Ireland, the fourth of Margaret Bell Sherwood's and Edward John Bellenden Clarke's five children. After the death of her father, a coastguard, when she was 7, the family moved to Yorkshire, her mother's English home county. Apart from five years spent in South East Asia with her husband David Chambers McFall's regiment, Grand was based in England for most of her life, taking frequent working and recuperative holidays in France. She died at Calne in 1943, shortly before her eighty-ninth birthday. For details see Gillian Kersley, *Darling Madame: Sarah Grand & Devoted Friend* (Virago, 1983).

18 Olive Schreiner was born in Wittenberge, in what was then Cape Colony (South Africa since 1911), in 1855, as the ninth of twelve children. Her parents, Rebecca Lyndall, daughter of an English non-conformist minister, and Gottlob Schreiner, a German shoemaker, had been recruited to Cape Colony by the London

Missionary Society. Her father's professional inaptitude resulted in the dissolution of the family unit, initiating Schreiner into the unsettled life that was to become a characteristic feature of her existence. From the age of 12 she lived with various relatives and later earned her living as a governess. In 1881 she moved to England, where, with intervals spent in Continental Europe, she stayed until 1889. Back in South Africa, she married Samuel Cronwright in 1894. She returned to Britain in 1914 and remained there till shortly before her death in 1920. For details see Ruth First and Ann Scott, *Olive Schreiner* (André Deutsch, 1980).

19 Alice Mona Alison was born in 1854 into an affluent family on the Isle of Wight. Her parents later moved to Kensington in London. Her mother, Matilda Ann Jane Hector, came from a well-to-do family and had been born in Schleswig-Holstein (then part of Denmark, now in the north of Germany). John Alison, who was twenty-two years older than his wife, was a landowner, engineer and inventor. Caird appears to have been an only child. At the age of 23 she married James Alexander Henryson-Caird, a 31-year-old land-owning gentleman farmer from an old and distinguished Scottish family. His estate, Cassencary (now Castle Cary, near Creetown in Dumfries and Galloway), and its surroundings figure prominently in her fictional works. In 1884 she gave birth to her only child, Alister James Henryson-Caird. While her husband was mostly resident at Cassencary, Caird spent most of her time in London or abroad, predominantly France and Italy. She died in 1932. For details see Margaret Morganroth Gullette, 'Afterword' to Mona Caird, *Daughters of Danaus* (New York: Feminist Press, 1989), pp. 493–539, and my article 'Mona Caird (1854–1932): Wild Woman, New Woman, and Early Radical Feminist Critic of Marriage and Motherhood', *Women's History Review*, 5 (1996) 67–95.

20 See Sarah Grand, 'The New Aspect of the Woman Question', and Ouida, 'The New Woman', *North American Review*, 158 (1894) 270–6, 610–19, repr. in *LVMQ*, II. For the first usages of the term 'New Woman' prior to Grand's article see Michelle Elizabeth Tusan, 'Inventing the New Woman: Print Culture and Identity Politics During the *Fin-de-Siecle*', *Victorian Periodicals Review*, 31 (1998) 169–82.

21 W. T. Stead, 'The Novel of the Modern Woman', *Review of Reviews*, 10 (1894) 67, repr. in *LVMQ*, V.

22 Annie S. Swan, *My Life* (Ivor Nicholson, 1934), repr. in *SSPSG*, I, p. 345.

23 Edith Maxwell, in Harry Quilter (ed.), *Is Marriage a Failure?* (1888; New York: Garland, 1984), p. 22, repr. in *LVMQ*, I.

24 Olive Schreiner to Karl Pearson, 23 October 1886, in *OSL*, 109.

25 Mrs John Brown, 'Memories of a Friendship', in Zelda Friedlander (ed.), *Until the Heart Changes: A Garland for Olive Schreiner* ([Cape Town:] Tafelberg-Uitgewers, 1967), p. 29 (emphasis in original).

26 Sarah Grand, 'In the Days of My Youth: My First Success', *M.A.P.*, 22 May 1909, 493, repr. in *SSPSG*, I, p. 204.

27 Sheila Stowell, *A Stage of Their Own: Feminist Playwrights of the Suffrage Era* (MUP, 1992), p. 40.

28 Kersley, *Darling Madame*, pp. 110–11.

29 Elizabeth Crawford, *The Women's Suffrage Movement: A Reference Guide 1866–1928* (UCL Press, 1999), p. 90.

30 First and Scott, *Olive Schreiner*, p. 262.
31 Caird was a member of both clubs, and all three were involved with the Pioneer Club, whose badge (an axe) represented the idea of striking the death-blow at gender prejudice. See Sarah A. Tooley, 'Women's Progressive Clubs', *Humanitarian*, 11 (1897) 170, and Crawford, *The Women's Suffrage Movement*, pp. 126–7; see also Eva Anstruther, 'Ladies' Clubs', *Nineteenth Century*, 45 (1899) 508–611, and David Rubinstein, *Before the Suffragettes: Women's Emancipation in the 1890s* (Brighton: Harvester, 1986), pp. 222–3.
32 See Mona Caird, 'Ideal Marriage', *Westminster Review*, 130 (1888) 620, and Chapter 5 in this volume.
33 Sarah A. Tooley, 'The Woman's Question: An Interview with Madame Sarah Grand', *Humanitarian*, 8 (1896), repr. in *SSPSG*, I, p. 227.
34 Olive Schreiner to Karl Pearson, 23 March 1886, *OSL*, 74.
35 Mona Caird, 'A Defence of the Wild Women', *The Morality of Marriage and Other Essays on the Status and Destiny of Women* (George Redway, 1897), pp. 173, 171; repr. in *LVMQ*, I.
36 'My ideal is an equal care both physical and mental from both father and mother', Olive Schreiner to Betty Molteno, 11 October 1896, in *OSL*, 291.
37 Lyn Pykett, 'Portraits of the Artist as a Young Woman: Representations of the Female Artist in the New Woman Fiction of the 1890s', in Nicola Diane Thompson (ed.), *Victorian Women Writers and the Woman Question* (CUP, 1999), p. 128.
38 Ibid.
39 Penny Boumelha, 'The Woman of Genius and the Woman of Grub Street: Figures of the Female Writer in British *Fin-de-Siècle* Fiction', *English Literature in Transition*, 40 (1997) 177–8.
40 Deborah L. Madsen, *Rereading Allegory: A Narrative Approach to Genre* (Macmillan, 1995), p. 13.

Notes to Chapter 1

1 Sarah Grand, 'Should Married Women Follow Professions?', *Young Woman* (1899), repr. in *SSPSG*, I, pp. 121–2.
2 For a detailed discussion of Grand's eugenic position see Angelique Richardson, *Love and Eugenics in the late Nineteenth Century: Rational Reproduction and the New Woman* (OUP, 2003).
3 See Teresa Mangum's discussion of Grand's middlebrow politics in *Married, Middlebrow, and Militant: Sarah Grand and the New Woman Novel* (Ann Arbor: University of Michigan Press, 1998), pp. 12–35.
4 See Marilyn Bonnell, 'Sarah Grand and the Critical Establishment: Art for [Wo]man's Sake', *Tulsa Studies in Women's Literature*, 14:1 (1995) 123–48.
5 Frank Danby [pseud. of Julia Frankau], 'Sarah Grand's Latest Book', *Saturday Review*, 20 November 1897, repr. in *SSPSG*, I, p. 472.
6 Gladys Singers-Bigger, diary entry of 12 July 1928, cited in Gillian Kersley, *Darling Madame: Sarah Grand & Devoted Friend* (Virago, 1983), p. 183; Sarah Grand, 'In the Days of My Youth: My First Success', *M.A.P.*, 22 May 1909, 493, repr. in *SSPSG*, I, p. 201.

7 Margaret Beetham and Kay Boardman (eds), *Victorian Women's Magazines: An Anthology* (MUP, 2001), p. 32.
8 Grand, 'Should Married Women Follow Professions', in *SSPSG*, I, p. 121.
9 Ibid.
10 Sarah Grand, Foreword to *The Heavenly Twins* (Heinemann, 1923), repr. in *SSPSG*, I, p. 403.
11 See Richardson, *Love and Eugenics*.
12 Mangum, *Married, Middlebrow, and Militant*, p. 25.
13 Vera Brittain, *On Becoming A Writer* (Hutchinson, 1947), p. 180, cited in Andrea Peterson, 'Alternative Wifestyles: Vera Brittain's Feminist Journalism of the 1920s and the Influence of Olive Schreiner', in Ann Heilmann (ed.), *Feminist Forerunners: New Womanism and Feminism in the Early Twentieth Century* (Pandora, 2003), p. 23.
14 Elaine Showalter, cited in Karen Gold, 'Women Behaving Badly for the Good: Lisa Jardine Chairs a Discussion between Fay Weldon and Elaine Showalter on the Women's Movement', *Times Higher Educational Supplement*, 26 October 2001, 18.
15 Luce Irigaray, 'The Power of Discourse and the Subordination of the Feminine', in Margaret Whitford (ed.), *The Irigaray Reader* (Oxford: Blackwell, 1991), p. 124.
16 Sarah A. Tooley, 'Madame Sarah Grand at Home', *Young Woman* (1897) 84, repr. in *SSPSG*, I, pp. 242–3.
17 Margaret Beetham, *A Magazine of Her Own? Domesticity and Desire in the Woman's Magazine, 1800–1914* (Routledge, 1996), p. 116.
18 Sarah Grand, 'The New Aspect of the Woman Question', *North American Review*, 158 (1894) 270–6, repr. in *LVMQ*, II.
19 Grand, 'Should Married Women Follow Professions?', p. 124.
20 Grand, 'The New Aspect of the Woman Question', p. 276. For similar uses of the domestic housekeeping metaphor see Josephine Butler, Introduction to *Woman's Work and Woman's Culture: A Series of Essays* (Macmillan, 1869), p. xvii; Mona Caird, *OTW* (I: 51); Charlotte Perkins Gilman, *With Her in Ourland* (1916), in Minna Doskow (ed.), *Charlotte Perkins Gilman's Utopian Novels* (Associated University Presses, 1999), p. 280; Frances E. Willard, 'The New Ideal of Womanhood', *Woman's Herald*, 23 February 1893; Elizabeth Robins, *The Convert* (1907; Women's Press, 1980), p. 246. For 1890s maternalist social purity arguments see Claudia Nelson, '"Under the Guidance of a Wise Mother": British Sex Education at the *Fin de Siècle*', in Claudia Nelson and Ann Sumner Holmes (eds), *Maternal Instincts: Visions of Motherhood and Sexuality in Britain, 1875–1925* (Basingstoke: Macmillan, 1997), p. 99.
21 Sarah Grand, 'The Man of the Moment', *North American Review* (1894) 620–7, repr. in *SSPSG*, I, pp. 50–7.
22 Grand, 'The New Aspect of the Woman Question', p. 273. Schreiner makes a similar point in 'Three Dreams in a Desert' (*D*, 79–80).
23 Sarah Grand, cited in 'Leading Articles in the Reviews', *Review of Reviews*, 10 (July to Dec. 1894) 567.
24 Sarah Grand, 'Eugenia', *OMN*, p. 140, repr. in *SSPSG*, IV, p. 116.
25 M. M. Bakhtin, *The Dialogic Imagination: Four Essays* (1981), in Pam Morris (ed.), *The Bakhtin Reader: Selected Writings of Bakhtin, Medvedev and Voloshinov* (Edward Arnold, 1994), p. 78.

26 Ibid.
27 Jane T. Stoddart, 'Illustrated Interview: Sarah Grand', *Woman at Home*, 3 (1895) 248, repr. in *SSPSG*, I, pp. 211–12. See also Athol Forbes, 'Impressions of Sarah Grand', *Lady's World* (June 1900) 880–3, in *SSPSG*, I, pp. 257–60.
28 Sarah Grand, 'The Morals of Manner and Appearance', *Humanitarian*, 3 (1893), repr. in *SSPSG*, I, pp. 24, 25, 26.
29 Thus, while praising professional women 'speaking on public platforms, and taking their part in the movements of the time', she advised them to take a leaf out of the book of the average wife and mother and consider 'homes and families first'. See Sarah A. Tooley, 'The Woman's Question: An Interview with Madame Sarah Grand', *Humanitarian*, 8 (1896) 166, repr. in *LVMQ*, V.
30 Joan Riviere, 'Womanliness as a Masquerade', in Shelley Saguaro (ed.), *Psychoanalysis and Woman: A Reader* (Basingstoke: Macmillan, 2000), p. 73.
31 Stoddart, 'Illustrated Interview', 251, in *SSPSG*, I, p. 216.
32 'Sarah Grand and Mr. Ruskin', *Woman's Signal*, 25 January 1894, 57, repr. in *SSPSG*, I, p. 277.
33 Stoddart, 'Illustrated Interview', 250, 248, in *SSPSG*, I, pp. 214, 212.
34 See my discussion of the illustrations to Sarah Grand's 1894 short story 'Should Irascible Old Gentlemen Be Taught to Knit?', published in *Phil May's Illustrated Winter Annual* (repr. in *SSPSG*, III, pp. 301–10) in my *New Woman Fiction: Women Writing First-Wave Feminism* (Basingstoke: Macmillan, 2000), pp. 16–21.
35 Graham Law, 'New Woman Novels in Newspapers', in Margaret Beetham (ed.), *The New Woman and the Periodical Press*, special issue of *Media History*, 7:1 (2001) 17–31.
36 Stephanie Forward, *SSPSG*, II, pp. 3, 5.
37 One of Sarah A. Tooley's interviews – 'Madame Sarah Grand at Home', *Young Woman* (1897) 81–7 – also figures Grand in three poses (though only one locality, the drawing-room): the Victorian lady (as in Stoddart's 'Illustrated Interview', Figure 4), the intellectual (directing an unflinching gaze at the viewer) and the New Woman with her bicycle. See 'Madame Sarah Grand at Home', *Young Woman* (1897) 81–7. The fact that one of her photographs is replicated on both occasions, and that the pictorial material used is attributed to different photographers, suggests that not all of the pictures were taken by a photographer accompanying the respective interviewer but were presumably supplied by Grand herself.
38 Bakhtin, *The Dialogic Imagination*, p. 117.
39 Compare the 'subversive' 'Modern Girl' article in the *North American Review*, 158 (1894) 706–14, repr. in *SSPSG*, I, pp. 36–44, with Grand's stridently conservative argument in an article also entitled 'The Modern Girl' in the *Temple Magazine*, 2 (1898) 323–6, repr. in *SSPSG*, I, pp. 45–9. The latter is replicated in *The Modern Man and Maid* (Horace Marshall and Son, 1898), pp. 11–31, repr. in *LVMQ*, II.
40 Grand, 'The Modern Girl', *North American Review*, in *SSPSG*, I, p. 40.
41 Eliza Lynn Linton, 'The Girl of the Period', *Saturday Review*, 14 March 1868, 339–40.
42 Grand, 'Should Married Women Follow Professions?', *Young Woman*, 121; 'The Modern Girl', *North American Review*, 706, in *SSPSG*, I, p. 36 (emphases added).
43 Bakhtin, *The Dialogic Imagination*, p. 118 (emphasis in original).

44 Ibid., pp. 118, 120.
45 Letitia Fairfield, 'Mme. Sarah Grand', letter to the *Manchester Guardian*, 19 May 1943, 4, repr. in *SSPSG*, I, p. 568.
46 Katherine Tynan, *The Middle Years* (Constable, 1916), p. 380, repr. in *SSPSG*, I, p. 312.
47 'Death of Madame Sarah Grand', *Bath Weekly Chronicle and Herald*, 15 May 1943, repr. in *SSPSG*, I, p. 564; 'Sarah Grand, Novelist of the Nineties', *The Times*, 13 May 1943, repr. in *SSPSG*, I, p. 560.
48 Hugh E. M. Stutfield, 'Tommyrotics', *Blackwood's Edinburgh Magazine*, 157 (1895) 833–45, repr. in *LVMQ*, V.
49 Hugh E. M. Stutfield, 'The Psychology of Feminism', *Blackwood's Edinburgh Magazine*, 161 (1897) 107, repr. in *LVMQ*, V.
50 William Barry, 'The Strike of a Sex', *Quarterly Review*, 179 (1894) 295, 297, repr. in *LVMQ*, V.
51 Stutfield, 'The Psychology of Feminism', 107.
52 For a discussion of the inconsistencies in Grand's eugenic plot in these final novels see Mangum, *Married, Middlebrow, and Militant*, pp. 192–218.
53 Sarah Grand, 'Some Recollections of My Schooldays', *Lady's Magazine*, 1 (1901) 43, repr. in *SSPSG*, I, pp. 194–5.
54 Ibid., 43, in *SSPSG*, I, p. 195.
55 Tooley, 'Madame Sarah Grand at Home', 84, in *SSPSG*, I, p. 242.
56 Ibid.
57 For similar uses of the footbinding metaphor see Florence Nightingale, 'Cassandra', in Ray Strachey, *The Cause: A Short History of the Women's Movement in Great Britain* (Virago, 1988), p. 408, and *AF*, 172.
58 Mary Wollstonecraft, *Vindication of the Rights of Woman* (1792; Harmondsworth: Penguin, 1985), p. 132. See *TDLF*, 53–4.
59 Sarah Grand, 'Janey, A Humble Administrator', *Temple Bar*, 93 (1891) 199–218, repr. in *OMN*, 211–45, and in *SSPSG*, III, pp. 251–85.
60 Kersley, *Darling Madame*, p. ix.
61 An annuity left by a female relative paid for Grand's two years of schooling between the ages of 14 and 16. The 'dreadful sense of lassitude' and 'mental misery' evoked by the Royal Naval School at Twickenham is recreated in *The Beth Book*. In 'Some Recollections of My Schooldays' (*Lady's Magazine*, 1 [1901] 43, repr. in *SSPSG*, I, pp. 194–5) Grand wrote that the school 'meant a martyrdom to a girl of my temperament. We had none but the most babyish books; our recreation in the grounds was limited to monotonous walks up and down the gravelled paths; we had no games of any kind – nothing to develop our physique at all but the making of our little beds every morning and an hour's "deportment" once a fortnight. When we were taken out to walk for exercise, we went in classes, each like a sorry caterpillar, moving reluctantly.' Fortunately Grand's preceding years of freedom had bred an independence strong enough to resist all attempts to subdue her spirit: 'she was always up to mischief', Singers-Bigger later recorded Grand recalling, 'would climb out of the window ... to play on the lawn and go down to the kitchen for the breakfast bread and butter and take it upstairs' (Gladys Singers-Bigger, diary entry of 15 December 1935, in Kersley, *Darling*

Madame, p. 292). Grand was subsequently sent to a finishing school in Kensington, a more liberal establishment though geared towards marriage as the primary object in a woman's life. *The Beth Book* ridicules the art of small talk and the unhealthy beauty and fashion codes which were imparted to the girls, attacking the pretence and hypocrisy engendered by such teaching.

62 Kersley, *Darling Madame,* pp. 23–5.

63 Sarah Grand to Gladys Singers-Bigger, 29 April 1931, Bath Central Library.

64 The disruptive strategies adopted by these girls are reminiscent of the pranks of Grand's heroines Babs, Angelica and Beth. See Lyn Mikel Brown and Carol Gilligan, *Meeting at the Crossroads: Women's Psychology and Girls' Development* (Cambridge, MA: Harvard University Press, 1992), pp. 42–4.

65 Heather A. Evans, 'Power-Eating and the Power-Starved: The New Woman's New Appetite in Sarah Grand's *Babs the Impossible*', in Julia Hallam and Nickianne Moody (eds), *Consuming for Pleasure: Selected Essays on Popular Fictions* (Liverpool: Media Critical and Creative Arts, Liverpool John Moores University, Association for Research in Popular Fictions, 2000), p. 122.

66 Sarah Grand, Foreword to *The Heavenly Twins, SSPSG,* I, p. 404.

67 Anon., [review of *Babs the Impossible*], *Athenaeum,* 20 April 1901, in *SSPSG,* I, p. 494.

68 Disappointed with the 'vulgarised' American adaptation, Grand actually withheld her permission, only to find later that 'they had produced it under another name and had made a million dollars with it!' She had no better luck with *The Heavenly Twins:* the play on which she had collaborated with Robert Buchanan hit copyright problems and was not performed. See Gladys Singers-Bigger, diary entry of 8 August 1931, in Kersley, *Darling Madame,* p. 227.

69 Singers-Bigger, diary entry of 5 April 1931, in Kersley, *Darling Madame,* p. 225. It is, however, more than likely that the original script was substantially revised in the 1890s; this would particularly apply to the debate about the New and Old Woman (terms not in circulation until the early 1890s). See Kersley, *Darling Madame,* p. 103.

70 Grand's remark ('In the Days of My Youth', *SSPSG,* I, p. 202) that her first book (*Two Dear Little Feet?*) was followed by a 'plotty-plotty novel' and then by one which 'reads more like the scenario for a play' points to *Singularly Deluded* preceding *Babs.* Possibly she mixed up the chronology of these two texts; she also claimed that her first book had never been published. In light of the more positive aspects of the marriage plot in *Babs,* it is likely that *Singularly Deluded* followed rather than preceded this novel because it reflects the first signs of a marital crisis, hinting as it does at the unreliability, bizarre conduct and even potential violence of husbands.

71 Sarah Grand in conversation with Gladys Singers-Bigger, diary entry of 23 March 1930, in Kersley, *Darling Madame,* p. 214.

72 Grand, 'The New Aspect of the Woman Question', 276, in *SSPSG,* I, p. 35.

73 See Heather A. Evans, '"Nor Shall I Shirk My Food": The New Woman's Balanced Diet and Sarah Grand's *Babs the Impossible*', in Ann Heilmann (ed.), *Masculinities, Maternities, Motherlands: Defining/Contesting New Woman Identities,* special issue of *Nineteenth-Century Feminisms,* 4 (Spring/Summer 2001) 136–49.

74 Nightingale, 'Cassandra', pp. 407–8 (emphasis in original).
75 Evans, 'Nor Shall I Shirk My Food', pp. 136–7.
76 Sarah Grand, 'Marriage Questions in Fiction: The Standpoint of a Typical Modern Woman', *Fortnightly Review*, 375 (March 1898) 378, repr. in *SSPSG*, I, p. 77.
77 Grand, 'The New Aspect of the Woman Question', in *SSPSG*, I, pp. 30, 32.
78 Sarah Grand, 'The New Woman and the Old', *Lady's Realm*, 4 (1898), repr. in *SSPSG*, I, p. 75.
79 Ibid., p. 73.
80 Grand, 'The Morals of Manner and Appearance', in *SSPSG*, I, p. 25.
81 Sarah Grand to Professor Viëtor, in Ernst Foerster, *Die Frauenfrage in den Romanen Englischer Schriftstellerinnen der Gegenwart* (Marburg: N. G. Elwert'sche Verlagsbuchhandlung, 1907), repr. in *SSPSG*, I, p. 190.
82 Grand, 'The Morals of Manner and Appearance', in *SSPSG*, I, p. 25.
83 Sarah A. Tooley, 'Some Women Novelists', *Woman at Home*, 7 (1897), repr. in *SSPSG*, I, p. 255.
84 Grand, 'The New Aspect of the Woman Question', in *SSPSG*, I, p. 29.
85 See Evans, 'Power-Eating and the Power-Starved', p. 126.
86 'Babs, the Impossible', *Independent*, 28 March 1900, 733, repr. in *SSPSG*, I, p. 505.
87 Ibid., pp. 505–6.
88 W. T. Stead, 'Some Books of the Month: "The Beth Book"', *Review of Reviews*, 16 (1897), repr. in *SSPSG*, I, p. 464.
89 Ibid.
90 W. T. Stead's sensational revelations of paedophile rings and organised girl abuse in 'The Maiden Tribute of Modern Babylon' (*Pall Mall Gazette*, 6, 7, 8, 10 July 1885) led to a partial success for social purity campaigners when the Criminal Law Amendment Act raised the age of consent for girls to that of boys, 16. Stead was made to serve a prison sentence for his role in procuring a child. For an extract of the 'Maiden Tribute' series see Sally Ledger and Roger Luckhurst (eds), *The Fin de Siècle: A Reader in Cultural History c. 1880–1900* (OUP, 2000), pp. 32–8. See also Judith R. Walkowitz's detailed analysis of the case in *City of Dreadful Delight: Narratives of Sexual Danger in Late-Victorian London* (Virago, 1992), pp. 81–134.
91 Audre Lorde, 'The Master's Tools Will Never Dismantle the Master's House', *The Audre Lorde Companion: Essays, Speeches and Journals* (Pandora, 1996), pp. 158–61.
92 In *Powers of Horror: An Essay on Abjection* (New York: Columbia University Press, 1982, trans. Leon S. Roudiez) Julia Kristeva argues that the 'corpse … is the utmost of abjection … It is something rejected from which one does not part, from which one does not protect oneself as from an object' (p. 4). Like the abjected corpse (the knowledge of our own mortality), woman and the female body represent an 'Imaginary uncanniness and real threat' which 'beckons to us and ends up engulfing us' (p. 4).
93 Hélène Cixous, 'Castration or Decapitation?' (originally published as 'Le Sexe ou la tête?', 1976), in Shelley Saguaro (ed.), *Psychoanalysis and Woman: A Reader* (Basingstoke: Macmillan, 2000), p. 232.

94 Ibid.

95 Grand did not use her pseudonym until 1893, and she would certainly not have had any cross-references in mind when she was first working on this novel in the 1870s. It is possible that she adjusted her protagonist's name just before publication in order to introduce a pun on her authorial identity. The slippage between names and especially initials is a prominent plot element in relation to Gertrude's husband (Leslie Somers) and his double (Lawrence Soames).

96 See Mangum, *Married, Middlebrow, and Militant*, pp. 49–58.

97 Elaine Showalter, *The Female Malady: Women, Madness and English Culture, 1830–1980* (Virago, 1987).

98 Teresa Lynn Mangum, 'Feminist Fiction and Fictional Feminism: Sarah Grand and the New Woman Novel' (PhD thesis, University of Illinois, 1990), Chapter 2, p. 47.

99 John Donne, 'To his Mistress Going to Bed', l. 27, *John Donne: The Complete English Poems* (Everyman, 1985), p. 184.

100 Mangum, *Married, Middlebrow, and Militant*, p. 57.

101 Ernesto de Martino, cited in Catherine Clément, 'Sorceress and Hysteric', in Hélène Cixous and Catherine Clément, *The Newly Born Woman* [*La Jeune Née*, 1975], trans. Betsy Wing (MUP, 1986), pp. 19–20, p. 20.

102 As Clément notes, the tarantella inverts the social order, an inversion often inscribed into paintings which explore a 'magical anti-world' in which '[n]ature and culture [are] abolished, all bodies mingled: animals, fruits, and humans in the same intertwining. Flowers penetrate, fruits caress, animals open, humans are like instruments of this universal *jouissance.*' Ibid., p. 23; earlier citation from Jurgis Baltrusaitis, ibid.

103 Ibid., p. 21.

104 Ibid., p. 22.

105 Ibid., p. 24.

106 Ibid., p. 22.

107 Kersley, *Darling Madame*, p. 52.

108 Mangum, *Married, Middlebrow, and Militant*, p. 45.

109 Elaine Showalter, *Inventing Herself: Claiming a Feminist Intellectual Heritage* (Picador, 2001), p. 88.

Notes to Chapter 2

1 George Moore, 'Sex in Art', *Modern Painting* (Walter Scott, 1897), p. 226.

2 *HT*, 452, 456.

3 Hélène Cixous, 'Sorties: Out and Out: Attacks/Ways Out/Forays', in Hélène Cixous and Catherine Clément, *The Newly Born Woman* [*La Jeune Née*, 1975], trans. Betsy Wing (MUP, 1986), p. 83.

4 Sandra M. Gilbert and Susan Gubar, *The Madwoman in the Attic: The Woman Writer and the Nineteenth-Century Literary Imagination* (New Haven: Yale University Press, 1979), pp. 65–80.

5 Teresa Mangum, *Married, Middlebrow, and Militant: Sarah Grand and the New Woman Novel* (Ann Arbor: University of Michigan Press, 1998), p. 25.

6 Judith Fetterley, *The Resisting Reader* (Bloomington: Indiana University Press, 1978).

7 Cixous, 'Sorties', *Newly Born Woman*, pp. 85–6.

8 Elizabeth Rachel Chapman, 'Religio Feminae: A Foreword', *Marriage Questions in Modern Fiction, and Other Essays on Kindred Subjects* (Lane, the Bodley Head, 1897), p. xiii, repr. in *LVMQ*, II.

9 For a discussion of Cobbe's categories see Susan Hamilton's '"A Crisis in Women's History": Frances Power Cobbe's *Duties of Women* and the Practice of Everyday Feminism', in Ann Heilmann (ed.), *Words as Deeds: Literary and Historical Perspectives on Women's Suffrage*, special issue of *Women's History Review*, 11:4 (2002) 577–93.

10 May Sinclair, *Feminism* (Women Writers' Suffrage League, 1912). See Laurel Forster, '"Nature's Double Vitality Experiment: May Sinclair's Interpretation of the New Woman', in Ann Heilmann (ed.), *Feminist Forerunners: New Womanism and Feminism in the Early Twentieth Century* (Pandora, 2003), pp. 166–78.

11 [Margaret Oliphant], 'The Old Saloon' [review of *Ideala*], *Blackwood's Edinburgh Magazine*, 146 (1889) 257–8, repr. in *SSPSG*, I, pp. 386–7.

12 Margaret Atwood, *Survival: A Thematic Guide to Canadian Literature* (Toronto: Anansi, 1972), pp. 36–41.

13 Atwood, *Survival*, p. 38.

14 Henry Maudsley, 'Sex in Mind and in Education' (1874), in Louise Michèle Newman (ed.), *Men's Ideas/Women's Realities: Popular Science 1870–1915* (New York: Pergamon, 1985), pp. 77–86. For feminist rebuttals by Millicent Garrett Fawcett and Sophia Jex-Blake see Katharina Rowold (ed.), *Gender and Science: Late Nineteenth-Century Debates on the Female Mind and Body* (Bristol: Thoemmes, 1996). For Edward H. Clarke see extracts from his *Sex in Education; or A Fair Chance for Girls* (1873) in Susan Groag Bell and Karen M. Offen (eds), *Women, the Family and Freedom: The Debate in Documents*, 2 vols (Stanford: Stanford University Press, 1983), I, pp. 427–30.

15 Mona Caird, 'The Duel of the Sexes – A Comment', *Fortnightly Review*, 78 n.s. (1905) 111.

16 See also Grand's early short story 'Eugenia', later reprinted in *OMN* (1894), which begins with the artist-as-physician metaphor (p. 103; repr. in *SSPSG*, IV, p. 79).

17 As Trevor May notes in *The Victorian Domestic Servant* (Princes Risborough: Shire Publications, 1998), 'scarlet fever' was a contemporary pun on domestic servants' attraction to soldiers (p. 13).

18 Sarah A. Tooley, 'The Woman's Question: An Interview with Madame Sarah Grand', *Humanitarian*, 8 (1896) 168–9, repr. in *SSPSG*, I, p. 228.

19 William Barry, 'The Strike of a Sex', *Quarterly Review*, 179 (1894) 302–3; repr. in *LVMQ*, V.

20 See Elizabeth Robins, 'In Defence of the Militants' (1912), cited in Martha Vicinus, *Independent Women: Work and Community for Single Women 1850–1920* (Virago, 1985), p. 259.

21 Joy Dixon, *Divine Feminine: Theosophy and Feminism in England* (Baltimore: Johns Hopkins University Press, 2001), p. 3.

22 Rose Lovell-Smith, 'Science and Religion in the Feminist *Fin-de-Siècle* and a New

Reading of Olive Schreiner's *From Man to Man*', *Victorian Literature and Culture* (2001) 303.

23 Like Ideala's new religion, theosophy was a 'cosmopolitan movement [that] … developed in reaction to orthodox Christianity … [and whose] appeal lay in finding a common ground between many world religions, without necessarily subscribing to the tenets of any one particular religion'. See Gauri Viswanathan, 'The Ordinary Business of Occultism', *Critical Inquiry*, 27:1 (2000) 4.

24 For the seventeenth century see Stevie Davies, *Unbridled Spirits: Women of the English Revolution 1640–1660* (London: Women's Press, 1998); for the eighteenth and nineteenth centuries see Alex Owen, *The Darkened Room: Women, Power and Spiritualism in Late Victorian England* (Virago, 1989), pp. 12–13. For Joanna Southcott see also Diana Basham, *The Trial of Woman: Feminism and the Occult Sciences in Victorian Literature and Society* (Basingstoke: Macmillan, 1992), pp. 52–6.

25 Florence Nightingale, 'Cassandra' (written 1852), in Ray Strachey, *The Cause: A Short History of the Women's Movement in Great Britain* (Virago, 1988), p. 416.

26 Frances Swiney, *The Awakening of Women, or Woman's Part in Evolution* (1899; William Reeves, 1908), pp. 43–4, cited in Lovell-Smith, 'Science and Religion in the Feminist *Fin-de-Siècle*', p. 310.

27 For Swiney see Dixon, *Divine Feminine*, pp. 168–9. Christabel Pankhurst, 'Though That Killest the Prophets', *Suffragette*, 10 April 1914, 590, cited in Dixon, *Divine Feminine*, p. 204.

28 Ideala's irritation about lack of female solidarity probably reflects Grand's own sentiments as echoed in her last novel, *The Winged Victory* (1916): 'It is only exceptional women who are not brutal either in fact or feeling to each other. As a successful pioneer, expect women to ignore you, and think yourself lucky if they don't actually trample you to death in a stampede to secure for themselves the advantages you have won for them. … If you want things done, make the men your friends. … They are not, as a sex, niggling and petty like women' (*WV*, 384).

29 Mangum, *Married, Middlebrow, and Militant*, p. 64.

30 Teresa Lynn Mangum, 'Feminist Fiction and Fictional Feminism: Sarah Grand and the New Woman Novel' (PhD thesis, University of Illinois, 1990), p. 94. For a discussion of Claudia's function as 'feminist corrective' see *Married, Middlebrow, and Militant*, p. 79.

31 *AF*, 171.

32 Ruskin blocked the publication of *Ideala* by his own publisher, George Allen, who was impressed by the manuscript, scribbling on the manuscript that he 'didn't like the title' and 'couldn't bear queer people however nice'. Anything but discouraged, Grand felt so flattered by his comments that she kept the rejected manuscript. See 'Sarah Grand and Mr Ruskin', *Woman's Signal*, 25 January 1894, 57, repr. in *SSPSG*, I, pp. 275–6, and II, p. 225.

33 See Rita S. Kranidis, *Subversive Discourse: The Cultural Production of Late Victorian Feminist Novels* (Basingstoke: Macmillan, 1995), p. 89.

34 Luce Irigaray, 'Divine Women', in Morny Joy, Kathleen O'Grady and Judith L. Poxon (eds), *French Feminists on Religion: A Reader* (Routledge, 2002), p. 43.

35 Unlike the biblical God, the narrator would not banish the fallen Ideala from

Paradise (his home); rather, he would restrict social intercourse with others in order to enable her to visit him and his sister without the risk of being ostracised. Effectively, of course, this would maintain her in social isolation.

36 I have adapted Irigaray's concept of the female trinity as defined by the fusion of 'mother–daughter–woman' ('Divine Women', p. 47).

37 Irigaray, 'Divine Women', p. 44 (emphasis in original), p. 45.

38 Irigaray, 'Divine Women', p. 47 (emphasis in original).

39 'Evadne would kill a better work with her heaviness', Meredith commented when rejecting the manuscript in his capacity as reader for Chapman and Hall. Cited in S. M. Ellis, *George Meredith: His Life and Friends in Relation to His Work* (Grant Richards, 1920), pp. 210–11. Meredith's comments are repr. in *SSPSG*, I, p. 409.

40 Josephine Butler, 'Introduction' to *Woman's Work and Woman's Culture: A Series of Essays* (Macmillan, 1869), pp. lvi–lx.

41 Aemilia Lanyer, 'Eve's Apology in Defense of Women' (*Salve Deus Rex Judaeorum, 1611*), ll. 33, 35, in Sandra M. Gilbert and Susan Gubar (eds), *The Norton Anthology of Literature by Women: The Traditions in English* (New York: Norton, 1996), p. 43; see also *Salve Deus Rex Judaeorum*, ibid., pp. 41–2: 'all women deserve not to be blamed … by evil disposed men … [It] pleased our Lord and Savior Jesus Christ … to be begotten of a woman, born of a woman, nourished of a woman, obedient to a woman, and that he healed women, pardoned women, comforted women: yea, even when he was in his greatest agony … and also in the last hour of his death, took care to dispose of a woman: after his resurrection, appeared first to a woman, sent a woman to declare his most glorious resurrection to the rest of his Disciples.'

42 Diana Basham, *The Trial of Woman: Feminism and the Occult Sciences in Victorian Literature and Society* (Basingstoke: Macmillan, 1992), p. 56.

43 'That little man in black there say a woman can't have as much rights as a man cause Christ wasn't a woman. Where did your Christ come from? From God and a woman? Man had nothing to do with him! If the first woman God ever made was strong enough to turn the world upside down, all alone, together women ought to be able to turn it rightside up again.' Sojourner Truth, 'Ain't I a Woman?' (1852), in Margaret Busby (ed.), *Daughters of Africa: An International Anthology of Words and Writings by Women of African Descent from the Ancient Egyptian to the Present* (Vintage, 1993), p. 38.

44 John Kucich, 'Feminism's Ethical Contradictions: Sarah Grand and the New Woman Writing', *The Power of Lies: Transgression in Victorian Fiction* (Ithaca: Cornell University Press, 1994), p. 249.

45 The Tenor conceals his name – David Julian Vanetemple – from Angelica, who, to his great displeasure, discovers it on an envelope in his Bible (*HT*, 401–2).

46 For a close reading of the homoerotic nature of Angelica's interaction with the Tenor see my *New Woman Fiction: Women Writing First-Wave Feminism* (Basingstoke: Macmillan, 2000), pp. 129–36.

47 For an earlier version of this section see my essay on 'Narrating the Hysteric: *Fin-de-Siècle* Medical Discourse and Sarah Grand's *The Heavenly Twins* (1893)', in Angelique Richardson and Chris Willis (eds), *The New Woman in Fiction and in Fact: Fin-de-Siècle Feminisms* (Basingstoke: Palgrave, 2001), pp. 123–35.

48 Cixous and Clément, *Newly Born Woman*, pp. 154–6, p. 5.

49 On first catching a glimpse of her at her aunt's house, Galbraith reflects on Evadne's potential as a 'seventh wave': 'when the tide is coming in it pauses always, and remains stationary between every seventh wave, waiting for the next, and unable to rise any higher till it comes to carry it on; and it has always seemed to me that the tide of human progress is raised at intervals to higher levels at a bound in some such way. The seventh wave of humanity are men and women who, by the impulse of some one action which comes naturally to them but is new to the race, gather strength to come up to the last halting place of the tide, and to carry it on with them ever so far beyond' (*HT*, 99; see also 659). See Chapter 3 for a detailed analysis of the wave metaphor.

50 Elaine Showalter, *The Female Malady: Women, Madness and English Culture, 1830–1980* (Virago, 1987).

51 'Women, especially, object to have their sense of pleasure disturbed by painful thoughts, and they are ingenious in making excuses for themselves. They raise their selfishness in this to the dignity of a duty by describing it as an effort to keep their minds pure.' Sarah Grand, 'What to Aim At', in Andrew Reid (ed.), *The New Party* (Hodder Bros., 1894), pp. 355–6, repr. in *SSPSG*, I, p. 150. See also *THQ*, 6: 'The habit of endurance has become so inveterate in women that they will sit and suffer from evils they might quite easily remove … A woman will self-deny herself off the face of the earth … the consequence of it is doctors' bills' (in *SSPSG*, I, p. 157).

52 Josef Breuer, case study of Anna O., in Josef Breuer and Sigmund Freud, *Studies on Hysteria*, trans. James and Alix Strachey (Harmondsworth: Penguin, 1974), pp. 73–102. First German edition 1895, first complete English edition 1955.

53 Elaine Showalter, *Sexual Anarchy: Gender and Culture at the* Fin de Siècle (Bloomsbury, 1991), p. 134; Elisabeth Bronfen, *Over Her Dead Body: Death, Femininity and the Aesthetic* (MUP, 1992), pp. 3–14.

54 See Showalter, *The Female Malady*, pp. 147–55, and *Hystories: Hysterical Epidemics and Modern Culture* (Picador, 1997), pp. 30–7.

55 Silas Weir Mitchell, [from] *Fat and Blood: And How to Make Them* (1877), in Catherine Golden (ed.), *The Captive Imagination: A Casebook on The Yellow Wallpaper* (New York: Feminist Press, 1992), pp. 49–50.

56 Charlotte Perkins Gilman, 'Why I Wrote "The Yellow Wallpaper"?' (1913), in Ann J. Lane (ed.), *The Charlotte Perkins Gilman Reader* (Women's Press, 1981), p. 20.

57 Showalter, *The Female Malady*, pp. 75–8; Isaac Baker Brown, [from] *On the Curability of Certain Forms of Insanity, Epilepsy, Catalepsy and Hysteria in Females* (1866) and *On Some Diseases of Woman Admitting Surgical Treatment* (1866), in Sheila Jeffreys (ed.), *The Sexuality Debates* (New York: Routledge & Kegan Paul, 1987), pp. 11–41; see also Pat Jalland and John Hooper (eds), *Women from Birth to Death: The Female Life Cycle in Britain 1830–1914* (Brighton: Harvester, 1986), pp. 250–65.

58 For medical constructions of the hyper-sexed wife as vampire see William J. Robinson, *Married Life and Happiness* (1922), cited in Bram Dijkstra, *Idols of Perversity: Fantasies of Feminine Evil in* Fin-de-Siècle *Culture* (OUP, 1986), p. 334. For the under-sexed wife see William Acton, [from] *The Functions and Disorders*

of the Sexual Organs (1875), in Jeffreys, *The Sexuality Debates*, pp. 63–4.

59 Lyn Pykett, *The 'Improper' Feminine: The Women's Sensation Novel and the New Woman Writing* (Routledge, 1992), p. 175.

60 Sally Ledger, *The New Woman: Fiction and Feminism at the* Fin de Siècle (MUP, 1997), p. 115.

61 Acton, *The Functions and Disorders of the Sexual Organs*, p. 61.

62 Laura Marcus, 'Staging the "Private Theatre": Gender and the Auto-Erotics of Reverie', in Angelique Richardson and Chris Willis (eds), *The New Woman in Fiction and in Fact: Fin-de-Siècle Feminisms* (Basingstoke: Palgrave, 2002), pp. 136–49.

63 Charlotte Perkins Gilman, *The Living of Charlotte Perkins Gilman* (1935; Madison: University of Wisconsin Press, 1990), pp. 23–4. See also the title of Golden's *The Captive Imagination*.

64 Breuer and Freud, *Studies on Hysteria*, pp. 73, 80.

65 Ibid., p. 74.

66 Cixous, 'Exchange' [with Clément], *Newly Born Woman*, p. 154.

67 Ibid., pp. 80, 73, 88.

68 Melinda Given Guttmann, *The Enigma of Anna O.: A Biography of Bertha Pappenheim* (Rhode Island: Moyer Bell, 2001), p. 59.

69 The first English translation by A. A. Brill, *Studies in Hysteria: Selected Papers on Hysteria and Other Psychoneuroses* (published in New York in 1909) excluded Anna O.'s case study. See 'Editor's Introduction' to Breuer and Freud, *Studies on Hysteria*, p. 31.

70 Gillian Kersley, *Darling Madame: Sarah Grand & Devoted Friend* (Virago, 1983), pp. xi–xii.

71 For Anna O. see Breuer and Freud, *Studies on Hysteria*, p. 102; Lisa Appignanesi and John Forrester, *Freud's Women* (Virago, 1993), pp. 76–7; and Mikkel Borch-Jacobsen, *Remembering Anna O.: A Century of Mystification*, trans. Kirby Olson in collaboration with Xavier Callahan and the author (Routledge, 1996), pp. 9–10, 21–5. See also Guttman, *The Enigma of Anna O.*, pp. 75–100. For Gilman see Denise D. Knight (ed.), *The Diaries of Charlotte Perkins Gilman*, 2 vols (Charlottesville: University Press of Virginia, 1994), I, p. 385. For Grand see Kersley, *Darling Madame*, p. x.

72 Appignanesi and Forrester, *Freud's Women*, pp. 77–80.

73 See Borch-Jacobsen, *Remembering Anna O.*, p. 27, and Guttman, *The Engima of Anna O.*, pp. 129–52.; Gilman, *The Living*, p. 314, and Ann Lane, *To Herland and Beyond: The Life and Work of Charlotte Perkins Gilman* (New York: Pantheon, 1990), pp. 323, 352.

74 Her 'favourite among [her] books', *Ideala*, Grand noted in 1895, reflected her views 'more fully' than *The Heavenly Twins*. See Jane T. Stoddart, 'Illustrated Interview: Sarah Grand', *Woman at Home*, 3 (1895) 248–9, in *SSPSG*, I, pp. 212–13.

75 W. T. Stead, 'The Novel of the Modern Woman', *Review of Reviews*, 10 (1894) 67; repr. in *LVMQ*, V.

76 As Gillian Kersley reports (*Darling Madame*, pp. 72–3, 75, 105), six editions of the novel were published in 1893 alone, and by the end of the first two years 20,000

copies had been sold in Britain. In the United States, *The Heavenly Twins* sold 'at least five times as many copies' in its first year and entered the 'Overall Best Sellers' list, with 625,000 copies sold in the decade 1890–9 (Frank Luther Mott, *Golden Multitudes: The Story of Best Sellers in the United States* (New York: R. R. Bowker, 1947), pp. 181–2, 311). More than any other book, the novelist 'Rita' (Mrs Desmond Humphreys) recalled in 1936, it left its mark on the time, 'creat[ing] one of the greatest sensations of literature. It was reviewed, talked of, discussed wherever one went' (Rita, *Recollections of a Literary Life* [Andrew Melrose, 1936], p. 173). Translated into Finnish and Russian, the novel was reviewed by the Norwegian writer and playwright Björnstjerne Björnson, and letters mainly from women readers, but also from physicians, came flooding in from all over the world. Even decades later one Washington reader wrote in to say that she had read the novel once a year ever since she was 16. See Jane T. Stoddart, 'Illustrated Interview: Sarah Grand', *Woman at Home*, 3 (1895) 249, in *SSPSG*, I, p. 213, and Gladys Singers-Bigger, diary entry of 30 September 1934, in Kersley, *Darling Madame*, pp. 262–3.

Notes to Chapter 3

1 *BB*, 324–5.
2 Catherine Clément, 'Jouissances: Between the Angel and the Placenta', extract from *Syncope: The Philosophy of Rapture* (1994, French original 1990), in Joy Morny, Kathleen O'Grady and Judith L. Poxon (eds), *French Feminists on Religion: A Reader* (Routledge, 2002), pp. 199–200, 202 (emphasis in original).
3 Hélène Cixous, 'Sorties: Out and Out: Attacks/Ways Out/Forays', in Hélène Cixous and Catherine Clément, *The Newly Born Woman* [*La Jeune Née*, 1975], trans. Betsy Wing (MUP, 1986), pp. 88–9.
4 See Hélène Cixous, 'The Laugh of the Medusa', in Elaine Marks and Isabelle de Courtivron (eds), *New French Feminisms* (Brighton: Harvester, 1981), pp. 245–66.
5 Cixous, 'Sorties', p. 90.
6 Cixous, 'The Laugh of the Medusa', p. 247.
7 Lyn Pykett, *The 'Improper' Feminine: The Women's Sensation Novel and the New Woman Writing* (Routledge, 1992), p. 184.
8 In the local library Ideala discovers shelves of decadent texts that have evidently never been read: 'The works of art for art's sake, and style for style's sake, end on the shelf much respected, while their authors end in the asylum, the prison, and the premature grave ... nobody reads [these books]' (*BB*, 460–1).
9 Gauri Viswanathan, 'The Ordinary Business of Occultism', *Critical Inquiry*, 27:1 (2000) 15.
10 Rachel Blau Du Plessis, *Writing Beyond the Ending: Narrative Strategies of Twentieth-Century Women Writers* (Bloomington: Indiana University Press, 1985), p. 89.
11 Ibid., p. 89. See also Pykett, *The 'Improper' Feminine*, pp. 185–6, and Terri Doughty, 'Sarah Grand's *The Beth Book*: The New Woman and the Ideology of the Romance Ending', in Carol J. Singley and Susan Elizabeth Sweeney (eds), *Anxious Power: Reading, Writing and Ambivalence in Narrative by Women* (Albany: State University of New York Press, 1993), pp. 185, 190–1.

12 Pykett, *The 'Improper' Feminine*, p. 186.

13 Anonymous reviews of *The Beth Book*, *Review of Reviews*, 16 (1897) 621, and of *The Heavenly Twins*, *Review of Reviews*, 7 (1893) 543, both repr. in *SSPSG*, I; James Ashcroft Noble, 'The Fiction of Sexuality', *Contemporary Review*, 67 (1895) 493, repr. in *LVMQ*, V.

14 Penny Boumelha, 'The Woman of Genius and the Woman of Grub Street: Figures of the Female Writer in British *Fin-de-Siècle* Fiction', *English Literature in Transition*, 40 (1997) 173.

15 'It was as if he had recognised her; and she felt herself as if she had seen him before' (*BB*, 432). In *From Man to Man*, Rebekah first becomes aware of Drummond at a concert because his hand appears somehow familiar; later she realizes that 'the hand it reminded her of was her own' (*FMTM*, 446).

16 Schreiner left notes for a potential ending in a letter to Karl Pearson (see *OSL*, 93–4). Another ending is outlined by her husband Cronwright in the 'Publisher's Note' at the end of the novel (*FMTM*, 506–7).

17 Frank Harris and Frank Danby, 'Reviews: Sarah Grand's Latest Book', *Saturday Review*, 20 November 1897, 557–8, repr. in *SSPSG*, I, pp. 468–73. For Harris's gender politics during his editorship of the *Fortnightly Review* see Laurel Brake, 'Writing Women's History: "The Sex" Debates of 1889', in Ann Heilmann and Margaret Beetham (eds), *New Woman Hybridities: Femininity, Feminism, and International Consumer Culture, 1880–1930* (Routledge, 2004), pp. 51–73.

18 For details of the room-as-womb metaphor in New Woman fiction, specifically in *BB* and *FMTM*, see my *New Woman Fiction: Women Writing First-Wave Feminism* (Basingstoke: Macmillan, 2000), pp. 178–93.

19 See Teresa Mangum's detailed analysis in *Married, Middlebrow, and Militant: Sarah Grand and the New Woman Novel* (Ann Arbor: University of Michigan Press, 1998), pp. 37–49. For the dress metaphor in this text see also *New Woman Fiction*, pp. 122–4.

20 Judith Butler, *Gender Trouble: Feminism and the Subversion of Identity* (Routledge, 1990), pp. 6, 129.

21 Deas Cromarty, 'To the Author of "Beth"', *Young Woman*, 65 (February 1898) 235, repr. in *SSPSG*, I, pp. 494–7.

22 Patricia Murphy, *Time is of the Essence: Temporality, Gender, and the New Woman* (Albany: State University of New York Press, 2001), pp. 119–21.

23 For Gothic elements in Grand's late fiction see *Adnam's Orchard* (1912) and *The Winged Victory* (1916); here it is the lace maker Ella Banks who has the gift of clairvoyance.

24 See Janet Oppenheim, *The Other World: Spiritualism and Psychical Research in England, 1850–1914* (CUP, 1985); Alex Owen, *The Darkened Room: Women and Spiritualism in Late Victorian Britain* (Virago, 1989); Diana Basham, *The Trial of Woman: Feminism and the Occult Sciences in Victorian Literature and Society* (Virago, 1992), pp. 8, 108, 135; and Judith R. Walkowitz, *City of Dreadful Delight: Narratives of Sexual Danger in Late-Victorian London* (Virago, 1992), pp. 171–89.

25 See Owen, *Darkened Room*, pp. 4–12, 18–40, 202; Basham, *Trial of Woman*, pp. 22, 122–6.

26 Owen, *Darkened Room*, pp. 1, 19, 41.

27 Frederic Marvin, *The Philosophy of Spiritualism and the Pathology and Treatment of Mediomania* (1874), cited in Owen, *Darkened Room*, p. 149.

28 In 1870 Louisa Lowe, the estranged wife of an Anglican vicar, was committed to a private asylum, and kept confined for eighteen months in various institutions, on the grounds of spiritualist mania; Henry Maudsley admitted that her refusal to give up her intention of divorcing her husband for adultery had made it impossible for him to consider her release (Owen, *Darkened Room*, pp. 168–201). Some years later Georgina Weldon, a woman with strong views and (in her husband's eyes) an infuriating obsession with spiritualism, singing and her orphanage, narrowly escaped the same fate, and fought back by successfully prosecuting the physicians involved in her near-abduction (Owen, *Darkened Room*, pp. 160–7; Walkowitz, *City of Dreadful Delight*, pp. 171–89). The socialist feminist Edith Lanchester was certified insane in 1895 for her decision to live in a free union with her working-class lover, but was released after mounting protest by the Legitimation League; see Lucy Bland, *Banishing the Beast: English Feminism and Sexual Morality, 1885–1914* (Harmondsworth: Penguin, 1995), pp. 159–61.

29 Louisa Lowe, *The Bastilles of England, or The Lunacy Laws at Work* (Crookenden and Co., 1883); Georgina Weldon, *How I Escaped the Mad Doctors* (Tavistock House, 1882), both repr. in Roy Porter, Helen Nicholson and Bridget Bennett (eds), *Women, Madness and Spiritualism*, 2 vols (Routledge, 2003), I.

30 Basham, *Trial of Woman*, pp. 204–14; Sylvia Cranston, *The Extraordinary Life and Influence of Helena Blavatsky, Founder of the Modern Theosophical Movement* (New York: Jeremy P. Tarcher/Putnam, 1993), pp. xviii, 145.

31 Theosophical aspects have been variously noted in the work of William Butler Yeats, James Joyce, T. S. Eliot, E. M. Forster, D. H. Lawrence, Wassily Kandinsky, Piet Mondrian, Paul Klee and Paul Gauguin. In addition, Blavatsky's biographer Sylvia Cranston points to Blavatsky's influence on Jack London, Thornton Wilder, Gustav Mahler, Jean Sibelius, Alexander Scriabin, C. G. Jung's notion of the collective unconscious and Sigmund Freud's interpretation of dreams; see Cranston, *Blavatsky*, pp. 463–98, 515–20.

32 H. P. Blavatsky, *The Secret Doctrine* (1888), cited in Basham, *Trial of Woman*, p. 201. For previous references see Cranston, *Blavatsky*, p. xviii, and Owen, *Darkened Room*, p. 136.

33 Joy Dixon, *Divine Feminine: Theosophy and Feminism in England* (Baltimore: Johns Hopkins University Press, 2001), p. 150.

34 See Martha Vicinus, *Independent Women: Work and Community for Single Women, 1850–1920* (Virago, 1985), p. 260; Margaret Mulvihill, *Charlotte Despard: A Biography* (Pandora, 1989), pp. 35–6.

35 See Dixon, *Divine Feminine*, pp. 152–205.

36 Ibid., p. 7.

37 Maud Gonne MacBride, *A Servant of the Queen* (1938; Gerrards Cross: Colin Smythe, 1994), pp. 200–13.

38 Netta Syrett, *The Sheltering Tree* (Geoffrey Bles, 1939), p. 281.

39 Dixon, *Divine Feminine*, p. 6.

40 Basham, *Trial of Woman*, p. x.

41 H.P. *Blavatsky to the American Conventions 1888–1891*, cited in Cranston, *Blavatsky*, p. 146.
42 Blavatsky's first two books, *Isis Unveiled* (1877) and *The Secret Doctrine* (1888), frame the period between the writing and publishing of *Ideala* (1888).
43 Dixon, *Divine Feminine*, pp. 21–4.
44 Ibid., p. 154. See also the theosophist theory, outlined in 1910 by Charles Lazenby, that individuals changed sex after every seventh incarnation. Individuals who in their seven masculine phases had shown cruelty towards women would reincarnate, it was believed, as women facing particularly oppressive circumstances. See Dixon, *Divine Feminine*, pp. 112–13, 160.
45 Ibid., p. 27.
46 In her Mahatma Letters, for example, Blavatsky engaged in a sophisticated game of alternately and simultaneously undermining her own authority and that of the Mahatmas. See Dixon, *Divine Feminine*, pp. 27–8.
47 A. P. Sinnett (ed.), *Incidents in the Life of Madame Blavatsky, Compiled from Information Supplied by her Relatives and Friends* (1886; Theosophical Publishing Society, 1913), pp. 27–8.
48 Sarah A. Tooley, 'Madame Sarah Grand at Home', *Young Woman* (1897), repr. in *SSPSG*, I, pp. 241–2.
49 See Sinnett, *Incidents in the Life of Madame Blavatsky*, pp. 16–17.
50 Ibid., pp. 27–8.
51 H. P. Blavatsky, *The Theosophical Glossary* (1892), cited in Cranston, *Blavatsky*, p. 119.
52 H. P. Blavatsky, *Isis Unveiled: A Master-Key to the Mysteries of Ancient and Modern Science and Theology*, 2 vols (1877; Pasadena: Theosophical University Press, 1988), II, p. 588.
53 Blavatsky, *Isis Unveiled*, I, p. xxxvi.
54 The Pythagorean concept of metempsychosis, Blavatsky asserted, constituted the '"missing link" in the chain' of the modern theory of evolution; see *Isis Unveiled*, I, p. 9. Blavatsky considered Darwinian evolution to form only a small part in a much larger spiritual development; see H. P. Blavatsky, *An Abridgement of The Secret Doctrine*, ed. Elizabeth Preston and Christmas Humphreys (Wheaton, IL: Theosophical Publishing House, 1966), p. 196, and *Isis Unveiled*, I, pp. xxx–xxxi.
55 Cranston, *Blavatsky*, pp. 165–7. Blavatasky questioned the idea of reincarnation in the sense of the consecutive rebirth of the same individual other than in exceptional cases; see *Isis Unveiled*, I, p. 351, and her later explanatory article, 'Theories about Reincarnation and Spirits', *The Path* (November 1886), repr. in *Isis Unveiled*, II, Appendix pp. 31–44.
56 See 'Anthropogenesis' in Blavatsky's *Secret Doctrine*, II, especially Stanzas 4–7, 9–12. See also George Robb, 'Race Motherhood: Moral Eugenics vs Progressive Eugenics, 1880–1920', in Claudia Nelson and Ann Sumner Holmes (eds), *Maternal Instincts: Visions of Motherhood and Sexuality in Britain, 1875–1925* (Basingstoke: Macmillan, 1997), p. 63.
57 'A hundred struggle and drown in the breakers. One discovers the new world', Florence Nightingale, 'Cassandra', in Ray Strachey, *The Cause: A Short History of the Women's Movement in Great Britain* (Virago, 1988), p. 398. Compare with

Frances Power Cobbe's *Duties of Women* (Williams & Norgate, 1881, p. 22): 'An immense wave is lifting up women all over the world'; cited in Susan Hamilton, '"A Crisis in Woman's History": Frances Power Cobbe's *Duties of Women* and the Practice of Everyday Feminism', in Ann Heilmann (ed.), *Words as Deeds: Literary and Historical Perspectives on Women's Suffrage*, special issue of *Women's History Review*, 11:4 (2002) 580. See also Schreiner's equation of the women's movement with 'the foremost crust of a great wave of human necessity' in *W&L* (135), and Lady Hill's waves/tide metaphor in Gertrude Colmore's suffrage novel *Suffragette Sally* (1911; Pandora, 1984), p. 44: 'Individidual waves [are broken]: but the tide comes in. And individual women have been and will be broken: but woman will reach her destined place.'

58 Blavatsky, *Isis Unveiled*, I, p. xix, and II, p. 590.

59 Blavatsky, *Abridgement of The Secret Doctrine*, p. 170.

60 'First Object' of the Theosophical Society, cited in Dixon, *Divine Feminine*, pp. 3–4. See also Charles Johnston, 'Helena Petrovna Blavatsky', *Theosophical Forum*, 5 (1900), cited in Cranston, *Blavatsky*, p. 331: 'There are really no "inferior races", for all are one in our common humanity.'

61 'Races of men differ in spiritual gifts as in color, stature, or any other external quality.' Blavatsky, *Isis Unveiled*, II, p. 588. For details of the racist element in theosophist discourse see Dixon's *Divine Feminine*, especially chapters 5 and 8.

62 Dixon, *Divine Feminine*, pp. 8, 11.

63 For the Victorian construction of working-class women through the discourse of 'race' see Anne McClintock, *Imperial Leather: Race, Gender and Sexuality in the Colonial Context* (Routledge, 1995), pp. 104–20.

64 Blavatsky claimed to speak for her Tibetan Masters Koot Hoomi and Morya; see Viswanathan, 'The Ordinary Business of Occultism', 6.

65 Dixon, *Divine Feminine*, p. 106.

66 Hélène Cixous, 'The Laugh of the Medusa' (1976), in Elaine Marks and Isabelle de Courtivron (eds), *New French Feminisms* (Brighton: Harvester, 1981), p. 246.

67 The British membership records of the Theosophical Society (50 Gloucester Place, London W1U 8EA) cover the period from the late 1880s to 1923, but they are incomplete for the period 1923/4 until the mid-1940s. Grand appears neither under her pseudonym nor under her maiden or married names, and she is not listed in the index of members who either resigned or allowed their subscription to lapse. I am grateful to Mark Llewellyn for this information, and to Colyn Boyce and Barry Thompson for permitting access to the records. I would also like to thank Conrad Jamieson, Theosophical Society, for researching the handwritten records from 1880 to 1944.

68 Gladys Singers-Bigger, 'Ideala's Gift: The Record of a Dear Friendship' (diary), 15 May 1927, Bath Central Library.

69 Dr Charles Whitby who, in a *Freewoman* article of 1912, engaged in astrological and theosophical discussion, later wrote in his memoir 'Sarah Grand: The Woman and Her Work' that she was 'nothing if not spiritual-minded' and had a 'strong leaning towards mysticism'; *SSPSG*, I, pp. 332, 329. For Whitby's contribution to the *Freewoman* see Dixon, *Divine Feminine*, p. 114.

70 Sarah Grand to Gladys Singers-Bigger, 17 May 1936, in *SSPSG*, II, p. 227. See also

letter dated 10 May 1936, Bath Central Library. In the earlier letter Grand ironised her current indifference to reincarnation by putting it down to her withdrawal symptoms on giving up smoking, but on 18 July 1936 she recorded having read 'an approach to *Rudolf Steiner* by Miss Faulkner Jones, Lectures by Rudolf Steiner [and] *Reincarnation* by Rittelmeyer' (*SSPSG*, II, p. 231). She had also received an invitation from the Rudolf Steiner Society in London, probably because her step-granddaughter had recently joined the movement.

71 Sarah Grand to Gladys Singers-Bigger, 25 April 1936, in *SSPSG*, II, p. 225, see also n.1.

72 Gladys Singers-Bigger, 'Ideala's Gift', 18 April and 15 May 1927, Bath Central Library.

73 'I Can't Explain It' and 'Josepha Recounts a Remarkable Experience', both in *Variety* (1922), pp. 111–36 and 173–90, repr. in *SSPSG*, IV, pp. 287–334. For Grand's claim that these stories were based on her own experience see Gladys Singers-Bigger, 'Ideala's Gift', 3 June 1928, Bath Central Library.

74 Diana Burfield, 'Theosophy and Feminism: Some Explorations in Nineteenth-Century Biography', in Pat Holden (ed.), *Women's Religious Experience* (Croom Helm, 1983), p. 41.

75 See Stephanie Forward's chronology in *SSPSG*, II, p. 14.

76 Max Müller, 'Esoteric Buddhism', *Nineteenth Century* (May 1893), 767–88; references are taken from *www.blavatskyarchives.com/muller1.htm*, accessed on 23 September 2002. I am grateful to Paul Barlow for drawing my attention to this text.

77 Dixon, *Divine Feminine*, p. 52.

78 Ibid., pp. 68, 62, 41–2.

79 Ibid., pp. 44, 70, 68.

80 See for example George Moore, 'Sex in Art', *Modern Painting* (Walter Scott, 1897), pp. 226–37. For more details see also my discussion of 'Literary Degeneration' in *New Woman Fiction*, pp. 46–59.

81 See Annie Besant, 'The Legalisation of Female Slavery in England' (1876), in Sheila Jeffreys (ed.), *The Sexuality Debates* (New York: Routledge & Kegan Paul, 1987), pp. 91–9. As a free-love advocate, Besant had located herself at the opposite end of Grand's social purism, but both shared a concern in the oppressive and violent structures of marriage.

82 Adapted from the subtitle of Hélène Cixous's essay 'Sorties', in Cixous and Clément, *The Newly Born Woman*, pp. 63–132.

83 See Frank Harris's review of *BB*, *Saturday Review*, 20 November 1897, 557, repr. in *SSPSG*, I, pp. 468–9.

84 Cixous, 'Sorties', p. 92.

85 Ibid. (emphases in original).

86 Ibid., p. 93.

87 Pykett, *The 'Improper' Feminine*, p. 179.

88 Pykett argues that Beth's secret chamber is 'the realisation of a wish-fulfilment fantasy' involving author, character and reader simultaneously (*The 'Improper' Feminine*, p. 183). Interestingly, Grand's first independent home after she left McFall and established herself as a writer was a Kensington flat located on the top

floor; see Jane T. Stoddart, 'Illustrated Interview: Sarah Grand', *Woman at Home*, 3 (1895) 247, repr. in *SSPSG*, I, p. 211.

89 Grand, Preface to *OMN*, vi; Preface to *EM*, x, both prefaces repr. in *SSPSG*, IV, pp. 9–29.

90 Olive Schreiner, Preface to *AF*, n.p. See my discussion of the New Woman's 'aesthetic of resistance' in *New Woman Fiction*, pp. 67–71.

91 Emile Zola, 'The Experimental Novel' (1879), in Walter Greiner and Gerhard Stilz (eds), *Naturalismus in England 1880–1920* (Darmstadt: Wissenschaftliche Buchgesellschaft, 1983), p. 67.

92 The notion that aestheticism was an exclusively male-gendered movement has been revised by Talia Schaffer and Kathy Alexis Psomiades' *Women and British Aestheticism* (Charlottesville: University Press of Virginia, 1999), and Talia Schaffer, *The Forgotten Female Aesthetes: Literary Culture in Late-Victorian England* (Charlottesville: University Press of Virginia, 2000).

93 Teresa Mangum, 'Style Wars of the 1890s: The New Woman and the Decadent', in Nikki Lee Manos and Meri-Jane Rochelson (eds), *Transforming Genres: New Approaches to British Fiction of the 1890s* (New York: St. Martin's Press, 1994), pp. 47–66.

94 Rita S. Kranidis, *Subversive Discourse: The Cultural Production of Late Victorian Feminist Novels* (Basingstoke: Macmillan, 1995), p. 78.

95 Adrienne Rich, 'When We Dead Awaken: Writing as Re-vision', in Barbara Charlesworth Gelpi and Albert Gelpi (eds), *Adrienne Rich's Poetry* (1971; New York: Norton, 1975), p. 90.

96 The note left with the baby was written in an educated feminine hand (*HT*, 427).

97 Pykett, *The 'Improper' Feminine*, p. 185.

98 Mangum, *Married, Middlebrow, and Militant*, pp. 150–4; Penny Boumelha, 'The Woman of Genius and the Woman of Grub Street: Figures of the Female Writer in British *Fin-de-Siècle* Fiction', *English Literature in Transition*, 40 (1997) 172; Murphy, *Time is of the Essence*, pp. 115, 133–4.

99 Mangum, *Married, Middlebrow, and Militant*, p. 152.

100 Ibid., p. 151. For the analogies with suffrage writing see p. 188.

101 Mangum, 'Style Wars of the 1890s', p. 49.

102 For an earlier version of the subsequent discussion of Grand's personification of decadence see my essay on 'Wilde's New Women: The New Woman on Wilde', in Uwe Böker, Richard Corballis and Julie Hibbard (eds), *The Importance of Reinventing Oscar: Versions of Wilde during the Last 100 Years*. Proceedings of the conference at the Technische Universität Dresden, 31 August–3 September 2000 (Amsterdam: Rodopi, 2002), pp. 135–45.

103 For Lord Henry's 'pointed brown beard' see *Dorian Gray*, in *The Complete Works of Oscar Wilde* (HarperCollins, 1996), p. 381.

104 'Ponce' in its modern meaning did not come into usage before 1932; Alfred's surname may reflect Mayhew's use of the term 'pouncey' as a synonym for pimp. See Angelique Richardson, *Love and Eugenics in the Late Nineteenth Century: Rational Reproduction and the New Woman* (OUP, 2003), p. 111.

105 Angelique Richardson, 'The Eugenization of Love: Darwin, Galton, and New Woman Fictions of Heredity and Eugenics' (PhD thesis, Birkbeck College,

University of London, 1998), p. 194. See also *Love and Eugenics*, p. 125.

106 Mangum, 'Style Wars of the 1890s', p. 60.

107 Grant Allen, 'Plain Words on the Woman Question', *Popular Science Monthly* (1889), p. 172–3; repr. in *LVMQ*, V.

108 H. G. Wells, *The New Machiavelli* (John Lane, the Bodley Head, 1911), p. 411.

109 Arnold Bennett, *Our Women: Chapters on the Sex-Discord* (Cassell, 1920), p. 106.

110 'The Life Story of Sarah Grand', *Review of Reviews*, 16 (1897) 595, repr. in *SSPSG*, I, pp. 251–2.

111 Sarah Grand, 'In the Days of My Youth: My First Success', *M.A.P.*, 22 May 1909, 493, repr. in *SSPSG*, I, p. 203.

112 William Barry, 'The Strike of a Sex', *Quarterly Review*, 179 (1894) 295; repr. in *LVMQ*, V.

113 Barry, 'The Strike of a Sex', 297; 'Recent Novels' [anonymous review of *The Heavenly Twins*], *Spectator*, 25 March 1893, repr. in *SSPSG*, I, p. 423.

114 'New Novels: The Beth Book', *Athenaeum*, 27 November 1897, 744, repr. in *SSPSG*, I, p. 474.

115 Frank Danby, review of *BB* in the *Saturday Review*, 20 November 1897, 558, repr. in *SSPSG*, I, p. 473.

116 Janet E. Hogarth, 'Literary Degenerates', *Fortnightly Review*, 57 n.s. (1895) 586–92, repr. in *LVMQ*, V; Hugh E. M. Stutfield, 'Tommyrotics', *Blackwood's Edinburgh Magazine*, 157 (1895) 836, 840, repr. in *LVMQ*, V. For the contemporary discourse of decadence see Lyn Pykett, *Engendering Fictions: The English Novel in the Early Twentieth Century* (Edward Arnold, 1995), pp. 14–37; Sally Ledger, *The New Woman: Fiction and Feminism at the* Fin de Siècle (MUP, 1997), pp. 94–121; and my *New Woman Fiction*, pp. 46–53.

117 Grand's indictment of the decadent critic and would-be writer in *The Beth Book* echoes an earlier attack on George Moore, in 1888, by Robert Buchanan, who sneered at 'The Modern Young Man as Critic' for being 'a pessimistic follower of Schopenhauer, Zola, and Ibsen' and writing 'criticism run to seed' rather than literature proper. Buchanan went considerably further than Grand, associating Moore's degenerative aesthetics with the sexual violence of a Jack the Ripper. See Adrian Frazier, *George Moore 1852–1933* (New Haven: Yale University Press, 2000), p. 186.

118 Helen C. Black, 'Sarah Grand', *Pen, Pencil Baton and Mask: Biographical Sketches* (Spottiswoode, 1896), p. 71, repr. in *SSPSG*, I, p. 280.

119 'New Writers: Sarah Grand', *Bookman*, 4 (1893) 107, repr. in *SSPSG*, I, p. 272.

120 W. T. Stead, 'The Novel of the Modern Woman', *Review of Reviews*, 10 (1894) 67, repr. in *LVMQ*, V.

121 'Some Books of the Month' [review of *HT*], *Review of Reviews*, 7 (1893) 545, repr. in *SSPSG*, I, p. 431.

122 Kate Flint, 'Reading the New Woman', *Browning Society Notes*, 17 (1987–88) 60. See also Ernst Foerster, *Die Frauenfrage in den Romanen Englischer Schriftstellerinnen* (Marburg: N.G. Elwert'sche Verlagsbuchhandlung, 1907), p. 68.

123 Cixous, 'Sorties', pp. 85–6, 93.

Notes to Chapter 4

1 Hélène Cixous, 'The School of Dreams', *Three Steps on the Ladder of Writing* (1993), extracts repr. in Morny Joy, Kathleen O'Grady and Judith L. Poxon (eds), *French Feminists on Religion: A Reader* (Routledge, 2002), pp. 238–42.
2 *D*, 175–6.
3 *Athenaeum*, 10 January 1891, repr. in Cherry Clayton (ed.), *Olive Schreiner* (Johannesburg: McGraw-Hill, 1983), p. 78.
4 *OSL*, 142; *LOS*, 145, emphasis in original.
5 Joyce Avrech Berkman, *The Healing Imagination of Olive Schreiner* (Amhurst: University of Massachusetts Press, 1989), p. 215.
6 Olive Renier, *Before the Bonfire* (Shipston-on-Stowe: P. Drinkwater, 1984), p. 12.
7 Olive Schreiner to Ernest Rhys, early 1888, *OSL*, 136.
8 Carolyn Burdett, *Olive Schreiner and the Progress of Feminism* (Basingstoke: Palgrave, 2001), p. 48.
9 Deborah L. Madsen, *Rereading Allegory: A Narrative Approach to Genre* (Basingstoke: Macmillan, 1995), p. 29.
10 For a discussion of Schreiner's 'aesthetics of literary miscegenation' see Berkman, *The Healing Imagination*, p. 195.
11 *AF*, 141–51; *D*, 23–50.
12 Cixous, 'The School of Dreams', p. 238.
13 See Berkman, *The Healing Imagination*, pp. 44–68.
14 Olive Schreiner to W. P. Schreiner, 12 May 1912, *OSL*, 128.
15 Renier, *Before the Bonfire*, p. 12.
16 5 January 1886, *OSL*, 72.
17 30 January 1887, in Juliet Gardiner (ed.), *The New Woman* (Collins & Brown, 1993), p. 154.
18 Ever since S. C. Cronwright-Schreiner's distinctly unfavourable *Life of Olive Schreiner* (1924), Schreiner criticism has been bedevilled by his projection of her as an unbalanced woman artist perched between the extremes of genius and hysteria: 'one half of a great writer; a diamond marred by a flaw' (Virginia Woolf, 'Olive Schreiner', 1925, in Clayton, *Olive Schreiner*, p. 94). Woolf's equivocal appraisal has been rephrased by modern critics such as Elaine Showalter in *A Literature of Their Own* (Virago, 1978) and *Inventing Herself: Claiming a Feminist Intellectual Heritage* (New York: Simon and Schuster, 2001); Kathleen Blake in *Love and the Woman Question in Victorian Literature* (Brighton: Harvester, 1983); and even Schreiner's more sympathetic biographers, Ruth First and Ann Scott, in *Olive Schreiner* (André Deutsch, 1980). In *Sexual Anarchy: Gender and Culture at the Fin de Siècle* (Bloomsbury, 1990, p. 52) and *A Literature of Their Own* (pp. 194–8) Showalter compares her 'crippling psychosomatic diseases' to the symptoms Freud and Breuer described in their study of female hysterics, suggesting that Schreiner's life and creative ambitions were handicapped by her 'claustrophobia' and by an invalidism which translated into an 'evasion of work'.
19 Marion Friedmann, *Olive Schreiner: A Study in Latent Meanings* (Johannesburg: Witwatersrand University Press, 1955).
20 First and Scott, *Olive Schreiner*, pp. 61–3, 68.

21 Helen Bradford, 'Olive Schreiner's Hidden Agony: Fact, Fiction and Teenage Abortion', *Journal of Southern African Studies*, 21 (1995) 623–41.

22 Anne McClintock, *Imperial Leather: Race, Gender and Sexuality in the Colonial Context* (Routledge, 1995), p. 264.

23 Renier, *Before the Bonfire*, p. 13; see also Liz Stanley, *The Auto/biographical I: The Theory and Practice of Feminist Auto/biography* (MUP, 1992), p. 210.

24 Berkman, *The Healing Imagination*, p. 14.

25 Stanley, *The Auto/biographical I*, pp. 181–213.

26 R. C. Lehman, *Mr Punch's Prize Novels: New Series* (Bloomsbury, Agnew & Co., 1892), pp. 135–41. The satire is illustrated with a cartoon depicting a monstrously unsexed 'Tant' Sannie stewing Kraut' (Figure 11) in a manner evocative of cannibalistic rites associated with 'savage' races (a rather tame representative of which is figured in the background). Tant' Sannie is indicative of the anomaly of both the Boer (woman) and Olive Schreiner, the mannish authoress whose allegories are as inimical to the exquisite literary tastes of a civilised English readership as Tant' Sannie's 'Kraut' is to the refined English palate. The titles ('Gasps', 'Screams') and fictive authorial name ('Schreion', 'Schrei' being the German word for 'scream', an association very different from the German meaning of Schreiner's surname, 'carpenter') combine an allusion to the respiratory problems of an asthmatic ('gasping for breath') with an attack on the effusions of the screaming (and gasping) feminist sisterhood.

27 Ann Harries, *Manly Pursuits* (Bloomsbury, 1999).

28 Showalter, *A Literature of Their Own*, p. 197.

29 See Laura Chrisman, 'Allegory, Feminist Thought and the *Dreams* of Olive Schreiner', in Tony Brown (ed.), *Edward Carpenter and Late Victorian Radicalism* (Frank Cass, 1990), p. 126; and Stephanie Forward, 'The Dreams of Olive Schreiner', *Irish Journal of Feminist Studies*, 3 (1998) 69–70.

30 Constance G. Lytton, *Prisons and Prisoners: Experience of a Suffragette* (1914; East Ardsley: E. P. Publishing, 1976), p. 157.

31 Edith Lees, 'Olive Schreiner and her Relation to the Woman Movement' (1915), in Clayton, *Olive Schreiner*, p. 47. Vera Brittain, *Lady Into Woman* (Andrew Dakers, 1953), p. 215, and 'The Influence of Olive Schreiner', in Zelda Friedlander (ed.), *Until the Heart Changes* (Cape Town: Tafelberg-Uitgewers, 1967), p. 125. Charlotte Perkins Gilman, *The Living of Charlotte Perkins Gilman: An Autobiography* (Madison: University of Wisconsin Press, 1990), p. 168. See also Harriet Howe, 'Charlotte Perkins Gilman – As I Knew Her' (1936), in Joanne B. Karpinski (ed.), *Critical Essays on Charlotte Perkins Gilman* (New York: G. K. Hall, 1992), p. 76.

32 Olive Banks, *Faces of Feminism: A Study of Feminism as a Social Movement* (Oxford: Blackwell, 1986), pp. 13–27.

33 An early version of this section was published as 'Dreams in Black and White: Women, Race and Self-Sacrifice in Olive Schreiner's Allegorical Writings', in Heloise Brown, Madi Gilkes and Ann Kaloski-Naylor (eds), *White?Women: Critical Perspectives on Race and Gender* (York: Raw Nerve Books, 1999), pp. 181–99.

34 The first edition had sold out after only four days, and two further editions were

planned for the same month, Olive Schreiner wrote to her brother in January 1891 (*OSL*, 184).

35 Olive Schreiner to T. Fisher Unwin, 26 September 1892, *OSL*, 209.

36 Charlotte Perkins Gilman and Harriet Howe referred to the allegory as the title of the book; see Gilman, *The Living*, p. 168, and Howe, 'Charlotte Perkins Gilman – As I Knew Her', p. 75.

37 Scott McCracken, 'Stages of Sand and Blood: The Performance of Gendered Subjectivity in Olive Schreiner's Colonial Allegories', in Sally Ledger (ed.), *Women's Writing at the* Fin de Siècle, special issue of *Women's Writing*, 3:3 (1996) 231–42.

38 Like myself, Laura Chrisman infers the narrator to be female, while McCracken reads her/his lack of an unambiguously defined gender as an indication of 'the undecided nature of identity in culture in contrast with the overdetermined conditions that weigh down woman as actor' inside the frame; see 'Stages of Sand and Blood', 235; and Chrisman, 'Allegory, Feminist Thought and the *Dreams* of Olive Schreiner', p. 127.

39 Olive Schreiner to Havelock Ellis, 8 April 1884, *LOS*, 15.

40 For Schreiner's involvement with the Fellowship of the New Life see First and Scott, *Olive Schreiner*, pp. 144–5.

41 Lytton, *Prisons and Prisoners*, pp. 157–8.

42 Gilman, *The Living*, p. 168.

43 Howe, 'Charlotte Perkins Gilman – As I Knew Her', pp. 75–6.

44 In typological allegory the 'prophetic situation rather than the figure forms the allegory': a characteristic feature of the Old and New Testaments; see John MacQueen, *Allegory* (Methuen, 1970), p. 23.

45 Jack Tresidder, *The Hutchinson Dictionary of Symbols* (Oxford: Helicon, 1997), p. 134.

46 Frieda Fordham, *An Introduction to Jung's Psychology* (Harmondsworth: Penguin, 1990). I am grateful to Patrick Bridgwater for this reference.

47 Hans Biedermann, *The Wordsworth Dictionary of Symbolism* (Ware: Wordsworth, 1996), p. 2.

48 S. C. Cronwright-Schreiner, Introduction to *From Man to Man* (1926), *FMTM*, 495. For biblical revisionism in *From Man to Man* see Rose Lovell-Smith, 'Science and Religion in the Feminist *Fin-de-Siècle* and a New Reading of Olive Schreiner's *From Man to Man*', *Victorian Literature and Culture* (2001) 303–26.

49 Laurence Coupe, *Myth* (Routledge, 1997), p. 74.

50 Madsen, *Rereading Allegory*, p. 44.

51 See the metaphorical crucifixion scenes in Lytton's *Prisons and Prisoners* (p. 276), Gertrude Colmore's *Suffragettes: A Story of Three Women* (1911; Pandora, 1984), p. 278, and Constance Elizabeth Maud's *No Surrender* (Duckworth, 1911), p. 287. For a critical analysis of the use of religious discourse and imagery in suffrage literature see Kabi Hartman, '"What made me a suffragette": The New Woman and the New (?) Conversion Narrative', in Ann Heilmann (ed.), *Words as Deeds: Literary and Historical Perspectives on Women's Suffrage*, special issue of *Women's History Review*, 12:1 (2003) 35–50.

52 To protest against her preferential treatment which contrasted sharply with the

physical neglect and abuse of less well-connected prisoners, Lytton determined to scratch 'Votes for Women' into her chest (*Prisons and Prisoners*, p. 164). Emily Wilding Davison threw herself from the railing at Holloway prison in an effort, as Ann Morley and Liz Stanley have argued, to stop the torture of suffragette prisoners, and later died in her attempt to attach a 'Votes for Women' banner to the king's horse at the 1913 Derby. See Morley and Stanley, *The Life and Death of Emily Wilding Davison* (Women's Press, 1988), p. 158. For an analysis of the suffragettes' strategy of bodily sacrifice see Martha Vicinus, *Independent Women: Work and Community for Single Women 1850–1920* (Virago, 1985), pp. 247–80.

53 MacQueen, *Allegory*, p. 26.

54 Sylvia Pankhurst, 'Olive Schreiner', letter to the *Listener*, 53 (5 May 1955) 809; see also Edward Carpenter, *My Days and Dreams* (Allen & Unwin, 1916), pp. 230–1.

55 Lovell-Smith, 'Science and Religion in the Feminist *Fin-de-Siècle* and a New Reading of Olive Schreiner's *From Man to Man*', 311.

56 Burdett, *Olive Schreiner and the Progress of Feminism*, p. 83.

57 Chrisman, 'Allegory, Feminist Thought and the *Dreams* of Olive Schreiner', pp. 130–1.

58 Laura Chrisman, *Rereading the Imperial Romance: British Imperialism and South African Resistance in Haggard, Schreiner, and Plaatje* (Oxford: Clarendon, 2000), p. 143.

59 Among more recent criticism see McClintock's *Imperial Leather*, pp. 258–95; and Susan R. Horton, *Difficult Women, Artful Lives: Olive Schreiner and Isak Dinesen, In and Out of Africa* (Baltimore: Johns Hopkins University Press, 1995).

60 Carol Barash (ed.), *An Olive Schreiner Reader: Writings on Women and South Africa* (Pandora, 1987), p. 133.

61 See Christopher Wood, *The Pre-Raphaelites* (Weidenfeld & Nicolson, 1981), p. 44.

62 See Berkman, *The Healing Imagination*, p. 217; and Gerald Monsman, *Olive Schreiner's Fiction: Landscape and Power* (New Brunswick: Rutgers University Press, 1991), p. 29.

63 Burdett, *Olive Schreiner and the Progress of Feminism*, p. 100.

64 McClintock, *Imperial Leather*, p. 268.

65 Laura Stempel Mumford, 'Selfless Androgyny: Gregory Rose as "Virile Woman" in Olive Schreiner's *The Story of an African Farm*', *Women's Studies International Forum*, 8 (1985) 621–9. For Schreiner's notion of the virile woman see *W&L*, 92, 144–7.

66 Ruth Parkin-Gounelas, Afterword to *AF*, 298.

67 Edward Carpenter, 'The Intermediate Sex', *Love's Coming-of-Age* (Methuen, 1896), repr. *LVMQ*, II, pp. 126–7.

68 See also Parkin-Gounelas, Afterword, p. 299.

69 Burdett, *Olive Schreiner and the Progress of Feminism*, p. 37.

70 Susan Casteras, 'Painted Sermons: Religion and Victorian Visual Culture', paper delivered on 13 July 2001 to the 'Locating the Victorians' conference, Science Museum, London. For Hunt's painting see Wood, *The Pre-Raphaelites*, p. 43.

71 John Caspara Lavater (1855) *Essays on Physiognomy*, extract repr. in Jenny Bourne Taylor and Sally Shuttleworth (eds), *Embodied Selves: An Anthology of Psychological Texts 1830–1890* (Oxford: Clarendon Press, 1998), p. 15.

72 Bradford, 'Olive Schreiner's Hidden Agony', 634.

73 Ibid., 633.

74 In 'Olive Schreiner's Hidden Agony' Bradford makes a fascinating case for Schreiner's fictional response to autobiographical trauma, suggesting that what she was attempting to deal with in *AF* and all her other fiction was her own experience of teenage abortion.

75 See my *New Woman Fiction: Women Writing First-Wave Feminism* (Basingstoke: Macmillan, 2000), pp. 118–41.

76 R. Iron [Olive Schreiner], Author's Preface to *AF*, n.p.

77 *W&L*, 175. The section on the 'virile birth metaphor' draws on my article '"Over that Bridge Built with our Bodies the Entire Human Race Will Pass": A Rereading of Olive Schreiner's *From Man to Man* (1926)', *European Journal of Women's Studies*, 2 (1995) 33–50.

78 Jean Marquard, 'Olive Schreiner's "Prelude": The Child as Artist', *English Studies in Africa*, 22.1 (1979) 6.

79 Olive Schreiner to Mrs Francis Smith, October 1909, *LOS*, 291.

80 Tess Cosslett, *Woman to Woman: Female Friendship in Victorian Fiction* (Atlantic Highlands, NJ: Humanities Press International, 1988), p. 133.

81 Brittain, *Lady Into Woman*, p. 215; Lovell-Smith, 'Science and Religion in the Feminist *Fin-de-Siècle* and a New Reading of Olive Schreiner's *From Man to Man*', 312.

82 Sally Ledger, *The New Woman: Fiction and Feminism at the* Fin de Siècle (MUP, 1997), p. 84.

83 Laura Chrisman, 'Empire, "Race" and Feminism at the *Fin de Siècle*: The Work of George Egerton and Olive Schreiner', in Sally Ledger and Scott McCracken (eds), *Cultural Politics at the* Fin de Siècle (CUP, 1995), p. 59.

84 See Mrs John Brown, 'Memories of a Friendship', in Zelda Friedlander (ed.), *Until the Heart Changes* ([Cape Town:] Tafelberg-Uitgewers, 1967), p. 26, and Renier, *Before the Bonfire*, p. 12.

85 'All fine imaginative work is self-conscious and deliberate', Wilde declared in 'The Critic as Artist'; 'No poet sings because he must sing. At least, no great poet does. A great poet sings because he chooses to sing. ... [T]he work that seems to us to be the most natural and simple product of its time is always the result of the most self-conscious effort. ... [T]here is no fine art without self-consciousness, and self-consciousness and the critical spirit are one' *The Works of Oscar Wilde* (Spring Books, 1977), p. 866.

86 This inspirational experience is exemplified in 'The Child's Day', when during rote-learning Rebekah is suddenly struck by a flash of insight, to realise that the baby she had discovered is dead: 'In a moment, something had flashed on her! She knew now ... In an instant, she knew ... and with absolute certainty ... She knew ... at that moment – vaguely, but quite certainly – something of what birth and death mean, which she had not known before' (*FMTM*, 63–4).

87 Olive Schreiner to W. P. Schreiner, December 1896, *OSL*, 299.

88 Olive Schreiner to T. Fisher Unwin, 26 September 1892, *OSL*, 209.

89 See Sandra M. Gilbert and Susan Gubar, *The Madwoman in the Attic* (New Haven: Yale University Press, 1979).

90 'His own faculties and prejudice', Caird wrote in the Preface to *WOA* (I, ix–x), 'play the artist … The writer of fiction has to present … a real impression made upon him.'

91 '[T]he artist's ultimate other-worldly gesture', Susan Sontag writes in 'The Aesthetics of Silence', in *Styles of Radical Will* (Secker & Warburg, 1969), is that 'he frees himself from servile bondage to the world' (p. 6). I am grateful to Ceri Mills for this information.

92 Susan Stanford Friedman, 'Creativity and the Childbirth Metaphor: Gender Difference in Literary Discourse', in Elaine Showalter (ed.), *Speaking of Gender* (Routledge, 1989), pp. 80–2.

93 The room Beth discovers in the attic of her marital home appears to have been inhabited by a female predecessor, and Beth proceeds to furnish it with her aunt's belongings. See *New Woman Fiction*, pp. 184–9.

94 This is reflected in their differential responses to extreme conflict: if in one of her most desperate moments Beth fantasises about murdering her husband (*BB*, 428), Rebekah thinks of killing her children and herself (*FMTM*, 299).

95 Gillian Rose, *Feminism and Geography: The Limits of Geographical Knowledge* (Cambridge: Polity, 1993), p. 150.

96 'Sometimes she got out the little wooden box where she kept her papers – little songs and allegories, fairy tales and half-written essays' (*U*, 122).

97 Burdett, *Olive Schreiner and the Progress of Feminism*, p. 107.

98 Ibid., pp. 88, 97, 108.

99 Ibid., p. 38.

100 Renier, *Before the Bonfire*, 15; Carpenter, *My Days and Dreams*, p. 229.

Notes to Chapter 5

1 Adrienne Rich, 'When We Dead Awaken: Writing as Re-Vision' (1971), in Barbara Charlesworth Gelpi and Albert Gelpi (eds), *Adrienne Rich's Poetry* (New York: Norton, 1975), p. 90.

2 Catherine Clément, 'Sorceress and Hysteric', in Hélène Cixous and Catherine Clément, *The Newly Born Woman* [*La Jeune Née*, 1975], trans. Betsy Wing (MUP, 1986), p. 6.

3 Mona Caird to Lady Wilde, 27 June 1889, cited in Richard Ellman, *Oscar Wilde* (Harmondsworth: Penguin, 1987), p. 556.

4 For an exploration of Caird's synergies with radical and psychoanalytic second-wave feminism see my article on 'Mona Caird (1854–1932): Wild Woman, New Woman, and Early Radical Feminist Critic of Marriage and Motherhood', *Women's History Review*, 5 (1996), 67–95. Sections of my argument are reproduced in altered form in this chapter.

5 *FMTM* represents Schreiner's most passionate indictment of social Darwinism and celebration of Christian compassion and mother love through the language of evolutionary science: 'life has been governed, step by step, through the long march and advance in stages of life, by union; love and expansion of the ego to others has governed life' (209). 'Yes, the struggle has gone on and the fittest have survived. The fittest? – to survive; not of necessity the fittest in any other sense in

which we ... use the word. ... The fittest to survive – but the fittest for what else?' (214, 216).

6 Clément, 'Sorceress and Hysteric', p. 6.

7 Elizabeth A. Sharp, *William Sharp (Fiona Macleod): A Memoir*, 2 vols (Heinemann, 1912), I, p. 227.

8 W. T. Stead, 'The Novel of the Modern Woman', *Review of Reviews*, 10 (1894) 66–7, repr. in *LVMQ*, V.

9 Shulamith Firestone, *The Dialectic of Sex: The Case for Feminist Revolution* (Women's Press, 1979), p. 189.

10 Ibid., pp. 216–17.

11 See my book *New Woman Fiction: Women Writing First-Wave Feminism* (Basingstoke: Macmillan, 2000), pp. 145–8.

12 Judith Walkowitz, *City of Dreadful Delight: Narratives of Sexual Danger in Late-Victorian London* (Virago, 1992), p. 167.

13 Lucy Bland, *Banishing the Beast: English Feminism and Sexual Morality, 1885–1914* (Harmondsworth: Penguin, 1995), pp. 126–7.

14 M. Sharpe, 'Autobiographical History' (1889), *Pearson Collection*, cited in Bland, *Banishing the Beast*, p. 127.

15 See Olive Schreiner's letter to Karl Pearson, 23 March 1886, *OSL*, 74.

16 Olive Schreiner to R. Parker, 30 September 1885, *Pearson Collection*, cited in Bland, *Banishing the Beast*, p. 126.

17 Olive Schreiner to Karl Pearson, 23 March 1886, *OSL*, 74.

18 'Mrs. Mona Caird in a New Character', *Review of Reviews*, 7 (1893) 519.

19 Ellis Ethelmer, 'Feminism', *Westminster Review*, 149 (January 1898) 61.

20 Review of *The Morality of Marriage and Other Essays*, *Shafts* (1898) 24.

21 Vera Brittain, 'The Influence of Olive Schreiner' (1955), in Zelda Friedlander (ed.), *Until the Heart Changes* ([Cape Town:] Tafelberg-Uitgewers, 1967), p. 125.

22 Clementina Black, 'On Marriage: A Criticism', *Fortnightly Review*, 53 (1890) 586, repr. in *LVMQ*, I; and Elizabeth Rachel Chapman, 'Marriage Questions in Modern Fiction' (1896), *Marriage Questions in Modern Fiction and Other Essays on Kindred Subjects* (John Lane, The Bodley Head, 1897), p. 32, repr. in *LVMQ*, V.

23 'My Ideal of Marriage, by Mrs. Mona Caird', *Review of Reviews*, 1 (1890) 198.

24 Sharp, *Memoir*, I, p. 227. For Gilman see her diary entries of 3 July and 23 July 1899 in Denise D. Knight (ed.), *The Diaries of Charlotte Perkins Gilman*, 2 vols (Charlottesville: University Press of Virginia, 1994), II, pp. 783, 786; and Charlotte Perkins Gilman, *The Living of Charlotte Perkins Gilman: An Autobiography* (1935; Madison: University of Wisconsin Press, 1990), p. 62.

25 Ernst Foerster, *Die Frauenfrage in den Romanen Englischer Schriftstellerinnen der Gegenwart* (Marburg: N. G. Elwert'sche Verlagsbuchhandlung, 1907), p. 30.

26 David Rubinstein, *Before the Suffragettes* (Brighton: Harvester, 1986), p. 222.

27 Mona Caird, 'Ideal Marriage', *Westminster Review*, 130 (1888) 620. In the revised version of this article this passage was deleted (see 'The Future of the Home' in *MOM*, 117).

28 Sarah Grand, 'Marriage Questions in Fiction: The Standpoint of a Typical Modern Woman', *Fortnightly Review*, 69 (1898) 388, repr. in *LVMQ*, V; see also *SSPSG*, I, p. 90.

29 George Moore, 'Pruriency', *The Hawk*, 25 March 1890, cited in Adrian Frazier, *George Moore 1852–1933* (New Haven: Yale University Press, 2000), p. 202.

30 Sarah Tooley, 'The Woman's Question: An Interview with Madame Sarah Grand', *Humanitarian*, 8 (1896) 168, repr. in *LVMQ*, V, and *SSPSG*, I, p. 228. Grand here referred to Grant Allen's *The Woman Who Did*, but as Allen promoted sexual liberty for women, her point can be applied to Caird as well, bearing in mind, however, that Allen and Caird had very different agendas.

31 Mona Caird, *Personal Rights. A Presidential Address to the Forty-First Annual Meeting of the Personal Rights Association* (London: n.p., 1913), p. 5.

32 Elizabeth Cady Stanton, *Eighty Years and More (1815–1897): Reminiscences of Elizabeth Cady Stanton* (Fisher Unwin, 1898), p. 409. I am grateful to Helen Rappaport for drawing my attention to this statement.

33 Angelique Richardson, '"People Talk a Lot of Nonsense about Heredity": Mona Caird and Anti-Eugenic Feminism', in Angelique Richardson and Chris Willis (eds), *The New Woman in Fiction and in Fact:* Fin-de-Siècle *Feminisms* (Basingstoke: Palgrave, 2001), p. 204.

34 Judith Fetterley, [from] *The Resisting Reader*, in Mary Eagleton (ed.), *Feminist Literary Theory: A Reader*, 2nd edn (Oxford: Blackwell, 1996), p. 305.

35 Richardson, 'People Talk a Lot of Nonsense about Heredity', pp. 198, 206.

36 For Grand's involvement see 'Why I Am an Anti-Vivisectionist', *Anti-Vivisection Review*, (July 1909) 17.

37 Elizabeth Crawford, *The Women's Suffrage Movement: A Reference Guide 1866–1928* (UCL Press, 1999), p. 90.

38 Gladys Singers-Bigger, diary entry of 15 November 1931, in Gillian Kersley, *Darling Madame: Sarah Grand & Devoted Friend* (Virago, 1983), p. 229. Sylvia Pankhurst, *The Suffragette Movement* (Virago, 1984), p. 284. Among the other prominent women listed were H. G. Wells's and Thomas Hardy's wives.

39 Angela V. John, *Elizabeth Robins: Staging a Life, 1862–1952* (Routledge, 1995), p. 153.

40 Mona Caird, 'Militant Tactics and Woman's Suffrage', *Westminster Review*, 170 (1908) 528, 530.

41 Elke Schuch, '"Shafts of Thought": New Wifestyles in Victorian Feminist Periodicals in the 1890s', in Ann Heilmann (ed.), *Masculinities, Maternities, Motherlands: Defining/Contesting New Woman Identities*, special issue of *Nineteenth-Century Feminisms*, 4 (2001) 126.

42 See Mona Caird, 'Punishment for Crimes Against Women and Children', *Westminster Review*, 169 (1908) 553.

43 Mona Caird, 'A Ridiculous God', *Monthly Review*, 74 (1906) 46.

44 Caird, *Personal Rights*, p. 4.

45 Mona Caird, 'The Greater Community', *Fortnightly Review*, 104 n.s. (1918) 742–55.

46 Caird, 'Marriage', revised version, *MOM*, 108.

47 Charlotte Perkins Gilman, *Women and Economics: A Study of the Economic Relation Between Women and Men* (1898; Amherst, New York: Prometheus Books, 1994); *The Man-Made World, or, Our Androcentric Culture* (1911; New York: Johnson Reprint Corporation, 1971); Cicely Hamilton, *Marriage as a Trade* (1909;

Chapman & Hall, 1912); Olive Schreiner, *Woman and Labour* (1911); [Elizabeth Robins], *Ancilla's Share: An Indictment of Sex Antagonism* (Hutchinson, 1924).

48 Lisa Surridge, 'Marital Rape in Mona Caird's *The Wing of Azrael*', paper delivered to the Tenth Annual 18th & 19th Century British Women Writers conference, 20 April 2002, University of Wisconsin, Madison.

49 Harry Quilter (ed.), *Is Marriage a Failure?* (Swan Sonnenschein, 1888), repr. in *LVMQ*, I. For details see my article, 'Mona Caird (1854–1932): Wild Woman, New Woman, and Early Radical Feminist Critic of Marriage and Motherhood', *Women's History Review*, 5 (1996), 87–8, n.14.

50 Patricia Marks, *Bicycles, Bangs, and Bloomers: The New Woman in the Popular Press* (Lexington: University Press of Kentucky, 1990), p. 51.

51 ''Arry on Marriage', *Punch*, 29 September 1888, 156.

52 'Donna Quixote', *Punch*, 26 April 1894, 194.

53 Mona Caird, 'The Emancipation of the Family' (1890), in *MOM*, 59.

54 Mary Maynard, 'Privilege and Patriarchy: Feminist Thought in the Nineteenth Century', in Susan Mendus and Jane Rendall (eds), *Sexuality and Subordination: Interdisciplinary Studies of Gender in the Nineteenth Century* (Routledge, 1989), pp. 221–47.

55 For Caird's echoes of Mill see Richardson, 'People Talk a Lot of Nonsense about Heredity', p. 186, and Patricia Murphy, *Time is of the Essence: Temporality, Gender, and the New Woman* (Albany: State University of New York Press, 2001), p. 163.

56 Friedrich Engels, *The Origin of the Family, Private Property and the State* (1884; Junius, 1994).

57 For the private marriage contract see 'Marriage', 198. For Caird's vision of marriage as a friendship between equals see 'The Morality of Marriage', *MOM*, p. 145.

58 Caird, 'Defence of the So-called "Wild Women"', *Nineteenth Century*, 31 (1892) 814–15 (a revised version was later published in *MOM* under the title 'Phases of Human Development', pp. 195–239). The arguments that follow are also taken from the article, 818–19, 826.

59 Caird, 'Defence of the So-called "Wild Women"', 826; 'Morality of Marriage', *MOM*, p. 152.

60 Grand, 'Marriage Questions in Fiction', 388.

61 Caird, 'Morality of Marriage', 154–5.

62 For Schreiner's rejection of eugenics see *FMTM*, 209.

63 W. T. Stead, 'The Novel of the Modern Woman', *Review of Reviews*, 10 (1894) 64, repr. in *LVMQ*, V.

64 Unsigned review of *Pathway of the Gods*, *Athenaeum*, 1 October 1898, 450.

65 William J. Robinson, *Married Life and Happiness* (1922), cited in Bram Dijkstra, *Idols of Perversity: Fantasies of Feminine Evil in Fin-de-Siècle Culture* (OUP, 1986), p. 334.

66 Virginia Stevens to Vanessa Bell, [25? July 1911] cited in James King, *Virginia Woolf* (Harmondsworth: Penguin, 1995), p. 180, p. 635, n.34.

67 Christopher Craft, '"Kiss Me with Those Red Lips": Gender and Inversion in Bram Stoker's *Dracula*', in Nina Auerbach and David J. Skal (eds), *Bram Stoker: Dracula* (New York: Norton, 1997), p. 459.

68　Virginia Woolf, *A Room of One's Own* (1929; Harmondsworth: Penguin, 1945), p. 31.

69　John Ruskin, 'Of Queen's Garden', *Sesame and Lilies* (1865; George Allen, 1891), pp. 74–121.

70　Lyn Pykett, *Engendering Fictions: The English Novel in the Early Twentieth Century* (Edward Arnold, 1995), p. 60.

71　Ibid.

72　In *The Daughters of Danaus* Professor Fortescue, a figure of the (older) New Man, falls for a hopelessly vacuous creature in his youth, even though the ideal New Woman (Valeria) was available. His attempts to convert his wife to feminism fail pitifully, resulting in her elopement and subsequent death. In *The Stones of Sacrifice* Alpin has to go through an infatuation with silly Elsie Bonner, an aesthetic version of the upper-middle-class daughter in search of a good match, before he perceives in Claudia a more suitable partner.

73　Clément, 'Sorceress and Hysteric', pp. 19, 20.

74　Ibid., p. 25.

75　Annie Besant, *The Ancient Wisdom* (Theosophical Publishing House, 1897), p. 4.

76　Joy Dixon, *Divine Feminine: Theosophy and Feminism in England* (Baltimore: Johns Hopkins University Press, 2001), pp. 150, 124.

77　Caird was granted her diploma (Blavatsky Lodge, membership seconded by B[ertram] Keightley) on 14 June 1904, and resigned on 19 January 1909. See the Theosophical Society European Section Register, VII, p. 52, Theosophical Society, London. I am grateful to Mark Llewellyn for this information, and to Colyn Boyce and Barry Thompson for permitting access to the records.

78　Dixon, *Divine Feminine*, p. 68.

79　Trapped literally and metaphorically in the house of patriarchy, Viola is fatally drawn to the 'Death Chamber', a room in a remote wing of her husband's castle in which an unfortunate ancestress was stabbed by her husband.

80　Premised as it is upon the patriarchal scapegoating and brutalisation of the innocent and oppressed, Christianity, Caird suggests, can only confound, never hold an attraction for, the humanist: 'How God could be willing to accept the pain and grief of one divine being as a substitute for the pain and grief of other guilty beings was what Viola could not understand. ... It was like the story of the young prince who, when he was naughty, had a little slave beaten in his stead, quite to the satisfaction of the royal father' (*WOA*, I: 57).

81　Gauri Viswanathan, 'The Ordinary Business of Occultism', *Critical Inquiry*, 27:1 (Autumn 2000) 17.

82　Ibid.

83　Rita S. Kranidis, *Subversive Discourse: The Cultural Production of Late Victorian Feminist Novels* (Basingstoke: Macmillan, 1995), p. 89.

84　Nancy Chodorow, *The Reproduction of Mothering: Psychoanalysis and the Sociology of Gender* (Berkeley: University of California Press, 1976). Chodorow argues that, in the traditional family, while girls remain in the world of the mother, and therefore 'experience themselves as continuous with others', boys 'define themselves as more separate and distinct' because they have to distance themselves from the mother in their attempt to rejoin the father, who has positioned himself outside of the family unit. She concludes that whereas the 'basic feminine sense of self is connected to the world, the basic masculine sense of self is separate' (p. 169). Dual parenting, she suggests, provides a powerful counterfoil to traditional psychological gender conditioning.

85 Carol Gilligan, *In a Different Voice: Psychological Theory and Women's Development* (Cambridge, MA: Harvard University Press, 1982), p. 136.

86 Ibid., p. 100.

87 Term adopted from the title of Betty Friedan's first chapter in *The Feminine Mystique* ([1963] Harmondsworth: Penguin, 1983), pp. 13–29.

88 For an application of Gilligan's gendered ethics to Grand's *The Beth Book* see Marilyn Bonnell, 'Sarah Grand and the Critical Establishment: Art for [Wo]man's Sake', *Tulsa Studies in Women's Literature*, 14:1 (1995) 123–48.

89 Mona Caird, *Personal Rights: A Presidential Address*. Delivered to the Forty-First Annual Meeting of the Personal Rights Association on 6 June 1913 (Personal Rights Association, 1913), pp. 8, 4, 6 (emphasis in original).

90 See my article 'Mona Caird', 77–8, 95. The high-born Scottish family into which Caird married would, with its lineage going back to the Lords Borthwick, have represented the force of tradition in her eyes (see Figure 15; the marriage between James Alexander [Caird] 'of Cassencary' and Alice Mona Alison, and that of their son, Major Alister James Henryson-Caird, is recorded on the bottom left-hand corner of the family tree).

91 'The worst part of all was the idea of sacrifice – that is *so* ancient'; Charlotte Perkins Gilman, *With Her in Our Land* (1916), in Minna Doskow (ed.), *Charlotte Perkins Gilman's Utopian Novels* (Associated University Presses, 1999), p. 319.

92 Oscar Wilde, 'The Critic as Artist', *The Works of Oscar Wilde* (Spring Books, 1977), p. 869.

93 For Gilman's eugenic vision see Janet Beer and Ann Heilmann, '"If I Were a Man": Charlotte Perkins Gilman, Sarah Grand and the Education of Girls', in Janet Beer and Bridget Bennett (eds), *Special Relationships: Anglo-American Antagonisms and Affinities* (MUP, 2002), pp. 178–201. For her ethnocentrism see Lisa Ganobcsik-Williams, 'Charlotte Perkins Gilman and *The Forerunner*: A New Woman's Changing Perspective on American Immigration', in Ann Heilmann (ed.), *Feminist Forerunners: New Womanism and Feminism in the Early Twentieth Century* (Pandora, 2003), pp. 44–56.

94 Mona Caird, *A Sentimental View of Vivisection* (William Reeves, 1896), p. 9. As Caird points out, this was the argument used to justify the Roman gladiatorial games.

95 Mona Caird, 'The Future of the Home' (*MOM*, 118). This essay was first published in 1888 under the title 'Ideal Marriage' in the *Westminster Review*, 130 (1888) 617–36.

96 Mona Caird to Professor Viëtor, 5 December 1896, in Foerster, *Die Frauenfrage*, p. 52, repr. in *LVMQ*, V.

97 'Galbraith' is an odd choice of name for a family marked out by patriarchally induced hysteria and mental paralysis, echoing as it does Evadne's perhaps not-so-benign physician-husband in Grand's *The Heavenly Twins*, a novel which enjoyed a substantial revival during and after the First World War. Like Grand's

'Lady Galbraith', the wife is a mere cipher in Caird's text, while the mental ill health of the daughters bespeaks the tragic inexpedience of the 'Galbraith cure'. If this was Caird's indictment of the bourgeois family, it also carried more than ironic undertones towards Grand's text and, by implication, Grand's complicity with dominant values.

98 Sigmund Freud, '"A Child Is Being Beaten": A Contribution to the Study of the Origin of Sexual Perversions', in Elisabeth Young-Bruehl (ed.), *Freud on Women: A Reader* (Hogarth Press, 1990), pp. 215–40.

99 Caird, 'Marriage', *Westminster Review*, 130 (1888) 197–8.

100 Margaret Atwood, *Survival: A Thematic Guide to Canadian Literature* (Toronto: Anansi, 1972), pp. 36–41.

101 David Lodge, *Nice Work* (Harmondsworth: Penguin, 1989), p. 83.

102 Havelock Ellis, *My Life* (Boston: Houghton Mifflin, 1939), p. 203. Translated, Goethe's motto reads: 'Lead a holistic, good, and beautiful life.'

103 Ellis, *My Life*, p. 203; Sheila Rowbotham and Jeffrey Weeks, *Socialism and the New Life: The Personal and Sexual Politics of Edward Carpenter and Havelock Ellis* (Pluto, 1977), pp. 145–6.

104 William Greenslade, *Degeneration, Culture and the Novel 1880–1940* (CUP, 1994), p. 26.

105 Rowbotham and Weeks, *Socialism and the New Life*, p. 177.

106 Ibid., p. 176; 'Marie Stopes', a Channel Four production in the series 'Secret Lives', 1995.

107 H. G. Wells, *The New Macchiavelli* (Lane, the Bodley Head, 1911), p. 411.

108 Karl Pearson, *The Ethic of Freethought* (Unwin, 1888), p. 389.

109 David Mitchell, *Queen Christabel: A Biography of Christabel Pankhurst* (Macdonald and Jane's, 1977), p. 277. For a detailed discussion of feminist involvement in the eugenics movement see Angelique Richardson, 'The Birth of National Hygiene and Efficiency: Women and Eugenics in Britain and America 1865–1915', in Ann Heilmann and Margaret Beetham (eds), *New Woman Hybridities: Femininity, Feminism, and International Consumer Culture, 1880–1930* (Routledge, 2004), pp. 240–62.

110 Katharine Burdekin, *Swastika Night* (1937; New York: Feminist Press, 1985).

111 Karl Pearson, reply to *Speeches Delivered at a Dinner held in University College, London, in Honour of Professor Karl Pearson*, 23 April 1934 (Cambridge: privately printed, CUP, 1934), p. 23. I am grateful to Carolyn Burdett for drawing my attention to this publication.

112 Catherine Clément, 'Sorceress and Hysteric', p. 6.

Notes to Chapter 6

1 Mary Daly, *Gyn/Ecology: The Metaethics of Radical Feminism* (Women's Press, 1979), pp. 39–40 (emphasis in original).

2 *SOS*, 411 (emphasis in original).

3 *DD*, 318–19.

4 See Adrienne Rich, *Of Woman Born: Motherhood as Experience and Institution* (1977; Virago, 1992), pp. 218–22; Luce Irigaray, 'And the One Doesn't Stir without

the Other', *Signs*, 7:1 (1981) 62.

5 Virginia Woolf, 'Professions for Women' (1931), in Michèle Barrett (ed.), *Virginia Woolf on Women & Writing: Her Essays, Assessments and Arguments* (Women's Press, 1979), pp. 58–60.

6 Raphael Patai, 'Lilith', *Journal of American Folklore*, 77:306 (1964) 308, 296–8, 303–4. I am grateful to Ceri Mills for drawing this to my attention. See also Marina Warner, *Managing Monsters: Six Myths of Our Time* (Vintage, 1994), p. 7.

7 '[T]hey did not perpetually go about together ... they did not intend to make the usual attempt to roll two people into one; they mutually respected one another's individuality, and recognized that, with all their essential unity, they had each a separate life to lead, and different needs and desires' (*OTW*, II: 144).

8 Adrienne Rich, 'Compulsory Heterosexuality and Lesbian Experience' (1980), in Ann Snitow, Christine Stansell and Sharon Thompson (eds), *Powers of Desire: The Politics of Sexuality* (New York: Monthly Review Press, 1983), pp. 177–205.

9 Ruth First and Ann Scott, *Olive Schreiner* (Women's Press, 1989), pp. 72–3.

10 J. Lempriere, *Lempriere's Classical Dictionary* (1788; Bracken Books, 1984), p. 416.

11 Julia Kristeva, 'Stabat Mater' (1977), in Morny Joy, Kathleen O'Grady and Judith L. Poxon (eds), *French Feminists on Religion: A Reader* (Routledge, 2002), pp. 133–5.

12 Patai, 'Lilith', 308, 309–10.

13 Luce Irigaray, 'The Forgotten Mystery of Female Ancestry' (Italian original 1989), in Joy, O'Grady and Poxon, *French Feminists on Religion*, p. 72, pp. 68–75. See also Robert Graves, *The Greek Myths*, 2 vols (Folio Society, 1996), I, pp. 91–7.

14 Hélène Cixous, 'The Laugh of the Medusa', in Elaine Marks and Isabelle de Courtivron (eds), *New French Feminisms* (Brighton: Harvester, 1981), p. 252.

15 Irigaray, 'And the One Doesn't Stir without the Other', 67.

16 The idea of an unconventionally close relationship between two women and a man who shared a deep mutual affection may have been inspired by Caird's own experience. Elizabeth and William Sharp's house in Hampstead, a 'two minutes' walk away' from Caird's according to Margaret Morganroth Gullette (Afterword to *DD*, 522), was called 'Wescam', after their three names: William, Elizabeth, Mona', and the trio welcomed Edith Wingate Rinder, another married woman and 'mother of Mona's god-daughter, Esther Mona' into their community (ibid.). In the winter of 1890–1 Caird and Rinder spent a holiday in Rome with the Sharps (ibid., 521, and William F. Halloran [Ed.] 'The William Sharp "Fiona Macleod" Archive', *www.sas.ac.uk/ies/Full%20Text%20Archive/Sharp/whowas.htm*, accessed on 29 June 2003; Halloran names Caird as Rinder's aunt). Rome proved to be of momentous importance to William Sharp: it was there that according to Ken Hinshalwood he 'became friendly with a lady whose personality symbolised to him the heroic women of Greek and Celtic days. As "Fiona MacLeod" he dedicated *Pharais* (1894) to her, a story full of "Celtic romance ... and the mysterious"' (*Discovering Scottish Writers*, Scottish Library Association, *www.slainte.org.uk/scotauth/sharpdsw.htm*, accessed on 29 June 2003). Although the exact identity of this mysterious object of desire remains open to speculation, Halloran suggests that she could have been Edith Rinder (*www.sas.ac.uk/ies/Full%20Text%20Archive/Sharp/whowas.htm*); the Greek and Celtic inspiration she proffered might also point to Caird herself. I am grateful to Mark Llewellyn

for drawing my attention to the internet sources.

17 See my *New Woman Fiction: Women Writing First-Wave Feminism* (Basingstoke: Macmillan, 2000), pp. 96–104.

18 For a discussion of Gilman's engagement with contemporary aestheticism in 'The Yellow Wallpaper' see Stephanie Forward, 'Charlotte Perkins Gilman's Yellow Wallpaper', *English Review*, 7:3 (1997) 34–6; and my essay, 'Overwriting Decadence: Charlotte Perkins Gilman, Oscar Wilde, and the Feminization of Art in "The Yellow Wall-Paper"', in Catherine J. Golden and Joanna S. Zangrando (eds), *The Mixed Legacy of Charlotte Perkins Gilman* (Newark: University of Delaware Press, 2000), pp. 175–88.

19 See Stephanie Forward, 'A Study in Yellow: Mona Caird's "The Yellow Drawing-Room"', *Women's Writing*, 7:2 (2000) 295–307, and her introduction to her collection *Dreams, Visions and Realities: Short Stories by Late-Victorian and Early Modernist Women Writers* (BUP, 2003), pp. xi–xxxii.

20 *DD*, 137.

21 Lempriere, *Lempriere's Classical Dictionary*, p. 216.

22 'Hiketides', *Kindler Lexikon*, ed. Wolfgang von Einsiedel, 8 vols (Weinheim: Zweiburgenverlag, 1984), IV, pp. 4439–41. See also 'Danaus' in John Warrington, *Everyman's Classical Dictionary* (Dent, 1961), p. 180.

23 Graves, *Greek Myths*, I, pp. 191–5.

24 Florence Nightingale, 'Cassandra', in Ray Strachey, *The Cause: A Short History of the Women's Movement in Great Britain* (Virago, 1988), pp. 402, 404, 399, 403.

25 Patricia Murphy, *Time is of the Essence: Temporality, Gender, and the New Woman* (Albany: State University of New York Press, 2001), p. 156.

26 Nightingale, 'Cassandra', p. 406.

27 Ibid., p. 405.

28 Sally Ledger, *The New Woman: Fiction and Feminism at the* Fin de Siècle (MUP, 1997), p. 28.

29 In her introduction to *The Morality of Marriage* (George Redway, 1897, repr. in *LVMQ*, vol. 1) Caird deploys a tongue-in-cheek counter-argument against the patriarchal trope of men's physical superiority, jusifying women's subjection by suggesting that women might decide to rid themselves of the males of the species when they are in their infancy (pp. 10–12). For a discussion of the Medea metaphor in *The Morality of Marriage* see Josephine McDonagh, *Child Murder and British Culture, 1720–1900* (CUP, 2003), Chapter 6.

30 Edith Hall, 'Medea and British Legislation before the First World War', *Greece & Rome*, 46:1 (April 1999) 42–77; Fiona Macintosh, 'Medea Transposed: Burlesque and Gender on the Mid-Victorian Stage', in Edith Hall, Fiona Macintosh and Oliver Taplin (eds), *Medea in Performance 1500–2000* (Oxford: Legenda, 2000), pp. 75–99. I am grateful to Josephine McDonagh for drawing my attention to these texts.

31 See McDonagh, *Child Murder and British Culture*, Chapter 6.

32 Lempriere, *Lempriere's Classical Dictionary*, p. 395.

33 Sarah Iles Johnston, Introduction to James J. Clauss and Sarah Iles Johnston (eds), *Medea: Essays on Medea in Myth, Literature, Philosophy, and Art* (Princeton: Princeton University Press, 1997), p. 5.

34 Euripides' *Medea* (Heinemann, 1912) calls on the 'Queen of Night', Hecate, to assist her in her dark designs (ll. 395–6, p. 315). For other references in this section see Graves, *Greek Myths*, II, pp. 560, 557, 543, 560, 557.

35 Graves recounts that when the Argonauts were menaced by a dragon, Medea used her magic to confound and pacify the monster, thus releasing the men into life and liberty; shortly after, she became responsible for the ruthless murder of her half-brother (ibid., pp. 544, 546). As Jan N. Bremmer argues in his essay 'Why did Medea Kill her Brother Apsyrtus?' (in Clauss and Johnston, *Essays on Medea*, pp. 83–100), by killing a male sibling who held authority in her life, Medea 'severed all ties to her natal home and the role it would usually play in her adult life', thus asserting her independence as an autonomous woman unbound to the norms of patriarchal family and society. In Caird's adaptation, the horror of Medea's fratricide is implicitly conjured up in Hadria's fear of involuntary matricide. By contrast, Christa Wolf's Medea (*MS*) is wrongfully accused of both brother-murder and infanticide, acts of abject violence instigated and carried out in each case by the law of the father and then displaced on to the rebellious woman.

36 Graves, *Greek Myths*, II, p. 544.

37 Euripides, *Medea*, ll. 1163–221, pp. 377, 379. See also Graves, *Greek Myths*, II, p. 557.

38 Graves, *Greek Myths*, II, p. 557.

39 Ibid.

40 Ibid., p. 558. See also *MS*, 216.

41 Sarah Iles Johnston, 'Corinthian Medea and the Cult of Hera Akraia', in Clauss and Johnston, *Essays on Medea*, pp. 50–8.

42 Graves, *Greek Myths*, II, p. 558.

43 Ibid.

44 Marianne McDonald, 'Medea as Politician and Diva: Riding the Dragon into the Future', in Clauss and Johnston, *Essays on Medea*, pp. 301–2.

45 Graves, *Greek Myths*, II, p. 558.

46 For other contemporary women artists inspired by Medea see Marianne Hochgeschurz (ed.), *Christa Wolfs Medea: Voraussetzungen zu einem Text. Mythos und Bild* (Bonn: Janus Press, 1997), section 'Arbeiten von bildenden Künstlerinnen und Künstlern', pp. 129–84. See also Margaret Atwood in this collection, 'Zu Christa Wolfs Medea', pp. 69–74.

47 McDonald, 'Medea as Politician and Diva', pp. 299–300.

48 Euripides, *Medea*, ll. 1082–9, p. 369.

49 Ibid., ll. 230–37, p. 303.

50 Mona Caird to Prof. Viëtor, 5 December 1896, in Ernst Foerster, *Die Frauenfrage in den Romanen Englischer Schriftstellerinnen der Gegenwart* (Marburg: N. G. Elwert'sche Verlagsbuchhandlung, 1907), pp. 52–3, repr. in *LVMQ*, V.

51 Christa Zorn, *Vernon Lee: Aesthetics, History, and the Victorian Female Intellectual* (Athens: Ohio University Press, 2003), p. 162.

52 Ibid.

53 Graves, *Greek Myths*, II, p. 527. This cauldron also appears in Wolf's *Medea*, where it serves to regenerate Jason and effectively save his life (*MS*, 63).

54 See Anthony Frederick Sandys's 'Medea' (1868), in Jan Marsh, *Pre-Raphaelite*

Women: Images of Femininity in Pre-Raphaelite Art (Weidenfeld and Nicolson, 1987), p. 117. In contrast, Evelyn de Morgan chose to represent Medea as a pensive figure walking towards the viewer inside a palace, holding a phial but otherwise dissociated from any signs of witchcraft; see her 'Medea' of 1889, in *Evelyn de Morgan: Oil Paintings* (De Morgan Foundation, 1996), Plate 24. John William Waterhouse's 'The Magic Circle' of 1886 (in Marsh, *Pre-Raphaelite Women*, p. 118) offers closer points of comparison with Caird's passage, although here the sorceress is placed outside rather than inside a cavern.

55 John Everett Millais' 'Autumn Leaves' (1856) symbolises human transience in its female child subjects gathering leaves to burn them against the backdrop of the sunset. See Christopher Wood, *The Pre-Raphaelites* (Weidenfeld & Nicolson, 1981), p. 38.

56 Cixous, 'The Laugh of the Medusa', p. 254.

57 Ibid., p. 247.

58 John Ferguson, *Euripides Medea and Electra: A Companion to the Penguin Translation* (Bristol: Bristol Classical Press, 1987), pp. 3–4.

59 Sigmund Freud, 'The Uncanny' (1919), in Victor Sage (ed.), *The Gothick Novel: A Casebook* (Basingstoke: Macmillan, 1990), pp. 76–7.

60 Murphy, *Time is of the Essence*, pp. 162–3.

61 Ibid., p. 171.

62 Ibid., p. 177.

63 Rich, *Of Woman Born*, p. 225.

64 Cited in Laurence Coupe, *Myth* (Routledge, 1997), p. 35.

Notes to the Conclusion

1 Roland Barthes, *Mythologies*, sel. and trans. Annette Lavers (French original 1957; Jonathan Cape, 1972), p. 135 (emphasis in original).

2 Ibid., p. 109 (emphasis in original), p. 112.

3 Ibid., p. 118.

4 Ibid., p. 120.

5 Ibid., p. 128.

6 Ibid.

7 Ibid., p. 142.

8 Ibid.

9 Ibid., pp. 145–8.

10 Ibid., pp. 150–4.

11 Ibid., p. 150.

12 Ibid., p. 151.

13 Ibid., p. 157.

14 Fatima Mernissi, *The Harem Within* (1994; Toronto: Bantham Books, 1997), p. 120.

15 Catherine Clément, 'Sorceress and Hysteric', in Hélène Cixous and Catherine Clément, *The Newly Born Woman* [*La Jeune Née*, 1975], trans. Betsy Wing (MUP, 1986), p. 6.

Index

Note: literary works can be found under the authors' names; page numbers in *italic* refer to illustrations; 'n.' after a page reference indicates a note number on that page.